TRAGIC THOUGHTS AT THE END OF PHILOSOPHY

Rethinking Theory

GENERAL EDITOR

Gary Saul Morson

CONSULTING EDITORS

Robert Alter
Frederick Crews
John M. Ellis
Caryl Emerson

TRAGIC THOUGHTS AT THE END OF PHILOSOPHY

Language, Literature, and Ethical Theory

Gerald L. Bruns

Northwestern University Press
Evanston, Illinois

Northwestern University Press
Evanston, Illinois 60208-4210

Printed in the United States of America

ISBN 0-8101-1674-X (cloth)
ISBN 0-8101-1675-8 (paper)

Library of Congress Cataloging-in-Publication Data

Bruns, Gerald L.
    Tragic thoughts at the end of philosophy : language, literature,
and ethical theory / Gerald L. Bruns.
        p.   cm. — (Rethinking theory)
    Includes bibliographical references and index.
    ISBN 0-8101-1674-X (cloth : alk. paper). — ISBN 0-8101-1675-8
(pbk. : alk. paper)
        1. Literature—Philosophy.   2. Literature—History and criticism—
Theory, etc.   3. Language and languages—Philosophy.   4. Literature
and morals.   5. Tragic, The.   6. Ethics.   I. Title.   II. Series.
PN49.B784 1999
801—dc21   99–21879
                                                                CIP

The paper used in this publication meets the minimum requirements of the American National
Standard for Information Sciences—Permanence of Paper for Printed Library Materials, ANSI
Z39.48–1984.

For Nancy Gaye Moore

Only what does not fit into this world is true.
—Adorno, *Aesthetic Theory*

Contents

Part III: Poetry and Philosophy inside the Everyday World

Preface

In 1981, in an essay entitled "Philosophy in America Today," Richard Rorty wrote: "One may expect that, by the end of the century, philosophy will have gotten over the ambiguities which have marked the last thirty years, and will begin to develop, once again, a clear self-image." By "ambiguities of the last thirty years" Rorty meant the post-positivist era when there was little consensus among Anglo-American philosophers as to what it was exactly that they should be doing. Prior to this period there was something like a common understanding that philosophy, whatever else it might be, was first of all philosophy of science. But by 1981 Arthur Danto, wondering why art should be something that there is a philosophy of, concluded that philosophy just *is*, if it is anything, philosophy of art. And this is the more true because art, having reached the end of its history, has turned into philosophy.

The essays in this book derive from a period, now all but over, when ambiguities of this sort provided a hearty meal almost every day. This was a time when Anglo-American philosophers began to take something more than a recreational interest in literature. The period started for me in 1979 with the publication of Stanley Cavell's *The Claim of Reason*, whose last line asks whether "philosophy [can] become literature and still know itself." This was the year in which Richard Rorty's *Philosophy and the Mirror of Nature* also appeared, with its idea that henceforward "one's self-identification as a philosopher will be purely in terms of the books one reads and discusses, rather than in terms of the problem one wishes to solve." Donald Davidson's "What Metaphors Mean" had just appeared in a recent volume of *Critical Inquiry*, Martha Nussbaum had just published her great essay on Plato's *Symposium* in a new journal called *Philosophy and Literature*, and Rorty's essay on "Philosophy as a Kind of Writing" appeared in *New Literary History*. Joe Margolis's *Art and Philosophy* would be published in 1980 and Alasdair MacIntyre's *After Virtue* in 1981, as would the second edition of Cavell's *Senses of Walden*, now really accessible for the first time and including two essays on Emerson. In 1982 D. Z. Phillips published *Through a Darkening Glass*, arguing that philosophers seem impoverished when it comes to giving accounts of moral dilemmas human beings actually have. Nussbaum pressed roughly this same point in her essay "*The Golden Bowl* as Moral Philosophy," which appeared in 1983 in *New Literary History*. And so it continued, with somewhat diminishing returns, through the next few years as these philosophers either enlarged and refined their views or drifted into other venues.

My sense is that Rorty's prophecy about philosophy at the end of the century is coming true. Whatever the ambiguities in philosophy's self-image that made this brief encounter of philosophy and literature possible, they are now dissolving in, among other things, the solution of philosophy of mind, with its fascinating controversies about brains, computers, and the problem of how we should treat imitation human beings once they become available. However, philosophy's self-image is not the concern of the essays here, which are basically the attempt of an English professor to make sense of such things as Stanley Cavell's interest in Shakespeare or Alasdair MacIntyre's interest in narrative. These interests are, it appears, ethical—in the various senses of this word that some of the following essays try to clarify. During the 1980s ethical theory was as compelling a subject as neurophilosophy is now. Meanwhile there remains the old question of language, which is where literary critics will always be found staring over philosophy's shoulders, especially if the philosopher is reading *Finnegans Wake*. But most intriguing perhaps is the question of what happens when philosophers begin looking at the world from ground level, that is, as inhabitants rather than as disengaged observers wondering what things would be like if no one were watching. Danto says that philosophy invented art in order to give reality something to be contrasted with. In certain moods I imagine that literature was invented to cure the poverty of description that seems always to have been a condition of philosophical argument (think of Socrates complaining against Protagoras and his stories). In working with the texts under study in this book I thought I had begun to discover what it would be for philosophers—moral philosophers, philosophers of mind, philosophers of art, even a neurophilosopher or two—to try a hand at the cure.

The essays in this volume were composed over the past fifteen years or so. All but two have been published before, and most of these have been revised and expanded since they first appeared. I am grateful for the responses, criticisms, and suggestions of many people—Sandy and Emily Budick, Marshall Brown, Joe Buttigieg, Stanley Cavell, James Conant, Arnold Davidson, Donald Davidson, Stanley Fish, Steve Fredman, Timothy Gould, Gary Gutting, Bruce Krajewski, Ed Manier, Don Marshall, Saul Morson, Martha Nussbaum, David O'Connor, Marjorie Perloff, Steve Watson, and Ewa Ziarek and Krys Ziarek. My special thanks to Erich Hertz, who read each of the essays in their revised state and made many helpful suggestions for improvement. And as always Jim Kincaid was a beacon for my thoughts.

Acknowledgments

Portions of the introduction first appeared as "The New Philosophy" in the *Columbia Literary History of the United States*, ed. Emory Elliott (New York: Columbia University Press, 1988); chapter 1 was first published in *Critical Inquiry* 11 (December 1984); chapter 2 appeared in *Arachnē: Revue interdisciplinaire de langue et de littérature* 3 (1996); chapter 3 was presented at a panel entitled "Law and Hermeneutics" during the annual meeting of the American Political Science Association in Chicago, September 1987, and first appeared as "Law and Language: A Hermeneutics of the Legal Text," in *Legal Hermeneutics: History, Theory, and Practice*, ed. Gregory Leyh (Berkeley: University of California Press, 1992); chapter 4 appeared in *Commitment in Reflection: Essays in Literature and Moral Philosophy*, ed. Leona Toker (New York: Garland Press, 1994); chapter 5 was originally presented at the conference "Neurobiology and Narrative" held at the University of Notre Dame in April 1990; a shorter version was published under the title, "Toward an Anarchic Theory of Literary History" in *Modern Language Quarterly* 57 (1996); an earlier version of chapter 6 was presented at a symposium on Martha Nussbaum's *Fragility of Goodness* held at the University of Tennessee in October 1988, and subsequently appeared in a special number of *Soundings* (72 [1989]); a version of chapter 7 was presented at a workshop on the institutions of interpretation at the Hebrew University of Jerusalem in June 1991 and is published here for the first time; chapter 8 first appeared in *Wallace Stevens: The Poetics of Modernism*, ed. Albert Gelpi (Cambridge: Cambridge University Press, 1985); a version of chapter 9 was published in *Critical Inquiry* 16 (Spring 1990); chapter 10 is an expanded version of a paper delivered at the annual meeting of the Society for the Advancement of American Philosophy, Albuquerque, March 4–6, 1997, and is published here for the first time.

Introduction

Theory, Practice, Proximity:
A Short History of the
End of Philosophy

Philosophy as science, as serious, rigorous, indeed apodictically rigorous science—the dream is over.

—Edmund Husserl

Indeed, in our day there is no end to the end of metaphysics.

—Emmanuel Levinas

We are by now too aware of the philosophical attacks on system or theory to place the emphasis in defining philosophy on a product of philosophy rather than on a process of philosophizing. We are more prepared to understand philosophy as a mode of thought that undertakes to bring philosophy to an end, as, say, Nietzsche and Wittgenstein attempt to do, not to mention, in their various ways, Bacon, Montaigne, Descartes, Pascal, Marx, Kierkegaard, Carnap, Heidegger, or Austin, and in certain respects Kant and Hegel. Ending philosophy looks to be a commitment of each of the major modern philosophers; so it is hardly to be wondered at that some of them do not quite know whether what they are writing is philosophy.

—Stanley Cavell

1. Theory

The idea that philosophy is a rigorous science—apodictically rigorous in the sense of being founded on something demonstrable, graspable, at all events more firm than passing opinion or uncontested talk—is traceable to the ancient belief that philosophy is something different from poetry, whose foundations are entirely inside of language. To be sure, like poetry philosophy is made of words. But whereas poetry circulates in the air as so many songs, stories, sayings, and memories of intoxicating human beings, philosophy is language that is (or wants to be) fixed, settled, rooted, hooked onto the world. Poetry is responsive to whatever it hears; philosophy is assertive of what is the case. Poetry is self-reflexive language, language in excess of its signifying function—material, figurative, nomadic language; philosophy is propositional form, a syntax without a vocabulary, a transparent looking-glass, a system of concepts. Poetry is spontaneous, open-ended, unrestrained by the law of noncontradiction; philosophy is rule-governed, self-contained, and just. The one is singular, contingent, refractory to categories; the other aspires only to what is necessary and universal. Poetry is porous, exposed, always captivated by whatever is otherwise; philosophy is disengaged and monadic, always careful to determine what counts as itself. So naturally we look for poets among the mad folk who roam the wilderness, whereas the philosopher is the transcendental observer occupying the seat of wisdom and judgment.[1]

These legendary distinctions, or caricatures, will never go out of date, partly because so much is to be learned by contesting them, as in our own intellectual culture with its interest in "leveling the genre distinction between philosophy and literature."[2] But philosophy and literature are not so much genres as limit-concepts. They are internal to one another's histories, starting with Plato's *Republic*, where the poet is excluded from the just and rational state that confers on the philosopher his once and future identity as "the guardian of rationality."[3] It was as such a guardian that Aristotle reconceptualized poetry so as to find a place for it within the organon or rule of discourse (a sort of purely formal version of Socrates' city of words). The concepts of mimesis and plot show that poetry is a kind of knowledge and that it hangs together like a kind of reasoning; so poetry is just and rational after all. Like philosophy, poetry is essentially Greek.

It is possible to argue that poetry has never recovered—or has but only just recently (see chapter 7)—from this reduction to logical or narrative form, which leaves open the question of what to do about the language in which poetry is spoken or, more exactly, written. The question of language has at any rate nagged poetry throughout its history (rhetoric, e.g., is chiefly an art of coping with the excess of words); and the same nagging has plagued philosophy, with its dreams of a *Lingua Philosophica*, that is, a language of pure notation unencumbered by material conditions. The reduction of philosophy to propositional style and argumentative form has always been vulnerable to the charge that philosophy is, nevertheless, as Richard Rorty puts it, "a kind of writing," by which Rorty means that philosophy is, whatever else it is, a cultural practice or product like any other (like the world?), and thus always materially embedded in what is merely historical and contingent.[4] So if the history of philosophy is, on the one hand, as someone has said, the history of rational inquiry, it can also, on the other, be studied as a history of *texts*, as if philosophy and literature, however different they might be, shared the same sort of history: one could call it a history of the excess of words, but one might also call it *modernity*, which is a condition in which the question of what counts as philosophy becomes what philosophy is chiefly about, just as the question of what counts as poetry becomes poetry's chief preoccupation. As Arthur Danto observes, it is precisely at this self-reflexive moment that the history of poetry comes to an end, since it has turned into philosophy.[5] Likewise when philosophy encounters its materiality, its historicity, its excess of words, it is doubtful, as Stanley Cavell says, whether it knows how to recognize itself.[6]

Possibly no one thing counts as philosophy nowadays. When in doubt consult the schools. It is at least clear that philosophy is, whatever else it is, a school curriculum: logic and methodology, epistemology, metaphysics, and, with philosophy visibly fading as one goes down the list, ethics, politics, religion, aesthetics, and so on to no definite term. Logic and methodology, etc. (but especially logic and methodology), make up a course of training that one has to go through to become a philosopher. A corollary of this program is that the traditional texts of philosophy—Hume's writings, for example, and Kant's—set an agenda of specifically philosophical problems. For example, here is a basic schoolroom question: is the world we know already made or is it of our own construction? On this question people divide into followers of Aristotle and followers of Kant, or into those who take what lies before us as it is given, or as it appears, and those who question whether anything just lies before us in the way we experience it. The basic idea of Kantian idealism, for example, is that our experience of the world is conceptual as well as empirical. Empirically, experience reduces simply to a chaos of undifferentiated sensations. If this is so, however, how is it that the world nevertheless appears intelligible to us, that is, how is it that we experience it as a world of objects extended in time and space and behaving more or less predictably according to the laws of physical science? What is the source of this intelligibility? Or, in Kant's own idiom, how is scientific knowledge (knowledge that is objective and logically valid) possible? An answer to this question cannot be derived from experience itself. It must be given a priori by determining the laws of cognition as such. One must, in effect, give an account of how the mind (or, more exactly, how reason) works. In the *Critique of Pure Reason* this becomes an account of the logical structures by which reality is constituted for us as an objective and therefore knowable entity. The word "constitute" here simply means to establish something as a determinate object. This is what the mind does in experience. The mind objectifies a world for itself by synthesizing the chaos of sensation according to the forms of space and time and the categories of substance, causality, and so on. Technically, this means that we are able, by means of transcendental idealism, to hold the position of empirical realism. Most people who call themselves realists turn out to be Kantians rather than Aristotelians. The mind in any case is, as Kant says, the sole author of what it experiences. Modernity, on a certain view, means living with the consequences of this sovereignty.

In this century a more elaborate version of Kant's constructionism was provided by Ernst Cassirer in his *Philosophy of Symbolic Forms* (1923–29). Cassirer recognized that Kant had construed the foundations of intelligibility too narrowly. "Not only science," Cassirer says, "but language, myth, art and religion as well provide the building stones from which the world of 'reality' is constructed for us, as well as that of the human spirit, in sum the World-of-the-I. Like scientific cognition, they are not simple *structures* which we can insert into a given world, we must understand them as *functions* by means of which a particular form is given to reality and in each of which specific distinctions are effected."[7] Or, in other words, the mind cannot be characterized purely in terms of scientific reason. The intelligibility of human culture as such, not just the intelligibility of science, requires that we postulate, Cassirer says, "a basic function of signification" as the foundation of all human activity. What is important to understand, however, is that this function is formative rather than mimetic: signification is a process of worldmaking. "Myth and art, language and science, are in this sense configurations *toward* being: they are not simple copies of an existing reality but represent the main directions of the spiritual movement of the ideal process by which reality is constituted for us as one and many—as a diversity of forms which are ultimately held together by a unity of meaning" (PSF107). It is true, Cassirer says, that we find ourselves therefore "in a world of 'images'—but these are not images which reproduce a self-subsistent world of 'things'; they are image-worlds whose principle and origin are to be sought in an autonomous creation of the spirit. Through them alone we see what we call 'reality,' and in them alone we possess it: for the highest objective truth that is accessible to the spirit is ultimately the form of its own activity" (PSF111). What is outside the activity of the spirit cannot be thought, but for Cassirer this is not so much a problem as it is "a fallacy in formulation, an intellectual phantasm. The true concept of reality cannot be squeezed into the form of mere abstract being; it opens out into the diversity and richness of the forms of spiritual life—but of a spiritual life which bears the stamp of inner necessity and hence of objectivity" (PSF111). The task of philosophy, as Cassirer understands it, is not to find a way outside the forms of signification. "If all culture is manifested in the creation of specific image-worlds, of specific symbolic forms, the aim of philosophy is not to go behind all these creations but rather to understand and elucidate their basic formative principle" (PSF113). The question of questions for philosophy is not whether these "image-worlds" of human culture are true; the question is rather the formal one of how they are made. This is the question that *The Philosophy of Symbolic Forms* tries to answer with its studies of the formative principles of language, myth, and science.

As it happens, this is also the regulative question of structuralist thinking. Essentially, what we call structuralism is just Kantian idealism with a displaced theory of the subject. It is idealism inscribed not in the language of German philosophy of the spirit but in the language of linguistics, semiotics, or the theory of signs. Thus whereas the German tradition thinks in terms of the relation of subject and object, mind and world, the structuralist tradition thinks in terms of signifier and signified and again in terms of the signifier and the system within which it operates. In both traditions, however, the relationship in question does not reduce to a copy theory of intelligibility or a mimetic theory of representation or signification; rather, intelligibility is a process of differentiation within an ensemble of discrete elements. In the German tradition these elements are empirical (the so-called data of sensation); in structuralism they are linguistic or, more accurately, semiotic, that is, elements within a system of differential relations. Intelligibility (that is, signification) is a product of relationships among signifiers and does not depend on anything outside the system, just as, in idealism, the world is said to be phenomenal in character and does not require to be grounded on a noumenon or Thing-in-itself. This allows the structuralists to speak not only of the construction of the world but also of the construction of the logical subject, the "I" of subjectivity. This last has been a particularly fruitful line of research in Freudian and Marxist inflections of structuralism, that is, in the work of Jacques Lacan and Louis Althusser. Here a theory of the unconscious, which is certainly the most powerful of the implications of Kant's philosophy, is brought into the foreground. To learn a language, for example, is to enter into a system of constraints, a symbolic order that structures both self and world, constituting them as what they are in consciousness. In this event, however, it is no longer accurate to speak of consciousness as itself constitutive or productive. On the contrary, it is the unconscious that is now to be described as a signifying system (that is, as a chain, place, or play of signifiers), or, at a higher level, as an ideological system, that is, a structure of images, myths, desires, genders, ideas, beliefs, values, or other cultural products whose modes of production are no longer spiritual and transcendental in Cassirer's sense but are embedded in the historically contingent social forces of labor, technology, and institutional operations and control. Our cognitive powers, in a word, are socially formed.

At this point, however, the intelligibility of the notion of intelligibility itself begins to require some propping up. For example, it is by no means clear that a structuralist's (basically Kant-like) account of the logic of signification will always remain consistent with norms of inferential and differential reasoning (or however norms of reasoning might be described). Indeed, on a certain view the linguistic turn that structuralism gives to Kant's philosophy is like a turn from logic to rhetoric, that is, away from a concern for the logical form of knowledge or of statements about the world toward the problem of figuration. This is quite visible in Roman Jakobson's reduction of signification to the metaphoric and metonymic poles of mental or linguistic functioning.[8] The historical point would be to see in this rhetorical bias a turn away from the tradition of Kant and Cassirer—the tradition of transcendental reason—toward the tradition of Friedrich Nietzsche where reason is radically historicized. For many this is just a turn away from philosophy itself. Nietzsche, after all, was a classical philologist who somehow did not find it contradictory to hold, as he did, that figuration or metaphor is the whole basis of intelligibility. Reason, language, the whole business of making sense of things—these are, according to the Nietzschean motto, "figurative all the way down." In a famous fragment from 1883–88 collected in *The Will to Power*, Nietzsche writes:

> Against positivism, which halts at phenomena—"There are only *facts*"—I would say: No, facts is precisely what there is not, only interpretations. We cannot establish any fact "in itself": perhaps it is folly to want to do such a thing.
>
> "Everything is subjective," you say; but even this is interpretation. The "subject" is not something given, it is something added and invented and projected behind what there is.—Finally, is it necessary to posit an interpreter behind the interpretation? Even this is invention, hypothesis.
>
> In so far as the word "knowledge" has any meaning, the world is knowable; but it is *interpretable* otherwise, it has not meaning behind it, but countless meanings.—"Perspectivism."
>
> It is our needs that interpret the world; our drives and their For and Against. Every drive is a kind of lust to rule; each one has its perspective that it would like to compel all the other drives to accept as a norm.[9]

If there is any interesting threshold between philosophy as rigorous science and postscientific or postanalytic philosophy, or between structuralism and post-structuralist thinking, it is just this Nietzschean idea that there are no transcendental standpoints, that reason is finite and historical, that consciousness is internal to the languages it uses to frame its representations of what it takes to be the world. In recent years this idea has taken the form of a radical questioning of the institutions of knowledge, as in the later writings of Martin Heidegger with respect to philosophy, the critique of rationality that the Frankfurt School adapts from Max Weber, and in the work of Michel Foucault with respect to the historicity of the human sciences. Hence also the variety of intellectual positions often lumped casually together as "deconstruction," where the idea (very roughly) is that language is not a logical system for constructing an intelligible and defensible description of reality but a historicized totality of texts—call them philosophy, science, literature, law, religion, or literary criticism—within which what gets counted as reality is in a state of constant, interminable, aporetic redescription (like a fabric that, Penelope-like, we weave and reweave in order to cope with whatever practical difficulty is at hand). However we figure it, whatever in nature or in culture we place before ourselves as an object of knowledge is always interpretable otherwise. Rorty calls this going from epistemology to hermeneutics and, more recently, liberal irony.[10]

Or (on Rorty's encouragement) one could call it pragmatism. At any rate a similar Nietzschean turn, but independent of Nietzsche, occurred within the tradition of logical empiricism that forms the backbone of Anglo-American philosophy, with its notion of conceptual frameworks. This notion is a basic corollary of an empiricist theory of language, where words have meaning, according to W. V. O. Quine, "only as their use in sentences is conditioned to sensory stimuli."[11] For Quine, however, language is holistic as well as empirical. It is a "fabric" of interwoven sentences, that is, a vast verbal structure held together by inferential reasoning as well as by a prejudice for the useful in favor of higher ideals. Another term for this vast structure is "theory," but it is more commonly known as a "conceptual scheme." A conceptual scheme is a way of organizing experience into a coherent picture of the world. It includes, Quine says, "all sciences, and indeed everything we say about the world" (WO12). However, the truth or falsity of what is said will, in practice, be determined by how congruously a statement fits into the total framework rather than by any single empirical verification. This is what Quine means by "the underdetermination of theory": more gets said about the world, and gets counted as true, than can be accounted for empirically. What we call "things," for example, are not the objects we encounter in experience but only "posits" called for by the particular conceptual scheme we happen to inhabit—call it the scheme of objectifying rationality. In a famous essay, "Two Dogmas of Empiricism" (1951), Quine has this to say about "objects":

> As an empiricist I continue to think of the conceptual scheme of science as a tool, ultimately, for predicting future experience in the light of past experience. Physical objects are imported into the situation as convenient intermediaries—not by definition in terms of experience, but simply as irreducible posits comparable, epistemologically, to the gods of Homer. For my part I do, qua lay physicist, believe in physical objects and not in Homer's gods; and I consider it a scientific error to believe otherwise. But in point of epistemological footing the physical objects and the gods differ only in degree and not in kind. Both sorts of entities enter our conception only as cultural posits. The myth of physical objects is epistemologically superior to most in that it has proved more efficacious than other myths as a device for working a manageable structure into the flux of experience.[12]

"Physical objects are conceptually imported into the situation as intermediaries": that is, they belong to the *logical* construction of the world. Or, in other words, what we have here is a sort of relativized and pragmatic Kantianism in which logical empiricism and behaviorism have replaced the German idealist account of rational functioning, with (materially, at least) no change in results. I say "relativized and pragmatic" because the upshot of Quine's argument is that a diversity of conceptual frameworks could be raised on the same empirical base, in which case the same sensory experience could in principle confirm rival theories. So on a certain view there is little to choose between a Homeric universe and the universe pictured for us in physics, or between myth and science, in terms of how each connects up with reality. Each is a reasonably self-consistent way of organizing experience, and, as Cassirer and the structuralists would say, the right question to ask about it is not whether it is true or false but how it is made, how it works, or how it is done. Questions of truth and meaning are internal to questions of structure. In *Ways of Worldmaking*, Nelson Goodman puts the structuralist's question from the side of Anglo-American philosophy, calling it "analytic constructionism."[13]

Call it what you will, however, constructionism ends up implying a plurality of criteria of rationality without telling you how to choose among them, that is, how to make your choice rational rather than arbitrary, interest-based, ethnocentric, emotive, or in any of a variety of ways historically contingent; and this makes the idea of a plurality of criteria of rationality itself sound a little self-contradictory, the more so if by reason you mean analytic and objectifying rationality, or the norms of inferential and differential reasoning. Cassirer's idea was that the same rationality— the formative power of the spirit—exhibits itself differently, but on a rising scale, in language, myth, and science, with science able to study language and myth because of its superior position on the scale. What saves science, or justifies it, is the idea of "same rationality," or rationality as such, however differently exhibited. For Cassirer, the historicity of reason—the different ways it builds a world for human beings—turns out to be Hegelian, that is, it means absolute reason coming to terms with itself, or becoming more like itself (more scientific), as time goes by. But what this means is that you do not choose among criteria of rationality—you do not choose to be mythic or scientific—rather history chooses for you. And so you have got to believe, as Hegel and Cassirer did, that you have pretty much arrived at the end of history.

The difficulty in determining reasons for such a belief has had important consequences in the social sciences, particularly in anthropology, where the problem has been to renounce primitivism, or the idea that history puts anthropologists in a transcendental position vis-à-vis those whom they study.[14] The structuralist anthropology of Claude Lévi-Strauss, for example, tries to produce a sort of non-Hegelian philosophy of symbolic forms by distributing the logic of myth and the logic of science along a common axis of differential signification (in other words, mutually incompatible surface structures reduce to the same logical form). However, the hard question is this: how do you study conceptual schemes (or cultures) whose criteria of rationality, or principles of construction, or schemes of intelligibility, are different from your own, particularly when this difference cannot be adjudicated by appeal to transcendental reason, philosophy of history, or a common axis of linguistic or mental functioning? Peter Winch tried to follow out this question from the standpoint of Ludwig Wittgenstein's later reflections on the social nature of rationality, where language is figured as a "form of life" rather than as a system for framing representations.[15] In "Understanding a Primitive Society" (1964), for example, Winch asks, "What is it for us to see the *point* of the rules and conventions followed in an alien form of life?"—where "alien" means rites of magic plainly offensive to the rules of logic.[16] Now what is interesting about this question is the way it is loaded, because asking about the *point* of rules and conventions is different from asking about their formal intelligibility or rational backup. Rationality is not just the application of criteria. It is as if Winch were turning structuralism into hermeneutics, where the idea that one can understand an alien form of life only by entering into it and living through it replaces the idea that knowledge means objectification and analysis. It was on this idea of understanding or *verstehen* that the German philosopher Wilhelm Dilthey tried to determine the validity of the human sciences (viz., we can only understand a text by reconstructing and reliving the experience that produced it).[17] The point here would be that a conceptual scheme can only be understood from ground level, or from the inside out, not from the outside as if from a transcendental standpoint. So participation replaces structural analysis. But this means that, among other things, understanding alien forms of life must confront serious obstacles, because it is by no means clear that one can simply cross a threshold from one scheme to another.[18] This is another way of putting the problem of the historicity or finitude of reason, and it is why understanding alien conceptual schemes—and perhaps understanding as such—always requires a liberal application of the principle of charity. This principle holds that for understanding to be possible we must always assume that what someone is saying is true (by our lights of what is true), even when we are not sure *what* someone is saying. Charity is what replaces belief in the universal distribution of reason or common axes of rationality, not to say transcendental standpoints of various elementary sorts. Charity is what compels Winch to posit as basic to the study of alien cultures what he calls "limiting notions"—notions of birth, death, sexuality. These are, he says, "notions which have an obvious ethical dimension, and which indeed in a sense determine the 'ethical space,' within which the possibilities of good and evil in human life can be exercised." For anthropology (but of course not just for anthropology), the significance of these notions "is that they are inescapably involved in the life of all known human societies in a way which gives us a clue where to look, if we are puzzled about the point of an alien system of institutions" (EA43). This simply means that if we want to understand other people we have to assume that they are sufficiently like us for us to learn something from them about what matters to us—as if our conceptual schemes were not cognitively relative with respect to the truth of things come what may, but ethically or responsively relative to each other. And perhaps this means that cultures are not sealed-off algorithmic structures (in other words, *not* conceptual schemes). Thus Winch stresses "the concept of *learning from*"; it is, he says, "closely linked with the concept of *wisdom*" (EA42), where wisdom means connecting up with how things are in a practical rather than theoretical way.

Wisdom means at least seeing the finitude of theory, or of reason, that is, seeing the human world as rational from within or from ground up, not from top down. This in a way is the argument of a famous essay by Donald Davidson, "On the Very Idea of a Conceptual Scheme" (1974). It is all very well to talk about conceptual relativism, Davidson says, but it is a different thing to make sense of it. The idea of "differing points of view" makes a kind of sense, "but only if there is a common co-ordinate system [a common axis] on which to plot them," that is, a nonideological place where knowledge of the kind Kant wanted, science rather than hermeneutics, is possible.[19] "We may accept the doctrine," Davidson says, "that associates having a language with having a conceptual scheme," but the problem is that "speaking a language is not a trait anyone can lose while retaining the power of thought. So there is no chance that someone can take up a vantage point for comparing conceptual schemes by temporarily shedding his own" (ITI185). And if we follow out Davidson's argument, which is that the "dualism of scheme and content, of organizing system and something wanting to be organized, cannot be made intelligible and defensible" (ITI189), we come to this: namely, that we have in our current intellectual environment a terrific surplus of conceptual-scheme theories—idealist theories of symbolic forms, structuralist systems of formal constraint, analytic conceptual holism, prison-house theories of language, ideology, and metaphysics, new historicist theories of cultural fabrics, Nietzschean perspectivism, internalist realism, theories of archives, paradigms, language games, webs of belief, narrative backgrounds, intersubjective assumptions, communicative communities, interpretive communities, reflective equilibriums, what-you-will: in short, a plenitude of structuralisms, and no bottom-line reason for holding any one of them.

2. Practice

At this point philosophers might be thought of as dividing into pure and impure Kantians, with not much to choose between them. Thus, from the side of purity, Martin Hollis says that, granting "the thesis about the construction of social reality," there has to be "on transcendentalist grounds that 'massive central core of human thinking which has no history,'" a core summarized "in the proposition that all men are rational," whence at least our constructions will be rational, whatever their content or surface details.[20] Meanwhile Nelson Goodman says, "With false hope of firm foundation gone, with the world displaced by worlds that are but versions, with substance dissolved into function, and with the given acknowledged as taken, we face the question of how worlds are made, tested, and known" (WWM7). A poststructuralist would be someone who asks: who are "we" who face the question of how things are made, and where are we situated? And why do we happen to face just this question? A poststructuralist, after all, is apt to be one who finds the question, well, unmotivated.

Whoever we are, we seem perilously close to what Martin Heidegger called "The End of Philosophy," which does not mean that philosophy (or, say, the history of reason) now stops but only that it stands out clearly now for what it is in all of its rigorous formality. Heidegger characterizes this formality as follows: "theory means now: supposition of the categories which are allowed only a cybernetical function but denied any ontological meaning. The operational and model character of representational-calculative thinking becomes dominant."[21] Cybernetically, thinking—rationality—is essentially rule-governed behavior; thinking means the development of procedures to replace the giving of reasons. "The end of philosophy," Heidegger says, "proves to be the triumph of the manipulable arrangement of a scientific-technological world and of the social order proper to this world" (TB59). The Newton of this social order was almost certainly Max Weber, who produced the first principia of bureaucratic culture, with its concern for regulations, procedures, effective management, operational guidelines, program implementation, career development, and technical innovation.[22] The end of philosophy, in other words, gives us not absolute knowledge but sound planning and cost-effective reasoning. Here reason is no longer Kant's transcendental unity of apperception or Cassirer's formative power of the spirit; it is reason as reason is figured today (in most university departments of economics, political science, sociology, and, if the truth be told, philosophy) in the form of "rational-choice theory," which is a reduction of rationality to a logic of calculation aimed at maximizing payoffs (a rational choice is one that most efficiently serves my interests). Basically the theory analyzes collective action on the model of the strategic behavior of individuals. It assumes, for example, that political decisions try to maximize the production of power and judicial decisions try to maximize the production of wealth. The goal of reason is success and, where applicable, a good conscience ("a rational individual," says John Rawls, "is always to act so that he need never blame himself no matter how his plans finally work out").[23] The theory excludes axiomatically any conception of noninstrumental relations between or among human beings, whence ethics, for example, reduces to the question of how far it pays to treat other people fairly.[24] As Rawls says, "envy tends to make everyone worse off" (TJ144).

As if the end of philosophy meant the deracination of reason, its debasement into merely instrumental control; but it also means, as in Heidegger's philosophy, a critical rejection of subject-centered rationality aimed at just the sort of systematic administration of people and things that rational-choice theory seeks to justify. Symmetrically with Heidegger, much of European thinking since World War II has been an inquiry into the consequences of a "rationalization of the world" in which, as Theodor Adorno and Max Horkheimer put it, conceptualization is only an instrument of domination.[25] I have already mentioned deconstruction, with its critique of integral rationality and its special feeling for the double bind (reason clutching itself with its own hand). The question is whether it makes sense to speak of reason freeing itself from the consequences of its own power. Jürgen Habermas thinks not, complaining that the critique of subject-centered rationality inaugurated by Heidegger and the early Frankfurt school and pursued across a wide front in poststructuralist philosophy and literary criticism entails "a performative contradiction" because of the way it abandons the propositional style of philosophical thinking.[26] However, as Rodolphe Gasché has argued, this underestimates the extent to which Heidegger's writings (or Adorno's or Derrida's) retain the force of argument while seeking richer conceptions of thinking, rationality, and critical reflection than our current intellectual culture provides.[27]

No one, not even Habermas, doubts the need for such conceptions, particularly in social and political theory and in moral philosophy. Bernard Williams, for example, has remarked how "the resources of most modern moral philosophy are not well adjusted to the modern world. . . . [This] is partly because it [i.e., moral philosophy] is too much and too unknowingly caught up in it [i.e., the modern world], unreflectively appealing to administrative ideas of rationality."[28] Instead of thinking in terms of rational actors operating systematically come what may, Williams argues for "a richer and more determinate view of what rational agency is, taking it to be expressed in living a specifically human life" (ELP29). Likewise Charles Taylor has argued that the recognition that "rational mastery means instrumental control" is not merely a negative questioning of reason, a Nietzschean denunciation of knowledge and bad faith that leads nowhere; it is an opening up of a world on the hither side of the sovereignty of the subject—a world of everydayness in which, among other things, we find ourselves involved with and, indeed, under the claim of both other people and the earthly environment of ordinary things.[29] Indeed, in Anglo-American as well as in European circles, contemporary awareness of the finitude of reason has demonstrably shifted the center of philosophical gravity away from the pole of logic and epistemology toward ethics, aesthetics, history, and politics, that is, away from the primacy of concepts, rules, and the laying bare of deep structures toward what used to be called the human sciences. Here dialogue replaces method; the give-and-take among human beings replaces the relationship between subject and object, signifier and signified, rule-governed behavior and overarching systems of integral relations. As Taylor says, our relation to the world is not reducible to framing representations of it; we deal with the world as agents within it.[30] Habermas himself follows this shift when he tries to subordinate the theory of cognitive-instrumental rationality to a theory of communicative rationality or praxis aimed at uncoerced consensus and problem-solving within the everyday lifeworld.[31]

Just so, to speak of a shift from logic to ethics and politics is mainly a short way of marking widespread contemporary recognition of the priority of practice over theory (where practice does not, pace Rawls, reduce to planning and calculating). Recall how cheerfully Quine accepted the equal intelligibility of Homeric gods and the laws of physics, saying only that, "qua lay physicist," he found it more workable, and to that extent more reasonable, to believe in the latter. Only within physics can a physicist practice physics, but what this means is that practice is no longer reducible to concepts of method and the construction of theories, or to what Karl-Otto Apel calls "methodological solipsism," which is the idea that "one person, alone, could at least in principle practice science." Rather, the practice of science is different from the logic of it; it presupposes social conventions mediated not by "the scientific rationality of operation on objects . . . but rather the pre- and meta-scientific rationality of intersubjective discourse mediated by explication of concepts and interpretation of intentions." Or, in other words, science presupposes hermeneutics, or the understanding of—practical involvement with—other people.[32]

This seems close to what Richard Rorty is getting at when he opposes solidarity to objectivity, or to what Cora Diamond is getting at when she says that understanding a concept means learning how to live with it, that is, how to participate in the form of life in which that concept has some application or point.[33] For both Rorty and Diamond this means, to be sure, accepting the contingency and alterability of our concepts, but even more interestingly it means learning that we do live, after all, without foundations—that, paradoxically, we do foundational things like practice science (a form of life like any other) without *Letztbegründungen*.[34] It was William James who proposed the notion of a plural universe (multiple and heterogeneous forms of life) as an alternative to rationalist claims that there is no world except the one that answers to the laws of physical science. James never doubted or concealed his commitment to scientific reason, but he understood that inhabiting a world is different from describing it, much less having a view of it that can take in everything at once. So instead of foundations, James spoke of engaging things at ground level, on the street, where the singular and irreducible is what is real in contrast to what can be subsumed by categories and distinctions. At ground level, as Bernard Williams says, we "stop talking about assessments of moral agency and talk rather about moral agency."[35] Likewise, according to the so-called Welsh school of moral philosophy, at the ground level our concern is with what moral agents do, not with how a moral spectator is to judge them or how a moral law is to guide them.[36] At ground level the moral spectator turns into the first person singular (that is, "me"), for whom, as Peter Winch says, moral clarity is possible "only through a sharpening of my perception of the particular circumstances which characterize my individual presence in the world"—and that means understanding "my practical involvement . . . with other human beings."[37] At ground level, as Cavell says, our relation with things (and certainly with other people) cannot be just one of knowing them.[38] But what other way is there? This may be the question of questions at the end of philosophy, a question that keeps philosophy open to the everyday world in which the rest of us find ourselves.

3. Proximity

The essays that follow presuppose—but also try to shed light on—this ground level of reality, in contrast to the level described by Thompson Clarke when he said that "we philosophers, apart from 'creating concepts' and providing their mental upkeep, are outsiders, standing back detached from concepts and items alike (even when items are aspects of ourselves), purely ascertaining observers who, usually by means of our senses, ascertain, when possible, whether items fulfill the conditions legislated by concepts."[39] What would it be for philosophers in Clarke's tradition to relocate themselves at ground level, no longer outsiders to the world but (in some nontrivial sense) inhabitants? Some evidence that might go into an answer to this question is provided by a number of Anglo-American philosophers who have recently had some interesting things to say about literature, which is, whatever else it is, a discourse that (like the law) engages the world at ground level where human beings find themselves in situations refractory to concepts, rules, and justified true beliefs. Mimetically, or at the level of narrative, literature is a richly detailed and endlessly expanding inventory of such situations under varieties of scrutiny. Looking past the traditional dismissive rhetoric that reduces literature to "folk psychology," we find a number of philosophers like Cora Diamond who wonder whether we could even come to know what a human life is like in the absence of the endless imagining of such a thing.[40] Literature keeps alive the concept of the human, shows its application, even though the concept may no longer be of much significance in what we think of as moral philosophy.[41]

At all events the essays in this book are mainly expository attempts to find out what philosophers who have taken an interest in literature have been up to, what they are getting at, and also what we can learn from them about literature and its differences from philosophy. This last issue usually means locating the limits of philosophical interest in literature, and the suggestion in this book is that these limits are frequently, but not always, limits of language. Philosophers divide into those who see, and those who don't see, that the language of literature is finally irreducible to its use as a form of mediation in the construction of meanings, concepts, propositions, narratives, and so on. Language is always a limit as well as a form of mediation (a fact that literature registers in often comic ways in its narratives, as I try to recall in chaps. 4 and 5). Much, if not most, of what I have written over the years has been an attempt to get clear about the relation of literature to its language.[42] I take this question up in this book at almost every chance I get, chiefly in chapter 7, which concerns the internal coherence among some writings by Arthur Danto, Stanley Cavell, and the work of a number of contemporary North American poets, some of whom sometimes think of themselves as writing "language poetry."

Poetry (so these poets argue, and so argues much of modern poetics) is made of words but is not (just) a use of them; that is, it is made of language but not of what we use language to produce—meanings, concepts, propositions, and so on. It is as much a response to language as a use of it, as if our relation to language were as much one of listening and responsibility as one of speaking. It is uncanny how Donald Davidson's notion of language intersects with this idea (see chapter 2). Moreover, it is in virtue of this irreducibility of language to its functions that poetry seems symmetrical with ethics, on a certain complicated view of ethics, one that stresses openness and responsibility as against rule-following and the justification of conduct, decisions, and beliefs. The essays that here make up roughly the second half of this book might be thought of as attempts to sort out different ethical theories in order to clarify ethics in terms of the engagement with what is singular and irreducible and therefore refractory, as poetry is, to meanings, concepts, rules, not to mention the propositional style of philosophical discourse itself. How far might ethics be thought of as occupying a border between philosophy understood as argument and poetry understood as refractoriness to concepts and rules? It is between these poles at any rate that much of narrative literature is to be found. Of course, this thought needs careful thinking, but my sense is that, if there is any interesting link between philosophy and literature, it would have to be seen at least partly in terms of poetry and ethics understood as openness and responsibility to the singular and irreducible, where poetry registers responsiveness with respect to language as ethics does to other people. The idea is to see the internal coherence between the linguistical and the ethical, even when these two dimensions of literature seem to interfere with one another at the level of the propositional and the descriptive.

"What happens to philosophy," Cavell asks, "if its claim to provide foundations is removed from it—say the founding of morality in reason or in passion, of society in a contract, of science in a transcendental logic, of ideas in impressions, of language in universals or in a formalism of rules?"[43] One answer seems to be: philosophy returns to earth. It recaptures an intimacy with the world that it had lost when it took up the task of legislating concepts. In *The Senses of Walden* Cavell complains against Emerson as the philosopher of the Oversoul that "he leaves me the habitual spectator of my world. That is where Emerson is always stuck, with his sense, not his achievement, of outsidedness, the yearning for the thing [the *Ding-an-sich*] to happen to him" (SW 102). Thoreau, on Cavell's reading, brings this "outsidedness" to ground level. Cavell's way of putting this is to say that whereas Emerson remains *apart* from the world, Thoreau is situated *next* to it, that is, in a relation of proximity rather than one of cognition. The idea would be to try to make sense of this distinction by figuring proximity as an ethical concept, as it is explicitly, for example, in the work of the French philosopher Emmanuel Levinas.

To be sure, it is hard to find a place for Levinas in a book on philosophers in the Anglo-American analytic tradition. Levinas is the major figure in a European philosophical tradition that holds that ethical reflection cannot be developed from an epistemological base or from the standpoint of self-interest. So the issue is what an ethical theory free of rules and calculation would look like. The basic Levinasian question is: what is it to encounter (or be encountered by) another? Sartre in his classic analysis of the look treats this as a cognitive event. To be seen, for example, is to become an object in another's world, a piece of furniture in another's consciousness.[44] Levinas maps onto this event another model: not the Greek or philosophical model of knowing but the Jewish biblical model of election, of being called out of the safety and comfort of one's house or homeland, into exile, taken into captivity, called to prophecy. It is important to stress that no one asks to be a prophet; election is not something I enter into (or not) as a result of rational deliberation. It is what happens to me. In this event I am no longer an "I" but a "me." Kafka understands this mode of election, sees the terror of it.

It is this model of election that structures Levinas's conception of the ethical claim. It is what defines the relation of proximity, which Levinas opposes to the notion of consciousness as this comes down to us from Kant, Hegel, and Husserl. Consciousness in this tradition means intentionality, transcendental constitution, conceptual mastery, cognition, representation, assertion, self-possession, the sovereignty or freedom of the rational subject, the agent of initiative who causes things to happen and from whom all things follow (the *arche*). Consciousness is that which confers meaning on the world and on others in it. But for Levinas consciousness in this sense "is not all there is to subjectivity."[45] There is also the condition of sensibility in which my relationship to the world is one of intimacy and passivity. Levinas calls a relationship of this kind "proximity."[46] Proximity is the condition of subjectivity in the mode of being touched; even perception is a mode of proximity rather than that of cognition. As Levinas says, "Perception is a proximity with being which intentional analysis cannot account for. The sensible is superficial only in its role [as a species of] cognition. In the ethical relationship with the real, that is, in a relationship of proximity which the sensible establishes, the essential is committed. Life is there. Sight is, to be sure, an openness and a consciousness, and all sensibility, opening as a consciousness, is called vision; but even in its subordination to cognition sight maintains contact and proximity. The visible caresses the eye. One sees and one hears like one touches" (CPP118).

However, proximity is an event as well as a relation. It has the anarchic character of an intervention in the order of things that I inhabit or over which I preside under the usual philosophical descriptions. "Proximity," Levinas says, "is anarchically a relationship with a singularity without mediation of any principle or ideality. What concretely corresponds to this description is my relationship with my neighbor" (OTB90). This is not a relationship that I bring about. It is an anarchic relation in the sense that "it happens," that is, it happens to *me* (the Levinasian world is not a Leibnizian world: it is a world in which, before anything else, you are someone to whom things happen, and in particular this means someone to whom *others* happen—an event that cannot be traced back to any rational order; like Meister Eckhart's rose, it is "without why"). Proximity is a relation outside intentionality. Levinas characterizes it as an "assignation," being approached, called out, summoned, accused; but he also thinks of it in terms of obsession (the condition of being gripped, fascinated, haunted, pursued, persecuted). What is overturned in proximity is my sovereignty, but not my responsibility, which is, so to speak, purified of every possibility of evasion (OTB101–2). Levinas likes to think of this event as one of exposure. In the ethical relation, the human relation par excellence, I am exposed to others.[47] For Levinas, this exposure to others gives the definition of the self: "the word *I* means *here I am* [*me voici*], answering for everything and for everyone." This condition of openness to others is, Levinas says, "the condition for all solidarity" (OTB117).

It is Levinas's idea that our relation to the world, and to others in it, is a relation of proximity. It is perhaps not a utopian state of affairs, since vulnerability with respect to the world is a condition of existence as such. However, this condition captures a conception of human finitude that cannot, on any argument I know of, be evaded. Let me conclude with a quotation from Emmanuel Levinas on proximity:

The proximity of things is poetry; in themselves the things are revealed before being approached. In stroking an animal already the hide hardens the skin. But over the hands that have touched things, places trampled by being, the things they have held, the images of those things, the fragments of those things, the contexts in which those fragments enter, the inflexions of the voice and the words that are articulated in them, the ever sensible signs of language, the letters traced, the vestiges, the relics—over all things, beginning with the human face and skin, tenderness spreads. Cognition turns into proximity, into the purely sensible. Matter, which is invested as a tool, and a tool in the world, is also, via the human, the matter that obsesses me with its proximity. The poetry of the world is inseparable from proximity par excellence, or the proximity of a neighbor par excellence. And it is as though by reference to their origin in the other, a reference that would obtain as an a priori structure of the sensible, that certain cold and "mineral" contacts are only privately congealed into information or pure reports. (CPP118–19)

I see in recent Anglo-American philosophy an acceptance of particularity—of singularity, even—that is closer to a Levinasian ethics of proximity, alterity, and responsibility than to the traditions of logic and empiricism, Kantian morality and British utilitarianism, in which this philosophy has its roots. What is more, this philosophy sees—or is close to seeing—literature as a place in which to engage this particularity conceptually and concretely, whether in the interests of language, practical reasoning, or ethical theory (or, as in the case of Cavell, all three together). Here philosophy seems to me to capture something essential about literature: namely that, as Levinas says, poetry is the proximity of language and the world, and is inseparable from the proximity of the neighbor, or the ethical relation as such.

Part I

The Proximity of Language

1

Loose Talk about Religion from William James

Metaphysics has usually followed a very primitive kind of quest. You know how men have always hankered after unlawful magic, and you know what a great part in magic words have always played. If you have his name, or the formula of incantation that binds him, you can control the spirit, genie, afrite, or whatever the power may be. Solomon knew the names of all the spirits and having their names, he held them subject to his will. So the universe has always appeared to the natural mind as a kind of enigma, of which the key must be sought in the shape of some illuminating or power-bringing word or name. That word names the universe's principle, and to possess it is after a fashion to possess the universe itself. "God," "Matter," "Reason," "the Absolute," "Energy," are so many solving names. You can rest when you have them. You are at the end of your metaphysical quest. But what do we know about nature?

—William James, "What Pragmatism Means"

1. The View from the Street

My purpose here is to ask about the way William James talks—as, for example, in *The Varieties of Religious Experience* (1902), the famous Gifford Lectures in which (as it appears) James attempted to rehabilitate religion as a subject fit for philosophical discourse, or as something still worth talking about.[1] Some hint as to what is to come is provided by the epigraph I have just given from "What Pragmatism Means," in which it sounds like James is taking a very traditional eliminativist line, not just about the emptiness of metaphysical language, but about the primitive or folk character of those who use it (P31). But it is no trouble to read this passage as a tacit defense of metaphysics precisely because it is as a magical rather than as a philosophical language that metaphysics works. So James talks about the "power-bringing" as well as the "illuminating" word or name. Whatever the rational pretense of metaphysics, its relationship to reality is finally practical rather than theoretical, and probably much the same could be said about magic. If there is a problem about metaphysics, it lies in its desire to overpower the world, to bring it under total conceptual control, regardless of consequences. James prefers local, more politic or micropolitical approaches. The task of language, as he never tires of saying, is not to describe the world but to help us come to terms with it just in the idiomatic sense of this expression, where truth or agreement with reality is something to be negotiated—something that will require revisions not only in the world but in ourselves. In this event it helps to remember that the world is made of people and not just of objects.

The question of how James talks in *The Varieties of Religious Experience* is complicated in several ways—first of all by his pragmatism, which he offers as a new way of justifying talk about things that are not always susceptible to rational or scientific accounting, and, second, by his pluralism, which in this case is an expression not so much of James's liberalism as of his historicism, of the idea that "there is no point of view, no focus of information extant, from which the entire content of the universe is visible at once" (P72). We are inhabitants of the world before we are spectators of it, and our spectatorship always remains internal to the world as it is lived. So perforce we are always in the position of having to speak more than one language more or less at the same time. And in the third place his talk is complicated by his radical empiricism, in which (among other odd features) experience is taken in an ethical and not merely in the traditional Lockean or sensationalist sense. Experience for James is Emersonian or romantic as well as Lockean—one German word for it would be *Erfahrung* (undergoing a transformation), another *Erlebnis* (lived experience). It is not just what occurs in sensation but what goes on in human life, what one lives through; even mystical experiences, for example, although they tend to obliterate sensation and so pose every sort of difficulty as to what they are experiences *of*, still count as real experiences because they are experiences that human beings keep having. In *Varieties* James cannot forbear asking everyone's question: what do religious or mystical experiences verify? what is their truth or foundation? what do they warrant or authorize? The last hundred pages of *Varieties* are riveted on this question of truth, which is a hard question because mystical or religious experiences are always private, inaccessible to observation, mediated by bizarre accounts in strange languages. But James knows that to worry about verification in any philosophical sense of universal and necessary statements about natural phenomena is already to have missed the main question, which is how to make sense of such experiences as are composed not of empirical sensations but of feelings that are irreducible to conceptual determination. One thing that seems to have attracted James to religious feelings is that, by his time (the age of Charles Darwin, Thomas Huxley, and Herbert Spencer), it had become difficult to know what to call these feelings—why, for example, call them religious at all? Why not call them neurotic or delusional feelings? This is surely the rational option, especially for a trained scientist like James, professor of physiology at Harvard and author of *The Principles of Psychology* (1890), who knows—and presumably wants to say—that our delusions and neuroses pass daily for religious feelings without our knowing it.

The problem, however, is not simply what to call these things; it is that James is *not* someone who speaks exactly of what he knows—*not* someone who says just what he would say if he were simply to speak his mind. What is more, he accomplishes this feat of duplicity without irony, as when he says (to take first a simple example) that "in delusional insanity, paranoia, as they sometimes call it, we may have a *diabolical* mysticism, a sort of religious mysticism turned upside down" (V426). If you read this sentence carefully, it may seem that James has got it wrong, and that he should have said, "in delusional insanity, *diabolical* mysticism, as they sometimes call it, we may have paranoia. . . ." This would have been a positive statement, a plain case of calling a thing by its real name. As the sentence stands, however, it is "they" who call it paranoia, whereas James talks like a theologian, saying that what we may have here (in what is sometimes called paranoia) is "*diabolical* mysticism," or a plain case of demonic possession.

The point is evidently that James's scientific beliefs do not exactly comprise a standpoint, outlook, or approach; he speaks from outside as well as from inside his analytic vocabulary. This "outside" is the side of the ordinary or the everyday, that is, outside philosophy, science, or learning. When in his lectures on pragmatism, for example, James says that pragmatism is a method rather than a philosophy, it turns out that he means that pragmatism is not a perspective *on* the world but a perspective *within* it, a view from the street rather than from the temple—a view from inside the "world of concrete personal experiences to which the street belongs [that] is multitudinous beyond imagination, tangled, muddy, painful and perplexed" (P17–18). From this perspective, it is always an open question as to how things are to be taken; from this perspective, if perspective is the word, things go by many names. Pragmatism is a way of fitting one's discourse to the situation in which one finds oneself rather than a method of squaring it with things at large; it is a philosophy of proximity. Not surprisingly, pragmatism thus has an internal kinship with rhetoric and hermeneutics, which are concerned with the application of, well, whatever seems applicable. Pragmatism, let us say, asserts the primacy of the applicable.

2. Speaking Many Languages at Once

Certainly as a scientist James is what one would call a noneliminative materialist, that is, not someone whose purpose is to eliminate theological discourse and to replace it with his own language of physiological description, which is the more natural language to use when describing experiences that are, after all, demonstrably physiological rather than demonic or divine. The point is that James's talk is frequently excessive with respect to his own scientific vocabulary, which naturally he depends on throughout, most obviously in the way the notion of the subconscious serves him as a premier explanatory concept for making sense of religious experiences—as in the experience of sudden conversions. "Psychology and religion are . . . in perfect harmony up to this point," James says,

> since both admit that there are forces seemingly outside of the conscious individual that bring redemption to his life. Nevertheless psychology, defining these forces as "subconscious," and speaking of their effects as due to "incubation," or "cerebration," implies that they do not transcend the individual's personality; and herein she diverges from Christian theology, which insists that they are direct supernatural operations of the Deity. (V211)

Or, again, of a certain sequence of amazing personal accounts, James says that "such quotations express sufficiently well for our purpose the doctrinal interpretation of these changes" (V229). But, he goes on,

> What, now, must we ourselves think of this question? Is an instantaneous conversion a miracle in which God is present . . . ? Or, on the contrary, may the whole phenomenon of regeneration, even in these startling instantaneous examples, possibly be a strictly natural process, divine in its fruits, of course, but in one case more and in another less so, and neither more nor less divine in its mere causation and mechanism than any other process, high or low, of man's interior life? (V230)

There is no mistaking the authoritative voice of science in these quotations, but neither is it any accident that, in the first quotation, James speaks not in his own voice but by means of a personification of psychology and that what he has to say in the second quotation takes the form of an extremely complicated question. This question is partly rhetorical and partly hypothetical, sufficiently closed to call traditional theological language into question yet sufficiently open all the same to allow James to conjure (in the manner of Thomas Carlyle) a sort of natural supernaturalism, that is, a middle way between an old manner of speaking (the language of miracles and divine intervention, which is, however, no less natural for being called divine) and the new (which is the language of covert mental operations that are, however, in a certain manner of speaking, no less divine for being entirely natural). Something is keeping James from speaking straightforwardly and without equivocation, as a scientist should.

It's tempting to say that James, on the occasion of the 1902 Gifford Lectures and addressing a heterogeneous audience in Edinburgh, Scotland, is speaking in tongues, as if on a kind of Pentecost, when everyone listening can hear the word in his or her own native language.

> When I say "Soul," you need not take me in the ontological sense unless you prefer to; for although ontological language is instinctive in such matters, yet Buddhists or Humians can perfectly well describe the facts in the phenomenal terms which are their favorites. For them the soul is only a succession of fields of consciousness: yet there is found in each field a part, or sub-field, which figures as focal and contains the excitement, and from which, as from a centre, the aim seems to be taken. (V195)

Here James looks like a man determined (one way or another) to be understood and who therefore instructs his audience as to how they may take him; yet he asks to be understood not simply according to his own intention and vocabulary but also according to theirs—for it appears that his intention has already accommodated theirs in virtue of the studied indefiniteness of his language. James speaks the language of the theologians, and yet he doesn't—not exactly. What we are given is something like the letter of this language, but the spirit in which it is to be taken is left open as between phenomenological and physiological alternatives, or between a literal and a figurative reading of, say, the word "Soul." Toward words of this sort the audience is encouraged to adopt a hermeneutical attitude, taking them now one way, now another, according to the contexts or situations they happen to inhabit. The relations of letter and spirit are everywhere unstable in *Varieties*.

In another of the pragmatism lectures from 1907, "Pragmatism and Humanism," James rehearses his favorite distinction between a rationalist and a pragmatist. A rationalist, James says, is someone who believes that reality stands ready-made before us and that the task of philosophy is to describe it purely and simply, as it stands, giving it not just in words but in *the only words possible*: giving it, in other words, its name. If reality is one, finished, and simultaneously entire, what need of many words? By contrast, the pragmatist is someone in need of many words—"a happy-go-lucky anarchistic sort of creature" who believes that the universe is open, pluralistic, "unfinished, growing in all sorts of places," now one thing, now another: in short, it is what James calls a "loose universe" (P125). "What we say about reality," James says, "depends on the perspective into which we throw it," which means that we must be prepared to speak in many ways, that is, not in names but in figures—able to figure things in different ways, perspectively, temporally, pluralistically. James asks: "what shall we call a *thing* anyhow?" (P122). What a thing is to be called is contingent on when and where it makes its appearance, and on where and how we stand as to the occasion of it, who we are and what we are like—and what our future demands of us. Accordingly, naming the thing becomes a complicated and, indeed, unfinished business, since it is the vast, endless, and irreducible array of contingencies that the naming of the thing must now try to take into account. The rationalist requires a thing to be named once for all—Adam's sort of naming—whereas the pragmatist favors the perpetual renaming of things, as if language had always to be updated in order to keep pace with a universe-in-the-making, or with the historicity of things, or with a reality that is never ontologically at rest, never sufficiently itself and whole ever to be adequately nameable: and in the bargain a reality from which we can never disengage ourselves sufficiently to gain what sometimes gets called a *philosophical* perspective, namely the perspective of the detached observer. Pragmatism is the philosophy that holds that we can never be philosophical with respect to reality. Our relation to it is just not one of observing and describing. Anyhow there is no calling a thing anything once for all because there is just no such thing as a once-for-all, at least not when one is situated inside of an ongoing reality, or history. A thing makes its appearance nowhere but within temporality and as nothing but a whatchamacallit (an *aliquid*); it does not possess on its own the logical status of thinghood. Things exist not in themselves but only in their versions, and a pragmatist differs from a rationalist by addressing versions of things, not their logical "sorts"—which is why it is always a difficult question as to what, exactly, a pragmatist is talking about. One always has to look to the situation of his or her discourse.

So the question that we come round to has to do with something like James's discursive preferences, which are only mainly, but not exclusively, for the language of psychology. Speaking in the *Varieties* about the appearance of light in experiences of conversion, James says: "I refer to hallucinatory or pseudo-hallucinatory luminous phenomena, *photisms*, to use the term of the psychologists. Saint Paul's blinding heavenly vision seems to have been a phenomenon of this sort; so does Constantine's cross in the sky" (V251–52). Yet it is characteristic of James that he will represent his preferred language as the language of another, that is, as a way of speaking that he makes use of for the occasion without, however, actually appropriating it or making it completely his own. James's attitude in this respect is classically rhetorical, especially as we recall the great premium that the rhetorical cultures of antiquity placed on the ability to adopt a plurality of roles or styles or to speak in many voices or languages as subject and occasion required. The rhetorician is never embodied in his or her statements. Thus James shows the same kind of reserve toward the language of psychology that he has for the traditional vocabulary of the theologians. The language of psychology, as James uses it, never acquires the status or authority of a philosophical language; it remains a rhetoric. None of its expressions is sufficiently grounded to be taken literally as it stands. Any expression will always be subject to interpretation, second thoughts, new sources of understanding, additions and corrections, individual enthusiasms—in short, it will always seem guarded, figurative, porous, and this is so for the very reason that a "loose universe" is not one thing but hangs together in countless different ways, like the weather (P85), and so calls for a language unconfined by theory. Or, as James puts it in "Pragmatism and Humanism," our experiences of the world "lean on each other, but the whole of them, if such a whole there be, leans on nothing. All 'homes' are in finite experience; finite experience as such is homeless. Nothing outside the flux secures the issue of it." Metaphysically, "this describes a tramp and vagrant world, adrift in space, with neither elephant nor tortoise to plant the whole of its foot upon. It is a set of stars hurled into heaven without even a centre of gravity to pull against" (P125). A loose universe is never logically stable. It is always turning into something else, another version of itself (tomorrow's, e.g.): a universe, in short, that in its turnings is more figurative than literal in its intelligibility. But (to speak fairly) what can the word "intelligibility" mean in this event?

3. The Hermeneutics of Pragmatism

In "Pragmatism and Common Sense" James expresses his admiration for those who say, as if he himself did not, that "no hypothesis is truer than any other in the sense of being a more literal copy of reality. They are all but ways of talking on our part, to be compared solely from the point of view of their *use*. The only literally true thing is *reality*"—and reality, from the standpoint of knowledge, is irreducible, mute, and indifferent to what we say about it (P93). Earlier I speculated that what attracted James to religious feelings was just this difficulty of knowing what to call them; they are, in this respect, just what reality is. In lecture 18 of *Varieties*, called "Philosophy," James says: "feeling is private and dumb, and unable to give an account of itself. It allows that its results are mysteries and enigmas, declines to justify them rationally, and on occasion is willing that they should even pass for paradoxical and absurd." And then, on the other side, there is philosophy: "philosophy takes just the opposite attitude. Her aspiration is to reclaim from mystery and paradox whatever territory she touches. To find an escape from obscure and wayward personal persuasion to truth objectively valid for all thinking men has ever been the intellect's most cherished ideal" (V432). But what hope is there for philosophy (versus persuasion) when "no hypothesis is truer than any other in the sense of being a more literal copy of reality"? What hope is there for "truth objectively valid" for all thinking people when all talk is rhetoric? "Feeling is private and dumb, and unable to give an account of itself," and therefore it falls to us to speak in its behalf, giving voice to feeling not as poets but as so many councillors summoned to representation. But how can we bring ourselves to speak when we know that this reality has no preference in itself for the ways we may talk about it and that it will (and does) give itself as happily to the theologians as to the psychologists?[2]

James's answer to this question prefigures Heidegger's argument that our relation to the world is practical rather than theoretical, that is, it is a relationship of involvement *with it* rather than one of knowing it in the sense of conceptual determination.[3] And, like Heidegger, James does not shrink from characterizing this practical relation hermeneutically as one of understanding and interpretation, where understanding is a matter of *taking* something *as* something—knowing the sense it makes in the situation in which we find ourselves *with* it, that is, taking it in relation to some purpose or task at hand in which the question of reality is *not* mute or indifferent but part of our ongoing, everyday, already-understood-and-interpreted life. Whereas, however, Heidegger speaks of our *circumspective* involvement with what is at hand, James (like Nietzsche) speaks as a perspectivalist, that is, still in terms of seeing even if relativized to a point of view, as in "Pragmatism and Humanism":

> In many familiar objects every one will recognize the human element. We conceive a given reality in this way or in that, to suit our purpose, and the reality passively submits to the conception. You can take the number 27 as the cube of 3, or as the product of 3 and 9, or as 26 *plus* 1, or 100 *minus* 73, or in countless other ways, of which one will be just as true as another. You can take a chessboard as black squares on a white ground, or as white squares on a black ground, and neither conception is a false one.
>
> You can treat the adjoined figure as a store, as two big triangles crossing each other, as a hexagon with legs set up on its angles, as six equal triangles hanging together by their tips, etc. All these treatments are true treatments— the sensible *that* upon the paper resists no one of them. You can say of a line that it runs east, or you can say that it runs west, and the line *per se* accepts both descriptions without rebelling at the inconsistency. (P121)

So one may speak, as Heidegger does, of the *as-structure* of perception.[4] As James says (on many different occasions) a thing is never simply *known;* it is always *known as*, where the *as* entails the whole context or web of circumstances in which the thing is encountered. The question perhaps is whether our relation with a thing (or with the world) can ever be adequately characterized merely in terms of propositions and descriptions, however multiple and various; or whether it is only narrative—multiple, variable *narratives*—that can capture the density and many-sidedness of our worldliness. The question is whether perspectivalism isn't more theory than practice, still concerned with representations rather than with actions.[5]

James sometimes negotiates a question of this sort by preferring "talking" to "seeing" as a way of characterizing the hermeneutics of our everydayness. Here is a famous passage from "Does 'Consciousness' Exist?" (1904), in which James speaks of the subjective and objective ways of taking (or talking about) an experience that is pure in itself, that is, not anything more than what goes on mutely or brutely or as you will:

> As "subjective" we say that the experience represents; as "objective" it is represented. What represents and what is represented is here numerically the same; but we must remember that no dualism of being represented and representing resides in the experience *per se*. In its pure state, or when isolated, there is no self-splitting of it into consciousness and what the consciousness is "of." Its subjectivity and objectivity are functional attributes solely, realized only when the experience is taken, *i.e.*, talked of, twice, considered along with its two differing contexts respectively, by a new retrospective experience, of which that whole past complication now forms the fresh content. (ERE23; WWJ177)

Subjectivity and objectivity belong not to the structure of things, nor to the way consciousness is put together, but to a certain way of talking about or construing experience, or a certain way of narrating or figuring it in order to make sense (or use) of it for some particular purpose. Subjectivity and objectivity are entries in a lexicon for interpreting experience. So, to speak strictly, we should speak of them in quotation marks as "objectivity" and "subjectivity," for they are words in the first place and, in the second, meanings in the sense of differences or terms of differentiation by which we are able to "discursify" experience or, in another metaphor, carve the marble of experience into a world (P119).

But James seems wary of metaphors of worldmaking that situate us outside the world. There is the question, for example, of where our words come from that we use to parse the world. How do we manage to have such things at our disposal? Lecture 18 ("Philosophy") of *Varieties* is one place where James addresses this question in a truly interesting way. Having said that "feeling is private and dumb, and unable to give an account of itself," he raises the question of how, then, to talk of feeling and whether we are able to speak *philosophically* on its behalf. What does *this* sort of talking amount to?

> I believe that philosophy will always have opportunity to labor at this task [that is, the translation of mute feelings into intelligible discourse]. We are thinking beings, and we cannot exclude the intellect from participating in any of our functions. Even in soliloquizing with ourselves, we construe our feelings intellectually. Both our personal ideals and our religious and mystical experiences must be interpreted congruously with the kind of scenery which our thinking mind inhabits. The philosophic climate of our time inevitably

forces its own clothing on us. Moreover, we must exchange our feelings with one another, and in doing so we have to speak, and to use general and abstract verbal formulas. Conceptions and constructions are thus a necessary part of our religion; and as moderator amid the clash of hypotheses, and mediator among criticisms of one man's constructions by another, philosophy will always have much to do. It would be strange if I disputed this, when these very lectures which I am giving are . . . a laborious attempt to extract from the privacies of religious experience some general facts which can be defined in formulas upon which everybody may agree. (V432–33)

John Stuart Mill, following Wordsworth, believed poetry to be the natural language of feeling, whereas logic and method give voice to reason; but for James feelings must be philosophized as well as poetized—or, in other words, we must not simply give voice to feeling, as in soliloquy or song, but must make sense of it. Philosophical talk is hermeneutical; that is, the task of philosophy is to construe or interpret religious feelings in order to overcome their inscrutability or reserve, their resistance to language and common understanding, as if such feelings were a dark or enigmatic text.

Here we come round again to our earlier question about what to call religious feelings, but now the question cannot be formulated in terms of mere naming and description. Religious feelings must undergo reconstruction in a language—but what language, exactly? James's answer is historical and cultural, that is, we can only speak in the language going on around us. "The philosophic climate of our time inevitably forces its own clothing on us." If you ask, Where do our vocabularies come from? here you begin to get your answer: they come from wherever language comes from, that is, they compose the human and already intelligible world in which we make our appearance and from which we acquire the whole common range of beliefs and practices that make up our human lives. This historicism is one of the major themes of James's pragmatism essays. In "Pragmatism and Humanism," for example, James distinguishes among three components of reality: sensations, relations, and *"previous truths"* (P118). "Previous truths" are constructions of reality that come down to us from the past, which are there to greet us when we are born, and which have claims on us analogous to the claims of our mother tongue: constructions, in other words, that are taken as authoritative (or *as* "reality") by the communicative community, the form of life or lifeworld, in which we are able to do such things as talk about reality. "The philosophic climate of our time inevitably forces its own clothing on us." None of us may speak as we please, not even to ourselves, and imagine that we have made sense of anything. Understanding, including and especially self-understanding, is social rather than mental.[6]

4. The Claims of Truth

In "Pragmatism's Conception of Truth," James says, "Realities mean . . . either concrete facts, or abstract kinds of things and relations perceived intuitively between them. They furthermore and thirdly mean, as things that new ideas of ours must no less take account of, the whole body of other truths already in our possession" (P102). James diverges completely from the Cartesian program of methodical progress in which a solitary mind sets out to construct a world for itself and proceeds by first eradicating all prior understanding or everything that has come down to it or is already in its possession. On the Cartesian model, authoritative discourse is that which begins as if no one had ever spoken before. By contrast, pragmatism presupposes a world received as well as made, the historical world as an ongoing and continuously transforming construction—Wilhelm Dilthey's "common sphere" into which we are woven and which we reweave in our turn. James recognizes the claims of tradition, but what he recognizes in particular is that these claims are not logically fixed but are historical and contingent; they are part of and (in view of the way they are always changing) they help to produce the unsettled or "open" nature of things. We are (being historical creatures) always answerable to the historical and cultural situation in which we find ourselves—which has been prepared for us (made intelligible for us) by those who have already passed this way—but we are not determined by it in a way that holds us fast, because what is historical about our situation is just that it is composed of things that are growing strange, or dying out, or emerging for the first time and competing for advantage. Unlike Dilthey's common sphere, pragmatism's world is multiple, heterogeneous, porous, inwardly striated, alive with conflicts of interpretation. It is easy to say that religious feelings must undergo construction in a language currently in use, but not so easy to determine currency (or authority) in a world characterized by the historicality and contingency of the truth. What comes down to us from the past, after all, is not one language but a babel of rival and incompatible languages. The distinctive feature of tradition is always the conflict of interpretations; or in other words, the world is no less "loose" and going every which way for being already in place, surrounding us and constraining us in sometimes contradictory ways. This is what being historical means. And it is why, James thinks, pragmatism is the order of the day.

In this (James's) age of Darwin, Huxley, and Spencer, one thing that is going on around us is that traditional theological language (which is of course itself not one language but a family of conflicting tongues) is going out of traditional use— but it has not become anything (yet) like a Latin. On the contrary, it is becoming increasingly a purely vernacular as against a learned or enlightened way of talking about certain sorts of uncanny experience, like sensing the presence of the unseen.

It is an everyday rather than a learned language. It is at all events never likely to become so dead a language that we will never find occasions to use it; yet taken as it is (or simply as it comes down to us), it no longer seems adequate to its subject, or to our new acquaintances, or to the altering occasions of our interest in it. This is especially so when our interest in religious experience has begun to circulate through, among other new languages, psychology, which every day grows stronger in its explanatory power—so much so, James says, that it is in danger of explaining too much and understanding too little, as when, for example, it figures Saint Theresa as a common madwoman. "To the medical mind," James says, as if such a mind were not his own,

> [Saint Theresa's] ecstasies signify nothing but suggested and imitated hyp-noid states, on an intellectual basis of superstition, and a corporeal one of degeneration and hysteria. Undoubtedly these pathological conditions have existed in many and possibly in all the cases, but that fact tells us nothing about the value for knowledge of the consciousness which they induce. To pass a spiritual judgment upon these states, we must not content ourselves with superficial medical talk, but inquire into their fruits for life. (V413)

It might not be too much to describe *Varieties* as a vast pragmatic allegorization of religious experience, where allegory means the recontextualization of what is false or absurd so as to make it come out true. Saint Theresa might for all the world have been quite literally (that is, empirically) mad, but pragmatism provides a context in which it is possible to take the dead letter of her text in a new spirit. So James speaks of passing "a spiritual judgment" on her "ecstasies," where "spiritual" means putting aside "superficial medical talk" and regarding these ecstasies in terms of "their fruits for life." This hermeneutical turn from the empirical to the ethical is part of what Cornell West calls James's "evasion of philosophy." James described his pragmatism as, among other things, a theory of truth, but West is right to wonder whether at the end of the day "any 'truth' is left after James gets through with it."[7] For as West says, James reinterprets the true as the good, or as James himself puts it: "let me now say only this, that truth is *one species of good*, and not, as is usually supposed, a category distinct from good, and co-ordinate with it. *The true is the name of whatever proves itself good in the way of belief, and good, too, for definite, assignable reasons*" (P42).

Religion brings James up against the limits of the empirical, rather the way the anthropologist confronts these limits in the ethical claims that an alien form of life makes when it asks to be described in a language it can understand (a language in which it can recognize itself). At the outset of "Mysticism" (lecture 16), for example, James says: "whether my treatment of mystical states will shed more light or darkness, I do not know, for my own constitution shuts me out from their enjoyment almost entirely, and I can speak of them only at second hand" (V379). What is it, however, to speak of them at first hand? What James studies in *Varieties* are not religious experiences given as empirical phenomena but, rather, firsthand accounts of such phenomena. The point to mark is that these accounts are given almost entirely in the traditional language of theological discourse. These experiences come down to us, in other words, not as "pure" experiences that we may construe as we will in any language that is authoritative for us but as already interpreted experiences, that is, experiences that are already theological in their self-understanding. Or, to put it more exactly, these experiences are only so many traditional texts, especially in the second half of the "Mysticism" lecture which studies poems by Saint John of the Cross, autobiographies of Al-Ghazali and Saint Theresa, the *Upanishads*, and so on. The question that James faces is how far to take these texts in *their* terms and how far to rewrite them in his own. This is the classical hermeneutical dilemma. For it is clear that these texts must be reinscribed (in some sense) in order for us to arrive at their "truth"; yet it is also the case that we cannot simply efface these originals analytically without losing hold of our subject or, more to the point, without losing the hold (or the claim) that this subject has on us, which would be, it turns out, just to lose its "truth."

One could mention here the famous lecture, "On a Certain Blindness in Human Beings," which in part is about the anthropological problem of making sense of the sense other people make of their experiences. This essay is about the limits of a spectator-theory of knowledge, which cannot cope with the problem of cultural difference. James comes round here to the hermeneutical position of interpretive social science, which holds that understanding a human action means understanding the significance it has for the one who performs it. This understanding means bracketing empirical description in favor of some form of participation in the event to be described—"no man," says James, "lives in the external truth among salts and acids."[8] Hence in "On a Certain Blindness" James contrasts two sorts of observer, the empiricist and the poet, where the one is reduced to experiencing the unrelenting strangeness of the common and the everyday, whereas the other is open, porous, responsive, and engaged with all of its otherwise unremarkable details.

At a very interesting moment in "Mysticism," James quotes from an odd text by Madame Blavatsky, *The Voices of Silence:* "he who would hear the voice of Nada, the 'Soundless Sound,' and comprehend it, he has to learn the nature of Dhâranâ. . . . When to himself his form appears unreal, as do on waking all the forms he sees in dreams; when he has ceased to hear the many, he may discern the ONE"—and so on. Here is James's comment on this text:

These words, if they do not awaken laughter as you receive them, probably stir chords within you which music and language touch in common. Music

gives us ontological messages which nonmusical criticism is unable to contradict, though it may laugh at our foolishness in minding them. There is a
verge of the mind which these things haunt; and whispers therefrom mingle
with the operations of our understanding, even as the waters of the infinite
ocean send their waves to break among the pebbles that lie upon our shores.
(V421)

Of two ways of being an outsider, one is philosophical or methodological, as
by the adoption of an objectifying attitude that turns everything around you into
an analytic project. The other is social and historical (or, say, anthropological),
as when you are confronted by a language you cannot understand—an alien
or secret tongue whose sounds, depending on your attitude, may strike you as
comic, or as expressive without expression, or as purely formal as in music, filled
with "ontological messages" that are closed off to analysis. Insiders can hear such
messages; we can (at best) know only of their goings-on. Again, as in "On a Certain
Blindness in Human Beings," the implication is that understanding an experience
always means living through it. And in *Varieties* James finds himself in the (for
him) uncharacteristic condition of being external to life, peering at it through the
windows of alien texts.
    At all events the sensation of being haunted by alien or inaccessible meanings—this experience of the hermeneutical strangeness of religion, where sense is
not abolished but withheld or forbidden like a shibboleth—is present everywhere
in *Varieties*. "We recognize passwords to the mystical region as we hear them," James
says, "but we cannot use them ourselves" (V422). It is as if we had lost the use of
our native tongue but not the feeling of its claim on us: there is a "verge of the
mind" in which this strange language remains darkly familiar.
    Here we have the proper context for James's final lecture in *Varieties*, "Conclusions," in which (in a certain manner of speaking) James tries his own hand at
theological discourse. "We who have pursued such radical expressions [of religion],"
he says, "may now be sure that we know its secrets as authentically as anyone can
know them who learns them from another"—that is, not quite as an adept or initiate
but just at second hand, as if poised undecidably between faith and suspicion. It is
here that we learn how James intends to speak of God, or how he would use this
name, which is, it turns out, coterminous with the "truth" of religious experience, or
with that "common nucleus" to which all religious traditions testify in their several
ways and to which James will now testify as well (V486, 507).
    James's procedure is to construct a model of an experience (which he is careful
not to name) whose stages and horizons give a clue to its nature. The experience
is inaugurated by a feeling of "uneasiness," that is, "a sense that there is *something
wrong about us* as we naturally stand," and that this wrong can only be corrected "by

making proper connection with the higher powers" (V508). The question is, what are these "higher powers," exactly? James figures it this way:

> The individual, so far as he suffers from his wrongness and criticises it, is to that extent consciously beyond it, and in at least possible touch with something higher, if anything higher exists. Along with the wrong part there is thus a better part of him, even though it may be but a most helpless germ. With which part he should identify his real being is by no means obvious at this stage; but when stage 2 (the stage of solution or salvation) arrives, the man identifies his real being with the germinal higher part of himself; and does so in the following way. *He becomes conscious that this higher part is conterminous and continuous with a* MORE *of the same quality, which is operative in the universe outside of him, and which he can keep in working touch with, and in a fashion get on board of and save himself when all his lower being has gone to pieces in the wreck.* (V508)

So the "higher powers" are, on the one hand, a projection from within and, on the other, (just possibly) an emanation from without. Psychology is that discipline that studies these powers as projections from within us; the history of religious traditions figures them as emanations from the outside. It is, once again, a question of perspective, or of what is to be done, or perhaps of how one connects up with one's future. In any event, how one's experience of this something MORE is to be taken depends on where, and who, one is.

The question is: what does it mean to take this MORE as true? This is, in fact, how James desires to take it, and how he manages to do so provides as good a lesson in pragmatism (and the pragmatic way of talking) as one can be given.

The first thing to notice is that James's MORE is not quite a term of reference. It is, to be sure, the only name that James will allow himself to attach positively to the "higher powers" with which, in this saving experience, we feel ourselves to be in contact, but it happens that MORE is not a name, nor yet is it any sort of makeshift indefinite pronoun like Wordsworth's resounding "something evermore about to be." For James, the purpose of this word is to guide us up to (but not to carry us across) a threshold of definition where names can be put into play, if only in a manner of speaking (but for a definite, vital, or necessary purpose). The manner of speaking that we choose to employ in giving a traditional religious definition to the MORE is what James calls an "over-belief," that is, a case of (strictly or philosophically speaking) going too far, which is what all religious traditions enable us to do for the sake of our lives (V511). To be able to cross this threshold is to be able to act, saving ourselves when all our lower portions go "to pieces in the wreck."

It is for the sake of this saving action that James will (eventually) want to call this MORE by its traditional name of God, but taken as it stands, this sacred name is inaccessible to him. "Those of us who are not personally favored with . . . specific revelations," James reminds us, "must stand outside of them altogether." Whence James finds himself compelled to speak analytically, somewhat in the manner of (but not quite so definitely as) Frederic Myers, who speaks not of God but of the "*subconscious self*": "each of us [James quotes Myers] is in reality an abiding psychical entity far more extensive than he knows—an individuality which can never express itself completely through the organism; but there is always some part of the Self unmanifested; and always, as it seems, some power of organic expression in abeyance or reserve" (V514, 512). Myers speaks for James, who adds:

> Much of the content of this larger background against which our conscious being stands out in relief is insignificant. Imperfect memories, silly jingles, inhibitive timidities, "dissolutive" phenomena of various sorts, as Myers calls them, enter into it for a large part. But in it many of the performances of genius seem also to have their origin; and in our study of conversion, of mystical experiences, and of prayer, we have seen how striking a part invasions from this region play in the religious life. (V512)

There is, however, a crucial difference between Myers and James. Myers speaks of entities and objectifies the subconscious as a "Self," whereas James's characteristic terms of reference are "region," "horizon," "sides," and "fields of life." Recall that in the celebrated essay "Does Consciousness Exist?" James's conclusion is that consciousness does *not* exist, no more (one might say) than God does, *as an entity*. "*That entity*," James says, "*is fictitious*," for consciousness is not a substance but a field or region of experience—or, indeed, it is just ungrounded experience taken from a certain point of view (ERE37). Experience as felt is pure, but (as James puts it in "The Thing and Its Relations" [1905]) "the flux of it no sooner comes than it tends to fill itself with emphases, and these salient parts become identified and fixed and abstracted; so that experience now flows as if shot through with adjectives and nouns and prepositions and conjunctions" (ERE94). Experience becomes, in short, a spoken and intelligible extension of minds and objects, of inner and outer worlds, of higher and lower parts, of transcendent and immanent domains. If you ask, therefore, how James is able to speak of God (in whom he professes no definite belief), the answer is ironic from both the analytic and the religious points of view. For if minds and objects be permitted in experience, why not "higher powers"? Experience is fathomless and inarticulate in every direction; or, as James says, "Day follows day, and its contents are simply added. The new contents themselves are not true, they simply *come* and *are*. Truth is *what we say about* them" (P36).

"Let me then propose," James says in his conclusion to *Varieties*, "as an hypothesis, that whatever it may be on its *farther* side, the 'more' with which in religious experience we feel ourselves connected is on its *hither* side the subconscious continuation of our conscious life" (V512). The point not to be missed, however, is that the difference between hither and yon proves to be indeterminate: (the ghost of Emerson hovers and looms throughout—the Oversoul is, in so many words, redescribed as an Undersoul with no change in consequences): whence the freedom with which James now allows himself to speak:

> The further limits of our being plunge, it seems to me, into an altogether other dimension of existence from the sensible and merely "understandable" world. Name it the mystical region, or the supernatural region, whichever you choose. So far as our ideal impulses originate in this region (and most of them do originate in it, for we find them possessing us in a way for which we cannot articulately account), we belong to it in a more intimate sense than that in which we belong to the visible world, for we belong in the most intimate sense wherever our ideals belong. Yet the unseen region in question is not merely ideal, for it produces effects in this world. When we commune with it, work is actually done upon our finite personality, for we are turned into new men, and consequences in the way of conduct follow in the natural world upon our regenerative change. But that which produces effects within another reality must be termed a reality itself, so I feel as if we had no philosophical excuse for calling the unseen or mystical world unreal.
>
> God is the natural appellation, for us Christians at least, for the supreme reality, so I will call this higher part of the universe by the name of God (V515–16).

One way (the theological way) to take this passage would be to say that in it James appears to be a sort of residual Emersonian pantheist for whom God is pervasive, not perhaps through the whole of experience, but anyway through that portion of it that enables us to turn out to our best advantage. The defect in this interpretation is both large and small. It is large, because James's God is not any sort of coherent metaphysical divinity but only ("for us Christians"!) a certain apt way of talking about experience: apt in the sense of being (in the pragmatic way of speaking) *true* in the long run. The defect is small, however, for the very reason that talk, to be true, requires no metaphysical foundations, only a gainful prospect tracing to positive results. Pragmatism's "general notion of truth," James says, "is essentially bound up with the way in which one moment in our experience may lead us towards other moments which it will be worth while to have been led to. Primarily, and on the common sense level, the truth of a state of mind means this function of *a leading that is worth while*" (P98). Or, again, "The essential thing is the process of being guided. Any idea that helps us to *deal*, whether practically or intellectually, with either the reality or its belongings, that doesn't entangle our progress in frustrations, that *fits*, in fact, and adapts our life to the reality's whole setting, will agree sufficiently to meet the requirement. It will hold true of that reality" (V102).

Famously, Bertrand Russell objected to this notion of truth because there did not seem to him any reason for it. Pragmatism's conception of truth, from an analytic point of view, just doesn't help anyone to make the sort of claims that a theory of truth is supposed to underwrite: namely, claims as to what the facts are.[9] James can talk of God so freely as he does because his conception of truth, or of what it means to speak the truth of anything, is only epistemological in the long run, as if describing a future rather than a present world. I mentioned the ghost of Emerson. Stanley Cavell calls Emerson and Thoreau "philosophers of direction, orienters," and, just so, "truth," James says, "is an affair of leading" (P101).[10]

> Agreement [with reality] turns out to be essentially an affair of leading— leading that is useful because it is into quarters that contain objects that are important. True ideas lead . . . to consistency, stability and flowing human intercourse. They lead away from eccentricity and isolation, from foiled and barren thinking. The untrammelled flowing of the leading-process, its general freedom from clash and contradiction, passes for its indirect verification; but all roads lead to Rome, and in the end and eventually, all true processes must lead to the face of directly verifying sensible experiences *somewhere*, which somebody's ideas have copied.
>
> Such is the large loose way in which the pragmatist interprets the word agreement. (P103)

Truth, therefore, is not so much a way of construing reality rightly, much less of constructing it as if from scratch, as of inhabiting it coherently, which means keeping it workable or inhabitable over the long term, keeping past and future coherent with one another, by the way we act in it—and also by the way we talk in it: keeping coherent with others, being understood by them. At the end of the day truth is how we connect up with a world made of other people.

> All human thinking gets discursified: we exchange ideas; we lend and borrow verifications, get them from one another by means of social intercourse. All truth thus gets verbally built out, stored up, and made available for everyone. Hence we must *talk* consistently just as we must *think* consistently: for both in talk and thought we deal with kinds. Names are arbitrary, but once understood they must be kept to. We mustn't now call Abel "Cain" or Cain "Abel." If we do, we ungear ourselves from the whole book of Genesis, and from all its connexions with the universe of speech and fact down to the

present time. We throw ourselves out of whatever truth that entire system of speech and fact may embody. (P102–3)

As if knowing how to talk at all just meant knowing how to get on with one another—how not to blindside one another, and the world, with unheard-of speech.

2

Donald Davidson
among the Outcasts

Then he took it into his head to invert, no longer the order of the words in the sentence, nor that of the letters in the word, nor that of the sentences in the period, nor simultaneously that of the words in the sentence and that of the letters in the word, nor simultaneously that of the words in the sentence and that of the sentences in the period, nor simultaneously that of the letters in the word and that of the words in the sentence and that of the sentences in the period, ho no, but, in the brief course of the same period, now that of the words in the sentence, now that of the letters in the word, now that of the sentences in the period, now simultaneously that of the words in the sentence and that of the letters in the word, now simultaneously that of the words in the sentence and that of the sentence in the period, now simultaneously that of the letters in the word and that of the sentences in the period, and now simultaneously that of the letters in the word and that of the words in the sentence and that of the sentences in the period.

—Samuel Beckett, *Watt*

A celebrated analytic philosopher, Donald Davidson, has written some things that are apt to catch the attention of a literary critic.[1] For example, in an essay called "James Joyce and Humpty Dumpty," Davidson says that in *Finnegans Wake* "Joyce takes us back to the foundations and origins of communication; he puts us in the situation of the jungle linguist trying to get the hang of a new language and a novel culture, to assume the perspective of someone who is an alien or exile. As we, his listeners or readers, become familiar with the devices he has made us master, we find ourselves removed a certain distance from our own language, our usual selves, and our society. We join Joyce as outcasts, temporarily freed, or so it seems, from the nets of our language and our culture" (PA11). What's Davidson's interest here? In this chapter I would like to try to come to some understanding, in my own nontechnical way, of what sort of thing Davidson is getting at when he makes the *Wake* originary and foundational with respect to what happens in communication; and also what he is getting at when he makes the *Wake* radically liberating or alienating—placing us, vis-à-vis our own language and culture, in the classic theoretical position of W. V. O. Quine's "radical translator" or Davidson's own "radical interpreter."

A radical translator is one who confronts not just a language different from his or her own but one so historically and culturally removed from it that there would be, at least empirically, owing to the way sentences are embedded in networks of beliefs, no way of knowing when a translation from that language is right or wrong—no way, in other words, of choosing between rival and incompatible translations.[2] Translations of poetic texts are frequently radical in this sense. Much to the same point, a radical interpreter is one who tries to understand and interpret the sentences of someone who speaks a radically alien language. A theory of radical interpretation tries to formulate some principles that might show what it takes to do such a thing, and this includes (to take up the slack of indeterminacy) a principle of charity that stipulates, as a starting point for interpretation, widespread agreement of the other with ourselves as to how things are, or at least how they look. "This is accomplished," says Davidson, "by assigning truth conditions to alien sentences that make native speakers right when plausibly possible, according, of course, to our own view of what is right. . . . If we cannot find a way to interpret the utterances and other behaviour of a creature as revealing a set of beliefs largely consistent and true by our own standards, we have no reason to count that creature as rational, or as having beliefs, or as saying anything."[3] Charity apart, however, "radical" in this context means being outside the language one wants to understand and interpret, as if encountering intelligent life in another galaxy, or listening to a schizophrenic, or reading a poem. (What being an outsider means is what evidently needs to be clarified.)

It might seem an open question as to whether any two natural human ("earthly") languages meet the standard of mutual alienation that the word "radical" is meant to suggest, but Davidson thinks that because we speakers of the same language each have our own unique way of speaking it (each our own idiolect, each evidently his or her own rich repertoire of such things), we are sufficiently alien to one another for the principles of radical interpretation (e.g., the principle of charity) still to apply (ITI276–77). As Davidson says: "the problem of interpretation is domestic as well as foreign: it surfaces for speakers of the same language in the form of the question, how can it be determined that the language is the same? Speakers of the same language can go on the assumption that for them the same expressions are to be interpreted in the same way, but this does not indicate what justifies the assumption. All understanding of the speech of another involves radical interpretation. But it will help keep assumptions from going unnoticed to focus on cases where interpretation is most clearly called for: interpretation in one idiom of talk in another" (ITI125). Joyce's *Finnegans Wake* (eventually) helps Davidson bring this point home, since Joyce writes our language in such a way as to put us outside of it (or maybe, as Heidegger would say, he writes to show us where we already are: without a language). This suggests a nice postmodern allegory as to what poetry or literature might be for. Having, in our time, given up on metaphysical standpoints, logical foundations, dogmas of empiricism, theories of knowledge, refutations of skepticism, and the credibility of universals, or in short having abandoned the whole idea of getting outside of our own languages and beliefs, philosophers seem to be turning to literature to provide them with the critical distance, or sense of outsiderness, that they need in order to keep doing philosophy. Here one thinks of Richard Rorty's irony (philosophy's first alien disposition).[4] Of course Davidson might be after other sorts of quite ordinary, nonphilosophical outsiderness.

1. On Metaphor as Ecstatic Discourse

Some of what Davidson is after seems to peer out from different parts of his essay, "What Metaphors Mean" (1978), which claims not to find in metaphor anything out of the ordinary with respect to the proper everyday literal workings of language.[5] Specifically this means denying, quite un-Nietzsche-like, any semantic distinction between the literal and metaphorical. "No theory of metaphorical meaning or metaphorical truth can help explain how metaphor works. Metaphor runs on the same familiar linguistic tracks that the plainest sentences do. . . . What distinguishes metaphor is not meaning but use—in this it is like assertion, hinting, lying, promising, or criticizing" (ITI259). To get at what Davidson means, we might try saying that there are no metaphors outright but only sentences that we take in a certain way. As Paul Ricoeur says, "a metaphor does not exist in itself, but [only] in and through an interpretation."[6] For example, we might say, as Davidson does, that a sentence like "The law is an ass" has only one meaning, namely the literal meanings of its words ("The law is an ass" means the law is an ass), and as such the sentence is false or absurd. However, Davidson wants to stop right there at the literal for reasons that might not restrain a literary critic (or Paul Ricoeur), that is, he wants to say no more about what metaphors *mean* than that they do so literally, whereas the critic, to be about business, has a kind of obligation to say that the sentence becomes metaphorical when we transfer it to a context (such as Dickens provides) where it comes out true, or in which, appearances aside, it is true to say, in a manner of speaking, "The law is an ass."[7] What cannot be taken in one context must be taken in another.

As if metaphor required a holistic rather than an atomistic theory—in the sense that understanding "The law is an ass" does not require us to square properties of the law *(P)* with properties of an ass *(R)* (a futile exercise)—rather the sentence presupposes a background or fabric of interwoven sentences or "endless interlocked beliefs" (ITI157). These might be an array of narratives, or maybe a world and its histories, in terms of which (somewhere and to someone) it makes sense or is intelligible to say of the law that it's an ass. Making sense here might simply mean that we know of a sense, that is, a context or set of circumstances or conditions in which we believe it is true to say, *s* is *p*. We apply something like a principle of charity to "The law is an ass" when we think of Dickens as supplying the beliefs that enable us to interpret or recognize "The law is an ass" as a true statement.

This is too obvious to be wrong, but neither, in Davidson's terms, is it precise enough to be right. "The law is an ass" means simply that the law is an ass (a meaningless statement). Knowing English, knowing its rules and conventions, is (so we might say) all we need to know to know that "the law is an ass" means, absurdly, that the law is an ass. Unfortunately, to *contextualize* the statement, thinking to save it thereby from its absurdity, does not alter what the statement *means*. All contextualization (or, if you like, recontextualization) does tell us is what, in the event, someone—a speaker or interpreter of the sentence—means by it. All it says is how someone (Dickens, e.g.) might want to apply this piece of absurdity, or how we might take it in making sense of Dickens.[8] Davidson means to emphasize this distinction between the meaning of the sentence and the use of it, that is, H. P. Grice's distinction between sentence-meaning and user's meaning.[9] A whole theory of meaning or truth or language—for example, the idea that the meaning of a sentence is the meaning of its constituent words, or that the meaning of a sentence is its truth conditions—depends on it.[10] Metaphor is external to meaning and truth; it is, on at least one of Davidson's views of language, outside of language, outside of sentences, predicates, and references—in the land of "unfamiliar noises," as Rorty happily puts it.[11] But if metaphor is outside of language, maybe we are all outside of language.

Being outside of language doesn't mean that metaphors deserve interpretive charity (charity is reserved for speakers), but Davidson does think metaphors are pragmatic. His way of putting this is to say that what metaphors *can do* is cause a change in our relation to our world—not a conceptual change, of course, assuming we know what that means, but just a behavioral change in the way of our seeing things. For example, metaphors are famously unparaphrasable, but all this means is that when we try to break a metaphor down in order to get at its propositional core, we find that it means or, more accurately, involves, if anything, too much: its core is all over the place. Metaphor at all events is all on the surface. There is neither a core nor a logical form to it apart from what it literally says. Or, as Davidson says, all there is to a metaphor is what it "makes us notice" (ITI262). If what metaphors cause us to notice were delimitable—"finite in scope and propositional in nature"— we could paraphrase them. "But in fact there is no limit to what a metaphor calls to our attention, and much of what we are caused to notice is not propositional in character. When we try to say what a metaphor 'means,' we soon realize there is no end to what we want to mention" (ITI263). We could express this by saying that making sense of metaphor means making narrative rather than propositional sense, that is, it means giving the metaphor a context in roughly the way Dickens did when he created a world for "The law is an ass" to be, loosely, true of. No context, no metaphor: no background of presuppositions extending absurdly and indefinitely into the whole imaginable universe, no nothing. Metaphors taken in isolation ("John is an ox": every logician's favorite) are inevitably experienced as dead. Metaphors presuppose forms of life exhibiting novel-like density to Chinese travelers passing through; natives perhaps need to read novels to make them notice the density around them.

But it is evident (as we have seen) that Davidson does not think metaphors are interpretable in the way ordinary sentences are, except as sentences that are trivially false or absurd. Metaphors, technically but importantly, stop being sentences for him.[12] Like some New Critics (and, more recently, like Richard Rorty) he thinks that when a metaphor becomes interpretable, it dies—or vice versa: when it dies, we no longer have any trouble paraphrasing it.[13] Like some New Critics, he holds that the "real issue" lies not in what a metaphor means "but in the question of how the metaphor is related to what it makes us see" (ITI261), as if our relation to the world were one of seeing (and not, for example, rather more like our relation to a novel, where we are very close to inhabiting, or virtually inhabiting, an alien or perhaps not-so-alien world; imagine metaphors turning us out of the house).[14] But Davidson is thinking of metaphor now only to ward off Max Black's idea that metaphors have a "special meaning, a special cognitive content," that we can grasp conceptually (ITI262). So near the very end of his essay Davidson likens metaphor to Wittgenstein's "noticing an aspect":[15] "if I show you Wittgenstein's duck-rabbit, and I say, 'It's a duck,' then with luck you see it as a duck; if I say, 'It's a rabbit,' you see it as a rabbit. But no proposition expresses what I have led you to see. Perhaps you have come to realize that the drawing can be seen as a duck or as a rabbit. But one could come to know this without ever seeing the drawing as a duck or as a rabbit. Seeing as is not seeing that. Metaphor makes us see one thing as another by making some literal statement that inspires or prompts the insight. Since in most cases what the metaphor prompts or inspires is not entirely, or even at all, recognition of some truth or fact, the attempt to give literal expression to the content of the metaphor is simply misguided" (ITI263). "Insight" and "recognition" here are to be understood behaviorally (or behavioristically) rather than morally. Literary critics must try not to let this take all the sting or fun out of "The law is an ass." Like objects in the world, metaphors are important for the beliefs they cause. It seems important to add that causing beliefs is different from, and more important than, confirming them. I'm not sure Davidson wants to think of metaphors as *causing* beliefs in the way natural objects do, but if I understand his argument this is what metaphors accomplish. Metaphors are outside of language in the way the world is.

Davidson's idea of metaphor as noticing the world, causing us to see not just one thing differently but an endless array of things we might have missed, helps to loosen the hold that the idea of metaphor as seeing likenesses between two dissimilar objects has had on us since Aristotle's time. No one wants to give up the idea of seeing likeness between dissimilars, not even Davidson, but Davidson's account of metaphor causes us to see that the likenesses at work in "The law is an ass" are not between the law and the ass but between the world Dickens creates and the one we already inhabit: two law-governed, down-by-law worlds (the two may after all be pretty much the same world, which is what Davidson tries to explain to us about alternative conceptual schemes). Here is where, pace Davidson, one might try replacing or elaborating the concept of seeing as perceiving aspects, likenesses, or what-have-you, with a concept of moral recognition, seeing the *truth* of Dickens's characterization in the sense of recognizing our own reality in his fiction, seeing the justice or indeed the application of his characterization of the law (seeing, at all events, an alternative to the law's serious, straightforward self-image).[16] Confronted with this elaboration, of course, Davidson would most likely say, "It's very well, only you're no longer talking about metaphor but have gone over into what metaphor makes us see." Here the issue is one of force rather than of meaning.[17]

Just so. "Only within metaphysics," says Heidegger, "is there the metaphorical."[18] Heidegger's motto means that only in a culture or in a group pretty firmly in the grip of the law of noncontradiction would it occur to anyone (an Aristotle, e.g., or a Paul Ricoeur) to produce a theory of metaphor, the idea being that metaphors stand out as such only against the background of the law of noncontradiction, or that metaphorical interpretation is simply a way of saving self-contradictory statements before the law of noncontradiction by recontextualizing them; or maybe metaphor is just a way of applying or justifying the law of noncontradiction.[19] At all events metaphor certainly presupposes a logical order of things such as only philosophers could come by, that is, a world constructed according to categories, conventions, rules, conceptual frameworks, totalities of essences hanging coherently together, something in short like metaphysics. Davidson takes metaphor out of metaphysics; he's closer to Heidegger's asylum than he can dare imagine.[20] The virtue or at least interest of Davidson's account of metaphor as disclosive, open-ended, illimitable, irreducible to any propositional style of philosophical discourse, is that metaphor is no longer part of an organon but is something ecstatic—a discourse that, like poetry or literature, removes us "from our own language, our usual selves, and our society," causing us to see things (e.g., the law) from the outside, as aliens, which is to say (as with Dickens) satirically. In certain circumstances one can imagine that the real issue with metaphor is not what it makes us notice, nor what it expresses, but what it exposes, not just to our critical gaze but to our raucous, unprincipled laughter.

2. Talking without Language

Here are two theories as to how it is that our speech makes such sense as it does (how it is that we can make sense of what someone says). The first, the deep-structure theory, thinks of speech as a species of rule-governed behavior, where the rules (conventions, schemata, principles, regularities, contents of tacit knowledge) are internal to language, which works in some way like a self-regulating system. Sharing a language means sharing these rules, or this system, and, therefore, sharing the ability (or, more narrowly, the competence) to make sense of and to one another. This is the theory proposed, often quite elegantly, in various forms by analytic philosophy of language, Chomsky-style linguistics, semiotics, many different sorts of structuralism, neurophilosophy, and the cognitive sciences. The second, call it a poststructuralist or even, loosely, a deconstructionist theory, thinks of speech as an anarchic babel of multiple, heterogeneous, conflicting, mutually incomprehensible fragments of discourse on which order and intelligibility are imposed through the constructive, institutional, disciplinary forces of logic, rhetoric, metaphysics, various dominant rationalities (or culture, ideology, social relations, material conditions, and so on). This is the theory that comes down to us in various versions from Mikhail Bakhtin, Jacques Lacan, Michel Foucault, Jacques Derrida, Julia Kristeva, and many others; it is neatly adumbrated in Derrida's remarks on "the analytic experience of the pun."[21] It has never seemed to me that these two theories are analytically different from one another in any interesting way. Possibly an identifiable difference between the two theories concerns where the rules are. Is speech regulated from within like a logical system or from without like a well-ordered state? Both sides might just answer yes.[22]

Davidson on this question is an anarchist, someone who doesn't see speech and behavior as needing either deep-structure or material-structure regulation, for reasons that become clear in his essay, "A Nice Derangement of Epitaphs." Its argument is that standard deep-structure descriptions of our linguistic competence, including some of Davidson's own, are put in doubt by the fact that we have no trouble understanding such phenomena as malapropisms. "Malapropisms introduce expressions not covered by prior learning [i.e., knowing a language]. . . . Malapropisms fall into a different category, one that may include such things as our ability to perceive a well-formed sentence when the actual utterance was incomplete or grammatically garbled, our ability to interpret words we have never heard before, to correct slips of the tongue, or to cope with new idiolects" (PGR162).[23] Under "coping with new idiolects" we might include learning to read poetry, studying *Finnegans Wake*, and getting in tune with the speech of schizophrenics.[24]

Prior learning, knowing (let us say) a language—what Davidson calls the interpreter's "prior theory" (my expectation as to what you or anyone would mean by *x*)—is helpful and even necessary in many cases, but in any given instance, given the idiosyncrasy of expression, the theory will have to be revised. It might even prove useless altogether and have to be abandoned in favor of a quite different theory got up on the spot. In certain respects this idea fits in with some commonplaces of hermeneutics, most obviously the idea of the hermeneutical circle.[25] In order to understand one another we have to change. Davidson says: "as the speaker speaks his piece the interpreter alters his theory, entering hypotheses about new names, altering the interpretation of familiar predicates, and revising past interpretations of particular utterances in the light of new evidence" (PGR168–69). So in the give-and-take of conversation we eliminate cross-purposes as to what our words mean, even if this means eliminating what our words meant elsewhere or previously, and even if this means eliminating what the dictionary says our words mean. We eliminate everything except what works in the moment at hand: "the theory we actually use to interpret an utterance is geared to the occasion" and most likely has no application beyond what this one occasion (or fragment within the occasion) composes for us (PGR168). Davidson calls this improvisation the "passing theory," which is just the theory I put together now to contextualize (i.e., interpret) what you are saying (PGR168). Davidson says: "what must be shared for communication to succeed is the passing theory. For the passing theory is the one the interpreter actually uses to interpret an utterance, and it is the theory the speaker intends the interpreter to use. Only if these coincide is understanding complete" (PGR169).

We can clarify an important aspect of what Davidson means by a passing theory by comparing it to Mikhail Bakhtin's statement that "every concrete act of understanding is active: it assimilates the word to be understood into its own conceptual system filled with specific objects and emotional expressions, and is indissolubly merged with the response, with a motivated agreement or disagreement."[26] Bakhtin continues:

> It is precisely such an understanding that the speaker counts on. Therefore his orientation toward the listener is an orientation toward a specific conceptual horizon, toward the specific world of the listener; it introduces totally new elements into his discourse; it is in this way, after all, that various different points of view, conceptual horizons, systems for providing expressive accents, various social "languages" come to interact with one another. The speaker strives to get a reading on his own word, and on his own conceptual system that determines this word, within the alien conceptual system of the understanding receiver; he enters into dialogical relationships with certain aspects of this system. The speaker breaks through the alien conceptual horizon of the listener, constructs his own utterance on alien territory, against his, the listener's, apperceptive background.[27]

Davidson puts this by saying that what goes into an interpreter's passing theory are clues that the speaker advances as to his or her intentions. "Let us look at the process from the speaker's side," says Davidson. "The speaker wants to be understood, so he utters words he believes can and will be interpreted in a certain way. In order to judge how he will be interpreted, he forms, or uses, a picture of the interpreter's readiness to interpret along certain lines. Central to this picture is what the speaker believes is the starting theory of interpretation the interpreter has for him. The speaker does not necessarily speak in such a way as to prompt the interpreter to apply his prior theory; he may deliberately dispose the interpreter to modify his prior theory. But the speaker's view of the interpreter's prior theory is not irrelevant to what he says, nor to what he means by his words; it is an important part of what he has to go on if he wants to be understood" (PGR168). What is worth remarking is that neither speaking or interpreting here is thought of as taking place on common ground that speaker and interpreter share beforehand. Both are exposed to one another on alien turf. Common ground, as Hans-Georg Gadamer would say, is what needs to be worked out, which is what building a passing theory comes down to.

Davidson stresses that a passing theory is not (or need not be thought of as) a language: "a passing theory is not a theory of what anyone (except perhaps a philosopher) would call an actual natural language. 'Mastery' of such a language would be useless, since knowing a passing theory is only knowing how to interpret a particular utterance on a particular occasion. Nor could such a language, if we want to call it that, be said to have been learned, or to be governed by conventions" (PGR169). Only for technical reasons is it called a theory at all (PGR163, PGR170).[28] Nor is a "prior theory" what we normally think of as a language, although what the expression "what we normally think of" means in this case needs some sorting out.[29] Davidson says: "for the prior theory has in it all the features special to the idiolect of the speaker that the interpreter is in a position to take into account before the utterance begins. One way to appreciate the difference between the prior theory and our ordinary idea of a person's language is to reflect on the fact that an interpreter must be expected to have quite different prior theories for different speakers—not as different, usually, as his passing theories; but these are matters that depend on how well the interpreter knows this speaker" (PGR171). So, at the level of communication, there is no one thing that can be called a "language," no L in the philosopher of language's theoretical sense of vocabulary, rules, and conventions. Hence Davidson's showstopper: "I conclude that there is no such thing as a language, not if a language is anything like what many philosophers and linguists have supposed" (PGR174). Here Davidson brings to mind Jacques Derrida's notion of the multiple languages that go into what we think of as a natural language, which is in turn connected to his idea that the difference between the way a philosopher talks (say Edmund Husserl) and the way a poet poetizes (say James Joyce) is that a philosopher tries to speak only one language at a time, and doubtfully succeeds, whereas speaking only one language at a time is a bona fide definition of poetic failure.[30] In any event, language can only be figured in the plural. ("If I had to risk a single definition of deconstruction," Derrida says, "one as brief, elliptical, and economical as a password, I would say simply and without overstatement: *plus d'une langue*—both more than a language and no more of *a* language.")[31]

Of course Davidson's plurality is obviously different from Derrida's in the sense that he never imagines anyone materially speaking many languages at once, only that (for him) there is no saying what language anyone is speaking at any particular time; rather an infinity of languages could be understood to fit any speaker's particular utterance on the occasion of him or her making it. In an essay entitled "The Second Person," Davidson says: "a feature of the concept of language as I have described it is that there must be an infinity of 'languages' no one ever has spoken or ever will" (WL256). As Davidson describes it, a language is "a complex abstract object, defined by giving a finite list of expressions (words), rules for constructing meaningful concatenations of expressions (sentences), and a semantic interpretation of the meaningful expressions based on the semantic features of individual words" (WL255). According to the usual rule of concepts, one might say that speaking a language means speaking whatever comes under this definition of language. But for Davidson *langue* is no longer internal to *parole* as a regulating system. Davidson reverses the one and the many. "To speak a language, one must speak from time to time, and these utterances must be consistent with the definition of some language. The trouble is that utterances are finite in number, while the definition of language assigns meanings to an infinite number of sentences. There will therefore be endless different languages which agree with all of a speaker's actual utterances, but differ with respect to unspoken sentences. What makes a particular speaker the speaker of one of these languages rather than another? And the problem may be worse still. For even if a speaker were (impossibly) to utter every sentence in some one language, many other languages would be consistent with his behavior, as Quine has maintained; and I agree" (WL257). So after the indeterminacies of translation and interpretation, the indeterminacy of language naturally follows. At any given moment I may not know what language you are speaking. Your behavior could fit any language.[32]

All very well. However, what we use, you and I, to communicate with one another, namely a theory got up on the spot of how I am to interpret you, or you me, need not be thought of as a language, however much it passes for one: "what interpreter and speaker share, to the extent that communication succeeds, is not learned and so is not a language governed by rules and conventions known to speaker and interpreter in advance; but what the speaker and interpreter know in advance is not (necessarily) shared, and so is not a language governed by rules and conventions. What is shared is, as before, the passing theory." Of course, "we could hold," Davidson says, "that any theory on which a speaker and interpreter converge is a language; but then there would be a new language for every unexpected turn in the conversation, and languages could not be learned and no one would want to master most of them" (PGR173). So instead of multiplying languages, Babel-like, Davidson buries the idea of language in the everyday, second-to-second practice of constructing passing theories.

In this respect Davidson is closer to Gadamer than to Derrida. Gadamer would be the first to say that no overarching theory—no "basic framework of categories and rules" (PGR171), no conceptual scheme, no system of tacit knowledge, no paradigm, no speech community, no set of rules and conventions, no establishment of meanings held in common—can be invoked to explain what is simply an event of practical rationality in everyday life (a simple but nonetheless central event: rationality just *is* interpretability). Gadamer would wonder why Davidson would cling to the word "theory" to characterize what we do. Practice is at all events untheorizable (i.e., no picking out all that goes into it). And likewise, at the end of the day, Davidson observes, "what two people need," he says, "if they are to understand one another through speech, is the ability to converge on passing theories from utterance to utterance" (PGR172–73). If we ask what sort of ability this is, we come up short: "no learnable common core of consistent behavior, no shared grammar or rules, no portable interpreting machine set to grind out the meaning of an arbitrary sentence" (PGR173)—in short, no "deep concept" (PGR153), no theory, can explain surface action. ("I have," says Davidson, "no better proposal.") Theory has, in so many words, disappeared into the everyday practice of theory-construction. As Davidson says,

> we have abandoned not only the ordinary notion of a language, but *we have erased the boundary between knowing a language and knowing our way around in the world generally.* For there are no rules for arriving at passing theories, no rules in any strict sense, as opposed to rough maxims and methodological generalities. A passing theory really is like a theory at least in this, that it is derived by wit, luck and wisdom from a private vocabulary and grammar, knowledge of the ways people get their point across, and rules of thumb for figuring out what deviations from the dictionary are most likely. There is no more chance of regularizing, or teaching, this process than there is of regularizing or teaching the process of creating new theories to cope with new data in any field—for that is what the process involves. (PGR173; my emphasis)

A passing theory is, practically speaking, an instance of *phronesis*, that is, of knowing how to carry on in an unprecedented situation where one cannot simply continue as before.[33]

3. A Hermeneutics of Nonidentity

If one were to ask, what replaces rules (or language) as an explanation of how we understand one another, the answer would be nothing. Knowing a language, practically speaking, means knowing no more than how to keep up with the speech of someone not at all like us—not (necessarily) someone fixedly or determinately different from us (in the sense of being from another culture or planet whose ways, if we could get there, we could study and learn), but someone just like us who (just like us) goes off track quite frequently, most likely all the time, someone trackless or unpredictable in his or her way of speaking or behaving, someone whose way of speaking or behaving we no sooner pick up on than, Watt-like, he or she changes it. (And since I do not always, and maybe never, square with my future self—I may not always have the same language as I have now, depending how I want to be understood—radical interpretation may be needed for self-interpretation.)[34]

In "The Second Person" Davidson writes:

> If you (the interpreter) do not know how a speaker is going to go on, you do not know what language she speaks, no matter how much she has said up until now. It will not help to mention the fact that the speaker has performed according to expectations so far, or that she went to the same school you did, or belongs to the same culture or community, for the question does not concern the past but the future. Nor can we appeal to the idea that the speaker has mastered a set of conventions (which conventions?), or has learned a set of rules (which ones?). The concepts of conventions or rules, like the concept of a language, cannot be called upon to justify or explain linguistic behavior; at best these concepts help describe (i.e., define) linguistic behavior. (WL257–58)

But all that *not* knowing how a speaker is going to go on means is that we cannot interpret others in advance of their making their intentions known to us; whereas once they start speaking the wonder is that we have no problem following, no matter how strangely they speak. So long as they mean something, we can, on the passing-theory theory, and if we have our wits about us, pick up on it. That is, the philosophical wonder, as Wittgenstein might have put it, is that we don't need a concept of language to explain how this picking-up-on-it is possible; just a feel for ordinary life, or for the way ordinary human beings go on, will do it. The mistake is to assume that "ordinary" means "sameness" or "all alike"—this was Heidegger's mistake about the ordinary, namely that it is equivalent to *das Man*. It is close to the mistake Stanley Cavell warns us against when we overinvest in rules.[35]

Davidson's essay, "The Second Person," is obviously inspired by (or inspires his interest in) *Finnegans Wake* just insofar as Davidson rejects the assumption that "linguistic communication requires that a speaker go on in the same way as others do" (WL260). The sense (or senses) in which we share languages has little semantic application to the way we actually talk, but the philosophical distinction between deep and surface structure has not just obscured this fact but has trivialized how we do talk (and make sense) to one another, not in the least by making the waywardness, irregularity, heterogeneity, or unpredictability of our own talk seem defective with respect to philosophical pictures of rational discourse. Consider Habermas, for example. Of course, most of us take considerable trouble *not* to be wayward, irregular, heterogeneous, or unpredictable in the way we talk. As Davidson emphasizes, we talk in order to be understood, and notwithstanding that we frequently fail, we know (it is the best and oldest principle of rhetoric) that in order to be understood we must not merely speak the natural language of our audience but know (as a native knows) its beliefs, desires, fears (perhaps above all its fears), prejudices, narratives, metaphysics, or, in short, the natural history of its self-understanding.

Davidson on Joyce sheds light on the way in which poetry is not rhetoric—not, so to speak, public: not speaking the public's but an alien's language. And yet, importantly, poetry remains interpretable (therefore rational and, so to speak, accessible) after all: at all events poetry is not solitary singing in the sense that, as most philosophers appear to think, no one can get the hang of it. There is, of course, the loose question of whether poets have intentions in the sense that fits Davidson's technical sense of the word "intention." It does not appear that Davidson and Paul Valéry, for example, are at cross-purposes when Valéry says that in writing a poem his intention was not to say something but to make something.[36] And Davidson's theory would certainly be a curious piece of work if it could not be made to cover events in the history of poetry and art where clearly writers and artists, and not just those arriving after 1800, intend almost nothing else than *not* to go on as before, whatever the cost in intelligibility—where, in fact, the worst thing would be to be intelligible according to the idea of "going on as others do" (although in fact few artists probably fail to be intelligible in this nugatory sense). If I understand, Davidson's theory would win the day if it could sustain such blows to prior theories as Marcel Duchamp would regularly deliver, as when he purchased a pickax at his local hardware store and set it up in his studio as his latest composition. Davidson makes it clear that the history of ordinary language mirrors the history of art, and even avant-garde art, with no loss in understanding. Cavell has for some time been trying to clarify an insight of precisely this sort.[37]

In "The Very Idea of a Conceptual Scheme," Davidson argued famously against the possibility of conceptual relativism. He argued that we have no way of getting outside our own system to see how or even whether others are different from ours with respect to what systems systematize (experience, the world, something uninterpreted): "speaking a language is not a trait a man can lose while retaining the power of thought. So there is no chance that someone can take up a vantage point for comparing conceptual schemes by temporarily shedding his own" (ITI185). But now Davidson seems in a position to amend this thought, if only in a lateral direction. In "James Joyce and Humpty Dumpty," he uses *Finnegans Wake* to gloss Stephen Dedalus's assertion of outsiderness: "when the soul of man is born in this country there are nets flung at it to hold it back from flight. You talk to me of nationality, language, religion. I shall try to fly by those nets." What can it mean to fly by the nets of one's language, that is, get outside of what one cannot get outside of? Davidson considers Humpty Dumpty, who willy-nilly uses words as he pleases without regard to whether anyone will be able to understand and interpret him. But Humpty Dumpty is not outside of language; he is not speaking a language at all (using words willy-nilly, not bothering to be interpretable, is not speaking a language [PA4]). Joyce's method is different. In *Finnegans Wake* words are broken down and reassembled into new words that are then combined vertically as well as horizontally to form multiple contexts superimposed one on another in a vast system of punning ("he piles word on top of word, reference on reference, sly hint on crass joke, personal allusion on top of classical quotation" [PA8]). In Derrida's formulation, Joyce speaks many languages at once, without, however—and this is the trick—without descending into nonsense or uninterpretability. Rather, Joyce's text is overdetermined. Bible-like, there is nothing, not the least letter or particle of the text, possibly not even a typographical error, that is not meant to be interpreted. The text is error-free, no matter what. So, once started, one cannot stop understanding and interpreting, although it is hard to get started so long as one holds to one's own idiom. Rather one has to become an adept at *Wakean* language—which, metaphor-like, causes us to be different from one another, not to say from ourselves.

This at all events seems the burden of Davidson's inquiry into what one could mean by flying by the nets of one's language and culture. "By fragmenting familiar languages and recycling the raw material Joyce provokes the reader into involuntary collaboration, and enlists him as a member of his private linguistic community. Coopted into Joyce's world of verbal exile, we are forced to share in the annihilation of old meanings and the creation—not really *ex nihilo*, but on the basis of our stock of common lore—of a new language. All communication involves such joint effort to some degree, but Joyce is unusual in first warning us of this, and then making the effort so extreme" (PA11). In other words, Joyce restores the force of the word "radical" in "All understanding of the speech of another involves radical interpretation" (ITI125): "Joyce takes us back to the foundations and origins of communication; he puts us in the situation of the jungle linguist trying to get the hang of a new language and a novel culture, to assume the perspective of someone who is an alien or exile" (PA11).

4. Up from Deep Structure

Is there a moral to this story? Perhaps it is just the idea that there is nothing wrong with how we talk. "A record of natural speech," Chomsky says, "will show numerous false starts, deviations from rules, changes of plan in mid-course, and so on. The problem for the linguist . . . is to determine from the data of performance the underlying system of rules that has been mastered by the speaker-hearer and that he puts to use in actual performance."[38] By contrast, Davidson's linguist is a linguist of the surface, a linguist without universals, a linguist of pure performance, a linguist who plays rather than rules. Davidson's linguist could be imagined as saying, "A record of natural speech would be a poem." So perhaps one could extract from this linguist a way of clarifying the thesis widely and variously pressed in much of modern and contemporary North American poetry and poetics, namely that there is nothing unpoetic about ordinary ("unpoetical," prosaic) everyday speech. The poetical is not something added to language; it is not a manipulation of formal features to produce a discourse that deviates from the norm of everyday usage (or even from prose).[39] Language is already poetical the way sound, as John Cage says, is already musical. It depends on our listening rather than on our speaking.

The Canadian poet Steve McCaffery, making very interesting use of one of Georges Bataille's ideas, thinks of language as an economy, a body of energy, rather than as a system of rules, as if the deep structure of language were somatic rather than syntactic or semantic.[40] Language as such is a general economy over which we try to gain control in order to produce statements that can be cashed in at local discursive institutions or "restricted economies" (e.g., law, medicine, religion, science, government, business, communication industries, the university, and so on through the various social formations of the historical world). Rules, grammars, codes, categories, conventions, constraints, standard operating procedures—in other words, what we think of as the logical structures of discourse, or what Davidson calls "prior theories"—belong to these institutions or restricted economies and not to language. So there are rules, but these are social and political rather than linguistic and universal. Linguistic competence is acquired the way one acquires a law degree or political office. When we fly by the nets that constrain us, these nets are not spread out at the level of "language" and "culture" (concepts too large to be intelligible) but are local, multiple, heterogeneous, intersecting, finite, historical, and infinitely manipulable, like the stock market. Following Wittgenstein, one could call these nets "forms of life," but unlike Wittgenstein one wouldn't have any reason to call them languages. Language, if it is anything, is the material energy that circulates through these systems like Foucauldian power through the capillary networks of a society. As Gilles Deleuze says, its structure, insofar as we could trace it, would be more like that of a rhizome than that of a tree. McCaffery, among other poets like him, wants us to think of poetry as a conservation of this energy rather than a conversion of it to the productive ends of communicative praxis. Or say that poetry is the excess energy of language, language that cannot be or in any event is not converted to use. Hence the motto of modernist poetics, that poetry is made of words but is not (just) a use of them. Poetry is resolutely noninstrumental with respect to language; it is speech attuned to the materiality of language. As McCaffery says in a poem called "Lyric's Larynx": "It is sound more so than meaning / That binds the body to language"—as if finally our bodies were as linguistical as our words.[41] Davidson's picture of communication as something that can be improvised on the spot without dependence on prior theories helps us to get in the mood of this way of thinking about language.

Davidson's picture is rather wonderfully utopian. It is a picture of free speech, linguistic energy converted into social contact rather than into the production of concepts, meanings, propositions, schemes of thought, and other portable and more or less reusable structures of mediation. Notice that it is not so much a picture of a world absolutely without concepts, meanings, and so on, as it is a picture of communication that does not need these things in order to happen. So it becomes possible to think of a poem, even the most fragmentary and obscure, as communicative without being a product constituted of images, metaphors, emotive expressions, self-fulfilling intentions, repressed wishes, principles of equivalence, foregrounded phonemes, floating signifiers, semantic thicknesses, or whatever we think of as the basic formal ingredients of verse. Poets have been patiently trying to explain this to us for most of this century. The intelligibility of poetry is closer to the intelligibility of everyday life when two people encounter one another in passing and, well, make up a passing theory. As if poetry were "the cry of its occasion" after all. Let every passing theory find a poem.

3

Law and Language: Ronald Dworkin, Critical Legal Studies, and the Hermeneutics of the Legal Text

All by itself the logos does not make language.
—Martin Heidegger, *Introduction to Metaphysics*

On my (admittedly incomplete) reading of recent legal theory, one question appears to urge itself with special force: what is a legal text? This is not a formal question about genres of legal composition, say the writing of opinions or statutes, nor is it (just) a question about the canonization of certain sorts of binding texts, or about what it is for a text to be binding; rather, it is a question about the various competing textual models that have turned up in recent arguments about what the law is and how it is to be understood. This is an open-ended question. Indeed, in our current intellectual environment, the textuality of the law entails a questioning of law itself.

There are, if I understand, roughly two poles of thought here that can help to orient one's thinking. On the one hand, there is the idea that the legal text is to be construed on the model of the logical proposition, that is, as a statement that can be judged as (in some sense) true or false according to the rules of consecutive reasoning; and, on the other, there is the idea that the legal text is always historically embedded and politically motivated, so that it is no longer possible to take the law simply as the product of reason and argument: one must also (always) construe it according to categories of materiality—power, technology, social relations, sexual difference, and so on.

So on the one side there is someone like Ronald Dworkin, whose views are developed elegantly in two books, *A Matter of Principle* and *Law's Empire.*[1] Dworkin takes it that the law is made of propositions and that the main task of "analytic jurisprudence" is to determine the sense and force that these propositions have (MP146). As it happens, however, Dworkin wants to take this idea a half step back from legal positivism, where everything reduces to rule-governed behavior; but he doesn't, of course, want to go so far back as relativism and skepticism, which call into question the possibility of "right answers in hard cases" (MP143). So he takes recourse to what he calls the "aesthetic hypothesis," where a legal text is said to be like a literary work produced by many authors, each of whom is determined, as of one mind, to create "the best work of art." Literary interpretation, as Dworkin understands it, is aesthetic interpretation, that is, "an interpretation of a piece of literature [that] attempts to show which way of reading . . . the text reveals it as the best work of art" (MP149). The legal equivalent of such a work of art would be a legal proposition, or chain of propositions, that exhibits what Dworkin calls "legal integrity." "Law as integrity," he says, "asks judges to assume, so far as this is possible, that the law is structured by a coherent set of principles about justice and fairness and procedural due process, and it asks them to enforce these in the fresh cases that come before them, so that each person's situation is fair and just according to the same standards" (LE243). On this model, the right interpretation of a legal text would be that which shows it to be the best, that is, shows it in the best light possible with respect to the principle of integrity. The idea is always, whether writing or interpreting the law, to make the law express itself. Analytically, or by analogy with analytic philosophy of language, this means laying bare the deep structure of the law, that is, the "coherent set of principles" that make the law semantically intelligible and judicially forceful—in a word, just. The task of analytic jurisprudence, in other words, is to describe, or enforce, the law of the law.

On the other side there is someone like Peter Goodrich. In a book called *Reading the Law: A Critical Introduction to Legal Method and Techniques*, Goodrich says that "Legal discourse is . . . simply one of many competing normative disciplinary discourses, discourses of morality, religion, and social custom, to which it is closely related and from which it draws many if not all of its justificatory arguments. It is a discourse which should ideally be read in terms of control—of dominance and subordination—and of social power-relations portrayed and addressed to a far more general audience than that of law-breakers and wrong-doers alone."[2] For Goodrich, the legal text must always be historicized, that is, it always needs to be situated within the states of affairs in which it helps power to circulate in the desired direction. Goodrich himself approaches the law in terms of the history of its canonizations as so many binding or coercive texts, like Justinian's *Corpus Iuris*, which Goodrich regards as something of a prototype of the legal text because "it wrote down," he says, "an archaic and alien law for political and ideological reasons; that it subsequently became the object of an almost mystical awe had more to do with the political needs of the later western governments than it had to do with the substantive legal content of the codification as a whole" (RL32). The lesson of the history of law, he says, is that the force of the law is independent of its sense. The law expresses itself in the form of power, not reason, despite the claims of legal doctrine "to a logic of law and of law-application." Goodrich writes: "innovations in ideology, changes in the manner in which the legal community represents and justifies its social and political roles, should not blind the student of legal texts to the fact that the claim that there is a strict logic of legal interpretation or the belief that 'legal reason' can alone provide 'correct' answers to legal problems are nothing more than exaggerated (dogmatic) assertions that the law be respected and obeyed" (RL141). He interprets the law as if its deep structure were the will to power.

Borrowing from Mikhail Bakhtin, Goodrich describes the language of the law as a "unitary language," that is, a system of usage that stands outside of and tries to control "the conflicting usages and differently oriented accents of social dialogue" (RL188). It translates social reality into its own terms in order to control it. These terms, moreover, are themselves "open to intentional manipulation, that is, to multiple possible usages." Goodrich's idea is that the indeterminacy of legal language—where words like right, duty, obligation, corporation, and contract are capable of a broad and heterogeneous range of application—means that legal language is more a rhetoric than a code; that is, it is a rhetoric disguised as a logic.[3]

For someone like Dworkin, or more explicitly Owen Fiss, this is nihilism.[4] But Goodrich would call it criticism. "What is at issue . . . in the debate as to law and criticism is not so much the reality of the meanings and values wearily peddled by the legal doctrinal community but rather whether or not it is desirable to allow the profession to continue to transmit those values and doctrines, that ideology and those myths, without being made explicitly accountable for the political choices underlying the development of the law" (RL219). This is also Roberto Unger's point in his book *The Critical Legal Studies Movement*. The indeterminacy of legal doctrine—which is to say the idea that such basic notions as property, contract, rights, freedom, democracy, and so on, can receive and in fact have always received "alternative institutional embodiments"—is emancipatory rather than destructive. It opens up the possibility of a theory of legal practice as the mounting of arguments among alternative social or institutional ideals, as against the underwriting of tradition or the established order by means of ritual appeals to precedent and the internal necessity of rules.[5]

Now it is interesting, and perhaps not accidental, that both sides—the formal or aesthetic and the critical or historical—think of themselves as having got "beyond hermeneutics." On the one side, there is in the analytic tradition, as part of its self-definition, the idea that interpretation is what has to be got away from or brought under rigorous argumentative control so that as little as possible, if anything, remains left open to it. Interpretation is always a tacit admission of the failure or shortfall of knowledge and reason. The very idea of legal interpretation weakens our sense of the law's legitimacy. Insofar as interpretations are necessary, they should be strict and final. We need to determine the *logic* of interpretation.

Thus, for people like Dworkin, hermeneutics is simply a synonym for relativism and skepticism because (he thinks) it denies the possibility of right answers in hard cases. Hermeneutics is too much in love with rhetoric, too suspicious of logic. It is, someone like Fiss would add, what people like Unger and (especially) Goodrich are in favor of, namely, the end of rationality and therefore the legal order as we know it. For people like Goodrich and Unger, on the other hand, hermeneutics is a method of getting the present to correspond to the past: in Goodrich's words, "hermeneutics preserves tradition and constantly endeavours to emulate or repeat the logic of a past culture" (RL165). It is a method of resolving, or suppressing, conflicts of interpretation; it is the production of single-mindedness or monological agreement; it is the erasure of difference and the construction of hegemony. Hermeneutics is what formalists and objectivists, whatever they think they are doing, are actually doing. Thus the one side would point to Hans-Georg Gadamer's idea that we always understand differently if we understand at all, with its (alleged and allegedly nihilistic) implication that the meaning of the legal text changes with its interpretation; whereas the other side would point to Gadamer's attempt to rehabilitate the notions of authority and tradition and to his classicist claim that we are always within the *normative* embrace of what comes down to us from the past.[6] So hermeneutics is either radical or reactionary; it seeks either to undermine the logic of the law and legal application, or it seeks to mystify the law as a body of original meanings and authoritative doctrines handed down from a divine origin through successive generations of priestly interpreters.

I think that both sides are pretty wrong about hermeneutics, but no matter. My interest here is not to try to correct them. I do think, however, that both sides need to be pushed further into hermeneutics in order to accomplish the tasks they set for themselves. My thought is that legal theory generally needs to loosen up its notion of rationality, and that Gadamer's notion of hermeneutics, which attempts (among other things) to clarify the practical rationality of life in terms of *phronesis* as against procedural and instrumentalist reasoning, shows at least that one does not have to choose between uncritical, implausible accounts of legal reasoning and apocalyptic visions of crisis, irrationality, skepticism, nihilism, and despair.[7] On the other side I would have to say that one ought not to confuse tradition with the institutions that try to control it. Gadamer's idea is that what comes down to us from the past, including the law, always exceeds our efforts to fix its meaning. Law as tradition is always excessive with respect to law as institution. Tradition is more dissemination than perpetuation. The idea of holding fast to an original construction is not how hermeneutics understands tradition.[8]

As for the law, one can begin with the proviso that hermeneutics does not think of it in terms of the conceptual or methodological interests of the legal theorist, still less in terms of the strategic interests of legal or judicial practice; rather, the concern is with the conditions in which these interests are pursued.

Put it that the interests of hermeneutics are more ontological than technical. A "hermeneutics of the law" in this respect would not be the same as a theory of it. On the contrary, hermeneutics is apt to seem a little too wayward or free in its thinking with respect to the law (or indeed any subject). This will certainly appear the case when it comes to the question of law and language, or what in hermeneutics would be called the linguisticality (*Sprachlichkeit*) of the law.

Gadamer, for example, likes to think of language as the medium of human existence: existence—ordinary, everyday, "factical" existence—is linguistical. But it remains an open question how this linguisticality is to be understood, because linguisticality is heterogeneous and irreducible, that is, untheorizable—rather the way *parole* or natural languages are untheorizable.[9] From the theoretical standpoint of, say, Husserlian phenomenology, structural linguistics, analytic philosophy of language, and most literary criticisms, *Sprachlichkeit* is a nonidea; it lacks ideality, or portability from context to context. In order to have a theory of language or even a grammar of any sort, one has to reduce language from linguisticality; that is, one has to have distinctions between *langue et parole*, or between deep and surface structures, between system and event. This is true even of ordinary language philosophy, which, in order to count as a theory, has to bring linguisticality under analytic control by exposing the deep structures (the locutionary, illocutionary, and perlocutionary forms) that govern what we say when. This is the task of John Searle's speech-acts theory, in contrast to Stanley Cavell's development of ordinary language philosophy, which no longer appears to have anything to do with language (but everything to do with linguisticality).[10] Meanwhile Heidegger, whose thinking goes very much against the grain of deep-structure analysis, says that none of our theories of language has anything to do with language in its ontological character as Saying (*Sage*). "Saying," he says, "will not let itself be captured in any statement."[11] One wonders what would happen if one began thinking this way about the law.

From the standpoint of hermeneutics it is certainly not enough to think of linguisticality on the model of logical grammar as so many deep structures, codes, conventions, tacit rules, systems of constraint, paradigms, intersubjective arrangements, and so on.[12] This is not to say that grammar is a mere fiction, or that there are no such things as linguistic rules, since obviously there are, but what is their point? One thing is that such structures help to keep linguisticality under control. They inscribe linguisticality in such a way as to make it rational and intelligible (controlled and predictable); without such "rules" we cannot imagine that sense could be made of anything. Language would always be getting away from us, as, of course, it inevitably does anyway. One can think of the law (or of any discipline) as an institution or mode of discourse that tries to bring linguisticality under the rule of reason. The law belongs to the region of disciplinary as against sovereign power—power justified in terms of its ends rather than its origins. One can think of poetry or literature (not as Dworkin does but much more loosely) as a region of discursive practices designed to let linguisticality go in Heidegger's sense of *Gelassenheit*, letting-be, stepping back from representational-calculative thinking, giving up the rule of the word.[13] Such discourse tends to mark its borders with things like *Finnegans Wake*, a text of intersecting surfaces across which one moves in nonlinear fashion, say from pun to pun—a text that grammarians then try all the harder to rationalize by showing how, despite its crazy surface, it is (whew!) law-governed after all.[14] Meanwhile, by contrast, there are, strictly speaking, or in principle, no puns in the law; anyhow none intended.[15] But the law is surely as ambiguous in this respect as in any other, because the law has, so to speak, its upside: it belongs to linguisticality—the vast, weather-system world of discourse—as much as anything does. So perhaps one could speak of the anarchy (versus the lawlike deep structure) of the legal text. When one reflects on the language of the law, or, say, its textuality, one begins to sense what this might entail. But does any legal theorist ever seriously reflect on the language of the law? What would it be to do such a thing?[16]

Here we arrive at the threshold that Gillian Rose, in *Dialectic of Nihilism: Post-Structuralism and Law*, urges us not to cross, for on the way to language madness lies.[17] But other voices are more challenging—for example, Reiner Schürmann's provocative *Heidegger on Being and Acting: From Principles to Anarchy*, with its call "to live without why."[18] What would it be to formulate the question of the legal text, not aesthetically or critically, but from within an open and uncertain (anarchic) space?

The question of textuality provides this sort of space because it is a question about rationality with respect to thinking and discourse as such, and not just a question about texts as structural objects that one identifies as literary or legal or rule-governed or whatever. Or perhaps one could put it that the question of the legal *text* is a question about how the institution of law copes with the weakness of language, or what Plato called "the weakness of the logos,"[19] that is, how it tries to bring language under control or how it tries to constrain or limit the ability of language to get away from us and to say something different from what we mean when we speak. There is an obvious sense, after all, in which linguistic competence is a utopian idea. The word "text," as it comes down to us in recent theory, is a dystopian word about the resistance of the word to the competent (rule-governed, deep-structured) human subject; that is, it is about the excessiveness or uncontainability of the word with respect to the categories—the logics and fixtures, the symbolic orders and overarching systems, the schemes and paradigms and frameworks, the deep structures and intersubjective arrangements—that explain how we make sense of things.[20] The text in fact is the way poststructuralists try to conceptualize linguisticality. This conceptual effort carries them, as the saying goes, "beyond structuralism" into hermeneutical anarchy. At a certain point along the way this movement entails the recognition that the task of any discipline or institution or culture or symbolic order is to bring textuality, and also therefore meaning, under control (for the problem of textuality is not nonsense but too much sense). One might say that control of meaning is the first meaning, the origin or *arche*, of law: *logos*. It is controlled usage. But what of the weakness of the logos? The weakness of the logos, or of the law, is just that, starting with itself, it cannot bring everything under control.[21]

This implies a language (or a dark side of language) very different from current prison-house theories that figure it as lawlike all the way down, that is, as a deep-structured, self-regulating system, as *langue* and, at a higher level, as culture, ideology, symbolic order, or metaphysics. I mean that the very idea of the weakness of the logos implies a language that is the *other* of system or which breaks free of system, a language that is more like historicality than totality, a language that is untheorizable, whose workings cannot be rationalized, a language of infelicities or *délire*, a language opaque to the analytic gaze, a language whose deep structure cannot be laid open to view because it is all surface, a language that Frege thought no one could ever or would ever want to have a philosophy of, a language that is more letter than spirit, more body than mind, more earth than world, a language of excess and residue, of libidinal density and sacred rage—a language not, saving some considerable cultural adjustments, for speaking.[22]

Naturally the very idea of law presupposes the repression or unthinkability of such a language, this dark side (or nonthought) of language, even as such a language presupposes the unthinkability or, at least, the end or limit of the law—not to say the end of philosophy or metaphysics or of all such thoughts of beginnings and endings. It is easy to see that such a notion of language is self-contradictory, that is, it confounds the very idea of language, which is, in current theory, nothing if not modeled on the very idea of law (the model of the self-regulating system). Indeed, it is a little odd to be asking about the legal text, because the answer to this question is already given in our lawlike theories of language. The notion of an untheorizable language, of a language not for speaking—call it a paralanguage or a parody of language, an apocalyptic or end-of-language language, the mystified language of a negative theology (that is, a language in which to avoid speaking), the language of *Finnegans Wake*, *délire*, Heideggerian *Sage* (whatever that is)—is just anarchic, that is, a nonnotion: an idea no one could have and still have what is called an idea.[23] But if, from the standpoint of hermeneutics, it has never made much sense to conceptualize linguisticality in terms of the linguistic competence bestowed by grammars, codes, conventions, or other models drawn from the idealist warehouse of deep-structuring systems, what are we to think?

It might make greater sense to think of language the way Bakhtin does, that is, as a heteroglossia, a Babel of conflicting tongues that are, however, not sealed off from another but porous, intersecting, caught up in a dialogism that cannot be idealized as a basic I-thou communication or intersubjective transference of identities but is rather the historically embedded, finite, and contingent condition of linguisticality that has always got us talking at cross-purposes. In a word: anarchy.

How to understand this anarchy? I mentioned that Goodrich associates the legal text, or the law, with Bakhtin's conception of unitary language. This is an obviously important insight, but it needs some qualification. Bakhtin figures language, not as a total system immanent in local discursive effects, but as a plurality of social or "verbal-ideological" languages, a heteroglossia agitated by a play of centripetal and centrifugal forces.[24] In Bakhtin's favorite metaphor, language is "stratified"; it is multilanguaged or irreducibly heterogeneous. There is always more than one language in language.[25] The task of describing this stratification of language is impossibly difficult, but very roughly Bakhtin breaks things down into generic, professional, and social "languages" (DI288–300). The tension or conflict between unitary and heteroglot forces is applicable in every one of these discursive regions. "Unitary language," Bakhtin says, "constitutes the theoretical expression . . . of the centripetal forces of language . . . and at every moment of its linguistic life it is opposed to the realities of heteroglossia." The heteroglossia is centrifugal, anarchic. Unitary language is lawlike: "a common unitary language is a system of linguistic norms. But these norms do not constitute an abstract imperative; they are rather the generative forces of linguistic life, forces that struggle to overcome the heteroglossia of language, forces that unite and centralize verbal-ideological thought, creating within a heteroglot national language the firm, stable linguistic nucleus of an officially recognized literary language" (DI270–71). The point to remember is that each language in the heteroglossia is itself caught up in a conflict between centrifugal and centripetal forces, or between unitary language and heteroglossia. And this applies to the language of law as well as to any of the "socio-ideological" languages that make up not just one's native tongue but the linguisticality of existence. So we must imagine the law, for example, not as a unitary language purely and simply, since there is no such thing, but also as always struggling to bring its own centrifugal forces, its "dialogized heteroglossia," under control. The distinction I made earlier between law as tradition and law as institution would only be an abstract, preliminary way of characterizing the stratification and irreducibility of the legal text. Indeed, the intertextuality of legal tradition implies stratification beyond description, as if the law were a vast text whose center is everywhere and whose circumference is hypothetical; a text that is in a constant state of heterogeneous reinscription owing to random semantic disturbances occurring everywhere; a text that generates countless reformulations of the question of what counts as a legal text; a text that is expanding in unpredictable directions and according to laws invalidated as conceived; a text, in short, that is multiple and conflicting, charged with competing systems and contradictory meanings, a thoroughly historicized text. The whole idea of a legal institution would consist in the attempt to unify and centralize this heteroglossia into something coherent and manageable.[26]

Doubtless this is a vision of the law only an anarchist or nonexpert could have. Experts are to be counted on as having clearer, cleaner, uncrazy views:

> Sentimental lawyers cherish an old trope: they say that law works itself pure. The figure imagines two forms or states of the same system of law, the nobler form latent in the less noble, the impure, present law gradually transforming itself into its own purer ambition, haltingly to be sure, with slides as well as gains, never worked finally pure, but better in each generation than the last. There is matter in this mysterious image, and it adds to both the complexity and the power of law as integrity. (LE400)

Of course, Dworkin writes this for outsiders like me in order to reassure me concerning the fundamental, self-regulating, one-shouldn't-hesitate-to-say Hegelian rationality of the law. But the argument currently going on in legal theory between aestheticism and criticism is testimony to the "dialogized heteroglossia"— let us say the linguisticality—of the legal institution. Legal tradition is not a monological unfolding of the idea; it is "a Tower-of-Babel mixing of languages" (DI278), an always highly charged environment of intersecting (bisecting and dissecting) dialogues in which the very idea of law itself is in constant revision— in play, as hermeneuts say, that is, contested, irreducible, resistant to conceptual determination, always in question, open to unforeseen contextualizations. As if the task of legal theory were not to conceptualize the law but simply to know where to look for it among its different and singular configurations; as if to understand the law would always be to understand it differently; as if understanding the law would be hardly distinguishable from the study of its situatedness, its historicality, its exposure to *Wirkungsgeschichte*.

One thing a hermeneutics of the law would look for is where the arguments are and what is being contested against which competing backgrounds or traditions of thinking. A hermeneutics of the law would not be a theory of it but an event in which the question of the law is opened up, placed in question, no longer resolvable in its usual terms but, on the contrary, released from the terms in which it is familiar to us, exposed to what look like crazy ideas, made radically questionable. From the standpoint of hermeneutics, the law is a *Sache*, the thing in question, the matter for thinking (*not* the object of description and analysis). As such it can only emerge in a space that is logically anarchic, what Gadamer calls a place of "open indeterminacy" where the thing is suddenly otherwise than we thought (TM325–30). The law, like most subjects (justice, the good life, politics, philosophy, the right decision, *Hamlet*—whatever makes us think, or anyhow think twice), belongs to this space, that is, it is always contested, always in question. A hermeneutics of anything always begins by detaching the thing in question from its dogmatic contexts, the fixed or institutionalized ways of thinking it. So the idea in the present case would be not to resolve the conflict of interpretation between aestheticism and criticism (as if merely seeking a right answer in a hard case) but to enter more deeply into it, to search out the events in which it occurs and to understand them as one would understand a contest or argument—because, after all, it is an argument in which one is implicated or involved even if (especially if) one is not a legal scholar.

One way of being implicated—of being caught up in the argument, brought up short by it in Gadamer's sense of finding oneself exposed and called on to respond—is in terms of one's gender. Indeed, a hermeneutics of the law is just what begins to happen when, for example, Catharine MacKinnon's polemical argument about the maleness of the law cuts across or through the serene aesthetic surface of legal integrity and liberal legal reasoning: "the law," she says, "sees and treats women the way men see and treat women."[27] Here is how MacKinnon analyzes the "deep structure" of the legal text:

> Formally, the state is male in that objectivity is its norm. Objectivity is liberal legalism's conception of itself. It legitimizes itself by reflecting its view of existing society, a society it made and makes by so seeing it, and calling that view, and that relation, practical rationality. If rationality is measured by point-of-viewlessness, what counts as reason will be that which corresponds to the way things are. Practical will mean that which can be done without changing anything. In this framework, the task of legal interpretation becomes "to perfect the state as mirror of the society." Objectivist epistemology is the law of the law. . . . The rule form, which unites scientific knowledge with state control in its conception of what law is, institutionalizes the objective stance as jurisprudence.[28]

Here the law is no longer inhabiting a separate domain of the spirit (the disinterested realm of the "judicial stare") but is construed as a "social discourse" whose underlying form cannot be adequately described in terms of the norms and conventions, the schemes of arrangement, of a logical and coherent order.[29] On the contrary, critical theory turns the law as a unified and coherent system upside down, or inside out, so that the logical form of the legal text now constitutes a "surface structure" that authorizes a social subtext, namely the various institutions of the law and their discursive operations and effects. This upside-down law is what Goodrich's *Legal Discourse* takes for its subject: "rules of statutory interpretation and the doctrine of precedent, together with the much more detailed and generally less than explicit features of the 'legal art' of interpretation and argumentation within specific legal disciplines or bodies of law (the role and status, for example, of Equity or of specific principles, presumptions, customs and maxims), together combine to determine an institutional and discursive hierarchy of authorisation over who may think and speak and what may be thought or said." Goodrich is thinking here particularly of the law school, which doubles as the medium of access to legal discourse and as the source of a powerful mystification that covers up the groundlessness of such discourse: "the apparently determinate ordering of legal texts according to an institutionalised, social ontology of sources of law, shields legal discourse from the potential threat of having to justify the form and content of the exercise of administrative power in terms of any discourse other than the traditional, patriarchal, and essentially *a priori* or given, legitimation internal to the legal hierarchy itself" (LD173).

Understood in this way as social rather than propositional discourse, the law is without ground ("without why"); it is not a system working itself pure but a play of surfaces, a heterogeneous cultural practice that cannot be formally reduced but needs to be studied locally in terms of its position and effects within specific social and political situations. The hard part is getting clear about the consequences entailed in such a view of legal study. One consequence is evidently the end of analytic jurisprudence, not in the sense that such jurisprudence now stops or abandons as useless its deep-structure style of analytic rigor; rather, it means that now we see (in a way we have otherwise seemed to miss) the obviously narrow limits of such jurisprudence, with its flattened theories of language and text. Doubtless, from the analytic standpoint, the law-as-social-discourse idea exposes the law to skepticism—only now it no longer makes much sense to locate the law in skepticism's way, that is, it no longer makes sense to think of the rationality of the law as (just) cognitive and propositional. One is reminded here of Cavell's insight that the truth of skepticism, its moral, is that our relation to the world is not one of knowing, or what we think of as knowing, but instead entails something very like Heidegger's idea of letting-go.[30] So as a first step one ought to unhook the law from such venerable distinctions as the one between logic and rhetoric, not to mention the one between knowledge and power. Here critical theorists might try working out the sense in which law as social discourse is not just technical or strategic, that is, not just a species of instrumental reasoning deployed within the confrontation of adversaries. The idea of the repressiveness of the legal text, so prominent in Goodrich's critical analysis, needs to be loosened up by some further reflection on the fragmentariness of the legal text, its multifariousness, its surplus distribution within or across heterogeneous forms of life, its labyrinthine character, its comedy, its inherently utopian content, its ironic, satirical, and even subversive relation to efforts to represent and control it—say its uncanny ability to disclose other, unprecedented sides of itself: its anarchy as well as its open- or multi-endedness (its being "without why"). Here the law is not a genre within the prison-house of language but instead subscribes to the freedom of linguisticality—as if the main idea with respect to the law were not the order and coherence of logical systems or the integrity of beautiful works of art, much less the power of hegemonic superstructures bearing down on us from every side, inside as well as out; as if indeed the idea worth thinking about were the relation of law and freedom: the way the law, confounded as it is, brings us down or sends us up and sometimes even lets us go, comic rascals that we are.

Part II

The Limits of Narrative

4

Literature and the Limits of Moral Philosophy: Reflections on Alasdair MacIntyre's Project

Without making any boast of it Sancho Panza succeeded in the course of years, by feeding him a great number of romances of chivalry and adventure in the evening and night hours, in so diverting from himself his demon, whom he later called Don Quixote, that this demon thereupon set out, uninhibited, on the maddest exploits, which, however, for the lack of a preordained object, which should have been Sancho Panza himself, harmed nobody. A free man, Sancho Panza philosophically followed Don Quixote on his crusades, perhaps out of a sense of responsibility, and had of them a great and edifying entertainment to the end of his days.

—Franz Kafka, "A Parable"

What we say about the relation between moral philosophy and literature will obviously depend on whose moral philosophy we are looking at, and also on what sort of thing we take literature to be—a hard task because literature is not any one sort of thing, even less so than is moral philosophy. But the interesting question here may not be the obvious one of what theory or definition or genre of literature is appropriate to moral reflection. Among literary people, after all, it is hardly controversial that a literature of character and action, or in other words narrative and dramatic literature, is what constitutes ethical reality, since this literature shows us (as nothing else does) what a human life is. Storytelling, just to put it dogmatically, is human life's only mode of intelligibility. But for a certain kind of philosopher this assertion is controversial in a fundamental way. It raises, for example, a question that has never really been settled, nor perhaps even clearly understood, namely the one that Plato formulated in the *Republic* about the incompatibility of philosophy and poetry. When philosophy imagines a world for itself in which people are rational and just according to rationally defensible concepts of justice and rationality, what sorts of discourse will it accept in its world, and what will be excluded?

Exactly what is the sense of this question? It is important to see it in the first place as a question about the relation between philosophy and nonphilosophy, or a question about philosophy and its limits. For example, near the end of his introduction to *Being and Time*, in which he had been trying to determine the proper "way of access" to the question of Being, Heidegger pauses to defend his own "awkwardness and 'inelegance' [*Unschöne*] of expression" by saying that "it is one thing to give a report in which we tell about *beings*, but another to grasp beings in their *Being* [ein anderes ist es, über *Seiendes* erzählend zu berichten, ein anderes, Seiendes in seinem *Sein* zu fassen]." And to illustrate what he takes to be the self-evidence of his distinction, Heidegger asks us to "compare the ontological sections of Plato's *Parmenides* or the fourth chapter of the seventh book of Aristotle's *Metaphysics* with a narrative section [erzählenden Abschnitt] from Thucydides."[1] On a certain view of philosophy, one instituted by Plato and nailed down for modernity by Kant, philosophy is that which goes around behind stories to the thing itself *(die Sache selbst)*. The story is what philosophy excludes as part of its self-interpretation, or its answer to the question of what counts as itself.

From Kant we inherited a distinctive kind of moral philosophy, one concerned with the question of what rules it is rational for a human being to follow, in contrast, say, to the question of what sort of human being it might be rational, or good, for a human being to become. But in the last decade or so this rule-oriented type of moral philosophy has begun to be contested by another sort, one represented, for example, by volume 13 of *Midwest Studies in Philosophy*, which is devoted to the topic, "Ethical Theory: Character and Virtue."[2] The genius loci of this topic is Alasdair MacIntyre, a sort of postmodern Victorian sage and author of three books, some parts of which I want to touch on in this essay: *After Virtue: A Study in Moral Theory* (1981), *Whose Justice? Which Rationality?* (1988), and *Three Rival Versions of Moral Inquiry* (1990).[3] MacIntyre's project in these books and in a number of related articles can be described as an attempt to rebuild moral philosophy following what MacIntyre takes to have been its disintegration during the entire course of its modern history, or since about 1630, but possibly since the fourteenth century—a disintegration not just not compensated for, much less reversed, but actually accelerated by the development of a modernist morality of rules divorced from any social and cultural background. What MacIntyre proposes is a moral theory based on concepts of character and virtue as opposed to a theory based on the idea of a disengaged moral agent who calculates what ought to be done (or, more often, *not* done) on the basis of universal, or universalizable, maxims.[4] What is it to be a certain kind of person, and what constitutes the good, or excellence, of that kind—that is, when has a person fulfilled the ideal or goal or purpose *(telos)* of a certain way of life?

The critical point for MacIntyre's argument is that questions of this sort cannot be framed in universal terms; they are intelligible only against the background of a particular culture in which specific characters and virtues are socially embodied, that is, lived and practiced in ongoing forms of life, or what MacIntyre likes to refer to as traditions "in good working order" (WJ7). There is no such thing as morality as such, only local and contingent forms of life. Indeed, even the concepts of character and virtue themselves are historically embedded and can hardly be made sense of apart from the story that MacIntyre tells in *After Virtue*, and again in much greater detail in *Whose Justice?* of their origin and development in Homeric and Athenian (and also Augustinian and medieval) cultures. MacIntyre points to the double moral of this story as follows: it is "first of all that morality is always to some degree tied to the socially local and particular and that the aspirations of the morality of modernity to a universality freed from all particularity is an illusion; and secondly that there is no way to possess the virtues except as part of a tradition in which we inherit them and our understanding of them from a series of predecessors in which series heroic societies hold first place" (AV119). As it turns out, this is quite a statement, since what it asserts is that having a moral philosophy at all means recovering an ancient Greek and specifically Aristotelian way of thinking, especially as this is mediated (that is, criticized and corrected) by the history of philosophy at least through the fourteenth century. Recovery of Aristotle, or of the Aristotelian tradition, is MacIntyre's goal.

Three points are important here. Let me cite them and then take them up separately, with special attention to the first and third. The first is that a morality of character and virtue is essentially a morality of storytelling, since only stories can show what it is to be a human being, have a character, and pursue the good of that character. Narrative, one might as well say, is foundational for moral philosophy. Second, MacIntyre contrasts his Aristotelian morality of character and virtue with our present state of affairs, which is defined by the incoherence of our moral concepts and the interminability of our moral disputes. Here is where MacIntyre seems to reenact the prophetic role of the Victorian sage (Thomas Carlyle, Matthew Arnold, John Ruskin), for whom the fragmentation of the present was to be judged, if not against the actual, historical unity of past cultures (classical Greek, hellenistic, medieval), then at least against an ideal of unity that these cultures could help us to articulate. Finally, the idea that morality does not possess metaphysical foundations—that is, that it is not transcendental as Kant thought but is internal to culture and history and therefore multiple and contingent in heterogeneous ways—raises the question of whether morality is therefore *merely* traditional, subject at best to anthropological study, or whether it can be justified on rational grounds. Historicism is all very well, but moral philosophy remains a discipline of reflection and judgment that asks whether we are justified in holding our views and practicing our practices. In the postmodern crisis of rationality, MacIntyre emerges as a determined defender of reason.

Three points, then—and I want to emphasize that what follows is not so much a literal exposition of MacIntyre's texts as my attempt to work out, somewhat in my own language, and perhaps in somewhat more detail, what he is getting at, starting with his concepts of character and narrative, which MacIntyre himself develops in ways that remain fairly sketchy and abstract.[5]

1. The Rationality of Narrative

Basic to a morality of rules is the concept of a self as an autonomous, self-motivating, self-interpreting, self-regulating agent.[6] The Kantian subject legislates for itself independently of social conditions. Action is always internal to such a self; all the rest is mere behavior. So much, one might say, is the lesson of romantic poetry, where character means self-consciousness. One might well let the nineteenth-century dramatic monologue stand as the corresponding genre of the Kantian subject, whose formal existence as a disembodied voice reaches a kind of desperate fruition in Samuel Beckett's *Unnamable*.[7] And of course everyone can speak to the ways in which character and events in modern fictional narrative are often peripheral to the inward drama of the narrator. An instructive text in this regard is J. Hillis Miller's *Form of Victorian Fiction*, where the novel is understood explicitly as a genre of consciousness ("Not isolated consciousness, not consciousness at grips with natural objects, not consciousness face to face with God in meditation, but consciousness of the consciousness of others—this is the primary focus of fiction").[8]

In a morality of character and virtue, character is not consciousness but *ethos*. Here what matters is the concept of a way of life. We know from studies by Hermann Frankel, Bruno Snell, Eric Havelock, and others that the ancients had no very special notion of the self—had no word for it, really—but the concept of a life *(bios)* was very powerful.[9] In Plato's *Apology* Socrates defends himself by telling the story of his life, or rather of his *way* of life, that is, the course of conduct he has consistently pursued, namely spending his life in philosophy, examining his own life and compelling others to give accounts of theirs. But what of Socrates himself? Like Alcibiades we want very much to open him up and look inside, and no doubt what we should find if we did so would be very beautiful, but what is hidden about Socrates is not Socrates, who is only what his life discloses. Of course, we see this life in action in the dialogues, where Socrates plainly fulfills romantic criteria of character as a self-conscious subject expressing itself *in propria persona*, but basic to the character of Socrates is the persistent ironic displacing of this subject, who claims not to be speaking for himself or in his own voice (as in the *Symposium*, where he impersonates Diotima). As Socrates says in the *Apology* and elsewhere, he is nothing in himself (a gadfly, a midwife), and while his saying such a thing is certainly ironic, this irony is not a mask or a rhetorical strategy or a style that Socrates might put on or take off at will. Ironic is what Socrates is all the way down—it is his character *(ethos)*, or more accurately it is what characterizes his life in all of its aspects—his physical appearance, his dress, his homely speech, his relations to other people, and also his way of doing philosophy, for the *elenchos*, questioning, is an intrinsically ironic action, since its effect is to demystify and unmask, and there is no getting around behind it. A point worth thinking about here is whether the commonplace distinction between individual and type has much application when character is a feature of a life rather than of a self.

Against a Kantian background, character and virtue reduce to mental qualities or psychological traits that knobs on a head might reveal, but in antiquity they are what a life exhibits and also, therefore, what give a life its internal coherence (its *way*). *Bios* is the medium of character, where character is not so much a type all by itself as an ethical difference, a relative position within a moral system, which is what Aristotle means by virtue (and also vice) in the *Nicomachean Ethics*, and which he explicates by means of characters in the Theophrastian sense, as in his portrait of the magnanimous man. It has always seemed to me a little odd that literary critics, who as a matter of course study the *Poetics*, with its very interesting idea that you can have tragedy without character, very seldom read the *Nicomachean Ethics*, which seems foundational for the creation of literary character throughout much of literary history, and which could very well stand in place of Aristotle's lost treatise on comedy. One might digress here on the extent to which a morality of character and virtue is inherently comic, and whether tragedy might not be one of its limits. (MacIntyre, for example, thinks it a weakness of Aristotle's system that it excludes the possibility of a conflict among virtues or between competing goods and therefore cannot accommodate the idea of tragic conflict [AV153]. How far are Sophocles and Aristotle compatible? Perhaps not very. Arguably philosophy itself is necessarily comic; there can be no such thing as a tragic philosopher.) A decent scholar would probably have no difficulty in showing Aristotle's dependence on traditions of Greek comedy (see *Nicomachean Ethics*, 1128a).[10] At any rate the differentiation of virtues along an axis of excess and deficiency produces not only an integrated, self-contained moral scheme but also, in the way Aristotle explicates this scheme, a great gallery of fools, knaves, and heroes, whose systematic relation to one another, as in the case of the *eiron* and *alazon*, discloses some fairly basic features of dramatic structure, including, of course, the basic structure of the Socratic dialogues. The point to mark is how character and virtue in the Aristotelian sense translate necessarily into narrative and dramatic action, especially in the cases of excess or deficiency. Prodigality shows itself, for example, not only in the character of the wastrel but as a kind of "progress" that Hogarth would later memorialize. Every vice and virtue has its own story to tell and is intelligible in no other way, and vice may always have the greater moral to point. But these tales can only be told in a culture that makes use of them.

People without character, that is, without ethical definition, can be said to be lifeless, not of course biologically, but in the sense that their existence is featureless and unmemorable, except perhaps for what goes on around them. There is no story that can be told about such people, although modern writers have had a go at it, as did Robert Musil in one of modernity's greatest satirical creations, *The Man without Qualities* (1930), a narrative without end that has some marvelous bitter comments on the modern self—

> For the inhabitant of a country has at least nine characters: a professional one, a national one, a civic one, a class one, a geographical one, a sex one, a conscious one, an unconscious and perhaps even too a private one; he combines them all in himself, but they dissolve him, and he is really nothing but a little channel washed out by all these trickling streams, which flow into it and drain out of it again in order to join other little streams filling another channel.[11]

One remembers Hannah Arendt's distinction in *The Human Condition* between action and behavior, where the one produces stories, the other statistics.[12] The old Heraclitean saying that character is fate has several applications in this context. It can mean, of course, that someone who possesses a character in Aristotle's sense is doomed in the sense of being *typed*, or even *fixed* in Jane Austen's sense of being no longer capable of growth or change (hardened in the way of a libertine, e.g., and judged so by society), or *marked* in the Sophoclean sense, not simply in the way lame-footed Oedipus is marked but more decisively in the way Antigone turns out to be as bull-headed as her father. In any case the saying seems to affirm a crucial link between character and the outcome of a life, and one could say that it is the business of narrative to explore this linkage, to show the forces at work. The upshot of character and virtue is the way they give a person's actions definition and point, a capacity for fulfillment, or what Aristotle, and MacIntyre after him with great emphasis, call *telos*. *Telos* is not a simple idea; it seems easier to trivialize than to make sense of it—it seems to be more than simply "the good at which all things aim" (*Nicomachean Ethics*, 1094a)—but at least one point would be that *bios* is not just a biological process or even a causal sequence that can be plotted but, as I have said, a *way*, that is, something practiced as well as experienced (something about which one can say that there's a point to it, done for a purpose: life is accidental; a way of life is intentional). For the ancients a life was made of deeds (*pragmata*), not experiences. For example, many things happen to Odysseus—one damn thing after another without much plot—but his story is not about what happens to him or what he experiences; it is about how he *responds* to situations, how he (characteristically) *acts*: one could just as well say, how he practices his existence, come what may. Odysseus *is* the coherence of his actions, a coherence defined by a specifically heroic inventory of virtues—courage, strength, cunning, trickery, an essential blood-thirstiness, marred perhaps by an occasional lack of restraint—but what draws these virtues out is what draws Odysseus out, calls him forth, and that is not so much the immediate challenges at hand as finally Ithaca, so that on a certain view Odysseus remains incomplete—not fully himself, not fully brought out—until that moment near the end when he throws off his beggar's disguise and (really for the first time) lets the true Odysseus appear, an Odysseus restored to the *eudaimonia* of his household. The point being, among other things, that a whole character requires a whole life, or, as Aristotle says, no happiness without a sense of completion (*Nicomachean Ethics*, 1100a); and the argument is that only narrative can give us this sense of the whole, of actions and events not just stopping but achieving completion.

It is not too much to say that rationality consists before everything else in the ability to make lists and tell stories. If, as Wilhelm Dilthey said, meaning is the reciprocal relationship between parts and whole, then narrative and the list are foundational for meaning.[13] Certainly the rationality of narrative consists in the way it contextualizes the random and contingent details of life, and this means in particular the contextualizing of human action (AV195–96). As for what contextualizing means: analytic philosophers in the tradition of W. V. O. Quine (and this includes several large parts of Alasdair MacIntyre) like to speak of conceptual schemes, that is, totalities of propositions and beliefs woven together by inferential reasoning. A culture, on this view, is simply a totality of propositions and beliefs that hang together (without large or fatal internal contradictions) to form a coherent picture of the world. Statements are true or false depending on how they fit into this total scheme or picture, or in short not as they separately agree with reality but as they agree with one another. "Holism" is the watchword. Quine thinks of conceptual schemes on the model of a scientific theory, that is, as a total system of scientific propositions touching reality on its periphery and surviving on the basis of its internal coherence. The difference between modern culture and antiquity (so Quine thinks) is the difference between a conceptual scheme made up of scientific propositions and one made up of stories that, however fantastic in themselves, nevertheless hang together without fatal contradiction to form a coherent picture of reality.[14] Naturally literary people cannot wait to say that the difference between myth and physics comes down finally to a formal difference between two genres of narrative between which there is nothing metaphysically to choose; and Quine, if I understand, would agree, though he would find the point too trivial to make. In any event, as no one proposition is true or false by itself but only as it fits within the total framework, so no one story can be told by itself but always entails allusion to a comprehensive cycle of stories or interlocking narratives.

Narrative in any case is the linchpin of MacIntyre's moral theory, and *After Virtue* has a number of straightforwardly Aristotelian things to say about it, starting with the idea that "Narrative history of a certain kind turns out to be the basic and essential genre for the characterisation of human actions" (AV194).[15] The minute you start talking about people you're in the game, namely the practice of making sense of conduct, action, and life. This is a moral and not just literary or aesthetic practice, and, as Patricia Meyer Spacks has shown, even gossip points a moral whether idle or not. MacIntyre says that a story is not something we tell after the fact but something we must take ourselves to be living in the first place if our lives are to make any sense at all. "It is because we all live out narratives in our lives and because we understand our own lives in terms of the narratives that we live out that the form of narrative is appropriate for understanding the actions of others. Stories are lived before they are told—except in the case of fiction" (AV197). Not that fiction is ancillary to life in any way that is easy to understand. For in fact our lives are lived against a cultural background of narratives—fictional, historical, philosophical, religious, legal, joking—such that an incident, experience, action, stage, or kind of life will depend for its intelligiblity on the way it connects up with this background. For MacIntyre, we become what we are only by internalizing the narratives of our culture: "We enter human society, that is, with one or more imputed characters—roles into which we have been drafted—and we have to learn what they are in order to be able to understand how others respond to us and how our responses to them are apt to be construed. It is through hearing stories about wicked stepmothers, lost children, good but misguided kings, wolves that suckle twin boys, youngest sons who receive no inheritance but must make their own way in the world and eldest sons who waste their inheritance on riotous living and go into exile to live with the swine, that children learn or mislearn both what a child and what a parent is, what the cast of characters may be in the drama into which they have been born and what the ways of the world are. Deprive children of stories and you leave them unscripted, anxious stutterers in their actions as in their words" (AV201). Hence also the anthropological point that "there is no way to give us an understanding of any society, including our own, except through the stock of stories which constitute its initial dramatic resources" (AV201).

Still, one might try to imagine a story-free culture. But in an essay called "Against Dryness" (1961), Iris Murdoch thought that we need imagine no such thing because we are such a culture, the twentieth century being, by contrast with the eighteenth and nineteenth, a century of narrative impoverishment, of novels without characters and of documents without plots—a fact that mirrors, she says, exactly our moral and political destitution.[16] "We have," Iris Murdoch says, "suffered a general loss of concepts, the loss of a moral and political vocabulary" (AD46). We are no longer able to tell stories that would show us how our concepts are to be used or to what situations they might apply. "We need more concepts in terms of which to picture the substance of our being; it is through an enriching and deepening of concepts that moral progress takes place" (AD49). But (for Murdoch) what this means is that we need something like the restoration of the nineteenth-century culture of the novel. Much to the same point, in a recent essay entitled "Relativism, Power, and Philosophy," MacIntyre himself has proposed that what distinguishes modern from premodern languages is their "detachment . . . from any particular set of canonical texts," such as the Homeric poems or the Bible, that would form the background for, and so render intelligible and forceful, a coherent set of norms, beliefs, and schemes of rational justification.[17] I'll come back to this point.

In addition, for MacIntyre personal identity is an effect of storytelling. To have a personal identity is to be the subject of a narrative. It is to be able to respond when "asked to give a certain kind of account of what one did or what happened to one or what one witnessed at any earlier point in one's life at which the question is posed" (AV202). The rationality of narrative consists not only in its power of contextualization, which rescues us from randomness and contingency, but also because it makes life responsive or responsible to interrogation in some fundamentally Socratic or philosophically satisfying way. There is a link between narrative and justice in the accountability that narratives enable our lives to achieve, as if one could rewrite Socrates' motto to the effect that a life not capable of a narrative rendering is not a life worth living: a point that both Freud and Samuel Beckett would certainly affirm. Narrative in any case makes us responsible in the sense that it puts us in a position of being able to interpret and explain, compare and choose, but most of all to answer back when questioned about our actions. Gadamer says that to understand a text is to understand the question to which it is an answer; the same appears to be true of the understanding of narrative, which seems to presuppose what Mikhail Bakhtin might call a dialogically agitated social environment. As MacIntyre says, "I am not only accountable, I am one who can always ask others for an account, who can put others to the question. I am part of their story, as they are part of mine. The narrative of any one life is part of an interlocking set of narratives. Moreover, this asking for and giving of accounts itself plays an important part in constituting narratives. Asking what you did and why, saying what I did and why, pondering the difference between your account of what I did and my account of what I did, and *vice versa*, these are essential constituents of all but the very simplest and barest of narratives" (AV203). Or, again, in *Three Rival Versions* MacIntyre says: "So my identity as one and the same person [throughout my life] requires me on occasion to make intelligible to myself and to others within my communities what it was that I was doing in behaving as I did on some particular occasion and to be prepared at any future time to reevaluate my actions in the light of the judgments proposed by others. So part of being one and the same person throughout this bodily life is being continuously liable to account for my actions, attitudes, and beliefs to others within my communities" (TRV196). But suppose one lived in a community in which it was bad form to put people on the spot like this? (Imagine a language whose grammar systematically excluded the possibility of questioning: would this be a rational language? To imagine a language is to imagine a form of life.) On MacIntyre's account, a culture of storytelling resolves into a Socratic culture of contestation and argument, a dialectical or self-interrogating culture—a philosophical utopia in which everyone owes everyone else an account of their own utterances, actions, beliefs, preferences, tendencies. We might contrast it with, let us say, a Jane Austen world in which everyone goes out of their way to avoid giving pain, even when pain is richly deserved. In Jane Austen's world people do not interrogate one another; rather they read one another's most subtle gestures and unprepossessing small talk as complex narratives of how things are.[18]

But above all the rationality of narrative consists in its *teleological* structure; or, as Beckett says in *Texts for Nothing*, "It's the end what gives the meaning." For MacIntyre the question of questions is: "in what does the unity of an individual life consist?" (AV203). The answer is ultimately Odyssean: "the unity of a human life is the unity of a narrative quest. Quests sometimes fail, are frustrated or abandoned or dissipated into distractions; and human lives may in all these ways also fail. But the only criteria for success or failure in a human life as a whole are the criteria of success or failure in a narrated or to-be-narrated quest. A quest for what?" (AV203) Well, the very notion of the quest implies the good as that which underwrites it. The concept of the good is internal to the very idea of quest (contrast the phenomenon of fleeing or escape), which is a way of saying that the quest is intelligible in itself, whatever it is a quest for, with different cultures or cultural periods having a different sense of what is worth pursuing, if anything—one recalls Dante's Odysseus, who is tired and simply wants to stay put. But quests (like questions) are sometimes open and therefore in constant need of redirection. MacIntyre makes a very good point in this connection when he says that "the medieval conception of the quest is not at all that of a search for something already adequately characterised, as miners search for gold or geologists for oil. It is in the course of the quest and only through encountering and coping with the various particular harms, dangers, temptations and distractions which provide any quest with its episodes and incidents that the goal of the quest is finally to be understood. A quest is always an education both as to the character of that which is sought and in self-knowledge" (AV204).

Yet this very line of thought suggests the possibility of a distinction between quest cultures and cultures that dispose themselves toward the future differently. Arguably the quest is an essentially Greek (that is, Homeric and Aristotelian) concept, whereas wandering is a distinctive feature of the biblical life. Biblical characters go not so much on quests as into banishment or exile, and their return from such things is often characterized less by adventure or forward movement than by waywardness and backsliding. Much to the same point, the sojourn rather than the journey defines the character of much biblical experience. Waiting and expectation, confinement and hope, longing and hearkening ("How long, O Lord?"), despair and forsakenness: these are essentially apocalyptic forms of life defined by a future that no present action can help to bring about. Martin Luther, with his doctrine of faith alone, grasped this in a twinkling. Or, again, instead of the quest there is the life of repetition and common routine set apart by a sudden supernatural intervention, like the hierophany of the burning bush that turned a shepherd into Moses. Kafka's tales are powerful satirical renderings of the form and spirit of biblical narratives. Biblical narratives are notoriously spare, laconic, truncated, multiple, discontinuous. Instead of an unfolding narrative the Bible is more likely to give us multiple examples of a single, isolated, critical moment of dramatic intensity that redefines the past and leaves us exposed to a radically uncertain future.[19]

However, to return to the issue at hand: what matters to MacIntyre is the pattern of narrative progress, that is, of advancement or movement toward resolution. For him, narrative is rational to the extent that it is structured propositionally like an argument pursued on a question that needs deciding. Narratives, like arguments, are ways of working out a problem, that is, allegories of rational deliberation in which doing what is right often comes down to the resolving of contradictions. For MacIntyre, human life and history are intelligible, and so worth living, insofar as they have the form of rational inquiry. In fact there seems to be no formal difference between rational inquiry and narrative quest. And if we imagine an entire culture structured in this way, that is, as a shared, communal, or collective life whose unity is that of an ongoing narrative quest, a "common pursuit," we will have some notion of what MacIntyre means by tradition ("a living tradition . . . is an historically extended, socially embodied argument, and an argument precisely in part about the goods which constitute that tradition" [AV207]). Exactly what this means is of primary importance because for MacIntyre morality—that is, an answer to Aristotle's question about what the good life is for human beings—is always and necessarily internal to a tradition, such that if a moral scheme is to be rational and defensible, it can only be on the basis of the prior rationality, and hence justifiability, of the tradition of which it is a part.

2. The Incoherence of Modernity

As I have suggested, an essential component of MacIntyre's moral theory, and what finally shapes his idea of narrative (and of history and tradition), is the analytic concept of a conceptual scheme. In an essay called "Epistemological Crises, Dramatic Narrative, and the Philosophy of Science" (1977), MacIntyre writes: "consider what it is to share a culture. It is to share schemata which are at one and the same time constitutive of and normative for intelligible action by myself and are also means for my interpretations of the actions of others. My ability to understand what you are doing and my ability to act intelligibly (both to myself and others) are one and the same ability. . . . It is these schemata which enable inferences to be made from premises about past behaviour to conclusions about future behavior and present inner attitudes. They are not, of course, empirical generalisations; they are prescriptions for interpretation."[20] "Epistemological crisis" meanwhile is a term of art in the history and philosophy of science. It is what happens when we find that the prescriptions on which we have relied no longer work, or are in competition with rival schemata—or, as MacIntyre says, when we "come to recognize the possibility of systematically different possibilities of interpretation, of the existence of alternative and rival schemata which yield mutually incompatible accounts of what is going on around [us]" (EC454). This happens all the time when we travel to foreign countries, but MacIntyre gives the example of Hamlet, who returns "from Wittenberg with too many schemata for interpreting the events at Elsinore. . . . There is the revenge schema of the Norse sagas; there is the renaissance courtier's schema; there is a Machiavellian schema about competition for power. . . . Until he has adopted some schema he does not know what to treat as evidence; until he knows what to treat as evidence he cannot tell which schema to adopt" (EC454). Imagine living in a world in which the events of one's experience can be accommodated by a number of mutually incompatible narratives. (In fact this is the world according to Derrida.)

For MacIntyre, modernity is such an overinterpreted world. It is a complex cultural condition characterized by ongoing epistemological crises in every sphere of life but nowhere more disastrously than in the sphere of moral action. In part this chronic state of crisis derives from what MacIntyre calls "the Enlightenment project" (AV34), which in essence is, or was, the modernist's rationalistic dream of a nonideological, nontraditional, story-free culture in which everything is intelligible and defensible on the basis of universal principles, rather the way nineteenth-century science thought itself intelligible, or the way Marxism thought it could make itself intelligible in contrast to mere views of the world. "It is of the essence of reason," MacIntyre says, "that it lays down principles which are universal, categorical and internally consistent. Hence a rational morality will lay down principles which both can and ought to be held by all men, independent of circumstances and conditions, and which could be consistently obeyed by every rational agent on every occasion" (AV43). The pursuit of such a rational morality required beforehand the emancipation of everyday life from moral schemes handed down from the past, and this meant in particular the repudiation of Aristotle ("Aristotelianism is *philosophically* the most powerful of pre-modern modes of moral thought" [AV111]). The first half of *After Virtue* argues that the Enlightenment project not only failed to provide such a rational morality but also that it had to fail, history being what it is, and that the major consequence of this failure is that we are all pretty much in the condition Hamlet found himself in when he returned to Elsinore, namely the condition of someone who has no coherent conceptual scheme, or rather too many schemes, in which to sort out the events and experiences of life or to understand and justify the actions either of himself or those of other people (someone incapable of rational inquiry and reduced to antic dispositions). Actually our condition is worse than Hamlet's. All we have at our disposal are "the fragments of a once coherent scheme of thought and action" (AV53), that is, we have moral concepts but no intelligible background, no coherent system of narratives, to instruct us as to their use, or that shows us, in Cora Diamond's phrase, how to live with them.[21] It is not, however, as Murdoch thought, that we suffer an impoverishment of narratives. MacIntyre's idea is interestingly like Derrida's: we have too many narratives—too much literature, too many competing and incompatible schemes, systems, models, paradigms, frameworks, ideologies, language-games, forms of life, too many unfused horizons.[22] Call these things what we will, we inhabit a world that is pretty much like the one Nietzsche described in the texts gathered together in *The Will to Power*, namely a world constituted as a conflict of interpretations in which everything that happens, whatever exists or is said or done or experienced, is always interpretable otherwise, with the constructions of the most powerful tending to prevail.

Hence we are thrown back (says MacIntyre) on what moral philosophers call "emotivism," or "the doctrine that all evaluative judgments and more specifically all moral judgments are *nothing but* expressions of preference, expressions of attitude or feeling, insofar as they are moral or evaluative in character" (AV11). Emotivism is not widely defended as a moral theory, but, as MacIntyre says, "to a large degree people now think, talk and act *as if* emotivism were true" (AV21), so that it is not too much to say that it has become *the* moral outlook of modernity. Emotivism means "Do this because I approve of it." The task is then to get people to do it, and accordingly emotivism requires a strong and often institutional reliance on instrumental, strategic, administrative reasoning. "The sole reality of distinctively moral discourse [in our culture]," MacIntyre says, "is the attempt of one will to align the attitudes, feelings, preferences, and choices of another with its own" (AV23). In a wonderful chapter in *After Virtue*—a tour de force of social criticism—MacIntyre shows how our culture has embodied its emotivist norms in identifiable characters or social types: the Aesthete, the Manager, and the Therapist. The moral identity of each of these types is determined by the exercise of some form of manipulative reason. The novels of Henry James are brilliant anatomies of the first type. As MacIntyre says, "James is concerned with rich aesthetes whose interest is to fend off the kind of boredom that is so characteristic of modern leisure by contriving behaviour in others that will be responsive to their wishes, that will feed their sated appetites" (AV23). In a similar way, "The Manager treats ends as given, as outside his scope; his concern is with technique, with effectiveness in transforming raw materials into final products, unskilled labour into skilled labour, investment into profits." Likewise the "Therapist . . . treats ends as given, as outside his scope; his concern also is with technique, with effectiveness in transforming neurotic symptoms into directed energy, maladjusted individuals into well-adjusted ones. Neither manager nor therapist, in their roles as manager and therapist, do or are able to engage in moral debate. They are seen by themselves, and by those who see them with the same eyes as their own, as uncontested figures, who purport to restrict themselves to the realms in which rational agreement is possible—that is, of course, from their point of view to the realm of fact, the realm of means, the realm of measurable effectiveness" (AV29). Or, as MacIntyre otherwise puts it: "the contemporary vision of the world . . . is predominantly . . . Weberian" (AV101), after Max Weber, the Newton of bureaucratic systems, and the rationalization of the world. The point is that in a world of Nietzschean perspectivism in which everything is interpretable otherwise, depending on the preference or outlook of the solitary individual subject, the only social order possible is essentially technical and administrative. (Compare Heidegger's analysis of modernity as the age of representational-calculative thinking aimed at totalization and control; or Hannah Arendt's idea that the modern age is an age of housekeeping.)[23] Instead of arguments about things that matter, we argue about operations, procedures, methods, programs, and how to calculate their efficiency and results. On questions that do matter, for example on the question of abortion, interminable debate and legal stalemate give way inevitably and destructively to strategies of harangue, force, and coercion.

To gain a feeling for what is at issue in this Nietzschean-Weberian state of affairs, MacIntyre asks us to compare Aristotle's *Nichomachean Ethics* with its modern counterpart, namely Erving Goffman's sociological analyses, as for example in *The Presentation of Self in Everyday Life* (1959). "The unit of analysis in Goffman's sociology," MacIntyre says, "is always the individual role-player striving to effect his will within a role-structured situation. The goal of the Goffmanesque role-player is effectiveness and success in Goffman's social universe is nothing but what passes for success. There is nothing else for it to be. For Goffman's world is empty of objective standards of achievement; it is so defined that there is no cultural or social space from which appeal to such standards could be made. Standards are established through and in interaction itself; and moral standards seem to have the function only of sustaining types of interaction that may always be menaced by over-expansive individuals" (AV108–9). So every moral situation has its own ad hoc norms, which in turn are mainly procedural norms for narrowing the terms of victory, that is, limiting the power of the contestants sufficiently to defer ultimate resolution of the question. This brings to mind the now hoary platitude of liberalism that it doesn't matter what we say or who is right so long as we keep talking to one another—which, along with the idea that we should avoid cruelty to one another, is essentially Richard Rorty's answer to Nietzsche.[24]

Rorty illustrates MacIntyre's point about our modern condition. He proposes an outlook or style called "liberal irony," and following Judith Shklar he characterizes liberal ironists as "people who think that cruelty is the worst thing we can do" (CISxv). The irony (for Rorty) is that "Don't be cruel" is not, and cannot be made into, a universal maxim; it is a preference among liberals but can't be expected of those, perhaps the majority of humankind, whose history and culture reserve a place for torture. "For liberal ironists," Rorty says, "there is no answer to the question 'Why not be cruel?'—no noncircular theoretical backup for the belief that cruelty is horrible" (CISxv). Nor is there any answer to the question of when to struggle against injustice and when to say the hell with it and retire to one's garden. That is, and this is Rorty's whole theme, the very idea of rational justification is pretty much a hopeless, because merely circular, business: one is always justifying this or that in terms of standards internal and peculiar to one's own culture and history. All one can hope for, or work for, is solidarity within one's own circle, or among those who think, for whatever reason, that cruelty is the worst thing we can do. But there is no way to secure this solidarity on anything like a philosophically defensible foundation. MacIntyre thinks otherwise, and one might well regard MacIntyre as attempting to save Rorty from himself by showing how solidarity can be rational and just without being transcendental. And this means showing how traditions can be rational, which is the task of MacIntyre's *Whose Justice? Which Rationality?*

3. Toward a New Republic

MacIntyre is a historicist of a certain qualified sort, that is, someone who does not think historicism is or has to be incompatible with some conception of a rational order of things. As a historicist he argues against the Enlightenment that standards of rational justification are internal to particular cultures and histories, and that there can be, moreover, rival, incompatible, equally compelling norms of rationality. Or, as he says, "There can be no rationality as such. Every set of standards, every tradition incorporating a set of standards, has as much and as little claim to our allegiance as any other." MacIntyre calls this "the relativist's challenge": "if there is a multiplicity of rival traditions, each with its own characteristic mode of rational justification internal to it, then that very fact entails that no one tradition can offer those outside it good reasons for excluding the theses of its rivals" (WJ352). Or, in other words, there are no reasons, other than personal preference or, at a higher level, ethnocentric reasons, for choosing between a culture of Jane Austen civility and a culture of terror.

MacIntyre had confronted the relativist's challenge earlier in a dispute with Peter Winch over whether a culture that relied on magical rites to make its crops grow could claim to be as rational as a scientific culture whose agriculture is based on laws of cause and effect.[25] MacIntyre had argued that it is all very well to speak of heterogeneous norms of rationality, but on the question of making crops grow we cannot help noticing and criticizing the unreason of magical beliefs and practices from the standpoint of our own modern Western practices, with their greater efficiency of production. We just know that magic doesn't enhance fertility. Winch countered by saying that the point of the magical rites is perhaps not efficiency of production but the expression of a culture's sense of the contingency of human life. A technological rationality is not obviously superior to a rationality aimed at reflection on the nature or meaning of human existence.[26] The point (says Winch) is that a technological culture like ours has something to learn from the magical tribe, namely that efficiency of production is not sufficient and maybe not even necessary to make life worth living. MacIntyre conceded nothing to Winch, but he seems to have taken Winch's point that a rational culture is one that can learn from an alien conceptual scheme that its own theories and practices are in need of correction, or even that what the alien culture possesses is just the set of concepts or practices that we need to work ourselves out of our own intellectual and moral dilemmas. The point is that our encounter with the alien scheme is analogous to an encounter with Socrates, which is to say that what such an encounter produces is exactly the self-criticism that we require in order to make our way into the future.

This is not very different from what MacIntyre argues in *Whose Justice? Which Rationality?*—a book that examines in some detail four traditions of rational inquiry (Aristotelian, Augustinian, Scottish Calvinist, and modern liberal, this last being an example of a tradition in positively bad working order), each with its own set of standards of rational justification. MacIntyre studies these traditions in order to put forcefully "the relativist's challenge" of how to choose among equally rational and justified forms of life. The answer to relativism is that one does not choose from God's point of view but rather only from within one's own tradition and history, which includes among other things the history of that tradition's internal difficulties or its ongoing and probably endless struggle to make itself coherent. Analytic philosopher that he is, MacIntyre is able "to contrast three stages in the initial development of a tradition: a first in which the relevant beliefs, texts, and authorities have not yet been put in question; a second in which inadequacies of various types have been identified, but not yet remedied; and a third in which response to those inadequacies has resulted in a set of reformulations, reevaluations, and new formulations and evaluations, designed to remedy inadequacies and overcome limitations" (WJ355). What this means in simple terms is that the test of the rationality of a tradition is its ability to resolve its ongoing epistemological crises (WJ362). Or, in other words, a culture or tradition is rational if it can solve its intellectual and moral problems. MacIntyre's idea is that it is not always the case that a tradition can manage such a resolution entirely on its own: its conceptual resources may be inadequate to what MacIntyre calls "its current problematic," that is, the "set of debates concerning a body of often interrelated problems for those inhabiting that [tradition], by reference to work upon which rational progress, or failure to achieve such progress, is evaluated" (RIC119; cf. WJ361). It is only in the encounter with an alien tradition that the rationality of a tradition can be measured. Since the matter wants careful stating, it will be important here to stick to MacIntyre's own words:

> For the adherents of a tradition which is now in this state of fundamental crisis may at this point encounter in a new way the claims of some particular rival tradition, perhaps one with which they have for some time coexisted, perhaps one which they are now encountering for the first time. They now come or had already come to understand the beliefs and way of life of this other alien tradition, and to do so they have or have had to learn . . . the language of the alien tradition as a new and second first language.
>
> When they have understood the beliefs of the alien tradition, they may find themselves compelled to recognize that within this other tradition it is possible to construct from the concepts and theories peculiar to it what they were unable to provide from their own conceptual and theoretical resources, a cogent and illuminating explanation—cogent and illuminating, that is, by their own standards—of why their own intellectual traditions had been unable to solve its problems or restore its coherence. The standards by which they judge this explanation to be cogent and illuminating will be the very same standards by which they have found their tradition wanting in the face of epistemological crisis. . . .
>
> In this kind of situation the rationality of tradition requires an acknowl-edgment by those who have hitherto inhabited and given their allegiance to the tradition in crisis that the alien tradition is superior in rationality and in respect of its claims to truth to their own. (WJ364)

This is very cunning, because on the one hand it acknowledges the truth of rel-ativism, namely that reason is plural and heterogeneous, yet on the other it affirms something like a cross-cultural rationality, or the idea that a culture can correct itself insofar as it is capable of self-criticism or of a critical relation with an alien culture whose rationality it acknowledges as superior to its own. I leave it to philosophers more adept at nice arguments than I am to determine whether a question isn't being begged here—whether, for example, MacIntyre doesn't just start out with problem-solving as being pretty close to what rationality is *as such* even though for historical reasons there is no such thing as rationality *as such*; or whether at the very least he does not simply assert that, whatever else rationality might be, the old Socratic idea of self-criticism and self-correction is what rationality qua rationality is, insofar as there is anything that distinguishes rational people (in any culture or historical period) from the rest of us. "Rationality, understood within some particular tradition with its own specific conceptual scheme and problematic," he says, "nonetheless requires *qua* rationality a recognition that the rational inadequacies of that tradition from its own point of view—and every tradition must from the point of view of its own problematic view itself as to some degree inadequate—may at any time prove to be such that perhaps only other resources provided by some quite alien tradition . . . will enable us to identify and to understand the limitations of our own tradition" (RIC201). I'm not sure I understand the difference between rationality *as such* and rationality *qua* rationality. In any case, MacIntyre says, "rationality requires a readiness on our part to accept, and indeed to welcome, a possible future defeat of the forms of theory and practice in which it has up till now been taken to be embodied within our own tradition, at the hands of some alien and perhaps even as yet largely unintelligible tradition of thought and practice" (RIC201–2).

It is certainly MacIntyre's thought that a rational culture or tradition would make its morality intelligible and justified in the same way that it explains and legitimates its science, namely, as the best theory so far, or the one that is best able to respond to criticism both from within its own history and, where it happens, against rival theories from another tradition (see, e.g., the appeal to the model of history of science, TRV149–51). What remains important is that no appeal to universals is required of a culture for it to rationalize its norms and practices. What *is* required is precisely what modernity is not able to provide, namely intellectual and moral coherence, or rather a conceptual scheme for moral action and reflection that is able to resolve its "problematic" and so progress in the manner of, say, physics, where the current state of the art is the best physics we have ever had, however things may be on Orbius Tertius. What MacIntyre's project proposes is a recovery of the moral coherence that characterized premodern cultures, that is, European cultures informed as they were until the seventeenth century by a philosophical tradition coming down from Aristotle and corrected along the way by Augustine and Aquinas. On MacIntyre's reading, this tradition was—until the Enlightenment's systematic repudiation of the very idea of tradition—as good an example as (and maybe the only example) we have of a rational, self-justifying tradition, that is, self-critical and self-correcting in a way that satisfies the theory of the rationality of traditions. *Three Rival Versions* gives the familiar example of Aquinas (familiar anyhow to anyone educated by the Jesuits), who confronted and is thought to have resolved the conflict of interpretations between Aristotelian and Augustinian histories of inquiry. He thus provides a success story to contrast with the failure of modernist universalism or encyclopedism to withstand the criticism of Nietzschean genealogy or historicism, and the failure of Nietzschean genealogy or historicism to do anything but expose the illusions of modernity.

That is, in short, rational moral theory and practice presuppose communitarian rather than universal principles. Belonging and participation replace ultimate foundation (*Letztbegründung*), where participation means sharing a common world, that is, a set of concepts, norms, beliefs, and practices, together with narratives that show what it is to share such and that show as well, one supposes, how to keep the whole system in good working order (how to keep things coherent, e.g., according to a theory of the narrative quest for the good, or of the rationality of traditions, or of the rational and just community). In *Three Rival Versions* MacIntyre puts it as squarely and unblinkingly as he can: "membership in a particular type of moral community, one from which fundamental dissent has to be excluded, is a condition for genuinely rational inquiry" (TRV 59–60).

So much the worse, one is tempted to say, for such a community.[27]

4. Culture and Anarchy

Let me conclude with two antithetical figures from Irish literary history, W. B. Yeats and James Joyce.

First consider Yeats, who responded (typically) to the fragmentation and anarchy of modernity by formulating a conceptual-scheme theory in the mythical language of a golden age: "I think that in early Byzantium, maybe never before or since in recorded history, religious, aesthetic and practical life were one, that architects and artificers—though not, it may be, poets, for language had been the instrument of controversy and must have grown abstract—spoke to the multitude and the few alike. The painter, the mosaic worker, the worker in gold and silver, the illuminator of sacred books, were almost impersonal, almost perhaps without the consciousness of individual design, absorbed in their subject-matter and that the vision of a whole people."[28] Art, morality, science: unity of culture is the condition in which these things are possible. I do not think it accidental that, Plato-like, Yeats excludes the contentious poet from his Byzantium, that is, a poet of a certain uncontrollable kind—namely, Shem the Penman, homeless and drunk, whose task it is to disarticulate the unity of culture by overloading the system with fragments of concepts, norms, beliefs, and narratives from everywhere and nowhere that neither begin nor end but expand uncontrollably in every direction by means of the perpetual introduction of random elements—words and parts of words from newspaper items, radio broadcasts, obscenities in Latin, nursery rhymes, billboard messages, a sophomore's half-filled bluebook, lunatic ravings, pub gossip, tax forms, conversations composed by Henry James, dirty limericks, printers' errors, philosophy's terms of art, a page (with words) from *Tristram Shandy*, movie subtitles, blasphemies from unknown religions, classroom lectures or the notes thereof, vile suggestions whispered in the dark, baby's first word, computer poems, biblical verses, assembly instructions translated from Japanese, and words both similar and dissimilar to the same effect. The Wakean aesthetic is not just the upside-down form of the Yeatsian; it is its natural and even necessary relation, as Shem is the brother of Shaun. If a culture accumulates too many "different, heterogeneous, and conflicting bodies of canonical texts from so many diverse parts of the cultural past that every one of them [has] to forego any exclusive claim to canonical status and thereby . . . any claim to canonical status at all" (RIC196), Shem is to blame. For Shem the Penman, Homer is a cultural fragment, the bricoleur's debris, not a norm for answering the question of what counts as poetry.

To put it differently, the difference between Shem and Shaun is that the one thinks of narrative as made of words, where words are apt to be refractory, whereas the other thinks of it as a form of mediation, that is, as a logic or mode of structuring in which, as Aristotle said of mimesis, *lexis* is inessential. As a rule Aristotelians do not believe in language, but there are exceptions.

For example, in his early essay "From the Prehistory of the Novel," the Russian critic and theorist Mikhail Bakhtin develops the idea that the formal, institutional genres of discourse by which cultures hold themselves together and are remembered are never as hegemonic or totalistic as they appear but are always contested by counterdiscourses of a certain explosive kind. Against the world of conceptual schemes, of narratives and propositions hanging together in coherent pictures of the world, of presiding institutions of science and philosophy and religion, of moral communities and Unity of Culture—against all of these in all of their multiple and heterogeneous versions there is "a great and diverse world of verbal forms that ridicule the straightforward and serious word in all its generic guises."[29] "It is our conviction," Bakhtin says, "that there never was a single strictly straightforward genre, no single type of direct discourse—artistic, rhetorical, philosophical, religious, ordinary everyday—that did not have its own parodying and travestying double, its own comic-ironic *contre-partie*" (DI53). No human culture can be intelligible and just except for philosophical reasons or, let us say, no just world exists except as it rests on philosophical foundations, even if, as in MacIntyre's project, these foundations have to be reconceptualized within the limits of historicism—rewritten as a theory of the rationality of traditions. Bakhtin's idea, however, is that rationality and justice always entail a problem of freedom insofar as the language of truth and the language of freedom cannot be organized into a single coherent discourse; rather, the one is defined by the exclusion of the other, which means that they are rival and incompatible but forever and necessarily linked. The nature of this linkage is not easy to describe (it may be that you cannot develop a theory of justice that would have enough room for a theory of freedom).[30] It is easiest (if not enough) to imagine that the linkage takes a parasitic form. Internal to every official or philosophically justifiable culture there is a culture of laughter, of misrule, disruption, and ridicule, whose energies are both uncontainable and inexcludable and therefore threaten to dissolve the world into frenzy and madness (just the sort of thing Plato warned us against).

The culture of laughter is not an aberration (nor dismissable as a modernity). The fact is you can't have a world acceptable to philosophy that doesn't cry out for Shem the Penman. Bakhtin, who is as much an Aristotelian in his own right as MacIntyre is in his, thinks of the culture of laughter as having, for all of its anarchy and centrifugal power, its own kind of unity and coherence—and therefore a *telos*: "I imagine this whole to be something like an immense novel, multi-generic, multi-styled, mercilessly critical, soberly mocking, reflecting in all its fullness the heteroglossia and multiple voices of a given culture, people, and epoch. In this huge novel—in this mirror of constantly evolving heteroglossia—any direct word and especially that of the dominant discourse is reflected as something more or less bounded, typical and characteristic of a particular era, aging, dying, ripe for change and renewal" (DI60). The task of laughter has always been to save us from philosophy.

"From the Prehistory of the Novel" sketches out a literary history from Homeric Greece through the middle ages whose canon is composed of highly protean "parodic-travestying forms" that are not to be confused with Literature (Literature in other words in Matthew Arnold's or Yeats's sense)—"a parodic poem is not a poem at all" (DI59)—but which aim rather at the profanation of literary tradition, the ridicule of Homer, Vergil, and the Bible, not to mention the mockery and confounding of those severe and narcissistic monologues we call philosophy and religion. But it is obvious that there can be no laughter without prior philosophical solemnity and self-importance, no laughter except at the expense of a philosophical republic. So it is no accident that, on Bakhtin's reading of literary history, the culture of laughter disappears at about the same time that, according to MacIntyre's narrative of the history of moral philosophy, moral philosophy goes to pieces. Except in a culture holding itself together according to a logic of exclusion—a culture, in MacIntyre's words, "from which fundamental dissent has to be excluded," or in other words a philosophical republic—there can be nothing needing or deserving of laughter, ridicule, and contempt. So Bakhtin: "in modern times the functions of parody are narrow and unproductive. Parody has grown sickly, its place in modern literature is insignificant. We live, write and speak today in a world of free and democratized language; [the] complex and multi-level hierarchy of discourses, forms, images, styles that used to permeate the entire system of official language and linguistic consciousness was swept away by the linguistic revolutions of the Renaissance" (DI71). These revolutions, as we know, were political as well as linguistic.[31] They made possible, via the the institutionalization of vernacular discourses, the liberalization of discourse as such, whence the disappearance of the classical genres. The chief discursive result of this was the formation of the novel, which is (although Bakhtin seems of two minds on this) a way of containing and controlling ancient discursive anarchy within formal if not entirely uniform and successful constraints. The novel, in effect, formalizes the contention between the discourse of truth and the discourse of freedom, or between an Aristotelian mimesis and an Aristophanic or Rabelaisian or Shandyist or Joycean disarticulation of the world. There can be (pace Martha Nussbaum) no such thing as an Aristotelian theory of the novel.

Here we may reach an impasse of sorts, as between two incompatible conceptions of narrative, one of which stresses concepts of unity, coherence, and the sense of an ending, the other stressing randomness, discontinuity, entanglement, open-endedness, and the multiplicity of versions. The one stresses deep structure, the other the thickness, complexity, and waywardness of linguistic mediation. The first is perhaps an Anglo-American or analytic concept of narrative, whose model is the proposition, the descriptive statement, the hypothesis, or some such account that makes a claim (of sorts) to truth; the other is a Continental or literary concept of narrative as the discourse of critical alternatives. ("That's not it, and that's not it, either.") A recent book by John McCumber says that "language is oriented to freedom as inherently as it is to truth. More so, indeed, because some language games are intrinsically emancipatory while—in spite of what we think philosophers have told us—none is intrinsically true." McCumber wants to argue "that freedom and truth are not only separate values served by speech, but that they are complementary; that language becomes, in certain senses, intrinsically emancipatory when truth claims are not made, and vice versa."[32] So there is a fundamental opposition between assertion and narrative after all. From the standpoint of truth only one assertion is allowed per single state of affairs, but this constraint does not hold for narrative. "Any narrative," McCumber says, "is . . . only one of many possible stories, and as more of these possiblities are actualized the better off, narratively speaking, we are. There is reason to believe that our store of philosophical narrative is presently rather low. . . . [The] reason for this is not want of intelligence and industry, but rather the conviction that narrative is a form of truth telling, that there can be only one true story, and that the proliferation of narratives would (as indeed it does) undermine the truth claim of any one of them. But narrative connecting is like a rope rather than a chain; there is no more need for different narratives to harmonize fully with one another than there is for all the strands of a rope to twist in the same direction at the same point" (PI12). The multiplicity of narratives, the absence of a canon of true stories, may produce a crisis of rationality, but such a crisis need not be taken apocalyptically as the onset of disintegration and madness (however much it might resemble this sort of thing) but rather as the work of outsiders from within whose task is to keep conceptual schemes loose, porous, irreducible, rich in backup potential, detached from sublime seriousness, maybe on rare occasions honest, but above all able to tolerate what is singular and refractory to categories, or, in other words, what won't or doesn't fit in.

5

Along the Fatal Narrative Turn:
A Cautionary Tale
for Neurophilosophers and
Other Eliminative Materialists

Late in September 1958, in a hotel in Stockholm, I set about writing this lecture for delivery a week later at the Brussels Fair. I recalled a remark made years earlier by David Tudor that I should give a talk that was nothing but stories. The idea was appealing, but I had never acted on it, and I decided to do so now. . . .

In oral delivery of this lecture, I tell one story a minute. If it's a short one, I have to spread it out; when I come to a long one, I have to speak as rapidly as I can. The continuity of the stories as recorded was not planned. I simply made a list of all the stories I could think of and checked them off as I wrote them. Some that I remembered I was not able to write to my satisfaction, and so they were not used. My intention in putting the stories together in an unplanned way was to suggest that all things—stories, incidental sounds from the environment, and, by extension, beings—are related, and that this complexity is more evident when it is not oversimplified by an idea of relationship in one person's mind.

—John Cage, "Indeterminacy"

1. "But Can Philosophy Become Literature and Still Know Itself?"[1]

By the "narrative turn" I mean roughly two related things. The first is that in recent years the concept of narrative has begun to have some interesting theoretical application in phenomenology, moral philosophy, cognitive psychology, and (somewhat unexpectedly) neurobiology and neurophilosophy, where narrative in some sense of this word takes the place of consciousness conceived as a kind of inward spectator of mental events.[2] What seems common to each of these disciplines is the idea that narrative is indispensable to having a self. For example, the neuroscientist Antonio Damasio, in an engaging book, *Descartes' Error: Reason, Emotion, and the Human Brain*, thinks of the brain as an organism capable of producing representations of objects and of a bodily self, but as also consisting of a "third-party neuron ensemble," a "metaself" or neural-based "subjectivity," that brings these two representations (Damasio calls them "protagonists") together in a kind of narrative. "This basic neural device," Damasio says, "does not require language. The metaself construction I envision is purely nonverbal, a schematic view of the main protagonists from a perspective external to both. In effect, the third-party view constitutes, moment-by-moment, a nonverbal narrative document of what is happening to those protagonists." It is interesting that Damasio insists on the point that this "narrative can be accomplished without language, using the elementary representational tools of the sensory and motor systems in space and time. I see no reason why animals without language would not make such narratives." Language simply makes possible a higher order of narrative that produces a "refined form of subjectivity. . . . Language may not be the source of the self, but it certainly is the source of the 'I.'"[3] It would be interesting to know more exactly what counts as language here.

Second and more specifically, however, the "narrative turn" refers to the antifoundationalist idea that things have histories rather than natures or essences, as in Alasdair MacIntyre's statement that "There can be no rationality as such."[4] Rather, rationality is internal to specific cultures and traditions, meaning that there is no such thing as rationality except against a background of specific cultural narratives that show what it is for anything or anyone to be called rational, show the use of the concept of reason, show what an argument is, show what the absence of rationality looks like, and so on. And so the possibility of rival and incompatible theories of rationality is something we have to think about. This puts it mildly, since an anthropologist studying multiple cultures might tell us that at the end of the day there is nothing (no one thing outside of local customs) that can pass for rationality ("But what sort of culture would think up a concept of rationality in the first place?"). Postmodernism is sometimes said to mean thinking such thoughts, as when Richard Rorty speaks of a turn from theory to narrative, meaning that, like narrative poets, we can alter a thing (anything: e.g., ourselves) by describing it differently, to which he adds that philosophy ought in fact to get into the business of redescription. For Rorty that means emancipation from obsolete concepts and beliefs, or being more interested in freedom than in truth.[5]

Obviously what is (not just critical but) fatal about this sense of the narrative turn is that philosophy is now liable to grow indistinguishable from literature—on a certain view of literature. This loss of distinction is a fate that MacIntyre is determined to escape, chiefly by constructing, and maybe also to some extent by trying to implement, a theory of a rational culture or rational tradition, a refurbished Plato's Republic from which literature (among other things) would have to be, not absolutely eliminated of course, but brought under severe communal constraints—philosophized, so to speak: kept consistent with norms that a rational culture would have to have, and this means at least kept or made consistent with the idea of coherence. The narratives of a rational culture would have to be kept coherent with one another, as in the now classical idea of a conceptual scheme, and a given culture's own story—its own history (to the extent that it is a rational culture)—would have to be a coherent narrative in which internal contradictions work themselves out over time, as if aiming toward a final end or the happiness of logical repose.[6] By contrast Rorty says that he embraces the transformation of philosophy into literature, which he describes as giving up the desire to know the truth in favor of the idea that we are "webs of beliefs and desires, of sentential attitudes—webs which continually reweave themselves so as to accommodate new sentential attitudes."[7] Where MacIntyre speaks of rational inquiry in terms of narrative coherence, making the story come out right, Rorty speaks of "inquiry as recontextualization," that is, the regular wholesale restructuring of our beliefs and desires (or of ourselves for short), not in pursuit of any end, say an ideal of the good or of being true to oneself or to the world, but simply as an expression of "the desire to dream up as many new contexts [as we can]. This is the desire [Rorty says] to be as polymorphous in our [descriptions] as possible, to recontextualize for the hell of it. This desire is manifested in art and literature more than in the natural sciences, and so I find it tempting [Rorty finds it tempting] to think of our culture as an increasingly poeticized one, and to say that we are gradually emerging from . . . scientism . . . into something better."[8] A poeticized culture would, if I understand, be governed by Ezra Pound's slogan, summarizing (so it appears) a version of literary modernism: "make it new!"

2. Rorty and MacIntyre in the Garden of the Forking Paths[9]

On a certain view, the differences between Rorty and MacIntyre resolve themselves into (among other things) a difference between two versions of holism, or maybe two versions of the Kuhnian theory of science, where the one stresses ongoing conceptual revolution ("for the hell of it") and the other stresses rational inquiry or self-criticism in pursuit of the best theory so far. Perhaps we can see in the argument between them (which of course I've had to imagine as best I can since the parties have no interest in pursuing it themselves) a way of preserving, in defiance of the narrative turn, the old (decidedly non-Aristotelian) distinction between the rational and the poetic, or between philosophy and poetry. Never mind that Rorty's grasp of the poetic is a bit of a grope in the dark; he seems at least right in suggesting that poetry is more interested in freedom than in truth, in a certain Anglo-American picture of truth, and that freedom at the end of the day is probably incompatible with rational coherence. My own idea, with all respect to current theory, is that historically and culturally (at least) philosophy remains a very different thing from literature. And the two are not just different; they are rival and incompatible regions of discourse, such that a philosophical community, say a just and rational human community (certainly a scientific community), would require, in some form, the *elimination* of literature, whereas by contrast a community in which freedom mattered before everything else, a community allowing for multiple languages and competing conceptual schemes, or say the perpetual introduction of random and Shandy-like narratives, would have a very difficult time being philosophical (on any recognizable theory of being philosophical).

One recognizable theory of being philosophical might be Jean-François Lyotard's definition of philosophy as, basically, governance by rules. "Philosophy is a discourse that has as its rule the search for its rule [and that of other discourses]."[10] The idea is that rules are for ruling in and ruling out so as to keep things straight. Imagine a culture that rules nothing out. The speculation here (see part 3 below) is that it might be in the nature of narrative to produce such a culture, and that a culture that tried to be philosophical would have a problem with this. A philosophical culture is one that prefers theories to examples of how things are or should be. A narrative turn in a philosophical culture would thus be something like a turn away from theories toward examples, perhaps along lines once suggested by Peter Winch when he argued, against Kant, that there is no such thing as good behavior without qualification—no good behavior as such—only examples showing the complexity of human judgment as to what might be the right thing to do under the circumstances. Moral philosophy is the study of this complexity, not a method for resolving it, say by producing a theory of the good, come what may. "All we can do," Winch says, "is to look at particular examples [of human conduct] and see what we *do* want to say about them; there are no general rules which can determine in advance what we *must* say about them."[11]

So, on this view, moral philosophy can only take place at the level of narratives of human judgments, not at the level of principles and rules that would guide judgment toward the right and the good. But then one has to ask, as a philosopher like MacIntyre would, what's so philosophical about moral philosophy?, since the upshot of Winch's argument is that moral judgments are not universalizable but are always located at the ground level of stories. The difference between theories and stories is that theories are in competition with one another for the role of best theory so far; that is, they logically organize themselves hierarchically, whereas stories or examples multiply horizontally much the way human history moves in its production of unprecedented situations whose moral complexities cannot be resolved from above.

However, here I want to study a slightly different version of this Platonic project of separating literature from philosophical culture, namely the idea that if literature is, in some sense, the background and medium of what neurobiologists call "folk psychology," and if folk psychology is, in contrast to neurobiology, just false—maybe even, as Paul Churchland says, "radically false," or as Stephen Stich says, "screamingly false"—then literature has to be, or should be, in some form, eliminated, certainly eliminated from neurobiology, psychology, philosophy of mind, but maybe indeed from all accounts, even the ordinary accounts, that we give of ourselves.[12] Where people think the line of elimination should be drawn is a good question; one might even think of it as a political question. I find it interesting that Rorty once subscribed to a form of this eliminativist view, namely the form disguised by the motto, "let a thousand vocabularies bloom and then see which survive."[13] This is the pragmatic Darwinian liberal's version of MacIntyre's self-correcting rational tradition—or say it's the laissez-faire naturalist's version of Jürgen Habermas's more plangent and grim-faced idea that (now more than ever after the narrative turn) it is the cultural task of philosophers to be "guardians of rationality," and this means guarding everyday human discourse or communicative praxis so that nothing from the separate domain of art leaks into it.[14] Communicative action requires transparency of language whose model is the propositional style of philosophical argument; literary or other forms of self-referential, noisy language are incompatible with this ideal of communicative action and need to be either excluded from the public realm of discourse or translated into it in some nondisruptive propositional way. What we call postmodernism is simply the crisis of rationality or enlightenment brought on by those who would level the genre distinction between philosophy and literature and who are determined to confound the logical differentiations among science, morality, and art. Let a thousand vocabularies bloom and then see which survive, says Rorty. Habermas by contrast is the horticulturalist who says, Let a thousand vocabularies bloom, but only within our Enlightenment garden, where it is the business of philosophy to organize and police these vocabularies so that they do not interfere with communicative praxis. But Rorty's thought is to drop the idea of "guardians of rationality" and to let our vocabularies take care of themselves, although a good liberal will want to encourage these vocabularies into obsolescence by, poetry-like, inventing new ones. (A good liberal also assumes that cultural history is like history of science or history of technology rather than literary history, since there is no such thing as obsolescence in literary history—unless it is Harold Bloom's theory of the obsolescence to which strong poets of the past threaten to consign poets of the present, whence poets of the present show their strength by creatively misreading or rewriting the strong poems of the past. Or words to that effect.)[15]

Nowadays Rorty describes himself as a "nonreductive physicalist" who believes that events like "Mozart composing a melody or Euclid seeing how to prove a theorem" can be described in terms of elementary particles.[16] "Nonreductive physicalism" looks like an attempt to replace the mind-body problem with a two-language theory, which is the theory that the same event can be described equally

well in physiological as well as intentional or phenomenological terms, where
these two sorts of terms are not synonymous or intertranslatable but rather form
a portion of a cultural heteroglossia—a multilanguaged or multicultural culture.
This means that physiological descriptions of brain processes entail no prejudice
against the discourses of musicians and geometrists, since music and geometry are
ongoing forms of life with their own up-to-date vocabularies; but it also means
that Rorty would find it easy to concede, or shrug off, Joseph Margolis's dualist
argument that "cultural phenomena are conceptually invisible to any and every form
of physicalism"; or, as Arthur Danto put it with respect to art, "To see something
as art requires something the eye cannot decry—an atmosphere of artistic theory,
a knowledge of the history of art, an artworld."[17] Things—the nonnatural sort of
things—are what they are only within the cultural narratives in which they mean
something. Coming to terms with what something means, means coming to terms
with a whole lifeworld or form of life, where "coming-to-terms" means "learning
to inhabit." So if events like "Mozart composing a melody or Euclid seeing how
to prove a theorem" can be described in terms of elementary particles, still we
wouldn't know these were the (cultural) events we were describing in terms of
elementary particles except against the background of narratives about which, not
being *just* nonreductive physicalists, we happen also to know a good deal—the way
Danto, for example, is able to know a very great deal about art history without
losing the good night's sleep of an honest physicalist: call this replacing the mind-
body problem with the twice-told tale of the double or secret life. One might
want to put it that the brain couldn't have anything to do with the composition
of music except in a culture in which composing music meant something; in a
music-free culture, imagining there to be such a thing, brain processes would
be occupied differently (which perhaps raises the question of whether the brain
is finally culturally constituted—a social construction as much as rationality or
justice is or, in other words, just another narrative). Perhaps this is just a naive or
confused way of saying that one language, that of physiological description, won't
translate into the phenomenological language of intentions—and vice versa. In
the same breath, it might be a way of saying that the concepts and practices of
human culture, including the concepts and practices of neuroscience, make sense
only against a background of narratives that show what it is to use these concepts
and perform these practices (that show, Cora Diamond would say, how to live with
them).[18] This is a version of Hubert Dreyfus's hermeneutical or practical holism that
redistributes the natural and the human sciences along the same anthropological
plane.[19] There is nothing very fatal about this redistribution unless one happens to
be a rule.

Still, on Rorty's theory the relationship between these two languages, the
physiological and the phenomenological, although no longer logically reductive,
is not negligible; it is, in its way, political, even politically liberal (in the sense

of liberating us, Descartes-like, from the prison-house of traditional theories). Rorty's idea seems to be that although physicalism may be (all by itself) blind to cultural phenomena, nevertheless it can cause these phenomena to alter their self-descriptions for the better, especially where these self-descriptions include eliminable words like "consciousness," "self," and various personal pronouns. No need (à la Habermas, or Churchland) to summon the philosophical police against these or other obfuscating words; rather we should simply allow them to die out as neurophysiology, poetry-like, invents new words to take their place. Remember that our nonphysicalist vocabularies, our cultural narratives, are to be thought of as vast webs of beliefs and desires that are constantly being rewoven in response to new stimuli, as for example when we (musicians and geometrists) acquire new beliefs, say the beliefs of nonreductive physicalists. So there is a sense in which, after all these years, Rorty is still a sort of eliminative materialist, although (unlike Churchland) he is more of the cheerful, easygoing, pragmatic sort that is willing to grant these phenomenological words such cash value as they may still have independently of nonreductive physicalist criteria. That is, Rorty hopes that physicalism will drive certain phenomenological concepts out of use, but, precisely because of where he stands on the fatal (no-turning-back) narrative turn, he cannot claim that physicalism gives us the true version of (or reduces to plain fact) what we thought these concepts had been accounting for, namely, why, among other things, we act as we do (why we are musical, for example). Rather, all he can liberally hope for is a conceptual revolution in which all of us, not just neurobiologists, give up phenomenological narratives and come round to the language of physiological description. So, ironically, when Rorty speaks of a poeticized culture replacing a scientistic one, what he finally means is that poetry will now do what heretofore, before the narrative turn, had been thought to be the job of reason, namely to bring our culture more completely in line with physical science, appropriating its language for our self-descriptions, or the stories we tell.[20]

This is not, appearances aside, strictly at odds with MacIntyre's program. Like Rorty, MacIntyre is a holist who thinks that things make sense because of the way they hang together, and as, among other things, a moral philosopher, he applies this idea to the problem of human action. No action makes sense all by itself, or just in terms of causes and reasons, but only as we contextualize it within a narrative history—narrative being, as MacIntyre says in *After Virtue*, "the basic and essential genre for the characterisation of human actions" (AV 194). He continues: "in successfully identifying and understanding what someone else is doing we always move towards placing a particular episode in the context of a set of narrative histories" (AV 197). A human form of life or human culture might be understood as comprising, or even as being constituted by, a store of such narratives. Moreover, we are ourselves intelligible only insofar as we internalize the narratives, including especially the characters that enact them, that our culture makes available to us. "We enter human society," says MacIntyre, "with one or more imputed characters—roles into which we have been drafted—and we have to learn what they are in order to be able to understand how others respond to us and how our responses to them are apt to be construed. It is through hearing stories"—the stock of stories that make up what we might call the cultural library or cultural archive—"that children learn or mislearn . . . what the cast of characters may be in the drama into which they have been born and what the ways of the world are" (AV201). Likewise we can call an action just only against a background of narratives that show what it is to act justly, or what a world bereft of justice looks like (e.g., *Hamlet*), or what happens when rival and incompatible theories of justice collide (*Antigone*). Justice as such may not be a concept whose extension can be closed by a frontier, that is, it may not finally, being so historical, be satisfactorily theorizable, but that does not diminish its importance for us so long as the stories concerning justice that inform our moral and political lives remain intelligible and forceful— lawlike in authority if not in form (or applicable, as we say in hermeneutics). So long as these narratives are seen to have application to our everyday experience, justice remains a living concept, a concept we know how to use or live with. A culture without narratives like *Antigone* and *Hamlet*, or one in which these and other similar narratives have come to seem pointless or unreadable, would not know what justice is.[21]

3. Tristram Shandy's Theory of Narrative

If our habitation within human forms of life, meaning at least our use of concepts (even the most scientific), is therefore mediated by narrative—which is essentially what the idea of the narrative turn comes down to—then there is some sense to the idea that our store of narratives has got to be protected or controlled. It is easy to see that science and philosophy are highly mediated, beautifully technical forms of such control—I call it: still faithful to Plato after all these years. MacIntyre, even more than Habermas, is worth studying for the way he articulates the dangers that our store of narratives faces—dangers that are *internal to narrative itself*, that is, inherent in the logical weaknesses of narrative, but that are, in addition, fatally exacerbated by modernity. These weaknesses are, first, that all narratives are mediated by language—are made of words, in other words—and, second, that narratives tend to proliferate incoherently so that a culture always faces the problem of having too many of them.

With respect to the first fatal fact: when MacIntyre in *After Virtue* says that in the modern world "the cultural place of narrative has been diminished" (AV211), he means that the historical tendency of modern narrative has been away from mimesis or fictional realism toward the condition of *Finnegans Wake* (or, more radically still, toward Gertrude Stein)—a movement whose corollary in literary study had been, until very recently, an increasing absorption in questions of writing and textuality. MacIntyre mentions (appropriately) the philosopher-novelist William Gass as a typically modern case in which the form of narrative is opaque rather than transparent, because narrative has become (for Gass) an art of language rather than of plot and character, that is, an art of the *materiality* of language—using this word in its nonphysicalist sense (so Gass: "narration is that part of the art of fiction concerned with the coming and passing of words—not the familiar arrangement of words in dry strings," that is, words in their musical rather than their propositional arrangements, where music is a metaphor for any nonsemantic form of discourse, or where the goal of discourse is not to say something but to make something). Gass is obviously the fellow Plato warned us about: "the purpose of a literary work," he says, "is the capture of consciousness," turning it *away* from the world toward the pure figures of art.[22]

Or one could put it that literary narratives are just bad information systems because they contain too much noise—or, more accurately, they don't just contain noise, rather they are constituted by it. Possibly one could deal with this problem by recourse to a concept like "self-organization from noise," which William Paulson has recently applied to literature as a way of bridging the gap between information theory and literary theory.[23] (The shorter course would be to consult John Cage, who says that noise is just a sound we don't know how to listen to.) Paulson draws on Jurij Lotman's *Structure of the Artistic Text:*

> Art—and here it manifests its structural kinship to life [one could as well say: its structural kinship to brains]—is capable of transforming noise into information. It complicates its own structure owing to its correlation with its environment (in all other systems the clash with the environment can only lead to the fade-out of information). This peculiarity of art . . . is related to the structural principle which determines the polysemy of artistic elements; new structures which enter into a text or the extra-textual background of a work of art do not cancel out old meanings, but enter into semantic relations with them. A structure that enriches the informational content of a text differs from a destructive heterogeneous structure in that everything heterogeneous which can be correlated in some way with the structure of the authorial text ceases to be noise.[24]

So in principle, perhaps, one could qualify or set limits to the empirical fact that every narrative is excessive with respect to its function, no matter what function we happen to assign to it.[25]

The second fatal fact (which is really only a way of making the first more interesting) is that narratives tend *not* to hang together like propositions in a conceptual scheme, or descriptions in a web of beliefs, or strands in a woven fabric; rather, they tend toward redundancy and fragmentation. By redundancy one can mean a number of things, starting with the idea that from the analytic standpoint of structures and rules narratives just tell the same old story, in which case, as the structuralists used to argue, we could in principle bring the history of narrative to an end simply by describing the rules of their production (although we see now perhaps that describing brain processes might do as well). The scientific materialist's version of redundancy is just the twice-told tale that folk psychology has not progressed beyond Sophocles.[26] A stronger version of redundancy can be found in Jorge Luis Borges's story, "The Library of Babel," where the universe turns out to be a vast library whose volumes "register all the possible combinations of twenty-odd orthographical symbols (a number which, though extremely vast, is not infinite): in other words, all that it is given to express, in all languages"— which means that the library contains the very words that I am now writing, including their several refutations and near-refutations, and also, among everything else, various rival and competing histories of neuropsychology from its simple or complex beginnings to the many versions of its gradual withering away or of its notorious and heroic final catastrophe or triumph.[27] Borges brings it home that the main question of narrative, the mystery of it, is why we keep at it, why we can't stop, pointless as it is, as if narratives were anarchic in the nature of the case ("without why," in Meister Eckhart's happy phrase); or as if Rorty's thoughts on obsolescence could never be (pace Harold Bloom) a bother to the storyteller.[28]

Or is it simply that what is lacking in such a library as Borges imagines, quite as much as in our own modernist (or, for all of that, postmodern) culture, is a set of master narratives that would give the law of storytelling forcefully enough to justify the elimination of the dreary surplus? (Giving the law of storytelling traditionally takes the form of a structuralist approach that reduces our surplus of narratives to mere surface structures governed by universal constraints, but it might just as well take the form of ruling that all narratives should conform to the genre of the quest-romance, which is essentially MacIntyre's Aristotelian theory of narrative [AV203–4].) MacIntyre's version of the tale of the incoherent library is given most explicitly in his essay "Relativism, Power, and Philosophy," in which he distinguishes between traditional and modern cultures by saying that whereas the former is governed by a coherent set of canonical texts showing how its language or its concepts are to be used, the latter is characterized by "the detachment of the language-in-use from any particular set of canonical texts." A "central feature" of modernity, MacIntyre says, is

the gradual accumulation . . . of so many different, heterogeneous, and conflicting bodies of canonical texts from so many diverse parts of the cultural past that every one of them had to forego any exclusive claim to canonical status and thereby . . . to any canonical status at all. [The principle here is that the force of the truth claims of our narratives diminishes as their number increases (supposing them to embody truth claims, which is something one cannot help supposing).] So the accumulation of Greek, Hebrew, and Latin texts at the Renaissance proved only a prologue not only to the annexation of Chinese, Sanskrit, Mayan, and Old Irish texts, and to the bestowal of equal status upon texts in European vernacular languages from the thirteenth to the nineteenth centuries, but also to the discovery of a wide range of preliterate cultures, the whole finally to be assembled in that modern liberal arts college museum of academic culture, whose introductory tour is provided by those Great Books courses which run from Gilgamesh to Saul Bellow via Confucious, Dante, Newton, *Tristram Shandy*, and Margaret Mead.[29]

So modern culture is like Joyce's Willingdon Museyroom in *Finnegans Wake* (or, like the *Wake* itself, a vast Echoland), whose moral might be that it's very well to let a thousand vocabularies thrive in order to see which ones survive, but what if (equally well, if equally jumbled) they *all* survive? One could speculate that postmodernism is simply the recognition that modernity is what MacIntyre says it is, an anarchy of storytelling: storytelling without why.[30]

Basically MacIntyre is Rorty without Rorty's belief in obsolescence; that is, in contrast to Rorty, MacIntyre sees that cultural history is more like literary history (or folk theory) than history of science (more like *Tristram Shandy*, neither beginning nor heading anywhere but merely cumulative and proliferating in every direction, undermining every possibility of truth claims), and that in order to get it (human history) to behave like history of science one has to intervene in human culture on behalf of a theory of the rationality of traditions, or of tradition as inquiry—that is, as "an historically extended, socially embodied argument" (AV207) of the sort that we discover in the history of physics.[31] The difference between Rorty's liberalism and MacIntyre's appeal to the rationality of traditions is just this difference between, on the one hand, staying out of harm's way, distancing oneself from the world ironically, trusting but never claiming that science will out, and, on the other, intervening in it with arguments or decrees (or whatever happens to work) in order to make human culture rationally coherent and thus justifiable at least in theory.

So much, one might say, for the superfluity of narratives. As for their fragmentation: from the anarchic or nonlinear standpoint of *Tristram Shandy* the fragment is born of the passion for leaving (that is, ruling) nothing out, as if there were nowhere at hand any criteria for excluding details, events, or anything at all as meaningless (no criteria, the dubious Nietzschean might say, for distinguishing the true from the false):

Could a historiographer drive on his history, as a muleteer drives on his mule,—straight forward,—for instance, from *Rome* all the way to *Loretto*, without ever once turning his head aside either to the right hand or to the left,—he might venture to foretell you to an hour when he should get to his journey's end; —but the thing is, morally speaking impossible: For, if he is a man of the least spirit, he will have fifty deviations from a straight line to make with this or that party as he goes a long, which he can no ways avoid. He will have views and prospects to himself perpetually solliciting his eye, which he can no more help standing still to look at than he can fly; he will moreover have various

> Accounts to reconcile:
> Anecdotes to pick up:
> Inscriptions to make out:
> Stories to weave in:
> Traditions to sift:
> Personages to call upon:
> Panegyricks to paste up at this door:

Pasquinades at that: All which both the man and his mule are quite exempt from. To sum up all; there are archives at every stage to be look'd into, and rolls, records, documents, and endless genealogies, which justice ever and anon calls him back to stay the reading of: —In short, there is no end of it; —for my own part, I declare I have been at it these six weeks, making all the speed I possibly could, —and am not yet born.[32]

One might put it that literature's habit of turning over every loose particle is required to compensate for philosophy's clenched genius for underdescription. But on the Shandyist theory, narratives are just geared to the singularity and randomness of things; they are tuned to the fact that randomness defies compressibility, so that the only way to describe the world would be to give a copy of it, say piece by piece, event by event, together with their alternatives; in which case it will naturally seem as if we will not only always have more narratives than we need, but also that every narrative will always seem obsessive with respect to its details (not to say obsessive with respect to its language, as in the case of James Joyce, whose career travels from documentary naturalism to *Finnegans Wake*, as if to encapsulate the history of the novel).[33] This is another way of saying that narrative is always excessive with respect to its function (whatever function we happen to assign to it)—the moral being, once more, that if we want our culture to be theoretically coherent we had better keep our narratives under Aristotelian control, constrained by logical form (transparent, e.g., as to plot and character) and interpreted allegorically so as to appear mutually compatible with one another or capable of hanging together like a conceptual scheme. Rorty's parallel moral simply substitutes being up-to-date for being coherent and, to arrive at a corresponding system for eliminating unwanted texts, replaces Aristotle and Kant with Darwin, Nietzsche, and John Dewey.

4. Tristram's Brain

In a controversial book, *Consciousness Explained*, the neurophilosopher Daniel Dennett says that the brain works as if it were a process of multiple narrations, where narration is like a large company of ancient scribes engaged (each one independently and without beginning or end) in the furious redaction of a text, as contrasted with the philosophical figure of the single, disengaged, logical ocularcentric homunculus producing proposition-like forms aiming at a true or at least coherent picture of a world:

> For instance, a discrimination of a picture of a dog might create a "perceptual set"—making it temporarily easier to see dogs (or even just animals) in other pictures—or it might activate a particular semantic domain, making it temporarily more likely that you read the word "bark" as a sound, not covering for tree trunks. As we already noted, this multitrack process occurs over hundreds of milliseconds, during which time various additions, incorporations, emendations, and overwritings of content can occur, in various orders. These yield, over the course of time, something *rather like* a narrative stream or sequence, which can be thought of as subject to continual editing by many processes distributed around in the brain, and continuing indefinitely into the future. Contents arise, get revised, contribute to the interpretation of other contents or to the modulation of behavior (verbal or otherwise), and in the process leave their traces in memory, which then eventually decay or get incorporated into or overwritten by later contents, wholly or in part. This skein of contents is only rather like a narrative because of its multiplicity; at any point in time there are multiple drafts of narrative fragments at various stages of editing in various places in the brain.[34]

So the brain does not register or construct perceptions or world-pictures, as traditional empirical and transcendental models have it; it does not even produce narratives on the standard theory of narrative as higher-order integrative discourse. It produces texts. Dennett calls this his "multiple drafts theory," which he opposes to what he calls the "Cartesian theater" or spectator theory, and which is something like a Shandyist as against an Aristotelian-Kantian model of how the brain works—in the sense that what the brain is said to produce resembles *Tristram Shandy* more than it does a conceptual fabric of propositions held together by inferential reasoning.[35] So far as I know, no philosopher or scientist, and not even Dennett himself, has quite realized the implications of this theory, which would amount to a radical inversion of the whole eliminativist project of neuroscience, or a reconceptualization of what counts as folk theory. Folk theory is now whatever conforms to the propositional attitude, whereas neuroscientific theory follows the Shandyist model of nonlinear or rhizomatic connectionism.[36] So literature replaces philosophy in the scientific scheme of things, but in a burlesque of what Rorty seems to be aiming at.

I say, "what the brain is said to produce resembles *Tristram Shandy*," but perhaps one can refine this formulation further by suggesting that what neuroscience presently confirms is Jerome McGann's conception of literary history (the only original and interesting theory of literary history produced in my lifetime). This is basically the idea that a literary text exists in its versions, and that poetic richness consists not so much in the multiplicity of meanings as in the multiplicity of texts that happen, sometimes accidentally, to go by the one name of a single monumental work, with no text or fragment thereof ruled out as an authorized version of the eminent thing in itself.[37] So the task of critical bibliography must remain external to every project of canonization. For the rigorous bibliographer, every text—every draft and fragment of manuscript together with every published version and even every anthologized excerpt, however garbled, of the monumental work—is equally authoritative, that is, equally worthy of study and equally foundational for critical and philosophical commentary, not to mention the construction of possible worlds. Every text is an open-ended horizon of multiple drafts, fragments, and versions whose extension, as Wittgenstein said of the concept of philosophy, cannot be closed by a frontier.

So we might, with Dennett's authority, imagine literary history as Tristram's brain—"a field of indeterminacies, with movements to be seen running along lateral and recursive lines as well as linearly, and by strange diagonals and various curves, tangents, and even within random patterns."[38] Taking a god's-eye, end-of-history view, literary history would look for all the world like one of Deleuze and Guattari's rhizomes: "it is composed not of units but of dimensions, or rather directions in motion. It has neither beginning nor end, but always a middle (*milieu*) from which it grows and which it overspills. It constitutes linear multiplicities with n dimensions having neither subject nor object, which can be laid out on a plane of consistency, and from which the One is always subtracted $(n - 1)$. When a multiplicity of this kind changes dimension, it necessarily changes in nature as well, undergoes a metamorphosis. Unlike a structure, which is defined by a set of points and positions . . . the rhizome is made only of lines: lines of segmentarity and stratification as its dimensions, and the line of flight or deterritorialization as the maximum dimension"—spreading out unpredictably to form an endless continent of unexplored but infinitely inviting plateaus.[39]

6

Tragic Thoughts at the End of Philosophy: Martha Nussbaum's Ethics of Particularity

In moral as in other branches of philosophy good examples are indispensable: examples, that is, which bring out the real force of the ways in which we speak and in which language is not "on holiday" (to adapt a remark of Wittgenstein's). It is needful to say this in opposition to a fairly well-established, but no less debilitating, tradition in recent Anglo-American moral philosophy, according to which it is not merely permissible, but desirable, to take trivial examples. The rationale of this view is that such examples do not generate the emotion which is liable to surround more serious cases and thus enable us to look more coolly at the logical issues involved. On such a view what is characteristic of the ways in which we express our moral concerns can be examined quite apart from any consideration of what it is about these concerns which makes them important to us. But "a moral issue that does not matter" is a mere chimera. The seriousness of such issues is not something that we can add, or not, after the explanation of what those issues are, as a sort of optional emotional extra: it is something that "shows itself" (again I deliberately echo Wittgenstein) in the explanation of the issues. And an issue the seriousness of which does not show itself will not be one that presents for our scrutiny those features of morality that we find philosophically puzzling.
    —Peter Winch, "The Universalizability of Moral Judgments"

1. Some P's and Q's in Ethical Theory

Let me begin with some elementary mapping. It seems possible to distinguish between two very different theories of the ethical. One theory—call it the P-theory—tries to characterize the ethical in terms of our beliefs, desires, values, principles, perceptions, actions, experiences, and so on. The other—call this the

Q-theory—tries to characterize ethics in terms of how we are with respect to other people or, more accurately, to the other as singular and irreducible. In the Q-theory the question at stake is how we respond to the claims that the other has on us rather than how we are able to justify the claims that we want to make on behalf of our beliefs, values, actions, commitments, and so on. The P-theory would argue that the rightness or wrongness of our response will follow from having right or wrong beliefs and values, the right or wrong perceptions and discriminations, right or wrong pictures of the good, so the idea to start with is obviously knowing right from wrong. This seems roughly to have been Kant's line. Claims are claims of reason, that is, rules. The Q-theory, however, would say that the claims of the other are in advance of reason, and that our beliefs, values, and rules often obstruct the workings of these claims, as if it were as much a function of our beliefs and values to protect us from the ethical as to bring us in line with it. For the point would be that the ethical is not a rule or measure or standard that one could get in line with. It is something much more difficult to live with than a set of principles.

Up until recently the P-theory has been the theory embraced by most analytic philosophers. The Q-theory meanwhile has belonged mainly to Continental thinking with its powerful critique of the subject, which is to say its critique of the whole idea of having beliefs, values, principles, and rules for deciding how to act.

Among recent P-theorists Martha Nussbaum is one of the more interesting because she has pretty much given up the idea that ethical theory has to be framed in terms of rules and beliefs, but meanwhile she still retains the idea that ethics is subject-centered. That is, ethics is still conceived in terms of a moral spectator, a perceiving agent, someone (to be sure) situated in circumstances calling for action or decision, but whose situatedness is still characterized in terms of seeing and describing a state of affairs. Nussbaum has laid out her ideas in a book called *The Fragility of Goodness* and again in a collection of essays, *Love's Knowledge*, where she says that "ethics is the search for a specification of the good life for a human being. This is a study whose aim, as Aristotle insists, is not just theoretical understanding but also practice. (We study not just for the sake of learning but also to see our 'target' and ourselves more clearly, so that we can ourselves live and act better.)"[1] "Specification" is the keyword here. Narratives like Henry James's *The Golden Bowl* can be counted as works of moral philosophy, Nussbaum says, precisely because they give close study to different theories of the good life by seeing how these theories compete with one another within complex, highly nuanced, often intricately tangled human situations. The moral agent, like the novelist, is "someone keenly alive in thought and feeling to every nuance of the situation" (LK143). Indeed, "the novel can be a paradigm of moral activity" precisely because it is "the intense scrutiny of particulars" (LK148). From James, Nussbaum says, one can learn that moral knowledge "is not simply intellectual grasp of propositions; it is not even simply the intellectual grasp of particular facts; it is perception" (LK152) in which "nuance and fine detail of tone" are everything (LK154). The idea here is that moral action or the moral life can never be reduced to rule-governed behavior or even to the application of received beliefs, values, and principles to the concrete situations in which we find ourselves; rather a "morality based on perception" (LK160) means the ability to see and respond to situations that are bewildering in the complexity of their particulars.[2] This doesn't mean that we don't have or need principles, values, and rules; rather a "morality of perception" is the ability to achieve a kind of equilibrium of the general and the particular—Nussbaum calls it a "perceptive equilibrium . . . in which concrete perceptions 'hang beautifully together,' both with one another and with the agent's general principles; an equilibrium that is always ready to reconstitute itself in response to the new" (LK182). In a "morality based on perception," our beliefs, values, principles, and rules are always revisable in light of new experience, which means that what we strive for is an attunement between rule and situation, and also between ourselves and our community of values (LK192).

Now against this a Q-theorist like Emmanuel Levinas would say ethics cannot even get under way until we get rid of the idea of "the primacy of perceptive intuition" (LK141); and that is because ethics means turning the subject of perceptive intuition inside out.

In *Totality and Infinity* Levinas characterizes ethics in terms of the relationship between myself and "the Stranger" over whom "I have no power. He [the Stranger, the Other] escapes my grasp by an essential dimension, even if I have him at my disposal. He is not wholly in my site. But I, who have no concept in common with the Stranger, am, like him, without genus. We are the same and the other. . . . The relation between the same and the other . . . is primordially enacted as conversation, where the same, gathered up in its ipseity as an 'I,' as a particular existent unique and autochthonous, leaves itself."[3] That is, in my encounter with the other my self-sameness, my self-possession, my self-identity as an *ego cogito*, my world and my spontaneous power of agency within it, is disrupted; I am, in the crucial simile, turned inside out "like a cloak," exposed to the other, radically resituated in a place of responsibility rather than that of cognition, intentionality, and agency.[4] This condition of responsibility is what Levinas calls ethics. "The strangeness of the Other, his irreducibility to the I, to my thoughts and my possessions, is precisely accomplished as a calling into question of my spontaneity, as ethics" (TI43). Gone therefore are all the basic characters of traditional moral philosophy: the moral spectator, the self-legislating rational agent, the calculator of ends and means, the emotive self, the theorist of the right and quester of the good, and so on. In their place stands a human being who is in excess of the subjectivity presupposed by knowledge, propositional attitudes, self-possession, self-identity, the unity of narrative, and the justification of conduct. This "more than I" recurs in those events when things happen to me, that is, when I am in the accusative rather than declarative position. To be approached, to be addressed, to be pursued—there are endless situations in which my relation to myself is to a *me*, someone who finds him or herself saying, "Who, me?" "The word 'I,'" Levinas says, "means *here I am* [*me voici*]" (OTB114): literally, "see me here," where "here" is the site of "a responsibility that is justified by no prior commitment" (OTB102). The "me" is the subject—the "I"—in the condition of exposure, "answering for everything and everyone" (OTB114).

Two things (at least) about this line of thought make it difficult for someone like Nussbaum to accept. One is that it opposes ethics to cognition, makes ethics the breakup of cognition, or what in *Otherwise Than Being, or Beyond Essence* Levinas calls "the breakup of essence" or the "breakup of identity" (OTB14). "Cognition," Levinas says, "is the deployment of [the identity of the] same. . . . To know amounts to grasping being out of nothing, or reducing it to nothing, removing from it its alterity"—depriving it of all strangeness, clarifying it (TI43–44). Cognition is "hence not a relation with the other as such but the reduction of the other to the same. Such is the definition of freedom: to maintain oneself against the other despite every relation with the other to insure the autarchy of the I. Thematization and conceptualization, which moreover are inseparable, are not peace with the other but suppression or possession of the other. For possession affirms the other, but within a negation of its independence. 'I think' comes down to 'I can'— to an appropriation of what is, to an exploitation of reality. . . . Possession is preeminently the form in which the other becomes the same, by becoming mine" (TI46). So there can be no "non-allergic relation with alterity" (TI47) within the subject-centered relation of cognition. Nussbaum would reject this, but at the same time she would (or ought to) see the point of disengaging ethics from essence, since in fact that is the whole point of her effort to rehabilitate ethical theory by reconceptualizing Aristotle's notions *aisthesis* and practical reasoning.[5] It is precisely to arrive at something like a "non-allergic relation with alterity" that Nussbaum wants to bring moral knowledge under the sign of love. Where Levinas speaks of proximity, responsibility, and the substitution of oneself for the other, Nussbaum speaks of intimacy.[6] But hers always remains a morality of the subject. The beneficiary of morality is not the other but the sealed-off *ego cogito* for whom perceptive equilibrium means release from moral isolation—from the mere "curiosity of the uninvolved gaze" (LK187).

The second reason why Nussbaum would find it difficult to engage Levinas's ethical theory is that hers is a comic theory while his is tragic. Ethics as the theory of the good life is necessarily comic: love's knowledge is not the sort of knowledge Oedipus or Lear suffer. Whereas for Levinas the breakup of essence or identity or the cognitive relation exposes the ethical subject in a terrible way: "vulnerability, exposure to outrage, to wounding, passivity more passive than all patience, passivity of the accusative form, trauma of accusation suffered by a hostage to the point of persecution, implicating the identity of the hostage who substitutes himself for others: all this is the self, a defecting or defeat of the ego's identity" (OTB15). Nussbaum would certainly find this excessive and intolerable, but one can also imagine her seeing the point of it, since in fact the whole argument of *The Fragility of Goodness* is that the good life for human beings entails vulnerability to luck. There is probably an unbridgeable difference between Nussbaum's vulnerability to luck and Levinas's exposure to outrage and persecution, and what makes the difference is that Levinas's ethical theory is above all an ethics of the Holocaust, that is, it presupposes a world of persecution and outrage— presupposes a world in which the Holocaust is not unthinkable, surprises no one, but gives the definition of the everyday.[7] Levinasian ethics presupposes catastrophe as an ontological condition, even as it presupposes skepticism as an unsatisfiable questioning that takes us out of the mode of self-sufficiency and control, as if the ethical were something hardly to be borne, like being human. Nussbaum speaks of the good life in terms of keen responsiveness and maintaining a delicate equilibrium the way Maggie Verver does in James's *Golden Bowl,* which is (on Nussbaum's reading of it anyway) a great comic novel. Responsibility for the other, however, is not part of Nussbaum's theory, which is a theory of the good life for me and mine. It is a very Greek theory, as befits a classicist and Aristotelian, whereas the ethics of the other, as Levinas shows in his Talmudic readings, is a very Jewish theory. Nussbaum speaks almost exclusively in terms of responsiveness to *situations,* whereas Levinas speaks of the Stranger who will not be done away with even though I murder him, who alters my self-relation by turning his face toward me, whose face turns me out in the open.[8] Here ethics concerns not the good life but the real one.

This preliminary contrast between Levinas and Nussbaum helps us to see some of the boundaries of a subject-centered ethics, but is not to be taken as a refutation of it. Difference is also in a sense proximity. The richness of Nussbaum's ethical theory is that one can take it as approximating a critique of the subject that is in certain respects symmetrical with Levinas's attempt to show that cognition "is not all there is to subjectivity" (OTB102). The ethical takes place at the level of sensibility rather than that of concepts and principles. "We live from 'good soup,' air, light, spectacles, work, ideas, sleep, etc.," Levinas says. "These are not objects of representation" (TI110). For Levinas, we do not "hook on to the world" as so many minds or brains; we inhabit it: "we relate ourselves to it with a relation that is neither theoretical nor practical. Behind theory and practice there is enjoyment of theory and practice: the egoism of life" (TI113). The trick is to see this as not just a trivial truth.

2. The Crisis of Modernity

Charles Taylor has shown how modernity begins with the cultural formation of a certain kind of human subject, "the subject of disengagement and rational control."

Disengagement is the key concept. It entails, on the one hand, the withdrawal of the subject from its own experience—indeed, from its own body; and, on the other, it entails the objectification of the world, starting with its own body and extending outward in all directions. The body is no longer internal to subjectivity but is constituted as an object subject to scrutiny and instrumental control. The same can be said for the subject's beliefs and experiences. Disengagement means that the subject's beliefs and experiences, its bodies and its feelings, its world, are no longer engaged from a first-person standpoint but from a transcendental standpoint of critical reflection. As Taylor says, "the modern ideal of disengagement requires a reflexive stance. We have to turn inward and become aware of our own activity and of the processes which form us. We have to take charge of constructing our own representation of the world, which otherwise goes on without order and without science; we have to take charge of the processes by which associations form and shape our character and outlook. Disengagement demands that we stop simply living in the body or within our traditions or habits and, by making them objects for us, subject them to radical scrutiny and remaking."[9]

Nussbaum's ethical theory is, by contrast, an ethics of reengagement that aims to reinsert the modern subject into its own experience, starting with its own body. Her point of departure is explicitly the intellect's inability to acknowledge its body, its sexuality, its temporality, its contingency, its complexity, its entanglement with other bodies, its refusal of reason, its *deinon*. This problem of the body is at the heart of her reading of *Antigone* with which *The Fragility of Goodness* begins, and which I wouldn't hesitate to call an allegory of the present, an end-of-philosophy story about the limits, which means the tragedy, of "the rage for control" (FG79). Indeed, *The Fragility of Goodness* is on a certain view dominated by the figure of Creon, who "made himself a deliberate world into which tragedy cannot enter" (FG58); that is, he created a city, an Ur-Republic, sealed off from contingency like a ship is sealed off from the sea:

> The image tells us that a city, like a ship, is a tool built by human beings for the subjugation of chance and nature. The city-ship, in the tradition of the image, is something safely water-tight, a barrier against imminent external dangers. Waves beat against its tides, currents toss its hull; clearly its intelligent makers must leave no gap, in the fabric, for the wildness of uncontrolled nature to penetrate. Reflecting on the image in this way, it would be easy to conclude that the task of the city, as life-saving tool, is the removal of ungoverned chance from human life. Ships and cities will recur together in the ode on the human being, as two inventions of this *deinon* creature, "all-devising," who subdues the world to its purposes. Creon, and the chorus in their early optimism, believe that human technological resourcefulness can overcome any contingency, short of death itself. But the suppression of

contingency requires more than the technology of physical nature: ships, plows, bundles, traps. It requires, in addition, a technology of human nature, a technology of practical reason. Contingency has long caused pain and terror in human life, never more so than when it causes a well-formed plan to generate conflict. Creon is convinced that the human being cannot bear this. . . . Fortunately, it is not necessary to bear it. The recalcitrant features of the world can be mastered by practical ethical rationality itself: by a constitutive rearrangement of practical attachments and ethical language. (FG59–60)

The key point here concerns Creon's reconceptualization of the practical as the technical, that is, as a program of mastery. What Creon runs up against, however, is not just the antagonism of Antigone but himself. Antigone is Creon's opposite, his (so to say) logical adversary, but his *other* is just his own body—as Nussbaum says, "In the end it is his own recalcitrant humanity that he fails to subdue. His education is, the chorus tells us, a taming; as in Creon's own example, 'blows' must be used to curb the spirit's pride. Unlike horse-taming, however, it ends not in mute obedience, but in understanding. Creon is forced, in particular, to acknowledge his love for his son and to see its separate value" (FG61–62).

It is interesting that in his *Introduction to Metaphysics* Heidegger reads the *Antigone* very much the way Nussbaum does, as a story about the origin of philosophy, that is, as a story about the attempt to bring the *deinon*, the overwhelming and the uncanny or strangest of all, under logical control or control of the *logos*, and about the resistance to such control, the reserve or withdrawal of *phusis*, which we translate as nature but which is probably untranslatable, as in the dark saying of Heraclitus: *phusis kruptesthai philei: phusis* loves to hide.[10] The trouble with Heidegger is that he understood this only as a problem of metaphysics and not as an ethical and political problem; but the ideal of logical mastery means that what we seal ourselves off from is not a world of things or beings (or Being); rather, we seal ourselves off from other people, from the community of others, and therefore also from our own ordinariness, our own body and its desires, our complexity and uncontrollability, everything that links us willy-nilly to the common world, the world held in common, the world of the Sophoclean chorus. Heidegger's critique of technology is a critique of logical mastery, but he opposes the Creonic ideal the way Antigone does, metaphysically, missing the point, not seeing the Holocaust, for example, as having to do with human beings. Like Antigone, Heidegger recognizes only earth and sky, gods and mortals. Human beings come into their own for Heidegger only in the mode of death. This is why there are no people in Heidegger's thinking. The same is true of Antigone.

Antigone resembles Creon just to the extent that she is obsessive and single-minded—perhaps one could say, metaphysical—in her reduction of life to a single project (the play, *Antigone*, is arguably a "critique of metaphysics"). She opposes Creon, but she is just as much a control freak as he is. Other people have no more place in her system than in his; or, rather, they will either be appropriated by her project, or they will have no meaning or reality. Nussbaum compares them this way: "Creon's strategy of simplification," she says, "led him to regard others as material for his aggressive exploitation. Antigone's dutiful subservience to the dead leads to an equally strange, though different (and certainly less hideous) result. Her relation to others in the world above is characterized by an odd coldness. 'You are alive,' she tells her sister, 'but my life *(psuche)* is long since dead, to the end of serving the dead.' The safely dutiful human life requires, or is, life's annihilation. Creon's attitude toward others is like necrophilia; he aspires to possess the inert and unresisting. Antigone's subservience to duty is finally the ambition to be a *nekros*, a corpse beloved of corpses" (FG65). What we have in the *Antigone* is a collision of two sorts of narcissism. The play doesn't take sides but grounds a critique of both in the ordinariness of the chorus, whose acceptance of complexity, of singularity and open-endedness, of randomness and contingency—alterity for short—contrasts sharply, that is to say morally and politically, with the whole idea of philosophical reduction that Creon and Antigone represent or anticipate. According to Nussbaum, "these people [the "they" of the chorus] experience the complexities of tragedy while and by being a certain sort of community, not by having each soul go off in isolation from its fellows; by attending to what is common or shared and forming themselves into a common responding group, not by reaching for a lonely height of contemplation from which it is a wrenching descent to return to political life. This entire ethical experience . . . stresses the fundamental value of community and friendship; it does not invite or even permit us to seek for the good apart from these" (FG70).

Here is where Nussbaum's characterization of Socrates begins to take shape. Creon, in a sense, constitutes the forestructure, the conceptual frame, for Nuss-baum's Socrates. It's not always a Socrates that I can recognize, but she makes it clear how we have obtained from Socrates, or confirmed in him (by reading him in a certain way), our idea of philosophy as self-sufficient, as that which seals us off from otherness or the uncontainable, as that which puts us in control. This is the representational-calculative Socrates of the *Protagoras*, the ascetic Socrates of the *Phaedo*, the totalizing, exclusionary Socrates of the *Republic*. This is the Nietzschean Socrates who marks the death of tragedy, and therefore the beginning (or say the end, the final cause) of philosophy.

Certainly the centerpiece of *The Fragility of Goodness* is the great essay on the speech of Alcibiades in the *Symposium*, which on Nussbaum's reading is indeed "a harsh and alarming book" (FG198), a horror show, since here we see a Socrates who has succeeded where Creon failed, a Socrates who is just no longer one of us, who no longer inhabits his body, lives in it no longer humanly but only philosophically—as if the *Symposium* were a fifth-century version of *The Invasion of the Body Snatchers*, where Socrates *looks* human enough, with his plainly comic features, but "drink [does] not make him drunk, cold [does] not make him freeze, the naked body of Alcibiades does not arouse him," a sleepless night leaves him clear-headed, primed for philosophy. "He goes about his business," Nussbaum says, "with all the equanimity of a rational stone" (FG199). Surely this is philosophy's wished-for body: impervious to the other, sealed-off even from its own otherness, so under control, so overwhelmed and overmastered by intellect that the human *deinon* has been replaced by another, otherworldly uncanniness, one with its own kind of transcendental seductive power that overmasters all who encounter it. It is this Socratic *deinon* that has seduced Alcibiades, who knows that if *he* had that sort of superhuman, all-controlling *sophrosune*, nothing could stop him, nothing could contain him, he would be master. Plainly what intoxicates Alcibiades about Socrates is just Socratic mastery and control, as if Alcibiades in his drunken (let us say, Nietzschean) wisdom had seen through the unassuming and apparently ungrasping self-possession of philosophy and uncovered its deep structure: as if the whole end of philosophy, just to use that phrase, were not knowledge and truth but power.

3. What Is *Phronesis*? (On the Conflict of Aristotelianisms)

The centerpiece of *The Fragility of Goodness*, as I have said, is Nussbaum's reading of the *Symposium*. Crucial to her argument, however, is her reading of the *Phaedrus*, in which she sees Socrates taking a step back from the theory of philosophy as self-containment in order to produce a theory of philosophy as "an inspired, manic, Muse-loving activity" that opens the philosopher to the particularities of human experience (FG226–27). This reading cannot be wrong, but where does it take us?

I have always read the *Phaedrus* as a seduction story in which Socrates, powerful as ever, wins young Phaedrus away from philology or the love of words to dialectic, or the mastery of language. The *Phaedrus* is an important text because it seems to show Socrates tampering with the Parmenidean ideal of philosophical silence, where nothing but questions can be justifiably put into words, and accepting (for philosophy) the limits of language and discourse, which means accepting the idea that philosophy might be discursive as well as purely (mutely) contemplative; the idea, in other words, that philosophy might be social and not a solitary, ascetic way of life (think of the *Symposium*, with its figure of Socrates standing all day in the snow, entranced by a philosophical problem). But how social? What is the political meaning of philosophy? In the *Phaedrus* the idea is not to get beyond language but to get control of it and therefore also control of those who are subject to it— and also, of course, control of those matters on which people never seem to stop talking: poetry, for example, or love, or madness. Talking has to stop sometime, says philosophy. So the idea is not just to brush talking aside but rather to bring it to a resolution, a philosophical closure. It is hard to see how this is different from the political program of the *Republic*.

But my way of reading the *Phaedrus* situates it within the history of rhetoric as Plato's effort to out-rhetoric rhetoric, to beat rhetoric at its own game by showing us what real power looks like, to produce the most powerful rhetoric of all, a philosophical rhetoric in which one learns to use words as Socrates does, stopping even the great Protagoras in his tracks: a philosophical *techne* of language where language brings not only interlocutors and audience to silence but also stabilizes its subject-matter, unpacking it according to the law of division, bringing it to order, bringing it under conceptual control, laying it bare for our inspection. By contrast, Nussbaum sees Socrates in the *Phaedrus* as working out a (philosophical) defense of madness, of emotion and desire and even of the body, retracting the severe asceticism of the *Phaedo*, the *Republic*, and the *Symposium*. I see Socrates bringing the subject of madness under the conceptual control of philosophical discourse, demystifying it, turning it into allegory, making it safe for philosophers. Nussbaum sees the *Phaedrus* as "our first example of . . . philosophical poetry" (FG227); I see it as philosophy's appropriation of poetry, its reduction of the other to the same ("philosophical poetry" is another name for allegory). To be sure, the discourse of philosophy is not the "propositional prose" that the Kantian tradition demands. Nussbaum is right to say that "Socratic knowledge is not itself simply propositional knowledge" (FG191); it is not just something produced by the *logistikon*. It is dialectical. It consists in bringing people and things under the control of the dialectical weave and exposing them to view.

Nussbaum reads the *Phaedrus* erotically as a love story, an allegory of Plato's own passionate attachment to Dion, and a recantation (but not for all of that a repudiation) of the severe Creonic philosophy of the *Protagoras*, the *Republic*, and the *Symposium*. It is a dialogue about "the moment of yielding in philosophy" (FG211); about ventilating the sealed-off analytic subject on behalf of "responsiveness" (FG211). "Responsiveness" is the key word—possibly *the* key word of Nussbaum's philosophy. The *Phaedrus* is about "openness" and "receptivity" (FG216). In the language of Heidegger and Stanley Cavell, it is about listening and acknowledgment, disowning knowledge (knowledge in the sense of cutting and grasping) in favor of "insight" (FG225). It is a dialogue about "cognitive emotion" (FG215) and about the "intellect as something more sexual" than we had ever imagined (FG217). It is about "the fusion of life and argument" (FG212)—as if Plato were now allowing for a philosophical subject that is not sealed off but porous and even situated, not to say *exposed*, at the end, or limit, of philosophy, where philosophy loosens a little the grip of its self-possession; philosophy at the point of being critical of itself, quarreling with itself for a change instead of with poetry and rhetoric. Here, one wants to say, is where philosophy should always be looking for itself instead of gazing blindly at the sun.

There is, to be sure, good hermeneutical sense to what Nussbaum is saying, and that is that dialectic is just *not* a thinkable enterprise for a sealed-off, mono-logical subject; *not*, in other words, something that the "self-sufficient philosopher" (FG230) could get into. If you're going to practice dialectic in the genuine Socratic way (in the open, in front of other people, *with* other people), you're going to have to loosen up a little, learn what motion is and responsiveness and listening. "Pure and stable contemplation" (FG217) allows you to withdraw into yourself, turtlelike, the way Socrates did on his way to the party or that day in the snow; but dialectic draws you out, *exposes* you, though perhaps not in a strong sense of exposure (the sense, e.g., that you get in tragedy, say in *King Lear*: think of the difference between Socrates in the snow and Lear raging in the storm).

Still, this picture of dialectic—although it is consistent with Nussbaum's thinking—belongs to a rather different sort of Aristotelian: Hans-Georg Gadamer, for whom *phronesis* is the key term in his conception of the rationality of hermeneu-tical experience.[11] A contrast between Nussbaum and Gadamer seems worth some elaboration. When Nussbaum speaks about "the fusion of life and argument," she is not talking about openness to the otherness of the other and living through the shattering of one's concepts but of the rootedness of the *Phaedrus* in Plato's life experience; that is, she wants to think of argument as life expression and as supplemented by particularity and example; and when she speaks of the intellect's need for motivation and the guidance of the passions, she is still thinking of the subject as a self-centered, monological ego, that is, something still self-contained, never less than self-motivating. Her ego is still the narcissistic ego communicating only with itself, as an intellect in touch with its emotions. The whole idea of "responsiveness" that is so crucial to Nussbaum's reading of the *Phaedrus* remains embedded in the language of empiricist psychology where "responsiveness" is ex-plicated as "stimulus-response," with the intellect receiving pulses of "information" from its nearby companions, appetite and emotion:

> [In] people of good nature and training, the sensual and appetitive response is linked with, and arouses, complicated emotions of fear, awe, and respect, which themselves develop and educate the personality as a whole, making it more discriminating and receptive. The role of emotion and appetite as guides is motivational: they move the whole person towards the good. But it is also cognitive: for they give the whole person *information* as to where goodness and beauty are, searching out and selecting, themselves, the beautiful object. (FG214–15)

Reception here is still the empirical reception of sensations by a solitary subject; it needs to be distinguished, for example, from "the idea of thinking as reception" that Stanley Cavell has developed in his studies of Emerson and Thoreau.[12] There is a crucial difference, I mean to say, between the reception of impressions and the reception, that is, the acceptance or acknowledgment, of other people. Nussbaum seems much closer to Walter Pater and the idea of reception as aesthetic experience than to Cavell, for Pater's problem was, indeed, how to particularize and enrich the personality of an essentially imprisoned ego, where openness, responsiveness, and receptivity are the features of a refined sensibility open to sensations, not the openness, responsiveness, and receptivity of the lover.

Of course linking Nussbaum with Pater is unfair and misleading. For what Nussbaum wants for her walled-in philosophical subject is love, not just rich experience. As Cavell says, our relation to the world is not one of knowing—not reception in the sense of receiving "information as to where goodness and beauty are, searching and selecting . . . beautiful objects." Rather, receptivity means acknowledging the other, opening ourselves to the other, exposing ourselves. But Nussbaum's lover, unlike Cavell's, does not "forgo knowing." The lover's task, she says, is not acceptance but "learning about the other person": it is "to know the other's character through and through" (FG218). A Levinasian might be right to object here that this is turning the other into a concept, "removing from it its alterity" (TI44). To know the other "through and through" is to neutralize the other. Knowing in this way "is not a relation with the other as such but the reduction of the other to the same" (TI46).[13] Here the thought one would want to pursue is that Nussbaum's lover needs to become less penetrating, has to learn not *techne* but *phronesis*, that is, responsiveness in the sense of being answerable to another's existence as against simply being sensitive to complexities of experience.[14]

What one misses in *The Fragility of Goodness* is an account of *phronesis*, where *phronesis* (practical wisdom) means, for example, knowing what friendship is. What sort of knowledge is this, and how does one acquire it? There is no *techne* for friendship. Some people don't know the meaning of the word "friendship," where knowing the meaning does not, of course, mean having a definition or analytically clarified concept but knowing what is called for in the way of action and conduct with respect to another person. Instead what we get is a mildly chilling chapter on "Non-Scientific Deliberation," in which *aisthesis* is made to do the work of *phronesis*: "practical insight is like perceiving in the sense that it is non-inferential, non-deductive; it is, centrally, the ability to recognize, acknowledge, respond to certain salient features of a complex situation" (FG305)—as if practical reason were still basically a sort of analytic operation, a short way of unpacking reality.

Of course, within the analytic tradition it would be hard to clarify the concept of *phronesis* except by analogy with the workings of perceptual consciousness and by comparison with scientific reasoning. For someone like Gadamer, however, it is precisely by distinguishing *phronesis* from the activities of a subject defined in terms of perception and information that sense can begin to be made of it.[15] The difference between Nussbaum and Gadamer on this question seems to come down to this: Gadamer's account of *phronesis* goes on explicitly in terms of the actions of a *situated* moral agent involved with other people, and, precisely because other people are involved, a careful distinction has to be preserved between *phronesis* and *techne*— a distinction that, for Gadamer, is already a central motif in Plato's writings, where dialectic is said to be *phronesis*.[16] Whereas for Nussbaum, *phronesis* has to be addressed strictly as a *problem* of rationality, that is, in terms of a model of scientific reasoning for which *phronesis* can never be rational enough, and so has to be supplemented by "a *techne* of practical reason" (FG311) in order to be logically justified.[17] So her account of *phronesis* becomes an account of "Aristotelian perception," that is, of "a perception that responds flexibly to the situation at hand" (FG312). Again, I am compelled to say that this is not wrong. For the logical empiricist, this reduction of the moral agent to perception is analytic, cutting away the extraneous to get at the essential. But from the standpoint of Gadamer's thinking, this reduction flattens out the notion of *phronesis*. It was precisely to get around behind the Kantian tradition, back to Aristotle, that Gadamer took recourse to the model of dialogue. *Phronesis* presupposes a dialogical, not a perceptual, relation with the other. Reading "Non-Scientific Deliberation" from Gadamer's standpoint makes one wonder where the people are in Nussbaum's conception of practical reason. One has reason to think that Nussbaum noticed this, too, and that this is why, in *The Fragility of Reason*, she appeals to tragedy as the place where moral philosophy is to be found. So when she appends to her account of "Non-Scientific Deliberation" a reading of Hecuba's speech in Euripides's *Trojan Women*, she is not, as she imagines, simply illustrating her argument, she is giving us the thing itself (FG312–17). And in certain of the essays in *Love's Knowledge* she seems to reconceptualize practical reason away from *techne* toward *phronesis*, understood as practical wisdom—knowing from experience what it is to exist in human situations that make claims on one's ability to act humanly and responsibly as well as rationally.

4. An Aristotelian Critique of Rational Choice

In his essay "Moral Integrity," Peter Winch argued against Kant's idea that "a piece of behaviour is morally right if and only if it has been performed for the sake of a rational principle itself, that is, according to Kant's argument, for the sake of duty." Winch's thought is that, on the contrary, there is no saying beforehand what counts as moral behavior in any given case. "All we can do," he says, "is to look at particular examples and see what we *do* want to say about them; there are no general rules which can determine in advance what we *must* say about them."[18] Moral knowledge consists of examples of how human beings act; it is a knowledge of the particular *perspectives* within which human beings make judgments about what to do. Moral knowledge is not a *guide* to right action; it is knowledge of the possibilities of right action that experience brings. And where experience falls short there is always literature to bring up the slack.

Winch's reflections derive from Wittgenstein's belief in the priority of examples over principles in making sense of what people do. In her essay, "The Discernment of Perception," Nussbaum arrives at much the same idea by way of Aristotle, whose conception of rationality, she says, captures as nothing else does "the sheer complexity of choosing well" (LK55). This complexity rules out rational-choice theories of deliberation modeled on planning and calculation.[19] Complexity means that the good life entails multiple and heterogeneous goods between which we often have to choose without having criteria at hand that will tell us how to proceed. At ground level the good life is often messy, but living the good life means making our way through "this messy state of things" rather than trying to bring it to order (LK59). The idea is not to reduce this heterogeneity to the Good as such but "to make the understanding of that heterogeneity a central part of the subject matter of deliberation" (LK60). This entails what Nussbaum calls "the priority of the particular" (LK66). Knowing how to negotiate complex situations calling for right action is not knowledge that can be captured in a system of rules. Not that Aristotle doesn't think rules are important, but for him rules are likely to be "rules of thumb, highly useful for a variety of purposes, but valid only to the extent to which they correctly describe good concrete judgments" (LK68). So an Aristotelian rule is more likely to resemble a proverb than a principle. On Nussbaum's reading of Aristotle, "priority in practical choice should be accorded not to principle, but to perception" (LK68). "The subtleties of a complex situation must be seized in a confrontation with the situation itself, by a faculty that is suited to address it as a complex whole. Prior general formulations lack both the concreteness and the flexibility that is required. They do not contain the particularizing details of the matter at hand, with which decision must grapple; and they are not responsive to what is there, as good decision must be" (LK69). This faculty for addressing situations in all their complexity is *aisthesis*. The question is: what sort of agent does the faculty *aisthesis* presuppose?

The answer entails a thesis about the worldliness of right action in hard cases. The process of reasoning in coming to a decision cannot work like a calculus. Rules and algorithms represent "a falling off from full practical rationality" (LK73), which for Aristotle is not reducible "to means-end reasoning" (LK73). Merely calculative deliberation is logical but empty; it needs to be filled phenomenologically by a sense of what it is to exist and act in concrete human situations—knowing what it is like to be a human being. In Nussbaum's terms, "the content of rational choice must be supplied by nothing less messy than experience and stories of experience. Among stories of conduct, the most true and informative will be works of literature, biography, and history; the more abstract the story gets, the less rational it is to use it as one's only guide. Good deliberation is like theatrical or musical improvisation, where what counts is flexibility, responsiveness, and openness to the external; to rely on an algorithm here is not only insufficient, it is a sign of immaturity and weakness" (LK74). *Aisthesis* in this respect presupposes *phronesis* as the moral condition of being experienced.

Hegel thought of experience as "skepticism in action," because it always entails negation: the world is otherwise than we thought. For Gadamer, this means that

> experience can never be science. Experience stands in an ineluctable oppo-
> sition to knowledge and to the kind of instruction that follows from general
> theoretical or technical knowledge. The truth of experience always implies
> an orientation toward new experience. That is why a person who is called
> experienced has become so not only *through* experiences but is also open
> *to* new experiences. The consummation of his experience, the perfection
> that we call "being experienced," does not consist in the fact that someone
> already knows everything and knows better than anyone else. Rather, the
> experienced person proves to be, on the contrary, somebody who is radically
> undogmatic; who, because of the many experiences he has had and the
> knowledge he has drawn from them, is particularly well equipped to have
> new experiences and to learn from them. The dialectic of experience has
> its proper fulfillment not in definitive knowledge but in the openness to
> experience that is made possible by experience itself. (TM355)

Experience does not produce positive knowledge of the kind that can be framed in statements of universal validity. It produces insight. Yet insight has a kind of universality about it. "Insight is more than the knowledge of this or that situation. It always involves an escape from something that had deceived us and held us captive" (TM356). As an illustration of what he means Gadamer invokes the motto of Aeschylus: *pathei mathos*, learning through suffering. "This phrase does not mean only that we become wise through suffering and that our knowledge of things must first be corrected through deception and undeception." It also means that what "a man has to learn through suffering is not this or that particular thing, but insight into the limitations of humanity, into the absoluteness of the barrier that separates man from the divine." As Gadamer puts it, "the truly experienced person is one . . . who knows that he is master neither of time nor the future. The experienced man knows that all foresight is limited and all plans uncertain. In him is realized the truth value of experience. . . . Experience teaches us to acknowledge the real. The genuine result of experience, then—as of all desire to know—is to know what is. But 'what is,' here, is not this or that thing, but 'what cannot be destroyed' (Ranke)" (TM357). Experience is, whatever else it is, knowledge of human finitude.

5. Comedy versus Tragedy

Recall the idea, proposed by the chorus in *Antigone*, that "nothing very great comes into the life of mortals without disaster" (FG75). What might this mean? No one, of course, can say exactly. We cannot answer this question, only reflect on it, meditate on it, search it out. Like questions of being or death, first things and last, the question of catastrophe and devastation is not one that we ourselves formulate, much less dispose of. We do not really know how to frame this question; it just looms and hovers over existence, circumscribes or limits it, and so belongs to it essentially. From a hermeneutical standpoint a question like this is a *Sache* that calls for thinking, which is just to say that what it calls for is *phronesis.*

Tragedy, let us say, is the traditional medium for reflection on this question, or say this insight that human greatness—maybe the human good—is tied to catastrophe.[20] Comedy, let us say, does not dispute the truth of this insight, but declines to participate in it, play it out, confirm it, bring it home. The task of comedy, after all, is to elude greatness and to accept the ordinary, what Cavell calls "living one's skepticism" (CR451); this is how comedy avoids horror (it can cope with death, but not with horror). Comedy prefers disguise to self-knowledge. Tragedy, by contrast, not only embraces the catastrophic insight but tries to enter into it as deeply as it can, not knowing where it will end up.

One thing that one learns from reading *The Fragility of Goodness* and *Love's Knowledge* is that Martha Nussbaum is essentially a comic thinker—as, in a similar way, is Stanley Cavell. Again and again, at every turn, she insists on the primacy of flexibility and responsiveness as virtues of practical reason. Her idea is that only flexibility and responsiveness will save us in the face of the contingency, the vulnerability, the fragility of existence. Disengagement, living a watertight existence, will only end us up destroying other people. As Levinas suggests, the Holocaust was arguably the greatest achievement of the ethics of disengagement and control.

This emphasis on flexibility and responsiveness reminds me of Susanne Langer's great studies of comic and tragic rhythms, where "the strain of maintaining a vital balance amid the alien and impartial chances of the world," is said to be "the essence of comedy." Here is what Langer says:

> The illusion of life which the comic poet creates is the oncoming future fraught with dangers and opportunities, that is, with physical or social events occurring by chance and building up coincidences with which individuals cope according to their lights. This ineluctable future—ineluctable because its countless factors are beyond human knowledge and control—is Fortune. Destiny in the guise of Fortune is the fabric of comedy; it is developed by

comic action, which is the upset and recovery of the protagonist's equilibrium, his contest with the world and his triumph by wit, luck, personal power,
or even humours or ironical or philosophical acceptance of mischance.[21]

Contingency, Langer says, calls for an intellect characterized by openness,
resilience, responsiveness to situations, knowing what the situation calls for and
how to answer. The comic hero is always the embodiment of resilience and
answerable style; he or she is the mirror of practical wisdom, of *phronesis*, in the face
of "a dreadful universe." The comic hero knows better than to try to conquer this
universe in the sense of appropriating it, Creon- or Ahab-like, and subsuming it
into self-possession or self-identity; he or she knows that the world is beyond one's
control, that one belongs to it and is defined by its limits. It is this belongingness,
this finitude, this ordinariness that philosophy has never been able to abide.

Borrowing from Cavell, one could say that the comic hero's relation to the
world is not one of knowing, or what we think of as knowing, namely conceptual
representation and control (CR243). Rather, the comic hero is one who has
learned to forgo knowing (something the tragic hero, like the philosopher, finds
unthinkable, more threatening than death itself) (DK95). The comic hero's relation
to the world is a relationship of thinking, thinking as reception, or in other words
not knowledge but acknowledgment, where the world is not just made of sensible
objects or situations calling for perception but is rather made up of other people.
Here forgoing knowledge means giving up disengagement and control; it means
what Heidegger means by *Gelassenheit*. It means giving up the desire to bend the
world to our will, to lay it bare and know it through and through. The world will
not be present to us in this way. This is what Lear and Othello discover, to their
horror, too late. One could say that what both tragic heroes lack is precisely this
comic acceptance of the world's, or reason's, finitude. Which is just to say that their
relation to this finitude, this limit of the human, is tragic rather than comic.

In tragedy one is exposed to something more than the world's contingency.
Bad luck is a comic, not a tragic phenomenon. In tragedy exposure is to something
called Fate, not Fortune or Contingency, and the main thing about Fate is that it
is fixed, like a limit. Fortune concerns the accidental and the contingent, the open
possibility, the freedom of possible worlds where things not only might have gone
otherwise but will, unpredictably, without final closure. But Fate concerns what is
necessary and inescapable, what (in Gadamer's words) cannot be done away with
(TM357). The comic hero flees Corinth but then sneaks back in, disguised, to
find out what's going on; the tragic hero flees and encounters his Fate, or what
he fled from, sought to hide from, seal himself off from, at the crossroads, too
blind or bullheaded to let it pass. Blindness and rigidity and a will to control, to
dominate or rule, are notorious features of the tragic hero, but above all there is his
refusal of the world, that is, refusal of its otherness, its resistance, its limits—the

limit it imposes on the powers of reason and control—"a metaphysical finitude," Cavell says, that the tragic hero blindly, fatally converts into "an intellectual lack," an inability to be certain, a skepticism that he tries to refute (CR493). But the "moral of skepticism," Cavell says, which is to say its truth, is that our relation to the world—say to Cordelia or Desdemona—is "deeper than knowing." As Cavell says, "what skepticism suggests is that since we cannot know the world exists, its presentness to us cannot be a function of knowing. The world is to be *accepted;* as the presentness of other minds is not to be known, but acknowledged" (DK95).

It is this otherness of the world, one wants to say, that the ancients called Fate. Fate is the other that calls for acknowledgment and acceptance, and of course it is that from which we always try to seal ourselves off. We can see here what Aristotle surely saw, namely a fundamental kinship between the philosopher and the tragic hero: what the philosopher examines is the moral weakness of the tragic hero, the willful blindness, the refusal of the other and of the ordinary. The tragic hero, like the philosopher, demands that the world be present to him—the real world, not the shady simulacrum that the rest of us (comically) inhabit. The philosopher demands a Desdemona of whose presence to him, of whose fidelity to his concept of her as "monumental alabaster," he can be absolutely certain.

Both Cavell and Nussbaum, however, want a philosopher who can love. Both recognize that this will take some doing, and principally what it will take is some considerable redoing of philosophy, or anyhow of philosophy's conception of itself as that discourse that presides over the world, suspicious of it, disdaining involvement, jealous of its position, fearing debasement into poetry and rhetoric, heaping contempt on the ordinary and the comic. So it is not surprising that both Cavell and Nussbaum have chosen to work the boundary between philosophy and literature, where the ability of philosophy to keep itself pure has always been most obviously questionable. For Nussbaum, literature is an indispensable component of a philosophy that tries to give an account of what the good life looks like. There is no giving this account just in terms of paradigms and rules. The account has to be particularized; it has to be multiple, heterogeneous, and revisable. Like the law, it has to be formulated in terms of concrete cases, to be porous, open-ended, under dispute, given to reinterpretation; otherwise it cannot have any sense and force, that is, any practical application, or say any just (justifiable) claim on human life. So it would make no sense to keep moral philosophy pure, that is, to seal it off within a discourse modeled on a *Grounding for the Metaphysics of Morals.* One has to say that the discourse of moral philosophy needs to be modeled on texts like *Antigone,* where competing claims as to what the good is meet head-on.[22]

This is a conception of the relationship between philosophy and literature that I share. One could not, I think, have anything like a philosophical understanding of justice independently, for example, of an understanding of *Hamlet* as a story of what it is to attempt to act justly, to restore justice, in a world so bereft of justice that even the best of human beings are incapable of *phronesis*. However, such a conception of an internal relationship between philosophy and literature remains incomplete. You can't have just one idea of literature. The limits of the Aristotelian view remain determined by the Platonic idea that there can be no such thing as a desire for knowledge and truth that does not depend on the repression of the desires that poetry arouses, in particular the desire for language, that is, philology in the etymological sense (the desire that fires Phaedrus)—a desire that is incompatible with propositional discourse, a desire that turns concepts into puns, that exists in a parodistic relation to any discourse that tries to justify itself as serious, rational, and faithful to reality. It is this Platonic view, where poetry sets a limit to philosophy, not just in a theoretical sense of logical delimitation but in the ontological sense of putting it at risk, that both Heidegger and Derrida have tried to recover *for* philosophy, as a way of shaking philosophy loose from the hoary dogmatisms of its self-conception. So far from leveling the genre distinction between philosophy and literature, they remind us that poetry is satirical with respect to philosophy, even as philosophy is allegorical with respect to poetry.

At the end of *The Claim of Reason*, Cavell asks whether philosophy could turn into literature "and still know itself" (CR496). Cavell himself has left this question unanswered; he may never take it up. I take it that the question is asking about what philosophy is willing to risk in opening itself up to whatever is not itself. At issue here is the question of whether there is an internal relation between poetry and skepticism that forces philosophy to confront its limits, say its finitude and historicality, its illusions about transcendence, its groundlessness. I think that the later Heidegger has tried, in his way, to take up this issue when he asks about what happens to thinking when it is exposed to poetry as *Dichten*, that is, poetry as the resistance of language to the rule of reason—poetry as the subversion of the *logos*.[23] His answer, if I understand, is that poetry turns thinking against philosophy, sets it free, that is, turns it loose so that it becomes indistinguishable from wandering. It is not that thinking turns into poetry. It is rather that poetry calls thinking into the open, where it can come into its own. But it is hard to imagine a philosopher, especially an analytic philosopher in the Anglo-American grain, who wouldn't recoil from this as from tragic horror (or is it comic lunacy?).[24]

6. On Philosophical Style

In a very interesting paragraph in her discussion of *Antigone*, Martha Nussbaum says that "The *Antigone*'s choral lyrics have an unusual degree of density and compression." Their structure, she says, "could be paralleled from other lyric poems, both in and outside of drama. It also bears a strikingly close relation to the compressed, dense, and riddling style of the major ethical thinker of the half-century preceding this play, that is, to the style of Heraclitus" (FG68–69).

What is the meaning of this density (*Dichte*)? Nussbaum puts this question in terms of an opposition between *Antigone*'s view of "the nature of learning and reflection" and Plato's. "We reflect on an incident," Nussbaum says, "not by subsuming it under a general rule, not by assimilating its features to the terms of an elegant scientific procedure, but by burrowing down into the depths of the particular, finding images and connections that will permit us to see it more truly, describe it more richly; by combining this burrowing with a horizontal drawing of connections, so that every horizontal link contributes to the depth of our view of the particular, and every new depth creates new horizontal links" (FG69). These two modes of reflection, call them the subsumptive and the responsive, correspond to two conceptions of the *psyche*. "The Platonic soul," Nussbaum says,

> will be directed, in its singleness and purity, to ethical objects that are single-natured and unmixed, themselves by themselves. The Sophoclean soul is more like Heraclitus's image of *psuche*: a spider sitting in the middle of its web, able to feel and respond to any tug in any part of the complicated structure. It advances its understanding of life and of itself not by a Platonic movement from the particular to the universal, from the perceived world to a simpler, clearer world, but by hovering in thought and imagination around the enigmatic complexities of the seen particular (as we, if we are good readers of this style, hover around the details of the text), seated in the middle of its web of connections, responsive to the pull of each separate thread. (FG69)

So density of style, the style of riddling complexity—call it *Dichten*—corresponds to the density of life, whereas lucidity of style, the so-called plain style of philosophical prose, is a product of the reduction or bracketing of life. Philosophy means bringing life under the rule of the proposition, reducing it to clarity and order, whereas poetry means entering into life, opening up to it, wandering loose within it, living through its reversals. Correspondingly, philosophical reading means allegorization, rewriting texts (all texts) as arguments about serious philosophical problems, unpacking the logical form of the text, taking texts as the embedding of propositions; whereas poetic reading means stepping back from the analytical attitude and entering into the mode of listening, hearing puns where philosophers see only concepts.

The pun, as Derrida says, is inaccessible to analytical reason; it is a discursive event that cannot be brought under rational control except by being repressed or excluded from discourse as such.[25] A carefully made pun is a contradiction in terms. Puns happen. They are not products of *poiesis* but moments when language gets away from us, runs loose, threatens to escape, leaving us at a loss for words (dumbstruck, which is a very different state from Parmenidean or Wittgensteinian silence—"That whereof we cannot speak, thereof . . ."). So it is no wonder that Socrates thinks of words as slaves that need to be tied down, whereas Heraclitus, by contrast, lets them go, lets them riddle and bemuse. This is the basis of Heidegger's distinction between words and terms (*Worte und Wörter*) and of Derrida's distinction between Edmund Husserl and James Joyce, or between geometry and *Finnegans Wake*: for the one, "Equivocity is the path of all philosophical aberration," whereas for the other equivocation is the whole end of writing, "utilizing a language that could equalize the greatest possible synchrony with the greatest potential for buried, accumulated, and interwoven intentions within each linguistic atom, each vocable, each word, each simple proposition, in all wordly cultures and their most ingenious forms (mythology, religion, sciences, arts, literature, politics, philosophy, and so forth)."[26] Naturally the question is whether one can philosophize in the form of punning. In effect, many of Derrida's philosophical texts are efforts to determine the limits to which philosophical writing can be taken—limits, many think, certifiably reached in *Glas*, where the effort to speak and write several languages and texts at once makes it (as Derrida himself indicates) a sort of philosophical *Finnegans Wake*.[27]

Socrates challenged the lovers of poetry to come, in plain prose, to its defense. Aristotle was the first to take up the challenge, and on the whole the history of reading has followed his lead. I see Heidegger and Derrida as reading the *Republic* and going in the opposite direction from Aristotle.[28] Instead of taking up the Socratic challenge, they take poetry to be exactly the dangerous, maddening thing Plato said it was, taking it, that is, as *Dichten*, as a darkening and thickening of discourse that establishes once for all the limit of philosophy, that which gives philosophy itself self-definition as the discourse of clarification, as the guardian of rationality, as the model or norm of a discourse that has got itself (and all that it takes up) under control. What Heidegger and Derrida want to know is, What will happen to philosophy if it refuses to repress or exclude *Dichten*? Will philosophy cease? Or will it turn into a version of itself heretofore repressed in the bargain of keeping discourse, and therefore itself, under control?

It is possible to see Nussbaum trying to work out something like an Aristotelian version of Heidegger's and Derrida's question. This means, in effect, a questioning of philosophical language that does not try go around behind Plato to Heraclitus but rather follows Aristotle down the middle path that seeks the just word—a word commensurate with the world and not (just) with the rules of an organon. So instead of turning to Joyce, Nussbaum turns to Henry James—the later James, whose style (on Nussbaum's reading) represents something like an Aristotelian version of *Dichten*, that is, a dense, riddling style that, nevertheless, a slow, careful reading can unriddle by working through the intricate ways of the text, paying close attention to the least and apparently most random detail. And what one unriddles is not simply a text but the world, that is, a human situation. The point is that there is a symmetry or decorum between the *Dichten* of discourse and the *Dichten* of human life. What Nussbaum proposes is a type of moral philosophy that starts out from, holds to, this equation; that is, a moral philosophy made up of

> texts which display to us the complexity, the indeterminacy, the sheer *difficulty* of moral choice, and which show us . . . the refusal of life involved in fixing everything in advance according to some system of inviolable rules. This task cannot be easily accomplished by texts which speak in universal terms—for one of the difficulties of deliberation stressed by this view is that of grasping the uniqueness of the new particular. Nor can it easily be done by texts which speak with the hardness and plainness which moral philosophy has traditionally chosen for its style—for how can this style at all convey the way in which the "matter of the practical" appears before the agent in all of its bewildering complexity, without its morally salient features stamped on its face? (LK148)

It is not surprising, therefore, that Nussbaum writes Aristotelian prose, as against the "dense and riddling" Heraclitean prose of Heidegger and Derrida. Her style is cool and transparent rather than apocalyptic or satirical, *of* the school rather than against it. It is what Geoffrey Hartman calls "the middle or conversational style" suited to the close company of familiars.[29] Is it too cool for her subject?

Interestingly, she puts the same question in regard to Aristotle's texts, which are famously "austere, forbidding, even drab." But that's not how she imagines them. "I myself now find in [Aristotle's] style a courageous straightforwardness and directness *vis-à-vis* 'the matter of the practical'; a serene restraint that expresses the determination to acknowledge these difficulties, to let them be there, and not to despair of human life because of them. In my interpretive writing here I have tried to convey this response" (FG392). Or, again: "a commitment to explanation is fundamental to all of [Aristotle's] philosophical works. If he respects the autonomous cognitive value of tragic poetry, he thinks, too, that the highest or most comprehensive understanding of their ethical content, the understanding that he calls 'understanding the why,' requires a philosophical reflection that will render the salient features of our ethical experience more perpicuous, that speaks to our sense of wonder and perplexity, striving to answer our 'why' questions" (FG393). This is the model Nussbaum thinks of herself as following. She has tried to write of tragedy in a way that is responsive to "the poetic features of the texts," that is, to "metaphorical and emotive language" (FG394), but not in a way that would compromise her commitment to explanation.

Still, one can't help thinking that something is being missed. Perhaps one could suggest what this something is by imagining the difference between someone who watches a tragedy and someone who bears witness to it. The one is outside, the other inside, the horizon of what happens. On the one hand, tragedy is a spectacle; on the other, it demands one's involvement, if only in the way of testimony. Nussbaum comes down on the side of sensitivity and responsiveness to the complexity of ethical situations. One has to open oneself to what human feeling can teach us about these situations. But one is always, finally, outside these situations, looking on, detached and speculative.[30] "Aristotle," Nussbaum says, "has a high regard for tragedy" (FG378). As an art form, yes, but how does one regard tragedy as something one lives through or as a catastrophe that calls one to account? Perhaps one could say the poet witnesses, the philosopher reflects. Martha Nussbaum speaks of a "serene restraint that expresses the determination to acknowledge [the difficulties of life], to let them be there and not to despair of human life because of them." Serenity and restraint: in what safe haven does the philosopher find such things?[31]

Part III

Poetry and Philosophy
inside the Everyday World

7

"The Accomplishment of Inhabitation": Danto, Cavell, and the Argument of American Poetry

In Memory of Sherman Paul

1. Toward a Poetics of Nonidentity

Modern poetics begins with the French poet Stéphane Mallarmé's belief that poetry is made of words, not of ideas. That is, a poem is made of language but is not, strictly speaking, a use of it. Poetry is made of words but not of any of the things that we use words to produce—concepts, meanings, propositions about the world, narratives, expressions of feeling, and so on. This does not mean that the poem lacks these things. It is only that the poem is no longer reducible to them; its definition can no longer be located in one or more of them. In other words, the poem is no longer reducible to other sorts of discourse; it cannot be made a branch of something else—part of an organon, for example, or a species of philosophy or rhetoric. In poetry language is no longer a form of mediation. So what is it, then?

The problem is how to tell that a piece of language is poetic. What is it that separates the poem from the nonpoem? Mallarmé tried to answer this question with an analytical distinction between poetic and ordinary speech, where the one is a formally self-contained system of relations, a beautiful work of art that occupies a space of its own—the white space of the printed page or, alternatively, the "poetic universe"—while the other is, well, just talk. Various traditions of rhetorical, romantic, and formalist-structuralist poetics have tried to clarify a distinction of this sort, not always successfully. As if denying the possibility of any such distinction, the American poet William Carlos Williams says that "A poem can be made of anything," even newspaper clippings.[1] Poetry is *internal* to the discourse of everyday life; it is not the product of a logic of exclusion but is conceptually, and therefore aesthetically, nondifferentiated.[2]

Williams's *Paterson* (1946–58), for example, is a poem made out of every sort of discourse imaginable, not all of it of Williams's own composition. Here is an excerpt from book 5, section 2 (which also contains a poem by Sappho and a letter from Ezra Pound):

> (Q. Mr. Williams, can you tell me, simply, what poetry is?
> A. Well . . . I would say that poetry is language charged with emotion. It's words, rhythmically organized. . . . A poem is a complete little universe. It exists separately. Any poem that has worth expresses the whole life of the poet. It gives a view of what the poet is.
> Q. All right, look at this part of a poem by E. E. Cummings, another great American poet:
>
> > (im)c-a-t(mo)
> > b,i;l:e
> > FallleA
> > ps!fl
> > OattumblI
> > sh?dr
> > IftwhirlF
> > (Ul)   (lY)
> > &&&
>
> Is this poetry?
> A. I would reject it as a poem. It may be, to him, a poem. But I would reject it. I can't understand it. He's a serious man. So I struggle very hard with it—and I get no meaning at all.
> Q. You get no meaning? But here's part of a poem you yourself have written: ". . . 2 partridges / 2 mallard ducks / a Dungeness crab / 24 hours out / of the Pacific / and 1 live-frozen / trout / from Denmark" Now that sounds just like a fashionable grocery list.
> A. It is a fashionable grocery list.
> Q. Well—is it poetry?
> A. We poets have to talk in a language which is not English. It is the American idiom. Rhythmically it's organized as a sample of the American idiom. It has as much originality as jazz. If you say "2 partridges, 2 mallard ducks, a Dungeness crab"—if you treat that rhythmically, ignoring the practical sense, it forms a jagged pattern. It is, to my mind, poetry.
> Q. But if you don't "ignore the practical sense" . . . you agree that it is a fashionable grocery list.
> A. Yes. Anything is good material for poetry. Anything. I've said it time and time again.

Q. Aren't we supposed to understand it?
A. There is a difference of poetry and the sense. Sometimes modern poets ignore sense completely. That's what makes some of the difficulty. . . . The audience is confused by the shape of the words.
Q. But shouldn't a word mean something when you see it?
A. In prose, an English word means what it says. In poetry, you're listening to two things . . . you're listening to the sense, the common sense of what it says. But it says more. That is the difficulty.)[3]

What counts as poetry when poetry is no longer discernible from a grocery list? Williams says that the answer is how we listen. As if there were more to a grocery list than the items that compose it.

It will be useful to enlarge our field of examples. Consider the famous case of David Antin's "talk poetry," as in the following from *talking at the boundaries:*

> "what am i doing here?"
> what is it that im doing here?   im trying to find out   how i
> could find out   and what im trying to find out is by
> essentially doing what i think talking does   that is
> talking and thinking may not be the same thing   but i see
> thinking as talking i see it as talking to a question   which
> may give rise to another question   and it may open up some
> terrain and lose some terrain and answers come up but theyre not
> the same answers[4]

The "talk poem," Stephen Fredman says, "challenges us to conceive of poetry, criticism, and philosophy as a single activity. Antin performs a talk poem by standing up in front of an audience and improvising speech around a certain intellectual territory, combining critical questions about the nature of poetry or art with philosophical speculations about the way language influences our behavior and thought, complementing these ideas by often humorous anecdotes about himself, his family, and friends."[5] And of course he also talks about what he is doing, inserting the claim that (at least this) talk counts as a poem:

> i mean if i were to come and read to you from a
> book you would consider it a perfectly reasonable form of behavior
> and its a perfectly respectable form of behavior   generally
> thought of as a poetry reading   and it would be a little bit like
> taking out a container of frozen peas   warming them up and
> serving them to you from the frozen food container   and that
> doesn't seem interesting to me because then i turn out to be a cook

and i dont really want to be a cook   i dont want to cook or
recook anything for anybody   I came here in order to make a
    poem   talking   to talk a poem   which it will be   all
other things being equal[6]

Philosophy distinguishes itself jealously from what is "just talk." But, on Antin's showing, not so poetry, which cannot or maybe just does not distinguish itself from mere talk. Yet by what sort of argument or line of thought could we begin to understand Antin's talk as poetry?

At a climactic moment in his *In Search of the Primitive,* Sherman Paul records his exchange of letters with George Butterick concerning David Antin's talk poetry. Paul and Butterick had been discussing the splendid moment at a symposium at the Library of Congress when Marjorie Perloff gave a paper on Antin that caused an outraged Harold Bloom to storm from the room.[7] Without exactly siding with Bloom, or in other words granting that Antin is not just to be brushed aside with a superior gesture, Butterick had wondered if there wasn't, nevertheless, a moral that Bloom was trying to point:

He [Antin] sure is on the right track: the primacy of story. I mean the guy's irrepressible. Imagine him in the CCNY cafeteria, circa 1952. But: Is it poetry? Need it be called such? Can't we reserve the term for something more formal (says the exponent of polymorphism)?

To which Paul responded:

I don't want the last word and this isn't the last word, by any means. *Is it poetry?*, lower case *p*, and less *formal,* or form-ridden, than the privileged upper case variety. How hard it is to come into the open, to cling to the advance, as Williams said. How much talk is still needed at the boundaries!

Ever since Emerson, whose lectures on all accounts are *his* poetry, American poetry has tried to get beyond fixity and determinism, to destroy arbitrary boundaries, in order to release the energy and impulse of creation and restore the self's place in the world. It has questioned both the sovereignty of mind and the closure of the universe, demanded an ever-greater inclusivity ("the common and low"), and favored an art of individual experience, witness, and truth. It has sometimes been performative. It has respected speech. I can imagine Emerson, whose trial as a poet was so severe, listening appreciatively to Antin in the CCNY cafeteria, gladdened again by the advent of another New York poet.[8]

So in the spirit of Emerson one might ask: what would poetry be if it were just the thing of which it is made (language, speech, talk) and not, so far as one could tell, something else (something set apart *as* Poetry and nothing else)? This is the question posed by much of modern and contemporary American poetry—perhaps initially by Gertrude Stein in *Tender Buttons* (1912), but with true theoretical aggression by the "language poets" (or L=A=N=G=U=A=G=E poets), whose texts are frequently composed of the common locutions of everyday life—yet composed in such a way that one imagines that ordinary language has grown conscious of itself without, however, showing any philosophical desire to be anything else (anything but ordinary, everyday talk).[9]

Here are three lines (yes, three) from David Bromige's poem "Lines" (1984):

> yes i do resent it
>
> ———————————
>
> when you use that word[10]

Or, again, take Tina Darragh's poem, "Raymond Chandler's Sentence" (1984)—which is about the poet's absorption in Raymond Chandler's remark that "I had to learn American just like a foreign language" (who doesn't? an immigrant, even a child of immigrants, might be tempted to ask; but Chandler was from England, and, in order to write mystery novels set in the seedier or ordinary reaches of Southern California, he had to sound the way people talk in these places, or perhaps the way they are made to talk in Hollywood movies from the 1930s):

> In "Bay City Blues"
> the detective is caught in a frame
> & tries to escape
> by climbing into the next room and dressing
> in someone else's clothes,
> even affecting another's voice
> But C has the tough cop spot
> him anyway & say
> "get dressed, sweetheart & don't fuss with your necktie.
> Places want us to go to them."[11]

Language poetry is, let us say, language about language, that is, not conceptually about language but (how should one say?) morally and politically responsive or receptive to the language in people's mouths—how people talk, come what may. A poem can be made of anything, depending on how one listens, which means that there is (in principle) nothing that cannot be counted as poetry. Poetry, unlike philosophy, is nonexclusionary. One might think of calling this a poetics of non-identity.

Such a poetics might pose a problem for a philosophy deeply committed to the idea of art as something (necessarily) discernible—something, for example, discernibly different from reality. Arthur Danto, a philosopher who doubles as an art critic, has tried to clarify a problem of this sort. "My thought," Danto says, "is that philosophy begins to arise only when the society within which it arises achieves a concept of reality." But this can happen "only when a contrast is available between reality and something else," and it appears that in the West the philosophical function of art is to constitute this something else.[12] Art gives reality something to contrast itself with, but unfortunately this in turn gives art the power to empty the concept of reality of its force, or detach it from its application, just by being the thing it is to be contrasted with. The classic example would be Marcel Duchamp's *Fountain,* which not only looks like but is, for all the world, a urinal.[13] A showing of Duchamp's work would occasionally look like a hardware store, and it seems important to acknowledge that he is not alone in this sort of thing but is simply giving definition to a whole culture of art, one in which art does not so much mirror the world as appropriate objects from its social and economic environment (Danto's favorite example is Andy Warhol's *Brillo Box*). Danto has some good lines that remind us of how "Picasso was famous for transfigurations of the commonplace. He had made the head of a chimpanzee out of a child's toy; a goat's thorax out of an old wicker basket; a bull's head out of bicycle parts; a Venus out of a gasjet—and so why not the ultimate transfiguration, an artwork out of a thing?" (TC46). What counts as art when the work of art is the very thing it pictures itself as being? Or when it is made up of things that are the very things it is supposed to be different from? Or, for that matter, the same as—Danto imagines a painter who loves a painting so much that he paints it, the way he does his mistress or his favorite rural scene in France (TC38).[14]

Here we seem to arrive at some sort of cognitive limit, perhaps more than one sort of limit. One cannot tell a work of art from a real thing just by looking at it, because the question is not what a thing looks like, nor even what it is, but how it is situated, and how taken. Every work of art presupposes an "artworld," in Danto's famous expression, which is a world constituted by concepts, theories, and narratives as to what counts as art. "What in the end makes the difference between [Andy Warhol's] Brillo box and a work of art consisting of a Brillo box," Danto says,

> is a certain theory of art. It is the theory that takes it up into the world of art, and keeps it from collapsing into the real object which it is (in a sense of *is* other than that of artistic identification). Of course, without the theory, one is unlikely to see it as art, and in order to see it as part of the artworld, one

must have mastered a good deal of artistic theory as well as a considerable amount of the history of recent New York painting. It could not have been art fifty years ago. But then there could not have been, everything being equal, flight insurance in the Middle Ages, or Etruscan typewriter erasers. The world has to be ready for such things, the artworld no less than the real one. It is the role of artistic theories, these days as always, to make the artworld, and art, possible. It would, I should think, never have occurred to the painters of Lascaux that they were producing *art* on those walls. Not unless they were neolithic aestheticians.[15]

Warhol's Brillo box, like Duchamp's *Fountain* before it, is a type of art of which not every Brillo box or urinal is a token. Danto puts this by saying that art is not a natural kind but a historical event, meaning that the essence of the thing is internal to the social and cultural (or institutional) space in which it is produced. All art, like all politics, is local and contingent.

Danto frequently cites Heinrich Wölflin's motto, "Not everything is possible at every time"—that is, "certain artworks simply could not be inserted as artworks into certain periods of art history, though it is possible that objects identical to artworks could have been made at that period" (TC44). So eventually debris from Etruscan or Jericho dumpsites end up as artifacts in museums. What is decisive between art and rubbish is the (Kripkean) concept of "causal history." When Duchamp, on what looks like a whim, pops into the local plumbers' supply for his latest composition, he disrupts the causal history of urinals and causes an ordinary thing to be art. "Tranfiguration" is Danto's name for this. An ordinary urinal remains ordinary by getting left behind in the causal history of mere urinals (urinals not purchased by Duchamp: urinals whose causal history ends with their manufacture, purchase, and urinary use, not with the end of the history of art). The ordinary urinal lacks, so to speak, the self-consciousness that Duchamp's urinal, whose causal history sets it apart in a studio rather than a men's room, achieves (TC48–49)—as if ordinary things could have uncommon destinies (and why not?). There comes a time in the history of art when we know better than to treat all urinals alike. It is no trouble to imagine or experience a word or an object, say a urinal, turning up in a form of life in which it is not thought to belong, but where, against all reason, it fits, it catches on. In ancient rhetoric this event is called a metaphor or transfer from one context to another. In *The Claim of Reason* Stanley Cavell calls it "projecting a word," which he takes to be one of the ordinary things that goes on in ordinary language.[16]

However, it is a nice question whether, alongside urinals and soup cans, there is any room in Danto's aesthetics for a poetry made of language (just language). In the *Poetics*, for example, Aristotle famously set aside language *(lexis)* as an inessential ingredient of poetic structure, and in this he has been followed by almost all philosophers and literary critics (but, at least since Wordsworth's time, by very few poets).[17] Something about the embeddedness of literature in language makes Danto want to affirm his Aristotelian ancestry, and so in an essay called "Philosophy as/and/of Literature," he defends the basically Aristotelian principle that literature is still part of the organon or logic of propositional discourse—still a branch of semantical theory and therefore made of things, not words (still mimetic after all these years). "Semantical theory," Danto says, "does the best it can to connect literature to the world through what, after all, are the only kinds of connections it understands: reference, truth, instantiation, exemplification, and the like, and if this means distorting the universe in order that it can *receive* literary representations, well, this has never been reckoned a heavy price to pay—has not been reckoned a price at all but a creative opportunity—and it remains to the credit of this enterprise that it at least believes that *some* connection between literature and the world is required" (PD145).

Semantics here means "possible-world" semantics, or modal realism, which does strike some philosophers as distorting the universe in literature's direction. "My contention," Danto says, "is that philosophical semantics renders literature true of possible worlds . . . in such a way that it would be history for any of them if actual instead of ours. As *Gulliver's Travels* would be just anthropology for a world in which there are Lilliputians instead of Melanesians" (PD154). In possible-world semantics, works of fiction are not false (not *not* factual, not *merely* fantastic, however fantastic); they are simply true of worlds different from our own. If I understand David Lewis, there is no warrant for saying that these other worlds don't exist. They are as real as ours (the one we inhabit); it's just that they aren't ours.[18] Danto says that works of fiction connect up with our world by way of their readers, which is pretty much the same idea as Paul Ricoeur's looking-glass theory of the text, where understanding a text does not mean going around behind it to retrieve some originating intention; rather, Ricoeur thinks of the literary text as projecting a possible world in front of itself, and that understanding means entering into this project, this space in front of the text, making it one's own. The reader's task, our task, is to reconnect text and world by appropriating the world in front of the text, that is, putting it, in some sense, into play, say by intervening in our world in order to change it in the text's direction (instead of changing the text in *our* direction, translating into our language, integrating it into our order of signification, which is how allegory moves).[19]

This is good hermeneutics, but doubtful poetics, since it reduces language (or literature) to its semantic or narrative function, whereas the poet is someone who is obsessed with what is irreducible in language (or literature). The poet Michael Davidson gives a straightforward narrative account of such an obsession:

> I have a kind of naive idea of what a fact is. To paraphrase Wittgenstein, it's a point of departure for further investigation. I think it began with my interest

in lists. At one point the idea of a list was a sort of ultimate autistic [artistic?] construct, because it would create the illusion of a random series that would relate immediately to my life. I would be able to go through my day and check off items on the list. They were words after all, but the syntax of the list was my activity [i.e., my daily life]. In that sense, it was a hermeneutic of reading the list. And then I began to realize that I wanted to tell stories; I wanted to describe events. And the problem, of course, occurred in the first few words: as I began to describe the event I was faced with my own language staring me back in the face. I simply couldn't describe. I found myself involved in the forms of mediation that were constantly coming up in front of me.[20]

Davidson writes as if language were both the form *and* the limit of mediation. Danto shows us a brief glimpse of his irrealist, non-Aristotelian side when he remarks in passing on the material aspects of artworks. "It is because," he says, "of these palpable features in excess of the features which make for semantical analysis that a work of art, even when straightforward narrative, cannot be collapsed into its content: there is something in the telling of the story which is more than the story told. It is for these reasons that even when a work of art is, as critics and literary theorists loosely say, 'referential,' it is never merely referential. For these reasons I speak of works of art as semi-opaque objects" (PD79). Can we make sense of the thought that poetry might be the irreducibility of language to its semantic features?

In analytic philosophy, opacity is less a concept than a covering term for whatever gets in the way of the perception of logical form or interferes with the unpacking of deep structures. In this tradition natural languages are conventionally described as opaque (or, more rigorously, *incoherent* and opaque). The language poets encourage us to think of poetry as a discourse that takes responsibility for the native opacity of everyday language, that is, for its native resistance or irreducibility to the logical functions of mediation that characterize our use of it. Naturally one thinks of famous cases, sometimes imaginary, like Flaubert's dream of "a book about nothing," a work from which the features that make for semantical analysis would have to be completely eliminated; but actual cases will serve— *Tristram Shandy*, Mallarmé's poetry, James Joyce's *Finnegans Wake*, Maurice Blanchot's *récits*, the later poems of Paul Celan. What is interesting about so many of the language poets, in contrast to these famous cases, is that they seek to remain within the opacity of natural language, neither to thicken nor reduce it by art but to write a poetry of the surface, a poetry of what otherwise—say in the making of art objects, or of narratives, or of concepts—is overcome or subsumed through mediation. In general the language poets affirm the opacity of natural language against what Lyotard calls "the ideology of communicational transparency" that goes hand in hand with the commodification of art, knowledge, experience, and so on.[21] (So Theodor Adorno: "the slick connoisseur who knows art like the inside of his pocket is the worst offender here because he distorts art, turning it into a completely transparent thing, which it is not.")[22] In "My Poetry" David Bromige writes: "the profound vocation of the work of art in a commodity society: not to be a commodity, not to be consumed."[23] This theme is sounded obsessively among the language poets—for example, in Charles Bernstein's "Three or Four Things I Know about Him" and Ron Silliman's "Disappearance of the Word, Appearance of the World."[24] Poetry contests the ideology of transparency, that is, it contests (under various names) an Aristotelian poetics that would assimilate poetry to the idea that language is reducible to its functions of mediation. As Bernstein says in his *ars poetica*, "Artifice of Absorption":

> The *thickness*
> of words ensures that whatever
> of their physicality is erased, or engulfed, in
> the process of semantic projection,
> a residue
> tenaciously in-
> heres that will not be sublimated
> away. Writing is not a thin film
> of expendable substitutions that, when reading, falls
> away
> like scales
> to reveal a meaning. The tenacity of
> writing's thickness, like the body's
> flesh, is
> ineradicable, yet mortal.[25]

"Writing," Stanley Cavell says in *The Senses of Walden*, "must assume the conditions of language as such; re-experience, as it were, the fact that there is such a thing as language at all and assume responsibility for it—find a way to acknowledge it."[26] What is it to take responsibility for language, that is, not just for the meaning of one's words but for the whole of them? If we imagine the materiality of language as a kind of flesh, then perhaps we can begin to understand the complexity of the claim to which the language poets are responding.

In "The Chinese Notebook" Ron Silliman says that "there is no useful distinction between language and poetry."[27] So how do we tell that a thing is a poem? We should imagine Silliman turning this question back at us: what makes us ask? Silliman's idea is that the question expresses nothing so much as a consumer's anxiety. We can imagine him saying that our relation to a poem isn't one of knowing (for sure) that it is one. We might know, of course, or we might not, but what sort of knowledge are we talking about, and what sort of person has such knowledge? Knowledge or ignorance of this sort seems to presuppose a certain kind of culture, an aesthetic culture or a culture of connoisseurship (compare Hugh Kenner on Andy Warhol and other counterfeiters)—call it a culture of experts charged with monitoring the art world to make sure that nothing gets passed off on the buying public.[28] What could be worse than a fake poem? But what would a fake poem look like? Implicit here is a concept of authenticity, but in what sort of world does this concept have application? For Silliman, language poetry throws its weight against the application of such concepts. And so he and his colleagues write (as Williams wrote) in such a way so as to situate us at the limits of knowing or, even more radically, outside the site of the knowing subject, outside our concepts, no longer in a position to say that the text at hand is authentic, faithful to criteria.

The result seems very close to what Stanley Cavell had in mind when, in "Music Decomposed" (1965), he made the observation that "the possibility of fraudulence, and the experience of fraudulence, is endemic to the experience of contemporary music. . . . I do not see how anyone who has experienced modern art can have avoided such experiences. . . . [The] dangers of fraudulence, and of trust, are essential to the experience of art. . . . Contemporary music is only the clearest case of something common to modernism as a whole, and modernism only makes explicit and bare what has always been true of art"—and that truth is that our relation with works of art is more like a relation with a person than with an object.[29] We have to have a life with contemporary music in order to experience it as music. What is having a life with a work of art (as if it were a person)?[30] According to Cavell's famous distinction, it is not a relation of cognition, grasping a thing by means of concepts, but one of responsiveness and acknowledgment—a distinction, Cavell's argument goes, that registers "the moral of skepticism": namely, that our relation to the world is not one of knowing it but rather one of inhabiting it.[31]

Imagine poetry withdrawing itself from our aesthetic gaze, not to say from our concepts, concealing itself in the obviousness rather than in the uniqueness, strangeness, or difference of its language. Language poetry teaches us that poetry is not an object for us. It is poetry that alters—displaces—the traditional site from which we approach it. It is not so much language that is recontextualized within the history of poetry (although Danto's analysis of transfiguration holds for language poetry as for Duchamp's urinal). It is rather that we as connoisseurs of poetry are recontextualized outside the world of aesthetic differentiation.

Many years ago the French philosopher Emmanuel Levinas remarked that, "paradoxical as it may seem, painting is a struggle with sight. Sight seeks to draw out of the light beings integrated into a whole. To look is to be able to describe curves, to sketch out wholes in which the elements can be integrated, horizons in which the particular comes to appear by abdicating its particularity. In contemporary painting things no longer count as elements of a universal order which the look would give itself, as a perspective. On all sides fissures appear in the continuity of the universe. The particular stands out in the nakedness of its being."[32] This thought sheds light on what language poets seem to be trying to find a place for in their work, namely, that which ordinarily gets excluded from poetry within the domain of aesthetic differentiation: call it the obviousness of language, or what we are poetically deaf to. In the *Philosophical Investigations* Wittgenstein writes: "the aspects of things that are most important for us are hidden because of their simplicity. One is unable to notice something—because it is always before one's eyes."[33] One might take this as the motto of language poetry, which is not so much a poetry of sight as a poetry of recognition, of listening and responding.

This comes out in an important essay, or talk, by Ron Silliman called "The New Sentence" (1979), which is in part about our inability to say what a sentence is, or to take any interest in it—or even to notice it. Silliman assembles a dossier of quotations in which experts from Saussure to Quine say that the sentence is external to language and so should be excluded from linguistics, literary criticism, and philosophy of language, where the sentence is always somehow less that the sum of its parts (is, e.g., not the same as a proposition, whose meaning is analyzable exactly into the meaning of each of its constitutive terms).[34] This suggests some common ground between poetry and the sentence (both inhabit the region of exiles). It is true that French structuralists like Emile Benveniste and Roland Barthes showed some interest in the sentence, which they took to be a unit of integration whose integration into units higher still suggested the possibility of linguistics of the text. In such a linguistics, however, the sentence remains a poor relation, occupying an empty space. In a similar way the sentence is external to the poststructuralist condominium—there is no such thing as a sentence when it comes to the textuality of the text, where there is only traversal and slippage. The sentence is simply the path of linearity that textuality disrupts. The sentence is indistinguishable from the fragment.

Now language poetry is, in so many of its versions, a poetry of sentences. Not of words or lines or texts but of sentences, as in Barrett Watten's "Complete Thought" (1982)—consult your first-grade grammar: what does a sentence express?

XIII
Connected pieces break into name.
Petrified trees are similar.

XIV
Everyday life retards potential.
Calculation governs speech.

XV
Rules stand out as illustrations.
People climb over piles of rock.

XVI
I am speaking in an abridged form.
Ordinary voices speak in rooms.

. . . .

XXXVIII
A straight road is unconvincing.
Not to kill the hero is a crime.

. . . .

XLIV
Candles stand up to icons.
Science gives feature to the world.[35]

Here is an excerpt from Lyn Hejinian's "My Life" (1980):

The coffee drinkers   The traffic drones, where drones is a
answered   noun. Whereas the cheerful pessimist
ecstatically   suits himself in a bad world, which is
                however the inevitable world, impossible of improvement. I
close one eye, always the left, when looking out into the glare of the
street. What education finally serves us, if at all. There is a pause, a rose,
something on paper. The small green shadows made the red jump out. Such
displacements alter illusions, which is all-to-the-good. Now cars not cows
on the brown hills, and a stasis of mobile homes have taken their names from
what grew in the valleys near Santa Clara. We have all grown up with it. If
it is personal, it is most likely fickle. The university was the cultural market
but on Sundays she tried out different churches.[36]

Is it poetry? It is, at all events, indistinguishable from prose—a feature or
condition that is basic to the Williams tradition, as Stephen Fredman explains
in *Poet's Prose*. Fredman's book is indispensable here because it studies the crucial
difference between "poet's prose" and prose that is poetic or arty: poet's prose is not
prose poetry. It may be indistinguishable from bad prose. It may even get boring
at times. (Silliman writes in "The Chinese Notebook": "If this bores you, leave.")[37]
The point is to keep the sentence from disappearing, from getting excluded from

poetry, and if this means extending the concept of the poetic so that nothing is excluded from it, well, *that* is what the "poetics" of the Williams tradition had been trying for from the start.[38]

Silliman explains that what is new about "the new sentence" is the way it resists totalization. It is *not* a unit of integration but resists our desire for paragraphs that are organized logically into so many conceptual orders or woven into fabrics of belief. "The sentences are all sentences," he says, "the syntax of each resolves up to the level of the sentence." But there is always a twist somewhere (Silliman calls it "torquing") that shifts the movement of the sentence away from totalities of one kind or another toward the singularity of the sentence itself. There are endless ways of "torquing," many quite simple—as simple as joking—as in the following from Bob Perelman's *a.k.a.*:

I was left holding the bag. I peered into it.[39]

This illustrates nicely the idea that there is no useful distinction to be made between language and poetry. Language itself is the poem.

Of course, Mallarmé thought no less. But among contemporary language poets language means ordinary language, whereas for Mallarmé it meant something quasi-transcendental: language as radically outside, not just purified of everyday use but outside all subjectivity and objectivity, outside culture and its discourses. Silliman, however, says that torquing "enables works of the new sentence a much greater capacity to incorporate ordinary sentences of the material world."[40] So David Bromige, as if in a tribute to Williams, borrows from a Sonoma newspaper to write "One Spring." Elsewhere, as in the line from *a.k.a.* just quoted, poetry remains at the level of the idiomatic expression. Silliman's own poetry is notoriously made of the locutions belonging to his everyday environment, and the point to mark is that the language is not external to the environment, not "about" it, but is internal to the stuff of everyday life:

I run into Watten in a lumber yard. When you get near the bottom the newspaper droops. The dog is happy rolling in the dirt. I am rapidly running out of lines. Small stainglass frog hands in the window. Meat by-products. Education designs the brain. Education redesigns the brain. Dry petfood is cereal. Ibid. A man tunelessly whistles, lugging garbage down three flights of backstairs. Jars, cans & spray-bottles sit in a kitchen window. I slap my hands clean. What you determine from the sound of unseen traffic is the general size of vehicle. Old broomsticks rotting on porch. Think of stitching as a mode of margin. Children scavenging crushed cans as a scout project. One million pennies from the National Endowment. Chickenwire on the fencetop to prevent entry.[41]

There is, one can see, something vaguely naturalistic about this poetry: it is documentary writing of a sort, but what it documents is the language of the everyday, that is, the language that *goes with* the everyday, where dry petfood *is* cereal. "A man tunelessly whistles, lugging garbage down three flights of backstairs": whistle while you work, say the Seven Dwarfs. "I slap my hands clean." And of course that's exactly what one does, and exactly what one would say, as if slapping one's hands clean were an idiomatic gesture, or say a piece of everyday practice that only the idiom can register. So the whole of the everyday is, in effect, drawn into the poem. Our contemporary form of life, in all of its gritty, commercial debris, is internal to the poem's horizon.

2. The Proximity of Poetry

Earlier I cited Danto's thesis that the difference between a work of art and a real thing from which it is indiscernible "is a certain theory of art. It is the theory that takes it up into the world of art, and keeps it from collapsing into the real object which it is. . . . Of course, without the theory, one is unlikely to see it as art, and in order to see it as part of the artworld, one must have mastered a good deal of artistic theory as well as a considerable amount of the history of recent New York painting." In "Aesthetic Problems of Modern Philosophy" (1965), Stanley Cavell takes up the question of atonal music, whose strangeness appears to extend the concept of music beyond anything known or knowable as music. What counts as music when there are rival and seemingly incompatible claims to being the thing itself? How does one settle such a question? Appealing to formal criteria is of no help, because criteria are already internal to the world (or worlds) which the rival musics presuppose. What Danto calls an "artworld," Cavell calls "a form of life," as in "To imagine a language is to imagine a form of life."[42] Between an artworld and a form of life there might be this difference, that our relation to a form of life is not theoretical:

> The language of tonality is part of a particular form of life, one containing the music we are most familiar with; associated with, or consisting of, particular ways of being trained to perform and to listen to it; involving particular ways of being corrected, particular ways of responding to mistakes, to nuance, above all to recurrence and to variation and modification. No wonder we want to preserve the idea of tonality: to give all *that* up seems like giving up the idea of music altogether. I think it *is*—*like* it.
>
> I shall not try to say why it is not fully that. I shall only mention that it cannot be enough to point to the obvious fact that musical instruments, with their familiar or unfamiliar powers, are employed—because *that* fact does not

prevent us from asking: But is it music? Nor enough to appeal to the fact that we can point to pitches, intervals, lines and rhythm—because we probably do not for the most part know what we are pointing to with these terms. I mean we do not know *which* lines are significant . . . and which intervals to hear as organizing. More important, I think, is the fact that we may see an undoubted musician speak about such things and behave toward them in ways similiar (not, I think, more than similar) to the ways he behaves toward Beethoven, and then we may sense that, though similar, it is a new world and that to understand a new world it is imperative to concentrate upon its inhabitants. (MW84)

The problem is, hermeneutically, the same as the anthropological one of trying to understand an alien culture: within the writing of poetry, as within the composition of music, there are multiple and heterogeneous forms of life among which agreement as to what counts as poetry or music or art cannot occur, that is, they are not reducible to one another or to some common ground or set of criteria; no translation manual will give us access to the thing itself. There is no overarching theory; rather theory is internal to local times and places.

This is as much as to say that there is no essence of poetry or of music or art, only local, contingent, heterogeneous practices of writing and composition distributed horizontally across the anarchic plane of "anything goes" rather than vertically in a canonical order of classical models that one learns to imitate (in order perhaps to supersede). Or, in other words, our relation to poetry or music is not determined by the legislation of our concepts; rather it is one of acknowledgment or recognition that comes from living with the thing, belonging to its world or, say, to its histories. As Cavell says, our counting the new music as music, our accommodating it, amounts to "naturalizing ourselves to a new form of life, a new world" (MW84). So the question of what counts as poetry that Antin and the language poets raise resolves itself into the question of what sort of migration we are being urged to undertake. What sort of conversion or transformation of ourselves are we facing? It is as if the main question as to what counts as art were not "What must one know?" but "How must one live?"[43]

The beginning of an answer to this question might be that what seems to characterize language poetry is that its poets reject, or at all events seem to interpret in marvelously ironic and satiric ways, the aesthetic principle of the ontological peculiarity of the work of art, or the idea, formulated flawlessly by Danto, that the work of art is necessarily, logically, external to the world. Doubtless Danto could find an argument that language poetry is still (in his sense) external to reality, but it is part of the uncanny realism of the language poets that they take such pains to situate their writing within the horizon of the ordinary, where things are not set aside as art. Thus the language of the language poets is internal to the situations in which it is learned; its projections are always, in Cavell's sense of the word, "natural" (not transfigurations of the commonplace but acknowledgments of it).[44]

Another way to put this would be to say that the materiality of the language of language poetry is not a product of art, as it is in the case of Mallarmé or Joyce's *Finnegans Wake*, or indeed as in the case of most poetry from almost any tradition, where writing consists in doing something to the language to set it apart from the everyday; rather, as per Williams's *Paterson*, for example, language registers the materiality of everydayness itself.[45] Only we shouldn't be misled by this "itself": everydayness is an open-ended category (or, in other words, not so much a category as a direction). As Marjorie Perloff suggests in her essay "Poetry and the Common Life" (1984), the common life is not a common denominator—not something to work down to: not a foundation and a norm.[46] Her essay is in part a reply to the poet Louis Simpson, who seems to want to think of the common life as foundational, like Wordsworth's "real language of men." The common life, Simpson thinks, is what poets like John Ashbery ignore (he forgets that Ashbery has a terrific poem about Daffy Duck). Perloff quotes Simpson's "26th Precinct Station," where the common life turns out to be a product of naturalism (a distinctively European aesthetic):

> One night Jake telephoned
> to say, "Mike has stabbed Lorna."
> He wanted me to call his lawyer . . .
> couldn't do it himself, he was tied up.
> I called the lawyer, who had just come in
> from seeing *Kismet*. We shared a taxi.
> All the way down to the station
> he kept humming "And This is My Beloved."
> Lorna recovered, and wrote a novel.
> Mike married and went to live in Rome.
> Jake Harmon died. But I remember
> the 26th Precinct Station.
> A black woman in yellow wig,
> a purple skirt, and stiletto heels;
> a pickpocket; a cripple
> arrested for indecent exposure.
> The naked light bulb; the crack in the wall
> that loops like the Mississippi at Vicksburg;
> the shadow of the cockroach
> under the baseboard, lurking, gathering his nerve.[47]

Here the common life seems sketched, as by a naturalist, that is, by a purely ascertaining observer, a maker of documents; whereas in the Williams tradition the common life is inhabited, not described. Perloff suggests roughly this sort of distinction when she opposes to Simpson's poem some poems by that unforgettable old beatnik, Kenneth Rexroth. Here is Rexroth's "The Signatures of All Things" (1950):

> When I dragged the rotten log
> From the Bottom of the pool,
> It seemed heavy as stone.
> I let it lie in the sun
> For a month; and then chopped it
> Into sections, and split them
> For kindling, and spread them out
> To dry some more. Late that night,
> After reading for hours,
> While moths rattled at the lamp—
> The saints and philosophers
> On the destiny of man—
> I walked out on my cabin porch,
> And looked up through the black forest
> At the Swaying islands of stars.
> Suddenly I saw at my feet,
> Spread on the floor of night, ingots
> Of quivering phosphorescence,
> And all about were scattered chips
> Of pale cold light that was alive.[48]

The title of Rexroth's poem is borrowed from Stephen Dedalus ("Signatures of all things that I am here to read"), but his poem is a constant allusion to Thoreau's *Walden*, and it inscribes Cavell's moral (in *The Senses of Walden*) that our relation to the common, the mean, and the low is not one of observing, as with a Joycean "scrupulous meanness." So poetry is, in this context, not incompatible with a sort of realism—not, to be sure, realism as an alternative to nominalism: not philosophical realism or realism as an aesthetics of correspondence or as a claim about art's cognitive power over empirical reality, but rather realism in the sense of *not* being sealed off from one's environment (think of a realist as one who has been exposed to reality; or think of realism in Cavell's sense of "taking an interest in one's experience").[49]

Realism from the site of habitation, not observation and description.

Thinking of Cavell, one is inclined to quote the following, from a poem by Gerald Burns, whose name is not misspelled (although mine frequently is). The poem is called "Letters to Obscure Men" (1975):

The quality of forties light
in B detective films
always coming through venetian blinds
the extra care with which they photographed
telephones as if they mattered
whether they rang or not
may be due, I thought, to German light men
growing up in small towns with gas lamps
and I've thought when Poe was on
the Broadway Journal shadows
must have been interesting in New York
but now I think that watching forties films
is not like watching fifties films
because we now ignore
the surface noise coming off the sound track
when nothing audible is on the screen
whereas when I was growing up
I loved to hear that sound
because it told me if you listen hard
the sound duration makes is audible
as we all watched the telephone
and heard it not ring.[50]

A poem about listening! But as if with Thoreau's, or John Cage's, or even Heidegger's ear: the sort of ear that language poetry calls for, as in Michael Davidson's "After the Dancers," from *The Prose of Fact* (1981):

He had a hearing fault,
a near ache
is that what you said?
he lost his left foot
they walked on the right side
the good one
they had a run through
or didn't, it didn't matter
one of their sides was missing
but present in the wings,
he heard them breathing
as a kind of wall
like light bulbs
always necessary

> when they turned them on
> it didn't matter
> but made a small clicking sound
> like an ear clearing[51]

Imagine being connected to the world by way of the ear rather than as purely ascertaining observers. This was Heidegger's idea, namely that we are in the world not as spectators but as belonging (*gehören*), where belonging is also the word for listening—"We have heard [*gehört*] when we belong to [*gehört*] to what is said," says Heidegger.[52] Moreover, listening is how Heidegger characterizes thinking, that is, at the end of philosophy the task of thinking can no longer be adequately conceived as conceptual representation or calculative reasoning, nor even as questioning, but as openness and responsiveness—an idea that Cavell picks up on when he links together Heidegger and Emerson: "the idea of thinking as reception . . . seems to me a sound intuition, specifically to forward the answer to skepticism [which Emerson meant it to do]. The answer does not consist in denying the conclusion of skepticism but in reconceiving its truth. It is true that we do not know the existence of the world with certainty; our relation to its existence is deeper—one in which it is accepted, that is, received. My favorite way of putting this is to say that existence is to be acknowledged" (SW 133).

The difference between Heidegger and Emerson (and Cavell) is that there are hardly any people in Heidegger's world. Heidegger sides with Heraclitus in saying that "You never hear properly so long as your ears hang upon the sound and flow of a human voice in order to snatch up for yourselves a manner of speaking. Heraclitus [rejects] hearing as nothing but the passion of ears."[53] By contrast, in the tradition Cavell is trying to recover for American philosophy, listening, reception, and acknowledgment are social, political, and ethical concepts. The ear connects us up with a world of other people. This seems to be the connection that is registered in language poetry, which is distinctive not so much for its voice as for its ear. But the poet's ear does not simply listen empirically in order to reproduce the world's sounds in the sounds of language (onomatopoeia). Rather the idea seems to be that whereas the speaking subject moves consecutively along syntactical lines, the listening subject is, like Tristram Shandy, nonlinear, open to distraction, indeed in a constant state of interruption, because a world organized according to listening is a world of simultaneous events that, unless one is ready to exclude most of what happens, one is bound to sort out into lists rather than into narratives and propositions, as in Ron Silliman's *What*:

> Over breakfast, three sisters
> speak at once. Sound truck
> on Fifth Ave is unintelligible

in midday traffic, tho signs read
Stop Union Busting Now.
I hear finches sing
in the magnolia while a blackbird
runs in the grass, dotted
with the white flower of clover.
An old man comes down
the stairs slowly,
putting one foot onto the next step,
then the other, both hands
on the railing. It's fathers flirt
with their infant daughters,
that's where that's learned.
Let's rake puns. Big robin
light on the branch and stares.
Cars pass. I sit
on an old porch swing,
held by chains
which are thoroughly rusted[54]

In his "Artifice of Absorption" Charles Bernstein lays down what seems to me a poetics of the ear (just to call it that) when he says that

In my poems,
I frequently use opaque & nonabsorbable
elements, digressions &
interruptions, as part of a technological
arsenal to create a more powerful
("souped up")
absorption. . . .[55]

Absorption is how the ear works, as against the selective eye that can focus things in and out of its world or simply close itself off. Eye contact is something one has to learn, whereas the ear is exposed to perpetual interference. A mote in the eye obliterates everything, but what sticks in the ear is something one cannot get out of one's head. Speaking several languages at once means speaking with the ear, as in the pun, a species of nonexclusionary discourse.

At all events a running theme in language poetry is that our relation to language is not by way of linguistic competence or the propositional attitude or as expressive agents. So writes the Canadian poet Steve McCaffery:

> It is sound more so than meaning binds
> the body to language[56]

The ear registers the excessiveness of language, or what McCaffery calls "the elsewhere of meaning," namely that which otherwise gets excluded by the operations
of deep structure—grammar, syntax, but also logic, rhetoric, and poetics, which
are artifices of elimination that work to bring discourse under control.[57] Whereas
language poetry, as Cavell says of Emerson's writing, is "the exercise not of power
but of reception" (SW 135).

Naturally poetry that is porous and receptive with respect to its environment is
likely to pose special problems of reading; that is, how one responds to such poetry
will depend in large part on how one stands with respect to its social and cultural
environment. On this point readers seem to fall roughly into two groups. Thus, in
his essay "Postmodernism, or the Logic of Late Capitalism," Fredric Jameson hears
in the language poets the schizophrenic logic of an overflushed capitalist nation-
state. Likewise the poet Eliot Weinberger, reviewing Ron Silliman's anthology
of language poets, In the American Tree, hears a narrow self-obsessed nationalism
indifferent to European or multicultural aesthetics ("it is rare in the extensive
critical writings of the 'language' poets to encounter any reference to foreign
poetry outside of Russian futurism").[58] Not surprisingly, readers of language poetry frequently register the cultural shock that occurs whenever cosmopolitanism
confronts the peculiar temporality, the randomness or fragmentation, of American
culture, particularly the way this culture is foregrounded in California (an obviously
mad place, an anti-Republic from which it is impossible to exclude anything: Los
Angeles is what Plato must have foreseen, to his horror, in the Athenian refusal
of metaphysics). California has always inspired apocalyptic arm-waving, as in
Adorno's and Horkheimer's famous polemic against the "culture industry" ("the
idolization of the cheap involves making the average heroic"), which is a nice tract
to read before taking up Cavell's Pursuits of Happiness. Whereas Horkheimer and
Adorno link Hollywood with Hitler's Germany, Cavell links it with philosophy,
or at least philosophy of a certain Emersonian sort. Here purely ascertaining
observation is put aside in favor of "taking an interest in one's experience," meaning
also one's everyday (as against once-in-a-lifetime) cultural inheritance; for example,
Cavell does not hesitate to link up Frank Capra with Immanuel Kant as a way of
introducing a discussion of the transgression of limits in It Happened One Night.[59]
Cavell is here coherent with the Williams tradition, with its self-conscious refusal
of cosmopolitanism—a refusal that situates Williams alongside Cavell's Emerson
("I embrace the common, I explore and sit at the feet of the familiar, the low. Give
me insight into today, and you may have the antique and future worlds. What
would we really know the meaning of? The meal in the firkin; the milk in the pan;

the ballad in the street; the news of the boat . . .").[60] Compare the "Prologue" to
Kora in Hell, with its idea of a museum of everyday paintings—

> I wish Arensberg had my opportunity for prying into jaded households
> where the paintings of Mama's and Papa's flowertime still hang on the walls. I
> propose that Arensberg be commissioned by the Independent Artists to scour
> the country for the abortive paintings of those men and women who without
> master or method have evolved perhaps two or three unusual creations
> in their early years. . . . Carefully selected, these queer products might be
> housed to good effect in some unpretentious exhibition chamber across the
> city from the Metropolitan Museum of Art.[61]

Williams suggests that that which gets excluded from the canon of authentic
productions itself could constitute a canon of inauthentic productions, and so on
without end, with every event inspiring, not a consequence, but an alternative
definition of what counts as art.

When Cavell asks, in The Senses of Walden, "Why has America never expressed
itself philosophically?" (SW33), this might sound, to the global ear, like your
basic hundred-dollar-a-plate jingo nationalism, but in fact the question is an
acknowledgment of historicality, like Emerson's "Self-Reliance," which sounds like
an isolationist tract ("the wise man stays at home"), but which is in fact about
America's difference from European culture, its discontinuity within the history of
the West, its refractoriness and uncontainability not just with respect to English
or Continental categories but with respect to categorial operations as such, or,
in other words, its failure to be one thing and whole. American difference from
European culture has always been a foundational theme in American literature
and criticism, which is inclined to figure this culture horizontally as an anarchic
distribution of communities and cultural centers rather than as a capitalist entity
or European-like nation-state controlled from the top down. Gordana P. Crnković
makes the interesting argument that for Eastern Europeans America has always been
imagined as a utopia constructed anarchically as a horizontal series, in contrast to
the Eastern European experience of a unitary, vertical culture in which questions of
what counts as poetry or music are settled from instituted power centers.[62] If this
Eastern European picture is, arguably, merely utopian, it is nevertheless symmetrical
with the utopia projected by American poetry itself.

This is the upshot of Stephen Fredman's argument in The Grounding of American
Poetry: Charles Olson and the Emersonian Tradition. For American poets, "ground" has
always meant a surface to be traversed rather than a position to be occupied or
a foundation on which vertical structures (churches, states, universities) are to be
raised.[63] Hence the enormous premium, mounting to an obsession, in American
poetry and criticism (as in Williams's Paterson, or Charles Olson's Gloucester poems)

on the "sense of place," where place is an open-ended list from which nothing can ever be excluded: beachtown and bordertown, mountains and desert, middle border and high plains, tidewater and backwater, sun-belt and rust-belt, main streets and mean streets, loops and beltways, Chinatowns and barrios and neighborhoods in various stages of cultural transfer—but also Mexico, Vancouver, not to mention the endless places of American exile. Walt Whitman taught us to make poetry out of lists of places, on the principle that the list is our only recourse in a world where space is more surface than container, where master narratives and deep structures have no application—a world that resists the analytic frame of mind, as if made for traveling rather than penetrating—

Under the bluffs of Oroville, blue cloud September skies, entering U.S. border, red red apples bend their tree boughs prop with sticks—
At Omak a fat girl in dungarees leads her big brown horse by the asphalt highway.
Thru lodgepole pine hills Coleville near Moses' Mountain—a white horse standing back of a 2 ton truck moving forward between two trees.
At Nespelem, in the yellow sun, a marker for Chief Joseph's grave under rilled brown hills—white cross over highway.
At Grand Coulee under leaden sky, giant red generators humm thru granite & concrete to materialize onions—
And grey water laps against the grey sides of Steamboat Mesa.
At Dry Falls 40 Niagras stand silent & invisible, tiny horses graze on the rusty canyon's mesquite floor.
At Mesa, on the car radio passing a new corn silo, Walking Boogie teenager's tender throats, "I wish they could all be California girls"—as black highway curls outward.[64]

—which is to say that how one reads a list like this depends on how one is situated, or how one moves. The cosmopolitan intellectual who writes essays like "Disneyland: A Degenerate Utopia" identifies one familiar site.[65] For the Jamesian expatriate, who is still something of a cultural norm for the American intellectual, each item on this list represents a closed or isolated world where writing becomes the natural language of exile.[66] My favorite version of this is Willa Cather's theory of Nebraska, whose hostile plains destroy the sensitive artist in a twinkling (*My Antonía*). For the Emersonian, by contrast, each place is an invitation to its own separateness and whimsy, and the question is whether it is an invitation one can bear to accept.
    It is against this (problematical) cultural background that Cavell, in *The Senses of Walden*, writes:

Study of *Walden* would perhaps not have become such an obsession with me had it not presented itself as a response to questions with which I was already obsessed: why has America never expressed itself philosophically? Or has it—in the metaphysical riot of its greatest literature? Has the impulse to philosophical speculation been absorbed, or exhausted, by speculation in territory, as in such thoughts as Manifest Destiny? Or are such questions not really intelligible? They are, at any rate, disturbingly like the questions that were asked about American literature before it established itself. In re-reading *Walden*, twenty years after first reading it, I seemed to find a book of sufficient intellectual scope and consistency to have established or inspired a tradition of thinking. One reason it did not is that American culture has never really believed in its capacity to produce anything of permanent value—except itself. So it forever overpraises and undervalues its achievements. (SW 32–33)

One of Cavell's own ways of interpreting this is to say that what Americans share is not a common culture; that is, "nothing of high culture is common to us," meaning that, among other things, "no text is sacred," no law is law of the land, no criteria are settled, the term "canonical" has no special application, as if American culture, whether philosophical, literary, utopian, or popular, were underived, without ground (without why), existing only in its versions, each of which would have to be studied, well, anthropologically.[67] The charge to look and see compels us to attach ourselves to the individual case, that is, it takes us out of the holistic attitude in which we deal with ideologies and conceptual schemes and forces us to consider things in their irreducible singularity, as one damn thing or place after another in no coherent order, where our task is not so much to represent and construe as to be open and receptive in the Cavellian (also Heideggerian) sense of "thinking as the receiving or letting be of something, as opposed to the positing or putting together of something" (SW 152).

In "Thinking of Emerson" Cavell says that "Emerson's and Thoreau's relation to poetry is inherently their interest in their own writing. . . . I do not mean their interest in what we may call their poems, but their interest in the fact that what they are building is writing, as it realizes itself daily under their hands, sentence by shunning sentence, the accomplishment of inhabitation, the making of it happen, the poetry of it. Their prose is a battle, using a remark of Nietzsche's, not to become poetry [presumably poetry with a capital *P*]; a battle specifically to remain in conversation with itself, answerable to itself" (SW 134). A decently trained American scholar would have no trouble translating this into Charles Olson's line of thinking about composition in the open, or composition by field as against linear or period composition, where one abandons the closed forms of literary tradition, sometimes called "closed Eurocentric forms" that do your speaking for you, and risks instead "a whole series of new recognitions" that refuse the legislation of our concepts and so might look like anything but poetry. As Olson says: "from the moment [the writer] ventures into FIELD COMPOSITION—puts himself in the open—he can go by no track other than the one the poem under hand declares, for itself."[68] No saying what happens next. "Whatever gets written," says Charles Bernstein, "gets written in a particular shape, uses a particular vocabulary & syntax, & a variety of chosen techniques. . . . Sometimes this process takes place intuitively or unconsciously (the pull of influence comes in here since somewhere in the back of your mind are models for what looks natural, personal, magical, mystical, spontaneous, automatic, dream-like, confessional, didactic, shocking). Sometimes it is a very conscious process. Anyway, you're responsible for what turns up."[69] "The accomplishment of inhabitation"—suppose we gloss this happy phrase as follows, partly summarizing Cavell: skepticism says, you can't tell the difference between poetry and talk, poetry and language, poetry and prose, good poetry and bad, art and non-art, art and reality, or (indeed) poetry and philosophy. Your criteria are without foundation; they float and drift across multiple horizons (the frontier in America is not a boundary but an opening). Whatever claim you make on behalf of whatever text (or canon) cannot be supported by an appeal to criteria. A poem can be made of anything.

To which Cavell might be imagined to respond: what you say is not to be refuted. A poem can be made of anything (translated into philosophy this means: the extension of the concept of poetry cannot be closed by a frontier)—only it does not follow therefore that anything goes, or that everything collapses into aporia. If we cannot distinguish between poetry and talk, poetry and prose, poetry and philosophy, this does not mean that they are indiscriminate or identical. What you say about criteria is true: they float and drift and fail to settle things once and for all, but all this means is that they do not decide for us independently of where we stand or where our history places us. The idea that not everything is possible at any time is simply a reminder that I am always situated, always historical, always the inheritor of certain parameters of poetry-writing or the making of artworlds. These parameters are my responsibility, and I express this responsibility by drawing them, these parameters, perhaps in defiance of the fear of exclusion, or the threat that others, seeing me draw (or write), will say that I have merely transgressed them to no purpose, that what I have done is not poetry or art. But my writing is not (before everything) answerable to them, and so I might have to give up the name of poet (capital P) in order to write what I do, much the way David Antin gives it up when he says that if Robert Lowell is what a poet is, then he (Antin) is not a poet.[70] Cavell likes to quote Emerson's "Self-Reliance" to this effect: "I would write on the lintels of my door-post, *Whim*" (SW 137).

So, to bring the point home, we may imagine poetry-writing by analogy with walking. In *Conditions Handsome and Unhandsome* Cavell writes:

Suppose one day I start sliding my feet one after another rather than lifting them (lots of people more or less do that now), or start skipping or hopping or goose-stepping or whirling once around on the toes of each foot in succession. If you question me about this perhaps I answer: "I've always meant to do this, you just did not know," or, "I didn't know what moving along the ground could be until now, the inclination is powerful and the results are wonderful." But suppose I answer: "I don't know what has come over me, I don't want this, the inclination is not mine, it mortifies me." Or just: "I'm doing the same as I've always done, the same as you do, making measured moves in a given direction under my own steam. I am not moving faster than walking, we are comfortably keeping up with one another—not like our acquaintance far back there who takes a step once a minute and calls that walking." Wittgenstein's comment seems in place here: "It would now be no use to say: 'But can't you see . . . ?'—and repeat the old examples and explanations" (§185). That is, I surely know everything about walking that you do. What you respond to as deviant behavior in me is a threat to me; what I do smacks a little of insanity and I will soon be kept, at least, out of most public places. You might put tremendous pressure on me to conform—do you think I do not know intolerance? I know very well the normativeness of the way things are done—and not just in this society (as though the normativeness were merely something justified by custom or morality); I know of no society that enjoys, or deplores the fact that it engages in, walking as I do, though I might explore for one.[71]

Compare Robert Creeley's "Was That a Real Poem or Did You Just Make That Up Yourself?"[72] No explanation, no theory, can account for the way one walks, which means that in walking we always risk ourselves, expose ourselves, for example to stares or ridicule or even arrest—picture the race-walking style at the Easter parade.

> God help him then
> if such things can.
> That risk
> is all there is.[73]

"I know of no society that enjoys, or deplores the fact that it engages in, walking [writing poetry] as I do, although I might explore for one." My thought is that the language poets give us a sense of what this might mean. In "Canons and Institutions: New Hope for the Disappeared," Ron Silliman takes up the problem of poets who disappear "from the public discourse and consciousness of poetry"— really the ancient or once and future problem of the unacknowledged poet. What counts as acknowledgment? The question of poetry finally comes down to this. Silliman attacks the edifice of a vertical culture—that is, the idea is that there is, or has been at least since the 1950s, a "process of public canonization" that is tied to the university study of literature and is therefore in the control of people like Helen Vendler, whose *Harvard Book of Contemporary Poets* has become oddly expressive of the poets it notoriously excludes—Charles Olson and Robert Duncan, for example, whom Silliman identifies as "outsider poets" who "perceived their own poetry as part of a larger project of constructing a new public canon, not necessarily more heterodox than that which they confronted [e.g., the old Oscar Williams *Little Treasury of American Poetry* widely used in the 1950s], but rather utterly different and extending well beyond the borders of poetry, the ultimate purpose of which was to have served as the foundation for a new paradigm of knowledge and agency in social life itself."[74] The important point is that "a new poetic canon, an alternative tradition," is not reducible to a new style or a set of recognizable formal features that enable us to tell (just by looking) that what we are looking at is a poem as such or a poem of a certain species; rather it comes down to the construction of a (local) poetic culture, a social grouping of poets who not only write but also read or listen to and study one another and, as in the case of the language poets, publish one another's work—and who provide, in their exchanges with one another, a discursive background against which their poems can be understood. So the poem is no longer a commodity that can be shipped anywhere but is internal to a collective or social achievement of habitation. Silliman's argument is that it is not enough for "outsider poets" to produce alternative anthologies (like Silliman's own *In the American Tree*) to counter those anthologies that carry the imprimaturs of university presses and large commercial publishing houses. There are plenty of anthologies. Likewise the point is not to win for the language poets recognition from critics like Vendler. To be sure, for Silliman the problem of the unrecognized poet is institutional. He takes it as analogous to the problem of radical or oppositional politics with respect to the Democratic Party—how to get the institution to acknowledge what is external to the legislation of its concepts. But as Silliman well knows, universities cannot be a substitute, and only rarely can they be an occasion, for poetic communities (San Francisco, Black Mountain, New York, Iowa City) in which the question of what counts as poetry can be addressed in a nontrivial way, namely, as Adorno might say, as a type of utopian social practice.

But then there will always be surperb poets whose lack of recognition derives from a kind of antique or Jamesian restlessness, the exiles, wanderers, misfits, whose audiences require a long time to form themselves, and perhaps never do, there being almost too much to know: for example, John Matthias, an American poet who, although formally very much in the tradition of open form that gives us language poetry—

E. has written to me once a year for eight years straight. This year it's about my poems. And his. His muse grows younger (he is over sixty-five) as mine begins to age. My attraction to quotation, commentary, pastiche: exhaustion? or the very method of abstention [from solitary singing?] that he recommends. Many days I'd be a scribe, a monk—and I, like monk and scribe, am permitted to append the meanings that my authors may have missed. "He abandoned himself to the absolute sincerity of pastiche": on Ekelöf, Printz-Pahlson. Otherwise? Poets know too much. We bring things on us. There is always an extra place at the table: the poem, as Ernie says, arranges it. . . .[75]

—nevertheless stands outside all the familiar "poetic communities." No doubt this is due to his having been expropriated (there seems no other word for it) by the British countryside, among other places, whence his sense of place is expressed by a kind of Brownian movement back and forth between Suffolk, England, and Indiana (a movement described in what he calls his "mid-Atlantic poems," the "Stefan Batory Poems," and the "Mihail Lermontov Poems," named after the ships that shuttled him between England and America). Matthias's poems are as much the product of the difficulty as of the achievement of habitation, which is perhaps why they are full of itineraries, trails, rivers, turns, crossings, explorers, traders, missionaries, pilgrims, not to mention modern exiles, drifters, refugees, lost friends, fugitives, poets hounded by authorities and, in general, people violently out of place ("Alexander Kerensky at Stanford"; "Paul Verlaine in Lincolnshire").[76]

It is worth a moment's reflection on how far poetry (American poetry in particular, where the metaphor of the open is foundational) is inspired by a terror of confinement—confinement, not, perhaps, as in Eurocentric theory, within history or the prison-houses of language, culture, and ideology, but, quite the contrary, confinement as being sealed-off, as in confinement to a self that, Descartes-like, lacks embodiment, or to a place that, say to the eye of a purely ascertaining observer, is blank, forbidding, uninhabitable, innocent of speech—a condition that forms the subject of Emerson's "Experience," with its reference to "this yet unapproachable America."[77] Whereas the language poets consult their ears, Matthias's difficulty of habitation is mediated by the names, the lore, and the layers of historical narrative and encyclopedic detail that attach to the places he crosses (from the Midwest to East Anglia to Scandinavia to Poland, and back again). So a place is, once more, a surface across which one moves rather than a container of objects; and, again, the surface is traversable only through its language—language in the sense of the words of other people, language aroused by reading and listening, whence the need for quotation, commentary, pastiche: the poem is the reception of this language, hence of the place it embodies. Matthias's collection of three long poems called *A Gathering of Ways*, for example, is an archeology of the multilanguaged discourse surrounding the waterways and trails (called "ley lines") used since neolithic times by travelers in East Anglia, the American Midwest, and Provence. The second of these poems, "Facts from an Apocryphal Midwest," is a pastiche of geography, geology, history, and local legend about American ley lines and rivers, for example the Old Sauk Trail and the Saint Joseph—Kankakee Portage, and, besides the Kankakee and Illinois, the Saint Joseph River near which Matthias lives but to which, all by himself, or as if (just) in his own voice, he could never belong.

Never having walked a foot along the banks of the St. Joseph river, I now followed [Francis] Parkman—who must have trudged virtually through my back yard on his visit to the area in 1867—followed La Salle who followed his Indian guide along the portage trail to the Kankakee marsh. With respect to the self, the solution seemed to be this: that I, who had little feeling for the place I would evoke and engage, should embody myself in a figure who had great feeling for it, who in turn embodies himself in the figure who initially explored the place, contended against it, and had perforce to fit his mind to the external world to survive and the external world to his mind to prevail.[78]

This is Matthias's way of reading himself into his own poem, where Parkman is characterized as follows:

The man who followed him [the explorer La Salle] in many ways was like him, and read his words, and read the words and followed all the trails of others who had passed this way before he did himself, but after him who was the first to come and was the object of his search. Charlevoix he read, and La Hontan. Tonty's own account, and Hennepin's, and all of La Salle's letters both to Canada and France. Transcripts, depositions. He too knew about insatiable ambition, pride and isolation, subduing all to an inflexibility of purpose. When his chronic and mysterious illness made his head swim and his joints swell, made his eyes so sensitive to light he could not read, his nights so sleepless that he could not even dream his shattered double's thousand mile trek from the lower Illinois back to Montreal, he had his friends read *to* him, tried to comprehend their strange pronunciations of the language of the texts and maps and manuscripts *de la France Septentrionale* which he followed to the Kankakee or Seignelay and then beyond.[79]

The self in this event is no longer the sealed-off punctual ego or purely ascertaining observer who monitors the lifeworld; it is a self embodied in another's words, as if there were no getting into the world—or, in other words, as if there were neither self nor a world for it—except through the mediation of other voices, other people, which is a nice interpretation of the moral of skepticism. And so it no longer makes sense to speak of a separate realm of subjective validity; rather this validity is now socially mediated as by an open, porous subject given as much to listening as to speaking. The special turn given to this line of thinking by John Matthias is that, like poetry, the self is excessive with respect to its boundaries: its habitations are on the way.

8

Wallace Stevens
without Epistemology

I shall whisper
Heavenly labials in a world of gutterals.
It will undo him.
            —Wallace Stevens, "The Plot against the Giant"

The word "epistemology" in my title is to be taken loosely to mean a concern for how the mind links up with reality. The question I want to ask is this: what happens to our reading of Wallace Stevens's poetry when the problem of how the mind links up with reality is no longer central for us the way it was for Stevens?

> She was the single artificer of the world
> In which she sang. And when she sang, the sea,
> Whatever self it had, became the self
> That was her song, for she was the maker.[1]

What is it no longer to take these lines as a touchstone?

Let me try to clarify this question by situating Stevens's poetry within the following history (or imaginary schema) of conceptual changes. There was a time when questions about nature, reality, or the world began to be reformulated as questions about mind, consciousness, imagination, or knowledge rather than as questions about God. This was the epistemological or subjectivist turn in Western thinking when (beginning, as the story goes, with Descartes's *cogito* and Kant's "Copernican Revolution") Mind or Reason or Spirit replaced Being as the "metaphysical centrum" of reality.[2] Then there came a time when questions about mind or consciousness (and therefore also questions about reality) began to be reformulated as questions about language. This was the linguistic turn, also known as the narrative turn, sometimes identified with the line, *n'est jamais present hors d'un système de différences*, or with the idea that our descriptions of the world remain internal to our vocabularies, ideologies, conceptual schemes, paradigms, cultural systems, forms of life, and so on. Finally, there came a time when questions about language (and also therefore questions about mind and reality) began to be reformulated as questions about social practice, political action, and ethical relations within singular, contingent, open-ended events of human history: questions, in short, about how people encounter one another in particular human situations. Call this the hermeneutical turn, where hermeneutics means something more than methods of textual interpretation, since it has to do with understanding as a mode of being (being with others in the proximity of the world). Here the issue is not so much how the mind links up with reality (or with language or a text or a cultural system) as how we link up with other people in everyday life.

We know—because Stevens teaches us—what it is to read his poetry when we no longer believe in God, the idea being that we have turned to his poetry in some sense *because* of this alteration in our system of beliefs. He shows his readers what this alteration comes down to. The lines

> The magnificent cause of being,
> The imagination, the one reality
> In this imagined world. (CP25)

will always remain foundational for any understanding of Stevens's poetry. It is also possible to read Stevens within the context of the linguistic turn—but not as easy: I tried to do this many years ago in unblinking defiance of the fact that language just didn't have much reality for Stevens. In order to read Stevens in this way one must recontextualize his poetry much the way J. Hillis Miller does when he says that in Stevens the imagination is not foundational but works like catachresis, that is, naming what cannot properly be named, using language to cover over the *mise en abîme*.[3] My question is: what happens when the reading of Stevens goes around still another bend?

From a hermeneutical or, let us say, ethical standpoint, the main problem for Stevens is not how the imagination works but what to do about other people. For example, one of the "Adagia" reads as follows: "life is an affair of people not of places. But for me life is an affair of places and that is the trouble."[4] What sort of trouble?

It is difficult to gain a sense of this question, because people are not a familiar component of Stevens's poetry, which is made rather of various sorts of imaginary landscapes and ideal objects of description. Stevens's poetry will always be a poetry of the spectator where the main thing is to see something or to construct something and thereby to count it as knowable or intelligible or valuable as a possession of one's own. What Stevens is after is something against which to strike attitudes and to have experiences. Stevens's poetry is a poetry of worldmaking in which "the

tongue is an eye" and the eye is a "silent rhapsodist."⁵ The tongue is meant for
experience rather than for discourse, as much for tasting as for talk; and the ear
is a "secondary" sense (CP374), especially when we are encouraged, as we almost
always are, to listen for sounds that cannot actually be heard. A good conversation
for Stevens is going to be a "Continual Conversation with a Silent Man" (CP359),
which is no doubt why we never learn what Ramon Fernandez has to say about
"the glassy lights" that master the night and portion out the sea (CP130).

Hugh Kenner was certainly right to say that there are no people in Stevens's
poetry.⁶ Their absence, however, is not inadvertent; on the contrary, the question
of others is a central preoccupation of Stevens's work. The problem of problems
for Stevens has not to do with the absence of people, but with their existence,
that is, their alterity with respect to imagination, their excessiveness with respect
to poetic worldmaking. It has to do with voices from nowhere and the uncanny
power that they have over us, and also with why we cannot abide them. Stevens's
poetry is filled with strange, unwanted, discordant, uncontrollable voices. He says,
"When the mind is like a hall in which thought is like a voice speaking, the voice
is always that of someone else" (OP168).

Naturally when we hear such a voice (sounding as if in a hallway or a corridor
of our own heads) we want to be able to say where it comes from, because being
able to identify its source will be a way of getting rid of it, and we want to be rid of
it. We know what it is to hear such a thing, and it's always frightening, because the
voice, after all, isn't coming from anywhere. It's just there where it doesn't belong.
It is our old nemesis, the disembodied voice, the voice out of nowhere, the voice
of the other or the outsider that has now somehow got inside us, sounding where
our own voice ought to be. We can neither objectify this voice nor appropriate it,
nor can we close ourselves off to it (the way we can to unwelcome sights); it is the
voice sounding at night or in darkness, and often it can simply mean that things
are going to pieces.

> No lamp was burning as I read,
> A voice was mumbling, "Everything
> Falls back to coldness,
>
> Even the musky muscadines,
> The melons, the vermilion pears
> Of the leafless garden." (CP147)

In a poetry of worldmaking this sort of voice is inimical. The best we can do
is to assimilate its antithetical character by calling it "apocalyptic."

An obvious place to engage this theme is with Crispin's experience in "The
Comedian as the Letter C":

> Here was the veritable ding an sich, at last,
> Crispin confronting it, a vocable thing,
> But with a speech belched out of hoary darks
> Noway resembling his. (CP29)

Much of Stevens's poetry is designed to keep Crispin's experience of otherness from happening. For Stevens, success in experience means hearing no one's voice but your own. You can then enter into a new world without any loss of self-possession:

> Out of my mind the golden ointment rained,
> And my ears made the blowing hymns they heard.
> I was myself the compass of that sea:
>
> I was the world in which I walked, and what I saw
> Or heard or felt came not but from myself;
> And there I found myself more truly and more strange. (CP65)

However, this experience (this monologue of worldmaking) is not just yours for the having. It requires you to silence the voice of the other by appropriating it (if you can) into your own interior discourse, as in "Two Figures on a Dense Violet Night," which sounds at first like a love poem but is really nothing of the sort:

> Be the voice of night and Florida in my ear.
> Use dusky words and dusky images.
> Darken your speech.
>
> Speak, even, as if I did not hear you speaking,
> But spoke for you perfectly in my thoughts,
> Conceiving words,
>
> As the night conceives sea-sounds in silence
> And out of their droning sibilants makes
> A serenade. (CP86)

It would be easy to multiply examples of this appropriation of the voice of the other by a discourse of the self that is in turn characterized as a monologue or song of worldmaking. Think of how often the metaphors of the choir and the chorus turn up in Stevens's poetry—rings of men, for example, chanting "Their boisterous devotion to the sun" (CP70). Stevens has many ingenious ways of silencing the "crackling of voices in the mind" (CP292) by converting such sounds into an ideal form that cannot be comprehended except by visual analogies, or by analogies with a soundless music reverberating in an ideal chamber, or by recourse to some figure of transcendence like the "central man," "a mirror with a voice, the man of glass, / Who in a million diamonds sums us up" (CP250). "Owl's Clover," arguably Stevens's most political poem, is rich in conversions of this sort:

> There each man
> Through long cloud-cloister-porches, walked alone,
> Noble within perfecting solitude,
> Like a solitude of the sun, in which the mind
> Acquired a transparence and beheld itself
> And beheld the source from which transparence came;
> And there he heard the voices that were once
> The confusion of men's voices, intricate
> Made extricate by meaning, meanings made
> Into a music never touched to sound. (OP54)

Remember what happens to that great metaphor of human social life in "Of Modern Poetry": "Then the theatre was changed / Into something else" (CP239). To be sure, the theater (or, in its converted state, poetry) "has to be living, to learn the speech of the place." It presupposes other people—"It has to face the men of the time and to meet / The women of the time. It has to think about war"—but only in order to subsume these public things into "something else," something more private, inward, and purely poetic:

> It has
> To construct a new stage. It has to be on that stage
> And, like an insatiable actor, slowly and
> With meditation, speak words that in the ear,
> In the delicatest ear of the mind, repeat,
> Exactly, that which it wants to hear, at the sound
> Of which, an invisible audience listens,
> Not to the play, but to itself, expressed
> In an emotion as of two people, as of two
> Emotions becoming one. (CP240)

This conversion of public dialogue and social interchange into private meditation, and of people into pure emotion, seems to me to summarize the whole point.

Don't misunderstand. I'm not talking about Stevens's conservatism, or his apparent indifference to social and political themes, or his intolerance of historical reality. I'm talking about "the delicatest ear of the mind" and what it refuses to hear, or what it represses. Two references may help to clarify things. The first is to Bakhtin's characterization of human discourse as a conflict between two forces, one that seeks "to unify and centralize the verbal-ideological world" in a single "unitary language" or authoritative monologue, the other that disperses discourse into a "heteroglossia," or what Bakhtin calls the "dialogized heteroglossia," in order to emphasize the constant give-and-take, back talk, and cross-purposes among the multiple and frequently incommensurable languages that make up human speech. It's again like the distinction between the work of Joyce and Husserl. Language in the world is structured like a conversation rather than like a grammar. It is the many-layered discourse of contrary voices in diverse tongues, each expressing its own "socio-ideological" outlook, its own temporal horizon, its own special history. It is not, as logic, linguistics, and philosophy of language would have it, a system that makes possible the endless creative production of new sentences. The task of logic, however, is to bring this heteroglossia under control; it is to reduce it to a single voice.

Interestingly, it was Bakhtin's view that poetry is on the side of logic and defines itself in relation to the pole of unitary language; it requires the silencing of heterogeneous voices—in contrast to the novel, which is heteroglot in its basic structure. Stevens's "The Novel" is a wonderful comic illustration of this idea:

The sun stands like a Spaniard as he departs,
Stepping from the foyer of summer into that
Of the past, the rodomontadean emptiness.

Mother was afraid I should freeze in the Parisian hotels.
She had heard of the fate of an Argentine writer. At night,
He would go to bed, cover himself with blankets—

Protruding from the pile of wood, a hand,
In a black glove, holds a novel by Camus. She begged
That I stay away. These are the words of José. . . .

He is sitting by the fidgets of a fire,
The first red of red winter, winter-red
The late, least foyer in a qualm of cold.

How tranquil it was at vividest Varadero
While the water kept running through the mouth of the speaker,
Saying: *Olalla blanca en el blanco,*

Lol-lolling the endlessness of poetry.
But here the tranquillity is what one thinks.

The fire burns as the novel taught it how. (CP457–58)

One can read "The Novel" as a parody of how a novel sounds, and also as a corresponding celebration of the sounds a noble rider makes ("How tranquil it was at vividest Varadaro"). And one can compare this to "Certain Phenomena of Sound," in which music appropriates the story that Redwood Roamer has to tell and turns the Roamer himself from a tale-spinner into a transcendental ego:

So you're home again, Redwood Roamer, and ready
To feast . . . Slice the mango, Naaman, and dress it

With white wine, sugar, and lime juice. Then bring it,
After we've drunk the Moselle, to the thickest shade

Of the garden. We must prepare to hear Roamer's
Story . . . The sound of that slick sonata

Finding its way from the house, makes music seem
To be a nature, a place in which itself

Is that which produces everything else, in which
The Roamer is a voice taller than the redwoods,

Engaged in the most prolific narrative,
A sound producing the things that are spoken. (CP286–87)

—or, in other words, another monologue of worldmaking.

As Bakhtin contends, "The poet is a poet insofar as he accepts the idea of a unitary and a singular language and a unitary, monologically sealed-off utterance."[7] Plainly, however, Bakhtin's thesis presupposes a European or Mallarméan poetics of elimination as against Williams's *Spring and All*, Eliot's *The Waste Land* ("He Do the Police in Different Voices"), Pound's *Cantos*—all heteroglot poems, loose and baggy monsters, whose multilanguagedness supplies the context for contemporary American talk- and language poetry. The poetry of Stevens, however, answers to Bakhtin's idea of what counts as poetry, a conception that is in fact fiercely held by most readers of Stevens. In his book on Stevens, at any rate, Harold Bloom lays it out brilliantly: "why do we read one poet rather than another? We believe the lies we want to believe because they help us to survive. Similarly, we read (reread) the poems that keep our discourse with ourselves going. Strong poems strengthen us by teaching us *how to talk with ourselves*, rather than how to talk to others."[8]

So a poem cannot be made out of anything, but rather means getting rid of everything but itself:

> A few final solutions, like a duet
> With the undertaker: a voice in the clouds,
>
> Another on earth, the one a voice
> Of ether, the other smelling of drink,
>
> The voice of ether prevailing, the swell
> Of the undertaker's song in the snow
>
> Apostrophizing wreaths, the voice
> In the clouds serene and final, next
>
> The gruntled breath serene and final,
> The imagined and the real, thought
>
> And the truth, Dichtung und Wahrheit, all
> confusion resolved, as in a refrain
>
> One keeps on playing year by year
> Concerning the nature of things as they are. (CP177)

"The world of poetry," Bakhtin says, "no matter how many contradictions and insoluble conflicts the poet develops within it, is always illumined by one unitary and indisputable discourse. Contradictions, conflicts, and doubts remain in the subject, in thoughts, in living experiences—in short, in the subject matter—but they do not enter the language itself. In poetry, even discourse about doubts must be cast in a discourse that cannot be doubted" (DI286). Thus it is not surprising that even the deconstructive Stevens of the late poems—the Stevens of J. Hillis Miller and Joseph Riddell, for whom ground turns into figure and back again— holds fast against Babel to the attitude of soliloquists, rhapsodists, choristers, and trees shouting in unison:

The trees have a look as if they bore sad names
And kept saying over and over one same, same thing,

In a kind of uproar, because an opposite, a contradiction
Has enraged them and made them want to talk it down. (CP522)

My second reference is to the first chapter of Geoffrey Hartman's *Saving the Text*, "Words and Wounds," in which Hartman speaks of the "ear-fear" that closes contemporary literary criticism off to the voice and to the power of the word to wound us (and perhaps also to heal or cure us) when we hear it—that is, when we open ourselves to it in an active listening.[9] Yet listening is not easy, because listening cuts against the grain of enlightenment and rationality. Hartman wants to recover the old idea that poetry is thaumaturgical—capable of wounding or curing in the way that curses and benedictions once did—but this requires that we read it with a "conscious ear" (CP141). The difficulty is that in reading this way we put ourselves at risk, for we expose ourselves to alterity. "When the mind is like a hall in which thought is like a voice speaking, the voice is always that of someone else": *that* is the experience of alterity. Stevens, it appears, knew it well, and liked it not at all.

Hartman's theme is "the vulnerability of the ear," and his thinking on this point shows the influence of Emmanuel Levinas, for whom the "saying" that occurs in dialogue is more than simply "a modality of cognition"—that is, more than simply the conveying of information with a view toward subsequent decoding by whoever happens along.[10] Dialogue does not consist in an exchange of views or a contest between them; rather, it consists "in the uncovering of oneself, in sincerity, the breaking up of inwardness and the abandon of all shelter, exposure to traumas, vulnerability."[11] Dialogue means the loss of subjectivity (a terrible loss for an idealist, since this means the loss of self, world—everything).

Hartman pursues this line of thinking as part of an ongoing quarrel with the structuralist's reduction of *parole* to *langue*. But in "Words and Wounds" he introduces the notion of the voice and its unsettling power over us in order to undo a puzzle in the connection that Derrida makes between speech and metaphysics. In Derrida's celebrated line about "the death of speech" and the beginning of writing one can see the resurgence of ancient anxieties about the voice that Enlightenment dreams of a philosophical language were meant to dispel, a philosophical language being the Husserlian or anti-Joycean one in which everything can be said exactly without need for interpretation. Derrida's early writings look like a powerful critique of philosophical language on behalf of speaking several languages at once, but the odd thing, as Leibniz and Bishop Wilkins knew, is that this is a language that can only be written: whence its power, that is, its ability to free itself from equivocation or to produce sentences whose meaning is determined by logical form or delimitable situations of use.

Writing represses, displaces, or demystifies the phenomenon of voice in order to emancipate us from bondage to divine or demonic presences, and it is in accord with this emancipation that univocity, agreement with reality (or the next best thing, freedom from illusion, or the knowledge that our fictions are only fictions), reflexivity, clarity of perception, self-certainty, orderly progress, hierarchical construction, and so on become possible. Jack Goody has spelled out this idea in *The Domestication of the Savage Mind*, in which he argues that literacy is specifically productive of the critical attitude that makes philosophical thought possible.[12] Writing displaces the attitude of listening. To put it as plainly as possible, writing is foundational for philosophy; or, as Stanley Cavell says, foundational for philosophy of a certain systematic kind—philosophy as argument, which is a species of discourse that presupposes the suppression of, among other things, the human voice. As Arthur Danto says in connection with Cavell but in reference to anyone's philosophy: "the voice does not penetrate the philosophy; the philosophy is the arguments. . . . This is the bottom line view of philosophy, that philosophy does not vary in any significant way depending upon whose fingers it comes out of or out of whose mouth it issues. The bottom-line view of philosophy is what underlies blind reviewing, and that means suppressing whatever does not on the bottom-line account belong to the philosophy. And that means, as I see it, the suppression of voice."[13]

Cavell finds very puzzling "Derrida's sense, or intuition, that bondage to metaphysics is a function of something called voice over something called writing; whereas for me it is evident that the reign of repressive philosophical systematizing—sometimes called metaphysics, sometimes called logical analysis—has depended upon the suppression of the human voice."[14] Hartman's reading of Derrida's *Glas*—a collage of texts by Hegel and Genet played off against one another by Derrida's punning commentary—reveals both the source of Cavell's puzzlement and how it may be resolved. Derrida may speak of the privileging of voice and the marginality of writing; but in order to make sense of him, one must see how his thinking turns inside out, since what he has done in *Glas* is to compose a text that works like an epitaph for philosophical language and the return of repressed voices (the voice of Genet, e.g., who is now made part of a dialogue with the monumental Hegel). *Glas* is nothing if not heteroglot. Following Cavell's insight and Hartman's line of thought, one could call *Glas* the closest thing in French to an American text, where an American text is that which is animated by alien voices—strange, unwelcome, unsettling voices that fail to cohere into a chorus. Hartman's word for such a feature is "glossolalia," or speaking in tongues, originally a sacred, now a poetic gift.[15]

Wallace Stevens is an American poet who does not compose American texts.
Indeed, it has been remarked often enough that Stevens composes the closest thing
in English to French texts—texts that, as in the case of Mallarmé, repress the voice
in favor of *écriture*.[16] Sound in such a text aspires not to the illusion of someone
speaking but to the formal conditions of music. Think of the character of sounds
in Stevens's verse. A score of dissertations must have made the point that Stevens's
ears are tuned to exotic noise:

> In Hydaspia, by Howzen
> Lived a Lady, Lady Lowzen,
> For whom what is was other things. (CP272)

Such sounds have been constructed as objects of aesthetic interest, making
no claim on anything but a contemplative ear; they are sounds that do not require
us to answer, sounds that we do not actually have to hear:

> Tell X that speech is not dirty silence
> Clarified. It is silence made still dirtier.
> It is more than imitation for the ear.
>
> He lacks the veritable complication.
> His poems are not of the second part of life.
> They do not make the visible a little hard
>
> To see nor, reverberating, eke out the mind
> On peculiar horns, themselves eked out
> By the spontaneous particulars of sound.
>
> We do not say ourselves like that in poems.
> We say ourselves in syllables that rise
> From the floor, rising in speech we do not speak. (CP311)

Which poet could be more easily substituted for the poet X—Mallarmé or
William Carlos Williams?

What is interesting about Stevens—and this is *his* strange, difficult way of
being an American poet—is the way in which he plays out the fear and repression
of alien voices as a sort of dramatic obsession. I have said that Stevens's poetry will
always be a poetry of the spectator where the idea is to see something. But the
point is that he is a poet troubled by the sort of poetry he is *not* writing, the poetry
he defines himself against (as in his antivernacular complaints against Williams).

This is the context in which I like to read "The Course of a Particular," with its ambiguous cry of the leaves:

> Today the leaves cry, hanging on branches swept by the wind,
> Yet the nothingness of winter becomes a little less.
> It is still full of icy shades and shapen snow.

> The leaves cry . . . One holds off and merely hears the cry.
> It is a busy cry, concerning someone else. (OP96)

Of all the sounds in Stevens's verse, the cry may be said to have a special character because it so often betokens otherness, as in "Not Ideas about the Thing but the Thing Itself," in which "a scrawny cry from the outside / Seemed like a sound in his mind" (CP534). In any event, the characteristic movement of Stevens's imagination is to convert otherness into aesthetic identity, whence the "scrawny cry" proves after all to be simply "A chorister whose c preceded the choir" (CP534)—not something alien, but rather a momentary dissonance, an unsynchronized sound. So, in "The Course of a Particular," the poet finally concludes that the cry we have heard is nothing to be alarmed about: it is not a "human cry" (CP96), and certainly not a divine one, but only leaves making their normal eerie sound:

> It is the cry of leaves that do not transcend themselves,
> In the absence of fantasia, without meaning more
> Than they are in the final finding of the ear, in the thing
> Itself, until, at last, the cry concerns no one at all. (CP96–97)

Or, in other words, in its "final finding" the poet's ear has dispelled its fear, but only by making familiar the otherness of the cry that initiates the poem. When "One holds off and merely hears the cry"—that is, when one simply listens—one is open to the voice of "someone else": it is only by converting to "the delicatest ear of the mind" that one can conclude, as the poet does, that "the cry concerns no one at all." No need to ask, Who's there?

The counterstatement of Stevens critics would be that all I've been saying is just a vulgar misreading, since plainly a poem like "The Course of a Particular" is what it has always been said to be: namely, a poem about the act of the mind vis-à-vis a certain phenomenon of sound. Nothing "repressive" is going on in the poem; rather, the "conversion" that I imagine taking place is simply the mind's normal work in making poetry possible. In this case the poem's obvious point is that poetry is not always possible—not, for example, in "the nothingness of winter," when the mind and its phenomena just don't come together. Otherness, in other words, reduces to disharmony:

> And though one says that one is part of everything,
> There is conflict, there is a resistance involved;
> And being part is an exertion that declines:
> One feels the life of that which gives life as it is. (CP96)

In short, the poem is a well-known poem of decreation and (more important) demystification:

> The leaves cry. It is not a cry of divine attention,
> Nor the smoke-drift of puffed-out heroes, nor human cry. (CP96)

That is what leaves sound like in "the absence of fantasia": they sound like leaves!

This certainly can't be wrong. On the contrary, it is entirely consistent with the poem in question precisely in the sense that it serves to reinforce the transcendental outlook that Stevens strives in poem after poem to preserve. My point is that the phenomenon of unwanted or discordant voices always threatens this outlook, and this is what Stevens's poetry teaches, particularly in the way in which other voices are obsessively aestheticized:

> Here in the North, late, late, there are voices of men,
> Voices in chorus, singing without words, remote and deep,
> Drifting choirs, long movements and turning sounds,
>
> And in a bed, in one room, alone, a listener
> Waits for the unison of the music of the drifting bands
> And the dissolving chorals, waits for it and imagines
>
> The words of winter in which these two will come together. (OP90)

Of course, it sounds bad, and is a sort of basic critical mistake, to question the Americanness of Stevens's texts simply on the basis of the systematic repression of alien voices, but I think that Stevens would have understood the point at once and would not have been surprised or dismayed by it. A poem that suggests as much is "Autumn Refrain," which contrasts the European nightingale with the American grackle, the literary and the vernacular, the written and the spoken, purity and disruption:

> The skreak and skritter of evening gone
> And grackles gone and sorrows of the sun,
> The sorrows of sun, too, gone . . . the moon and moon,
> The yellow moon of words about the nightingale
> In measureless measures, not a bird for me
> But the name of a bird and the name of a nameless air
> I have never—shall never hear. And yet beneath
> The stillness of everything gone something resides,
> Some skreaking and skrittering residuum,
> And grates these evasions of the nightingale
> Though I have never—shall never hear that bird.
> And the stillness is in the key, all of its is,
> The stillness is all in the key of that desolate sound. (CP160)

The poem is organized as a sonnet: (1) A grackle, let us say, is a blackbird meant to be looked at and counted, not to be heard; but in this country *that* is just what one must listen to, as against the melancholy song of the nightingale. To American ears, filled with the vernacular racket of grackles, the nightingale is just a word in a poem by Keats ("The yellow moon of words about the nightingale"). Our most poetic experience, in contrast to Keats's, is of the silence of departed grackles. (2) In "Autumn Refrain," the "skreaking and skrittering" of the grackles yields to the pure poetic measures of the nightingale—but notice that this displacement almost fails. Even after the grackles have gone, leaving the poet alone to imagine the poem he cannot hear, "something resides, / Some skreaking and skrittering residuum" that "grates these evasions of the nightingale." (And so we may speak once more of the return of the repressed.) (3) As always, however, the heteroglossia is appropriated by a unitary language; the mental echo left by the grackles is harmonized, or poetized. It is taken up in the last two lines by a music that only "the delicatest ear of the mind" could hear, namely, the nightingale's melancholy song: "the stillness is all in the key of that desolate sound." What counts as poetry is poetry of the mind; it is antivernacular—"speech we do not speak" (CP311). It is like the difference between "clickering" (CP28) and "immaculate" (CP128) syllables. "Skreaking and skrittering," like the "gibberish of the vulgate" (CP397)—this is the world we hear, until, like the man on the dump, we manage, if we can, to withdraw into our own voice:

> One sits and beats an old tin can, lard pail.
> One beats and beats for that which one believes.
> That's what one wants to get near. Could it after all
> Be merely oneself, as superior as the ear
> To a crow's voice? Did the nightingale torture the ear,

Pack the heart and scratch the mind? And does the ear
Solace itself in peevish birds? Is it peace,
Is it a philosopher's honeymoon, one finds
On the dump? Is it to sit among mattresses of the dead,
Bottles, pots, shoes and grass and murmur: *aptest eve:*
Is it to hear the blatter of grackles and say
Invisible priest; is it to eject, to pull
The day to pieces and cry *stanza my stone?*
Where was it one first heard the truth? The the. (CP202–3)

We perhaps need not go so far as to imagine the poet (or, indeed, the poem) as a windowless monad. Stevens here simply satisfies the idea of poetry as a region of subjective validity—of the "unrestricted commerce of the ego with itself"[17]— as against the idea that poetry, like subjectivity itself, requires the mediation of other people.

9

Stanley Cavell's Shakespeare

*It is very unhappy, but too late to be helped, the discovery that we have made, that
we exist.*

—Ralph Waldo Emerson, "Experience"

The principal concern of philosophy since Descartes and Kant is, arguably, how
we connect up with the world. Stanley Cavell is a philosopher who asks what
happens to this question when we imagine a world made of other people rather
than of objects studied by science or reduced to concepts by reason.[1] One thing
that evidently happens is that our relation to the limits of knowledge, or of reason, is
altered, or perhaps our understanding of these limits, or indeed of what knowledge
is—what its costs are—is turned in a direction philosophy is not accustomed to
follow. Near the end of *The Claim of Reason* Cavell says that at any rate he was "pushed
to pieces of literature to discover the problem of the other," because he found
"the problem largely undiscovered for philosophy," or at least English-speaking
philosophy (CR476). The pieces of literature in question are some of Shakespeare's
tragedies, which Cavell doesn't hesitate to think of as works of philosophy as well
as of literature, as when he says, for example, that "the advent of skepticism as
manifested in Descartes's *Meditations* is already in full existence in Shakespeare,
from the time of the great tragedies in the first years of the seventeenth century,
in the generation preceding that of Descartes" (DK3). In what follows I want to
find out what it is to understand Shakespeare in this way, that is, not so much as
philosophical texts but as literary texts that a philosopher finds it necessary or at
least important to study. Of course this raises some interesting questions about
what counts as philosophy, or as literature. What are the limits of each vis-à-vis
the other? Cavell appears to be someone who (in contrast, say, to Richard Rorty)
wants to preserve these limits rather than transgress or dissolve them. But more
interesting is the connection that Cavell makes between skepticism and tragedy.
Without claiming to match Cavell's views point for point, I would like to say what
Cavell's thinking with respect to Shakespeare is about, and also where it leaves us
on the question of philosophy and literature.

1. The Moral of Skepticism

Some sense of how Cavell thinks can be got from the speculation that there is an internal coherence between Descartes's doubt and Othello's.[2] The difference between them is perhaps that Descartes's doubt is comic. It is a methodical skepticism that emancipates him, or part of him, from the burden of the past, that is, from the weight, or blockage, of learning—the patrimony of Aristotle, for example, or indeed the whole Western philosophical tradition, with its endless, tormented school rehearsals and ecclesiastical controversies. Whereas Othello's doubt is, philosophically, something else, something closer to, made of the stuff of, skepticism itself. What Othello wants to possess and can never have (cannot in the nature of the case, because he is human) is Desdemona's own self-certainty of her fidelity, that is, her own self-experience of her love for him—a self-certainty or self-experience that has at least the philosophical force or foundational strength of the *cogito*. Remember that Descartes could doubt the existence, or validity, of everything, even his own body, but *not* his doubt. His very experience of doubting—which, oddly, he called thinking—was (to him) indubitable. With it he could prove the existence of the world, or anyhow of God; proving the existence of the human proved to be a separate problem that did not get clearly formulated until Mary Shelley's *Frankenstein* and E. T. A. Hoffman's "The Sandman."[3] We can imagine that Desdemona has no doubt, has what might be called a Cartesian certainty, of her faithfulness to Othello. This is the knowledge that Othello desires, what he is jealous of: imagine that he wants to not-doubt Desdemona as she not-doubts herself, as Descartes could not doubt his own existence. I mean that we must imagine Othello wanting to possess Desdemona's self-experience as his own; nothing short of this experience could confirm for him, beyond doubt, her fidelity. So jealousy, on this line of thinking, becomes the condition of skepticism, of not having the world present to us in the way of knowing, where knowing occurs in the intimacy of self-experience. What Othello and Descartes have in common is that, in order to overcome, or destroy, their doubt—in order to refute skepticism and to experience knowing (for sure)—they are willing to give up (in Othello's case, kill) the world (the other, the body, the human). Think of *Macbeth* (which is never far from Cavell's thoughts), where the desire to possess the world, to know it as one knows oneself, means refusing, or killing, the human in oneself. What is it to find one's humanness, one's ordinariness, one's nakedness, one's own self-intimacy, unendurable? Shakespeare's tragic heroes know—perhaps any tragic hero knows. Why does Oedipus put out his own eyes? To escape forever the experience of being seen.

In *The Claim of Reason* Cavell writes: "I do not picture my everyday knowledge of others as confined but as exposed" (CR432). Exposure to reality is what happens in *Hamlet*, although it occurs nowhere (anywhere, in any literature) so powerfully as in

King Lear, where it is what Lear fears more than anything, what he will do anything to avoid (so also, in his way, Othello, whose fear of exposure to Desdemona's sexuality is something Cavell calls special attention to). Plato knew that it is this sort of exposure, say to the wrong sort of desire, that the philosopher has to be sealed off from if philosophy, or knowledge—for example, seeing Justice, among other things, face to face—is to be possible. It is part of Hamlet's philosophical and also tragic misfortune that his encounter with Justice occurs *as* his exposure to its fragmentation and withdrawal, its *pseudos* and its other. Of course it is almost impossible to number the terrible consequences of Hamlet's desire for certainty (which is continuous with his desire not to expose himself to the world around him), but at least one lesson of *Hamlet* is, certainly, that our relationship to Justice is not one of knowing, much less having; and this, in Cavell's language, is also the lesson of skepticism—he calls it "the moral of skepticism, namely, that the human creature's basis in the world as a whole, its relation to the world as such, is not that of knowing, anyway not what we think of as knowing" (CR241).

But if not knowing, what? We might want to say, as Hamlet (prematurely) seems to assume, that we connect up with things by way of action, not thought (not acceptance)—say in the form of dumb shows that will *compel* how things are to expose themselves, lay themselves open to view, make us sure of them, justify us before the world; but Hamlet discovers straightaway that this is no answer, one still can't be sure enough, dumb shows and all; there is no making the world present to oneself, it always exceeds one's grasp. It is no trouble to think of Hamlet's play-within-a-play, or indeed his whole effort of revenge, as a burlesque of Baconian method, since Hamlet experiences, without quite realizing it, the inevitable shortfall of strategic thinking with respect to the world, particularly since the world is made of other people.

Cavell's idea, developed in *The Claim of Reason* and elsewhere, is that skepticism is a story about our disappointment with criteria, or perhaps our unsatisfiability in this regard, as for example when it comes to telling whether someone is in pain or, more drastically, whether someone is human. The skeptic is someone who says that we don't know, can't know, that we know this. That someone is human, the person whose deep eyes captivate me, seems plain enough; being human belongs to what Thompson Clarke, in his essay "The Legacy of Skepticism" (1972), calls "the level of the plain," which is also what Cavell calls "the ordinary." So long as we hold to the level of the ordinary (ground level) we seem safe enough, because, after all, skepticism does not address itself to the level of the plain; its audience is the self-defined rational subject, the one surely in the know. And between this subject and the ordinariness of the plain there exists a sort of allergic relation, since disengagement from the ordinary is what constitutes the *ego cogito,* makes it what it is. We philosophers, Clarke says, "apart from 'creating' concepts and providing their mental upkeep, are outsiders, standing back detached from concepts and items alike (even when items are aspects of ourselves), purely ascertaining observers who, usually by means of our senses, ascertain, when possible, whether items fulfill the conditions legislated by concepts."[4] Do things match up with meanings? Yes, for all practical purposes, but outsiders, "purely ascertaining observers," cannot know this, that is, are in no position to appeal to the level of everyday practice, having reflected themselves out of the ordinary. So they are left, for all practical purposes, without a world.

Cavell turns the "truth of skepticism" into an ethical concept by saying that what others ask of us is not our knowledge that they are present to us like desks or chairs, or that they fulfill the conditions legislated by our concepts of them; rather, as Hegel knew, they ask to be recognized. The essay on *King Lear* puts it squarely: "this is why we think skepticism must mean that we cannot know the world exists, and hence that perhaps there isn't one (a conclusion some profess to admire and others to fear). Whereas what skepticism suggests is that since we cannot know the world exists, its presentness to us cannot be a function of knowing. The world is to be *accepted;* as the presentness of other minds is not to be known, but acknowledged" (DK95). Acknowledgment is not an alternative to knowing, Cavell says, but an interpretation of it, even a critique of it, since acknowledgment is just what an outsider is in no position to give (QO8). Imagine living in a world in which people did nothing else but keep one another under surveillance. Possibly our world is more like this (Hamlet's world!) than we think. At all events acknowledgment means openness and acceptance of the other as such, that is, as other, as that which resists every effort on my part to reduce it to something containable within the legislation of my concepts. The other is excessive with respect to this legislation. It is this excessiveness, like the excessiveness of the philosopher's body, that skepticism has in mind when it questions the *ego cogito.*

2. From Text to Character

All of this might sound a little strange among up-to-date workers in the field of Shakespeare studies. Cavell is not afraid to go back to an older, romantic way of reading Shakespeare, before absorption in character gave way to the unpacking of textual and contextual systems. "The Avoidance of Love" is quite straightforward about this return: "what has discouraged attention," Cavell wants to know, "from investigations of character?" (DK40). Cavell is quick to say that he does not want to institute a new, or restore an old, critical method, one called putting "words back into the characters speaking them" (DK41). His question is rather what, in shifting attention from character to language or text or context, are we (ourselves, as readers) turning away from, or trying to avoid? Whatever it is, it is something very close to what ordinary language philosophy was trying to get back to by turning away from questions of propositional structure or logical form to questions of what people say in this or that situation (what people say when). So in fact it is not simply to Samuel Taylor Coleridge or A. C. Bradley that Cavell returns, but to J. L. Austin, for "the issue," Cavell says, "is one of placing the words and experiences with which philosophers have always begun in alignment with human beings in particular circumstances who can be imagined to be having those experiences and saying and meaning those words. This is all that 'ordinary' in the phrase 'ordinary language philosophy' means or ought to mean" (DK42). So the idea is to read Shakespeare by confronting his characters.

One of the regulating questions of "The Avoidance of Love" is why we are no good at this sort of reading, why we shy away from it in favor of purely formalist or historicist or other sorts of "approaches" that one might teach in school. The reasons, Cavell thinks, are not methodological; or, if they are, method is being used (as usual) to repress the moral, or the human. Part of his purpose in his reading of *King Lear* is to cure us of this repression, this neurosis of method, by getting us to live through the dramatic action of the play, as if all this while we had been missing, avoiding—refusing—its point. So what Cavell proposes is to think through, once more, some of the oldest and most wearisome questions about *King Lear*, principally the question of what motivates Lear in the first place—what, in other words, motivates the action of the play, including our own involvement with it.

The starting point is the question of seeing—what Paul Alpers, in a famous essay, called the "sight pattern," that is, the whole theory of the eyes in *King Lear*.[5] Our intellectual custom is to think of seeing in terms of perception or empirical adequacy. Cavell gets us out from under our empiricism by reminding us that, in *King Lear* as elsewhere, eyes are as much for weeping as for seeing, and also as much for recognizing other people as for perceiving material objects (this last being what most people think of when they think of themselves as seeing: the cat is on the mat). The portion of the sight pattern that interests Cavell has to do with the length to which people will go to avoid being seen. "The isolation and avoidance of the eyes," he says, "is what the obsessive sight imagery of the play underlines" (DK46). What is it to avoid another's eyes? Under what conditions, and by what strategems, will one do such a thing? In *King Lear* (as in *Oedipus the King*) one avoids another's eyes most famously by putting them out, but also, in various ways, by not looking back—by not recognizing, or answering (that is, by refusing) the appeal of another's look, or presence, or existence. The subplot of Gloucester's relation to his sons, mirroring, obviously, Lear's relation to his daughters, is a dialectic of avoidance: Gloucester will not recognize Edmund as his son; Edgar will not disclose himself to (will not allow himself to be recognized by) his father. Edgar's refusal to reveal himself, his delay on this score, however puzzling by itself, is a key to the play because the whole business of avoiding the eyes (the recognition) of another is the expression of a fear of exposure, or say the expression of a sort of foundational shame—a shame that cannot be accounted for by causal explanation (the way, e.g., Sartre tried to account for it by reminding us what it feels like when someone catches us looking through a keyhole): hence the enigma, but also the obviousness, of the opening scene of *King Lear*, in which Lear's behavior defies explanation, but is not implausible for all of that (we do, after all, follow his behavior, watch what comes of it). Foundational shame is, on Cavell's reading, what Lear feels; it is what sets the tragedy going.

"My hypothesis," Cavell says, "will be that Lear's behavior [in the opening scene] is explained by . . . the attempt to avoid recognition, the shame of exposure, the threat of self-revelation" (DK57–58). The opening scene is a ritual of avoidance that Cordelia explodes with her directness. (Cavell stages this scene, as others have, by imagining an oratorical performance, or competition, in which Lear, Goneril, and Regan address the assembled court rather than one another; whereas Cordelia, when she answers Lear so famously—"Nothing, my lord" [1.1.89]—speaks directly to him, conceivably looks him squarely in the eye, means to say something to *him*, without being intelligible in his terms.) Lear turns on Cordelia because he knows, or fears, from her directness, possibly from her look, anyhow from her refusal to play the game, that she can't feign feigning but genuinely loves him: and it is this love (Cavell thinks) Lear cannot bear. "For some spirits," says Cavell, "to be loved knowing you cannot return love is the most radical of psychic tortures" (DK61): a torture specially fitted to fathers, dispensers (so we seem) of children. The torture is that love, or the world, is not to be dispensed with: it always constitutes itself as a claim on our self-possession—a claim that disrupts our self-possession by forcing us out of the mode of knowing into that of answering, out of the mode of just seeing what is there before us, taking it in, into the mode of having to respond, of going out and owning up: what Cavell calls, crucially, *acknowledgment*. On the difference, and internal connection, between knowledge and acknowledgment, Cavell stakes himself as a philosopher.[6]

The question of what sort of philosopher Cavell is has been confused by efforts to link him up with Jacques Derrida. The similarities between them—superficially on the relation of philosophy and literature, more urgently on how they read Heidegger (they are, in their different ways, among Heidegger's best readers)— seem worth trying to sort out, but neither Cavell nor Derrida is up to this task: they are concerned mainly with their own histories, and find one another's writings opaque.[7] Much more to the point is the way Cavell's thinking coheres with the work of Emmanuel Levinas, principally in the ethics of alterity or responsibility to the other that Levinas develops in *Totality and Infinity* and again in *Otherwise Than Being*.[8] Whereas Cavell concentrates on the eyes, Levinas works out the question of the other in terms of our encounter with the face. The face for Levinas is the privileged mode in which the other presents itself. The face cannot be objectified, can never just be seen (unless we spy on it from behind a curtain or a mirror), because the moment I look at it I am transformed, that is, the moment I see it turned toward me, or possibly even not as yet regarding me, I am under a claim that puts cognition out of account: a claim, that is, that cannot be made intelligible by cognition, is incompatible with it. The face is irreducible, "refractory to categories" (TI40); it is, Levinas says, "present in its refusal to be contained" (TI194)—Cordelia's sort of refusal. "The face resists possession, resists my powers. . . . The expression the face introduces into the world does not defy the feebleness of my powers, but my ability for power" (TI197–98). Our relation to the face, to the other, is not one of knowing (cf. DK95); on the contrary, the face, like the world (*as* the world) requires me to forgo knowing—but all this means is that I can no longer maintain myself, except at cost (loss of the world, of intimacy with the world), in the condition of the sealed-off subject of epistemology (the detached observer, the transcendental spectator, the maker of stratagems and player of parts, the wearing of antic dispositions): as a consciousness I am, in Levinas's phrase, turned inside out "like a cloak."[9] It is this exposure that Cavell sees played out in the life of skepticism and in Shakespeare's tragedies.

3. The Step Back

Played out, interestingly, in such a way that we who watch, or read, cannot keep our critical distance except by shutting our eyes to what happens, remaining, as if concealing ourselves, in the dark. "What," Cavell wants to know, "is the medium of this drama, how does it work upon us?" Cavell answers with a highly condensed hermeneutical essay on reading (not watching) *King Lear:*

> My reading of *King Lear* will have fully served its purpose if it provides data from which an unprejudicial description of its "work" can be composed. One such description would be this: The medium is one which keeps all significance continuously before our senses, so that when it comes over us that we have missed it, this discovery will reveal our ignorance to have been willful, complicitous, a refusal to see. This is a fact of my experience in reading the play (it is not a fact of my experience in seeing the play, which may say something either about its performability or about the performances I have seen of it, or about the nature of performances generally). It is different from the experience of comprehending meanings in a complex poem or the experience of finding the sense of a lyric. These are associated with the thrill of recognition, an access of intimacy, not with a particular sense of exposure. The progress from ignorance to exposure, I mean the treatment of an ignorance which is not to be cured by information (because it is not

caused by a lack of information), outlines one motive to philosophy; this is a reason for calling Shakespeare's theater one of philosophical drama. (DK85)

Not much of this will make sense from the analytic standpoint of most forms of modern criticism, where the play is a play of signifiers rather than a play of characters or of people more or less like those we run up against in ordinary forms of life. Cavell's hermeneutics is a species of romantic hermeneutics, where understanding means understanding other people, not texts or meanings or even intentions, that is, understanding the other *as* other (someone outside my grasp).[10] What is romantic about romantic hermeneutics is that, like skepticism, it is an allegory of frustrated desire, namely the desire (in Schleiermacher's formula) to understand the other first as well as, then even better than, the other understands him- or herself. This, as I have mentioned, is Othello's desire—Othello is the first romantic as Cavell, on a certain view, is the last: else how is it that he understands the Moor so well? What Cavell understands, of course, are just those hermeneutical limits that Othello doesn't see, refuses to be bound by: limits imposed by the otherness of Desdemona and the claim this carries. In Cavell's reading this claim is mediated sharply by Desdemona's sexuality, which fills Othello with fear and loathing masked as jealous rage, because it is something (she is something) beyond his control; she exposes him to the part of himself he cannot conquer. As Cavell says, "He cannot forgive Desdemona for existing, for being separate from him, outside, beyond command, commanding, her captain's captain" (DK136). (*Othello*, on this reading, is an allegory of the philosopher and his body. One recalls Descartes's great line in the *Discourse*: "I then examined closely what I was, and saw that I could imagine that I had no body." This is, in a sense, our modernist version of philosophical asceticism: basic body denial.)

The idea, if I have it right, is roughly this: skepticism affirms, in Cavell's motto, "unknowableness from the outside" (DK29), which pretty much puts paid to any spectator theory of knowing. But we could interpret knowing more intimately, not as knowing another from the inside out, knowing secrets—this was still romanticism's desire, and Freud's: to turn the other inside out, exposing all that is hidden, laying the human being bare all the way down—but as turning ourselves inside out, which is what the idea of acknowledgment comes to, rather the way Heidegger's listening and Gadamer's openness and Levinas's "nonallergic" ethical relation imply a turning of the subject inside out, exposing it, giving up the will to explain and desire for absolute self-possession, dropping or setting to one side the Enlightenment project of conceptual control and technological production (whereby we try to shake down the threat of skepticism with theories of worldmaking). Cavell does not so much throw in with this Heideggerian critique of modernism as appropriate it on behalf of Emerson—

With his "jealousy," Othello's violence studies the human use of knowledge under the consequences of skepticism. This violence in human knowing is, I gather, what comes out of Heidegger's perception that philosophy has, from the beginning, but . . . with increasing velocity in the age of technology, conceived knowledge under the aegis of dominion, of the concept of a concept as a matter, say, of grasping a thing. In Kant this concept of the concept is pictured as that of synthesizing things, putting together appearances, yoking them, to yield objects of knowledge: Knowledge itself is explicitly, as opposed to the reception of sensuous intuition, an active thing—Kant says spontaneous; intuitions alone occur to us passively. . . . I have claimed elsewhere ["Thinking of Emerson"] that Emerson contests Kant on this fundamental ground of *The Critique of Pure Reason.* Or if Kant himself is ambivalent about this matter, then Emerson may be seen to contest the ambivalence, putting his weight on the side of receptiveness, of say, intelligible intuition. (DK9)

The key word is *receptiveness,* which might well serve as a partial translation of Heidegger's *Gelassenheit,* nonviolent thinking, letting-be or (as I prefer) letting-go, which comes out as "abandonment" in Cavell's reading of Emerson (SW136): abandonment, not as of children or tasks but rather as a giving up of oneself before these things (children, tasks, lovers, language, the world as made of other people)—a condition Plato, for example, could not, would not, distinguish from *wild* abandon, what poetry *(Dichten)* calls thinking into, as if away from philosophy, and which Emerson, with consummate Unitarian dignity, summarizes in his word *Whim* ("we cannot spend the day in explanation" ["Self-Reliance"]).

For literary criticism as we know and practice it, this would mean taking a "step back" (in Heidegger's metaphor) from the analytical attitude, or say the sort of methodological self-consciousness that asserts itself (Descartes-like, against all that has preceded it) in terms of "strategies" and "approaches" to a textual object or contextual or pantextual systems containing every conceivable network or region of discourse. In contrast to criticism as something strategic and instrumental, where even reader-response criticism is thought of as a technique, Cavell proposes, or "perversely insists," that we *confront* the characters whom we see on the stage (DK102). What this confrontation amounts to, whether it is anything that can be made intelligible in the languages of current critical theory, is something that needs to be worked out. Evidently, if I understand Cavell, we need to imagine putting ourselves, in some sense, in the presence of the characters we are reading about or watching, exposing ourselves to them as to something other than textual functions, occupying *their* present (DK104–5). This is something else besides psychological projection—but it is hard to know what it could mean, if it does not mean, in some very familiar sense, *identifying* with these characters, finding some internal connection with them, taking them as, in some sense, irreducible to mere representations—in other words, taking them as not really intelligible as (just) fictions. Not wanting to take characters as fictions, as mere products of imaginative projection, is what Cavell has learned from Othello's horrifying example of what his (Othello's) imagination did to Desdemona. It is what makes psychoanalysis interesting to Cavell as a critical language—a language, however, that he turns inside out, as if to place the Shakespearean text in the analyst's chair and ourselves on the couch. As if it were the task of tragedy to cure us of something—say of philosophy, or of literary criticism.

This would be Martha Nussbaum's view, for example, or her version of Aristotle's view, that what tragedy cures us of is exactly the sort of desire for self-sufficiency that someone like Socrates tries to arouse in us.[11] We recognize this desire in the very idea of "First Philosophy," in Descartes's *Meditations*, in Kant's "What Is Enlightenment?" and in Husserl's dream of a rigorous, self-justifying philosophy that watches over, criticizes, but finally claims to be outside of the human lifeworld (cf. Habermas on philosophy as "the guardian of rationality"). Literary critics don't quite see this desire at work in their methodological self-assertions, but not seeing this desire may be just the neurotic symptom Cavell is trying to understand and assuage. Cavell recognizes this desire in each of the plays he studies, each of them being readable as a version of philosophy's quarrel with itself—its quarrel over, for example, how much different it wants to be, can afford to be, needs to be, from literature: does it, for example, really want to seal itself off from whimsical, gay, uncontrollable language, repressing memorable stories and outrageous puns in favor of "the propositional style of philosophic discourse"?

4. Philosophy and Aestheticism

Cavell sees in the character of Coriolanus the philosopher who, like Socrates, cannot imagine sharing existence with ordinary human beings—cannot imagine abiding, seriously, with people who (as philosophers delight to say) "just talk" (DK140–41). Coriolanus is a figure, or instance, of the philosopher as rigorous male who desires self-grounding, that is, who finds himself loathsome just to the extent that he has to accept himself as fathered by someone else—someone not himself—fathered, one might say, in the ordinary way, between the sheets, and so belonging to the world, no different from the rest of us. Cavell's essay on *Coriolanus* (entitled "*Coriolanus* and Interpretations of Politics") tries out various sorts of critical questioning, including the question of what it is to understand, or even be, a Shakespearean play, and also the question of how to make intelligible the political impact of such a play—but what Cavell most of all wants to get at is, romantically, the *motivation* of the character, Coriolanus. And, as if in digression from the main issue, he hits squarely on it: "the mother relation is so overwhelmingly present in this play that we may not avoid wondering, at least wondering whether we are to wonder, what happened to the father" (DK156). Cavell lays out a number of speculations on this score ("in decreasing order of obviousness"), saving the best for last: "third, and so little obvious as to be attributable to my powers of hallucination, Coriolanus's effort at mythological identification as he sits enthroned and entranced before Rome is an effort—if one accepts one stratum of description I shall presently give of him—to come unto the Father. (I shall not go into the possibilities here, or fantasies, that a patrician matron is simultaneously father-mother, or that, in replacing his father, he becomes his own father.)" (DK157). But isn't this last possibility, becoming one's own father, the whole point? Isn't it, for example, the prime motivation of modern philosophy, not to say of modernity itself (with its foundational quarrel against the ancients duplicating or echoing philosophy's ancient quarrel with poetry)? What is the *cogito* if not a moment, or seeming experience, of self-fathering? What was the point of all that doubting?

It is worth a moment's reflection that the literary equivalent of the rigorous philosopher is the aesthete—for example, Stephen Dedalus, whose name is allegorical of his desire for "mythological identification," and who seeks in art a sacrament of transubstantiation that will redeem ordinary flesh and blood, transfigure it into something like a "human form divine," worthy of contemplation. It is no accident—indeed, it is requisite to the whole scheme of aesthetic modernity—that Stephen constructs, among other fantasies, a theory of Shakespeare in which (in Buck Mulligan's wonderful phrase) "He proves by algebra that Hamlet's grandson is Shakespeare's grandfather and that he himself is the ghost of his own father" ("—What, Haines said, beginning to point at Stephen. He himself?").[12] In the Scylla and Charybdis or library episode of *Ulysses*, the exposition of this theory gets a little garbled because Stephen, Simon D.'s son, and an ordinary Dubliner after all, is drunk, but enough of it gets through for us to pick out its deep structure: "fatherhood," Stephen says, "in the sense of conscious begetting, is unknown to man. It is a mystical estate, an apostolic succession, from only begetter to only begotten. On that mystery and not on the madonna which the cunning Italian intellect flung to the mob of Europe the church is founded and founded irremovably because founded, like the world, macro and microcosm, upon the void. Upon incertitude. Upon unlikelihood" (U207/170). Cavell has Coriolanus desiring, Christ-like, to "come unto the Father," sit at His right hand, transcendent to all beginnings (DK157). The only society Stephen, Coriolanus-like, can imagine for himself, the only order in which he can see himself really existing, is the Trinity, where he would fit in roughly where God the Son does, that is, as someone who is not fathered in any ordinary way but only begotten—the only begotten Son of the Father, who is Himself unbegotten, hence the uncaused cause, but only in virtue of his self-identity, his divine oneness, with the Son and the Holy Ghost.

What clicks in Stephen's mind is that only begotten and "onlie begetter" are of the same nature, consubstantial, present to one another from all eternity, belonging (in other words) to the same absolute present, enjoying the same absolute priority with respect to what is merely generated, the ground of all generations: "He Who Himself begot middler the Holy Ghost and Himself sent Himself, Agenbuyer, between Himself and others, Who, put upon by His fiends, stripped and whipped, was nailed like a bat to the barndoor, starved on crosstree, Who let Him bury, stood up, harrowed hell, fared into heaven and there these nineteen hundred years sitteth on the right hand of His Own Self" (U197–98/162). Students of the Jesuits will warmly appreciate Stephen's emphasis that he is embracing esoteric heresy here—"Sabellius, the African, subtlest heresiarch of all the beasts of the field, held that the Father was Himself His Own Son" (U208/171)—but the main point concerns the philosophical myth of *Letztbegründung* that this heresy so vividly clarifies. As Stephen says, Rome (read: Philosophy, or Modernity) represses—in a way, interestingly, that Judaism does not—the whole concrete fact of maternity, that is, ordinary nonmiraculous sexual generation, in favor of a self-grounding, self-contained, self-sufficient, patriarchal Being (uncontaminated by the sexuality of the other: Othello's dream). If you ask, Wherever did anyone get the idea of becoming a philosopher?, here you begin to get your answer. The idea of self-sufficiency could not, on a certain view, *not* have occurred to human beings.

Historically, Stephen's Shakespeare theory, like Cavell's, belongs to the same hermeneutical milieu as Bradley's and Freud's, where character is all in all, and where understanding, therefore, means understanding Shakespeare's characters as we understand ourselves and vice versa. Stephen's theory is a proto- or parapsychoanalytic theory to the extent that it depends on our seeing in Shakespeare's tragedies the deep structure of a family romance, where fathers and sons, wives and lovers, brothers and sisters, mothers and daughters torment, betray, and destroy one another within intricate, unstable networks of shifting, multiple, frequently splitting identities. It is this deep structure that binds us to these tragedies, implicates us in them as we are implicated, tangled, in our own lives. We can only remain detached observers by sealing ourselves off in analytic space, that is, in a purely technical, Cartesian self-consciousness, or else in the sort of aesthetic consciousness that Stephen aspires to, and within which he wants to remake the world, thereby ridding himself of it and of his own ordinariness in the bargain.

Stephen helps us to see the subtle but important difference between confronting a character, in Cavell's sense, and projecting oneself onto a character, appropriating him, reducing his otherness to one's own self-identity, situating him in one's own present. For Stephen is, in his way, *not* a detached reader of *Hamlet*, in whose hero he encounters his own disappointment with life and his own desire, amounting to a sense of mission, to revenge himself on it, set it right, be, therefore, his (true, consubstantial) father's son. There are two sets of equations in Stephen's *Hamlet* theory, one transcendental—

$$\frac{\text{God the Father}}{\text{God the Son}} \qquad \frac{\text{Daedalus ("old father artificer")}}{\text{Stephen ("The Daedalus")}} \qquad \frac{\text{Shakespeare (as the Ghost)}}{\text{Hamlet}}$$

—and one ordinary:

$$\frac{\text{Claudius}}{\text{Hamlet}} \qquad \frac{\text{Simon}}{\text{Stephen}} \qquad \frac{\text{Gertrude}}{\text{Stephen's Mother}}$$

What links the two planes is just the story of *Hamlet*, that is, a story of usurpation, infidelity, and sexual debasement in which ordinary life is finally exposed for what it is, a prison-house (a Dublin) in which mythological identity is displaced by an ironic naturalism. Whence there is nothing for it but to hang on to oneself as best one can:

> We walk through ourselves, meeting robbers, ghosts, giants, old men, young men, wives, brothers-in-love. But always meeting ourselves. The playwright who wrote the folio of this world and wrote it badly (He gave us light first and the sun two days later), the lord of things as they are whom the most Roman of catholics call *dio boia*, hangman god, is doubtless all in all in all of us, ostler and butcher, and would be bawd and cuckold too but that in the economy of heaven, foretold by Hamlet, there are no more marriages, glorified man, an androgynous angel, being wife unto himself.
> *Eureka!* Buck Mulligan cried. *Eureka!* (U213/175)

So, in the Joycean economy, Stephen's dream of self-sufficiency—of encountering in the real world the unsubstantial image of himself that his soul constantly beholds—finds its fulfillment, or anyhow one of its expressions, in Buck Mulligan's parody of a Shakespearean tragedy,

Everyman His own Wife

or

A Honeymoon in the Hand
(*a national immorality in three orgasms*)
by
Ballocky Mulligan
(U216/178)

Exactly where the coherence of philosophy and aestheticism takes place is pin-pointed by Cavell in his reading of Coriolanus, which turns, he says, on "an interpretation that takes skepticism as a form of narcissism" (DK143), where narcissism, as the dream, or desire, of self-sufficiency expresses itself as "a kind of denial of an existence shared with others," hence a denial of the political, which means principally (for Cavell) a denial of the human (DK143).[13]

This comes out also in Cavell's reading of *The Winter's Tale*, another family romance of jealousy and revenge, where the skeptical dilemma takes the form of not knowing, not being self-certain, that your son is your own: a dilemma that is the expression of a frustrated desire to be one's own son. What criteria are there for determining that this person before me is my son? This question is a version of the question about criteria that animates the first part of *The Claim of Reason*, which is about our inevitable disappointment with criteria, a disappointment played out in *The Winter's Tale* when Leontes examines the face of his son and fails to find any recognizable features there; so, not seeing himself, Narcissus-like, mirrored in that face—missing, in other words, the obvious moral to be drawn, that sonship requires acknowledgment in order to exist, not vice versa—he refuses recognition, rouses himself instead to jealousy, and sets the whole tragedy, or near-tragedy, in motion, according to a familiar economy: "taking jealousy as derivative of the sense of revenge upon life, upon its issuing, or separating, or replicating, I am taking it as, so to speak, the solution of a problem in computation, in which sons and brothers are lovers, and lovers are fathers and sons, and wives and mothers become one another" (DK213).

5. Cavell's Philosophical Hermeneutics

Cavell's intuition is that there is some internal connection between the condition of Shakespeare's tragic heroes, their narcissism, for example, and our relation to these plays, which we seek to make answerable to our methods. What's the point of our analytical desire to keep these plays, or perhaps these heroes, under our readerly control? We can't let them break out, Pirandello-like, of the frame in which they are intelligible to us the way, for example, that Iago is intelligible as a character out of the morality-play tradition, or as a Machiavel, or as something in some way intertextual. But why not? What are we afraid of? Why must we keep our distance? How can these characters hurt us? What's at stake in reading Shakespeare, where reading is no longer one of the methodological operations of an interpretive community? What is it to read Shakespeare (or any literary text) out of school?

Cavell points toward part of an answer when he asks about understanding "what a Shakespeare play is" (DK156). It is not like knowing an object but is rather like the encounter with another person. What this implies is very close to the dialogical notion of reading that Gadamer develops in his philosophical hermeneutics. By dialogue Gadamer means not just a certain kind of speech-situation—not a situation of intersubjectivity—but rather the *critical* condition in which, for example, characters in Plato's dialogues find themselves when they run up against Socrates, who puts them (and not just their answers to his questions) in question. This condition is one of openness, which is not the open-mindedness of liberal pluralism but exposure in a sense very like the one that Cavell gives this term: exposure to the other, in which our self-possession, or say our existence, is at stake.[14] This is not much different from the notion of exposure that turns up in the tradition of satire. There is a sense in which every literary text is satirical with respect to its readers. In Gadamer's hermeneutics this means that the text resists the conceptual framework in which we try to enclose it in order to make sense of it, that is, it resists our understanding and interpretation in just such a way as to bring into the foreground (expose) the historicality, the situatedness or conditioned character—the limits—of our hermeneutical situation. Gadamer speaks of this historicality in terms of prejudices, but what he has in mind is not just the subjective attitude of prejudgment and expectation but also the cultural formations, the social, political, and intellectual constructions, within which our encounter with the text occurs, and which the text always unsettles, always puts at risk, though we may miss it. Reading in this sense always resembles the working out, as if against the will of the reading subject, of a critique of consciousness. It is this critique that methodological reading programs of the sort one finds in literary criticism, including (paradoxically perhaps) the formal techniques of critique that one finds in various Marxisms and in Habermas, tend to repress.

Cavell formulates this idea according to a psychoanalytic analogy in which the text unfolds a narrative of our repression, or say a dumb show of our darkest secrets and deepest fears, as in the case of *Hamlet*:

> And we already know that the urgency for Hamlet in proving the Ghost's veracity is not alone to convince himself (at least) of Claudius's guilt but to avoid the only other conclusion—that his "imaginations are as foul / As Vulcan's smithy" (III.ii.83–84). It seems to me that our eagerness to believe the Ghost is fortified by a similar concern over the potentially foul condition of our own imaginations. Moreover, since Hamlet tortures and guides himself to put the Ghost's veracity to the proof, any unwillingness on this matter on our part suggests a claim to superiority over Hamlet's intellect that strains belief. I should say that I simply assume that by his "imaginations" Hamlet is referring not alone to Claudius as a murderer but to the vivid pictures he paints of Claudius as his mother's lover. (DK182)

It's important to emphasize that Cavell is *not* practicing psychoanalytic criticism here, that is, *not* proposing a psychoanalytic reading or interpretation of the play, but is, on the contrary, trying to say what it is for us, as readers, to *confront* (or not) Shakespeare's characters, to be exposed to them—caught, as if in a space in front of the text, with everyone suddenly watching us. The point would not, obviously, be to read Shakespeare in order to produce this exposure, supposing that we knew what this would mean in every instance of reading, but to recognize the extent to which our exposure is what occurs in the nature of the case, as if one could not exclude such an event from the act of reading (reading is not spying, or if it is, think of it as, Polonius-style, risky). Cavell likes to phrase this by saying that there is no reading that is not also a being-read. (What is it to be *seen* by a play? Perhaps Claudius knows, if he was watching.)

Cavell has tried to suggest what this might mean in his essay on the politics of interpretation, "Politics as Opposed to What?," where he says that what is political about interpretation is precisely its dialogical character, where the idea is that we cannot claim to have read a text, understood and interpreted it, unless we can say how it has read us, that is, unpacked us, laid us bare, opened us to critical scrutiny, that is, to a questioning to which we cannot adequately respond without being altered in some fundamental way. Gadamer calls this having a "hermeneutical experience," in which the encounter with the text subjects us to a dialectical reversal, a radical restructuring of our self-understanding that "always involves an escape from something that had deceived us and held us captive" (TM356).[15] Like Gadamer, Cavell wants to understand this condition of being read as redemptive or therapeutic, that is, emancipatory, releasing us from some species of mental bondage. "For most of us," Cavell says, "the idea of redemption or redemptive reading and interpretation will not be credible apart from a plausible model or picture of how a text can be therapeutic, that is, apart from an idea of the redemptive as psychological" (TO51). Our relation to the text in this event would not take the form of a projection but rather of a transference in which the text maps itself onto our own situation and gives it, so to say, a language in which it will out, like murder. Some such transference is what takes place in our reading of *Hamlet*, says Cavell, when it comes over us that "Hamlet's actions, not just his dreams, are our dreams" (DK190).

All reading starts out from our sense of alienation from the text. This is an old hermeneutical commonplace. But, like Gadamer, Cavell understands that this alienation is not a barrier to be overcome but a limit to be acknowledged. The idea is not to accommodate the text to our way of thinking but to recognize its alienness, its otherness, as a question put to us, such that understanding the text will mean understanding this question, what it asks of us. Cavell calls this, in his *Coriolanus* essay, allowing the text its autonomy, seeing it in its own terms (DK144), but this is not the same as objectifying the text and regarding it as an aesthetic object that is to be understood only in relation to itself, as autotelic; rather it means something like understanding the resistance of the text, its refusal ("Nothing, my lord"). In

"Politics as Opposed to What?" this otherness is characterized in terms of the *textuality* of the text, its implacable silence, its resistance to interpretation. How is it, Cavell wonders, that "the stillness of the text, or a text's self-containedness, should be interpretable politically as a rebuke and confrontation and be interpretable epistemologically as the withholding of an assertion, on which I have found the defeat of skepticism, and of whatever metaphysics is designed to overcome skepticism, to depend—as if the withholding of assertion, the containing of the voice, amounts to the forgoing of domination"? (TO51). This stillness, this self-refusal, this nonassertive reserve is exactly what Gadamer identifies as the Socratic dimension of every text that comes down to us in tradition, as if it were in the power of the text to reduce us to a state of aporia or bewilderment; as if the text, in the nature of the case, occupied the site that we normally reserve for philosophy understood as a species of radical questioning.[16] So it is not as if Cavell were leveling the "genre difference between philosophy and literature"; rather it is as if literature and philosophy were changing places.

At the end of his essay on *Othello* (which is also the last line of his book, *The Claim of Reason*), Cavell asks whether philosophy can become literature "and still know itself" (DK142). The answer to this question appears to depend on what we think literature is, something on which Cavell himself has remained silent, pointing, at most, to Shakespeare and *Walden* ("I mean *that* over there"), obviously not wanting to get hoist with his own petard. However, if we think of philosophy as something that can only begin in a response to an assertion, we can see the sort of difficulty poetry poses for philosophy, insofar as poetry retains its ancient character as the dark saying or *ainigma*, that which withholds its saying, refuses itself, resists exegesis, forces us into the allegorical posture of speaking on its behalf. This notion of poetry as the dark saying is one that the later Heidegger recuperates in his conception of poetry as *Dichten*, or that which thickens, darkens, grows dense or earthly *(Die Dichtung dichtet)*.[17] The problem with poetry is not so much that its representations are false as that its textuality or reserve, its self-refusal, situates philosophy on the site of the skeptical dilemma and threatens to prevent it from beginning. It plays, so to speak, Cordelia to philosophy's Lear. And so it must be banished.

10

The Last Romantic:
Stanley Cavell and the
Writing of Philosophy

How do we learn that what we need is not more knowledge but the willingness to forgo knowing? For this sounds to us as though we are being asked to abandon reason for irrationality (for we know what these are and we know these are alternatives), or to trade knowledge for superstition (for we know when conviction is the one and when it is the other—the thing the superstitious always take for granted). This is why we think skepticism must mean we cannot know the world exists, and hence that perhaps there isn't one (a conclusion some profess to admire and others to fear). Whereas what skepticism suggests is that since we cannot know the world exists, its presentness to us cannot be a function of knowing. The world is to be accepted; as the presentness of other minds is not to be known, but acknowledged.
—Stanley Cavell, "The Avoidance of Love: An Essay on *King Lear*"

This passage is very close to the conceptual center of Stanley Cavell's philosophy.[1] It occurs in an essay that interprets Shakespeare's *King Lear* as a play about human recognition, or the avoidance of recognition. Cavell offers something like an extended investigation of what the avoidance of recognition is like, what it means, what is so distinctively or crucially human about this event, why it is so tragic, why it is philosophically important. It's not too much to say that this question or family of questions about recognition, acknowledgment, and human responsiveness is what Cavell's whole philosophy is about—from his initial conversion to the ordinary language philosophy of J. L. Austin to his most recent book (*Contesting Tears*) on the film genre that he calls "the melodrama of the unknown woman."

Not everyone is comfortable with Cavell as a philosopher. One possible reason concerns the way Cavell splits the difference between Anglo-American and European ethical theories. In the one, the ethical consists in being or acting in accord with rules, codes, principles, models, beliefs, teachings, communities, theories of the good or the right, and so on. The ethical means getting straight about something and then acting accordingly. It is essentially subject-centered, rule-based, and given to calculative reasoning. The other kind of ethical theory concerns our involvement with other people. It emphasizes the claims others make on us and how we respond or fail (or refuse) to respond to them. The claims are not necessarily ones we are in a position to negotiate. They are often in advance of any beliefs or principles or justifications for acting (or not acting) that we may have. This second kind of theory (identified most often with the French philosopher Emmanuel Levinas) is sometimes called an ethics of alterity or an ethics of responsibility.[2] Cavell is an analytic philosopher for whom the priority of responsiveness and acceptance of others displaces the sovereignty of the cognitive subject. This seems to capture something of the radical spirit of Levinasian ethics. Yet Cavell remains a moral perfectionist who affirms in both Kant's name and Emerson's "the absolute responsibility of the self to itself" (CHxxvii). How responsiveness to others squares with this absolute responsibility will be one of the questions this chapter will try to address.[3]

A second reason Cavell seems eccentric as a philosopher is that, to all appearances, his philosophy is not made of arguments; instead it is composed of descriptions, readings, musings, fantasies, puzzles about words, imaginary conversations, improvisatory flights, obsessive returns to sentences from Emerson and Thoreau, and endless interpretations or reinterpretations of passages from Wittgenstein's *Philosophical Investigations*, which Cavell consults as if it were a scriptural text, not so much interpreting as seeking repeated guidance (as, e.g., from the line "What gives us *so much as the idea* that living beings, things, can feel?").[4] And, not the least, his work is made up of studies of film. Film-watching and philosophizing are not different things for Cavell. The reason they are not different seems to be that philosophy for Cavell has to do with careful attention to particular human situations and to what people say and do in them vis-à-vis each other. Is this a coherent picture of philosophy? Cavell's idea seems to be that the question of what counts as philosophy can't be foreclosed—there is no bottom line as to what philosophy is, because philosophy is, whatever else it is, a matter of writing in which the sound and look of philosophy matter as much to it as its arguments. This means (at least) that philosophy is to be located at the level of the singular and irreplaceable rather than at the level of the universal and the necessary. Hence Cavell's idea, advanced in his recent *A Pitch of Philosophy: Autobiographical Exercises*, that "there is an internal connection between philosophy and autobiography" (PPvii).

I want to try to make sense of this remarkable idea by showing how Cavell's ethical concern with responsiveness to others coincides with his formal concern with how philosophy is written (the coincidence seems intentional: Cavell refers explicitly to "the connection of writing and the problem of the other" [CRxiii]). What Cavell tries to do is to bring the Kantian "I think" down to earth and make it an autobiographical self of responsibility, that is, a self who is intelligible to itself and to others as a "who." One might clarify this last phrase initially by recalling that Kant's way of framing the question of ethics is to ask, What is man? Against Kant, Emmanuel Levinas asks, Who is *Autrui* (the other)? For Cavell both of these questions are embedded in the question of who I am (PH38): "'Who, or what, is this other?' . . . is tied to the question 'Who, or what, am I, that I should be called upon to testify to such a question?' How, and why, am I thrown back upon myself?" (CR429). What he calls "the absolute responsibility of the self to itself" is to give a philosophical answer to this question, and autobiography is one form, a principal form, that this answer takes.

1. Romantic Poetics

Poetics is that branch of criticism (or philosophy) that asks how a poem is written. This question entails the deeper problem of what sort of thing poetry is, and specifically how one tells a poem from a nonpoem. Cavell repeatedly (and from the start) approaches philosophy in something like the spirit of poetics, as in the foreword to *Must We Mean What We Say?* (1969), where he asks explicitly: "What is philosophy? How is it to be written?" (MWxxiii); and again, in the foreword to *The Claim of Reason* (1979), he says that his fascination with Wittgenstein's *Philosophical Investigations* "had to do with my response to it as a feat of writing" (CRxiii). What sort of writing?—"Why does he [Wittgenstein] write this way?" (e.g., confession and dialogue) (MW70)—and how exactly does this way of writing answer the question of what philosophy is? This is also the regulating question of *The Senses of Walden* (1972), which begins with Cavell's puzzlement as to "why [Thoreau's] words about writing in *Walden* are not . . . systematically used in making out what kind of book he had undertaken to write" (SW3). Likewise Cavell says that the difficulty of counting Emerson as a philosopher lies first of all in his writing, which is "indirect and devious" (QO34), "a kind of mist or fog" (NY78), or (like Martin Heidegger's prose) it exhibits "the wild variation and excesses of linguistic form that have always interfered with rationality" (CH38). Not to put too fine a point on it, "contradiction," Cavell says, "is the genesis of his [Emerson's] writing of philosophy" (NY81). But then why isn't his writing *anything but* philosophy?

It happens that the problem of philosophical writing isn't formal—isn't reducible, for example, to questions of logical or even of literary form, unless in the purely negative sense that "philosophy is not exhausted in argumentation" (QO109), nor (indeed) in anything else. Cavell asks, more than once, "How can philosophy . . . *look* like Emerson's writing?" (NY116). And again, in "An Emerson Mood" (1980): "isn't *lecturing* about philosophy an extraordinary, even bizarre, activity, neither a time of solitude nor of conversation? If we agree that it is bizarre, then do we know how *writing* philosophy is any the less bizarre? These doubts may usefully raise the question of the audience of philosophy, perhaps in the form of how philosophizing is to *sound*" (SW152). But how can the sound or look of philosophy matter? The answer is precisely that there is no deep-structure answer to the question of philosophical writing, that is, no saying beforehand, no theory—no philosophy of philosophy—that will give the answer to what counts as philosophy. "We are possessed," Cavell says, "of no standing discourse within which to fit anything and everything philosophers have said" (QO19). But it isn't merely that the question remains unsettled; it is that it *cannot* be settled—logically, philosophically, settled at the level of the universal and the necessary. On the contrary, the answer, for Cavell, comes down to Wittgenstein's line, which Cavell must have quoted a hundred times: "I am inclined to say: This is simply what I do" (PI§217).

How to make sense of this?

The general problem here is a familiar one in literary history. For example, romantic writing is sometimes thought of as a crisis or breakdown in the rhetorical system of genres that had been authoritative for European culture from Roman antiquity until the onset of modernity. As to what a poem is and how it should be written, Virgil was authoritative for Milton as he had been for Dante. Unless one happens to be a natural genius like Shakespeare, one becomes a poet by reading and imitating the classics:

> Be *Homer's* Works your *Study*, and *Delight*,
> Read them by day, and meditate by night. . . .

Or so says Alexander Pope. But by the end of the eighteenth century there is no longer any saying beforehand what a poem is by appealing to models and rules. On a certain Hegel-like view, poetry had now reached the end of its history—and had turned into philosophy, by which it is usually meant that poetic texts now with increasing regularity began to take the question of what counts as poetry, or how poetry is possible, as their subject.[5] Friedrich Schlegel called this self-reflexive writing "transcendental poetry" or "the poetry of poetry." "Other kinds of poetry are finished," Schlegel said, "and are now capable of being fully analyzed. The romantic kind of poetry is still in the state of becoming; that, in fact, is its real essence: that it should forever be becoming and never perfected. It can be exhausted by no theory and only a divinatory criticism would dare try to characterize its ideal. It alone is infinite, just as it alone is free; and it recognizes as its first commandment that the will of the poet can tolerate no law above itself. The romantic kind of poetry is the only one that is more than a kind, that is, as it were, poetry itself: for in a certain sense all poetry is or should be romantic."[6] Poetry is now untheorizable, that is, it is irreducible to genre descriptions. Poetry has a history, perhaps, but no essence.

The formal distinction of the romantic poem is that it has no form; or, put it that the romantic form par excellence is the fragment (a nonform). So romanticism is a species, perhaps *the* species, of aesthetic nominalism. The poem is no longer answerable to a concept; it cannot be justified like an assertion. It is answerable only to the poet who is, Kant-like, self-legislating, but whose laws, un-Kant-like, are local and contingent, more like eccentricities than rules and conventions ("This is simply what I do").[7]

As Coleridge said, "What is poetry? is so nearly the same question with, what is a poet? that the answer to the one is involved in the solution to the other."[8] So an inquiry into the conditions that make poetry possible will henceforward require something like autobiography, as in Wordsworth's *Prelude; or, The Growth of the Poet's Mind*. Part of the difficulty of counting Emerson and Thoreau as philosophers is that they write, so to speak, at the romantic level of poetry, that is, at the level of the local, the contingent, and the autobiographical (the level of what Cavell calls "my voice in my history" [CH64]): whatever final form or generic disposition their writing takes, it is rooted in the notebook, the diary, and the journal, which are not genres but places of writing; and what gets placed in them are not works but sentences. Emerson and Thoreau are, let us say, micro- rather than macrophilosophers, philosophers of the sentence rather than of the proposition, the argument, the system, the universal and necessary rule. They are philosophers who remain on the hither side of the universal and the necessary. (Or do they? Cavell speaks somewhere of romanticism as a universalizing of autobiography.)

The American poet Ron Silliman has remarked that the sentence is the most invisible of linguistic forms: logic, linguistics, philosophy of language take no interest in it because, as Saussure said, the sentence belongs to speaking, not to language.[9] Silliman says that what distinguishes the sentence from the proposition is its resistance to a logic of integration that would subsume it (make it disappear) into a totality—into an argument, say, or a conceptual scheme, or perhaps just a context. An Emersonian essay is famous for the way its sentences do not add up to an argument or any sort of conceptual whole, and the same may be said of Cavell's writing at least since *The Senses of Walden* (1972). The movement from sentence to sentence in Cavell is not continuous; it is dissonant. His sentences tend not to integrate themselves into larger units but to play off one another in ways that are hard to follow; and sentences tend to repeat themselves or their ingredients obsessively.[10] Just so, a sentence is, on Silliman's definition, a fragment, where a fragment is not something broken off from a whole but something external to the possibility of wholeness. When Wittgenstein says, in the preface to *Philosophical Investigations*, that he was unable to weld his remarks into a whole, he is testifying to the resistance of the sentence, or confessing that he is, whatever else he is, a philosopher of the sentence. But what would it be to locate philosophy at the level of the sentence, that is, at the level of the local, the contingent, and the autobiographical?[11] This is the fundamental question—or maybe effort—of Cavell's philosophy, namely to show that "there is an internal connection between philosophy and autobiography" (PPvii). Cavell has argued from the beginning that the procedures of ordinary language philosophy are inherently autobiographical: "if it is accepted that 'a language' (a natural language) is what the native speakers of a language speak, and that speaking a language is a matter of practical mastery, then such questions as 'What should we say if . . . ?' or 'In what circumstances would we call . . . ?' asked of someone who has mastered the language (for example, oneself) is a request for the person to say something about himself, describe what he does" (MW66). So philosophy is, possibly before it is anything else, self-knowledge or at least self-accounting. It is here, one might as well say, that most philosophers (most recently Arthur Danto) break with Cavell.[12]

At this point one could pause to describe Cavell's own writing in terms of Gertrude Stein's philosophy of composition: "begin again and again, prolong the present, use everything."[13] The first phrase is a recipe for fragmentation and has direct application to Wittgenstein's writing. The second is symmetrical with what Cavell confesses to be a "certain craving for parentheses" (MWx). Cavell imagines at one point "a book of philosophy [that] would be written with next to no forward motion, one that culminates in each sentence. This sounds like a prescription for a new music, say a new discourse [in which] the sentence is everything" [QO18–19]. The third echoes William Carlos Williams's motto: "a poem can be made of anything." Is the same true of philosophy? Imagine a philosophy made, for example, of descriptions of movies. There is a line of inquiry that needs to be developed here concerning Cavell's antithetical (or anyhow complicated) relation to the avant-garde. I once tried to show an internal coherence between Cavell and John Cage, principally on responsibility or responsiveness as the point where poetry and ethics intersect. Music is an acceptance of sound (and voice) as morality is an acceptance of others and of the everyday.[14] But pressing this argument runs up against Cavell's "Music Discomposed," which shows a good deal of impatience with the avant-garde scene of the late 1950s and early 1960s in which Cage was a leading figure.[15] The important fact remains that the avant-garde has always placed a great premium on the everyday, the fragmentary, and the singular. If the avant-garde is the preserve of the everyday, why bracket it off from one's thinking?

It is not surprising that Cavell has taken explicit recourse to romantic poetics (with its special attention to the fragmentary and the singular) in an attempt to clarify the question of how philosophy is written—and how this writing is different (if not always distinguishable) from poetry.[16] In Quest of the Ordinary engages this question of how philosophy is written from several directions, more than one of which intersects with the argument (common to romantic and modern avant-garde poetics) that a poem is made of language, but not of any of the things that we use language to produce: meanings, concepts, propositions about the world, narratives, expressions of feeling, and so on—hence the difficulty of fitting poetry to a genre. Poetry is, borrowing a phrase from contemporary poetics, "language as such."[17] How then to tell that a piece of language is poetic? The poet Stéphane Mallarmé tried to answer by way of a distinction between poetic and ordinary language. American poets from William Carlos Williams to the contemporary language poets (e.g., Ron Silliman) reject this distinction, arguing that "a poem can be made of anything," even (as in Williams's poem *Paterson*) newspaper clippings. There is nothing unpoetic about ordinary language. What if this is true even of language used in philosophy (i.e., that there is nothing unpoetic about it)? One could connect this with the difficulty of Cavell's own writing, with its aversion to argumentation and the construction of theories. The idea would be to construe a linkage by way of the concept of "listening," that is, of writing conceived not as assertion but as responsiveness or reception—which Cavell, after Emerson and Heidegger, is inclined to call "thinking" and, almost synonymously, writing (QO24–25). So much of thinking is attunement to language (what else, at any rate, is ordinary language philosophy?). The same, so poets like Williams say, is true of poetry.

In *The Senses of Walden*, Cavell, sounding for all the world like a language poet, says that "Writing . . . must assume the conditions of language as such; re-experience, as it were, the fact that there is such a thing as language at all and assume responsibility for it—find a way to acknowledge it" (SW33). This means three things: (1) "the conditions of language as such" means language as we find it: it is the language as spoken in the world around us, the discourse of everyday life, ordinary language (of course, what Cavell's notion of "ordinary language" entails remains to be clarified); (2) "re-experienc[ing] . . . the fact that there is such a thing as language at all" means experiencing its density, its materiality, its sound and its look, its irreducibility to logical form, its resistance to theory—something comparable perhaps to what Heidegger means by "having an experience with language," which is something that occurs when we realize that language is not under our control, that our relation to it is not cognitive and instrumental; so that (3) "assume responsibility for it—find a way to acknowledge it," means that our relation to language is as much one of listening as of speaking, of "being with" language rather than being in possession of it and, for example, deploying it as a system for framing representations.[18] Cavell speaks of the need to redeem language, not because there is something essentially wrong with it, but because of its enslavement (or, rather, our enslavement) to our institutions, or to our culture—Cavell mentions religion and politics, but he could just as well have mentioned (without having to cite Michel Foucault) all the social and cultural formations designed to constrain, discipline, and appropriate discourse for some higher authoritative purpose, including philosophy—think of Jürgen Habermas's definition of the philosopher as the "guardian of rationality" who stands watch over the human lifeworld.[19] This enslavement is something like a loss of privacy or loss of subjectivity, where "what goes on inside us now is merely obedience to the law and the voices of others—the business Emerson calls conformity, a rewriting of what Kant calls heteronomy" (CR45). Emersonian perfectionism is aimed at just this state of affairs, but what it requires is a turnaround (maybe even a turning upside down) of rationality itself.

2. Madness and Voice in Philosophy

Listening? Responsiveness? Is there a problem with what Cavell means by rationality (and hence philosophy)? Is he one of the "antirationalists" that people like Habermas and Martha Nussbaum warn us against?[20] After all it is true that, following Heidegger, Cavell takes up the question of thinking as something (like listening) that is not convertible into rationality without high cost.[21] In "Aversive Thinking," for example, Cavell explicitly links Emerson to Heidegger's critique of Kantian or subject-centered rationality:

> Emerson's image of clutching and Heidegger's of grasping, emblematize their interpretation of Western conceptualizing as a kind of sublimized violence. (Heidegger's word is *greifen;* it is readily translatable as "clutching.") Heidegger is famous here for his thematization of this violence as expressed in the world dominion of technology, but Emerson is no less explicit about it as a mode of thinking. The overcoming of this conceptualizing will require the achievement of a form of knowledge both Emerson and Heidegger call reception, alluding to the Kantian idea that knowledge is active, and sensuous intuition alone passive or receptive. (CH39)

Interestingly, Cavell reads Shakespeare's *Othello* as an allegory of conceptual violence, where Othello's "clutching" of Desdemona is given a gendered turn as "the violence in masculine knowing"—a knowing that cannot bear the thought of anything or anyone that is not internal to itself, part of its self-possession (DK8–11).[22]

Moreover, as in the case of Heidegger, madness is not an empty concept in Cavell's philosophy. In fact, in his essay on Beckett's *Endgame* Cavell comes out and says that "Every profound philosophical vision can have the shape [the sound and look] of madness" (MW126). (The question of madness is sharply foregrounded in *Contesting Tears,* a portion of which is a gloss on Derrida's statement, "I philosophize only in *terror,* but in the *confessed* terror of going mad" [CT62].) "Being Odd, Getting Even," for example, contains a reading of Edgar Allan Poe's "The Imp of the Perverse," which Cavell takes as, in part, a parody of Descartes's *Meditations on First Philosophy,* as when Poe's narrator says: "I well, too well understand that, to *think,* in my situation, was to be lost." Lost, because thinking here is not consecutive reasoning but a mode of responsiveness or attunement to one's surroundings (e.g., to one's language). Cavell illustrates this in what one might call an avant-garde or language-poet way by noticing that the text of Poe's story is littered with "imp-words" (or word-imps): "*impulse* (several times), *impels* (several times), *impatient* (twice), *important, impertinent, imperceptible, impossible, unimpressive, imprisoned*, and, of course, *Imp*" (QO124). Cavell's comment:

> "Word-imps" could name any of the recurrent combinations of letters of which the words of a language are composed. They are part of the way words have their familiar looks and sounds, and their familiarity depends upon our mostly not noticing the particles (or cells) and their laws, which constitute words and their imps—on our not noticing their necessary recurrences, which is perhaps only to say that recurrence constitutes familiarity. This necessity, the most familiar property of language there could be—that if there is to be language, words and their cells must recur, as if fettered in their orbits, that language is grammatical (to say the least)—insures the self-referentiality of language. When we do note these cells or molecules, these little moles of language (perhaps in thinking, perhaps in derangement), what we discover are word-imps—the initial, or it may be medial or final, movements, the implanted origins or constituents of words, leading lives of their own, staring back at us, calling upon one another, giving us away, alarming—because to note them is to see that they live in front of our eyes, within earshot, at every moment. (QO125)

Cavell's idea is that language is not something under our control, yet it is our responsibility, and this responsibility consists in *not* tuning out what is logically excessive in language, for example the sound and look of words and the way they echo and mirror one another, such that, for example, one ought to let the word *Begründung* in Wittgenstein's *Philosophical Investigations* stand as "begrounding," on the grounds that the English translation, "justification," "misses . . . the metaphorical strain" that circulates through section 217 ("If I have exhausted the justifications I have reached bedrock, and my spade is turned. Then I am inclined to say: 'This is simply what I do'"). Metaphorically, the idea of foundations turns into that of limits—does so, one might say, of its own accord, as if the turn were built into our language. (But there's no "as if": "In the series of words we call sentences, the words I will need meet me half way. They speak for me. I give them control over me" [CR122].)

Attunement to the sound and look of words is, however, not just poetical; it is, Cavell wants to say, philosophical, but philosophy as it occurs at the level of voice rather than at the level of rules, theses, arguments, and refutations. This is, if I have it right, Cavell's argument against Saul Kripke in "The Argument of the Ordinary": the sound of Wittgenstein's "voice" does not just resonate within his philosophy as an expressive aftereffect; it is constitutive of his philosophy, as voice is constitutive of philosophy as such.

How is this to be understood? Part of an answer to this question involves us in Cavell's attempt "to characterize philosophy in terms of the claim to speak for the human—hence in terms of a certain universalizing use of the voice" (PPvii). What sort of universalizing? In "The Argument of the Ordinary," after remarking on the play of voices in the *Philosophical Investigations*, Cavell says: "by now it is becoming clear that each of the voices, and silences, of the *Investigations* are the philosopher's, call him Wittgenstein, and they are meant as ours . . . ones I might find myself in. How else would the *Investigations* form its portrait of the human self, on a par with Locke's *Essay*, Hume's *Treatise*, Kant's *Foundations of the Metaphysics of Morals*, and, like Plato's and Freud's visions, a self that incorporates selves?" (CH83).

I think it is important to ask whether a "universalizing use of the voice" doesn't amount to a silencing of it for the very reason that voice belongs to the singular and irreplaceable, that which is (to borrow a phrase from Levinas) "refractory to categories," resistant to subsumptive thinking or the logic of conceptual construction. What's the point of seeking a philosophy that "renounces philosophical theses" (CH66), that rejects the idea of a disengaged rational ego exercising conceptual control of its world, that seeks an ethical theory based on responsiveness and acceptance rather than on the justification of rules and beliefs—what's the point of a philosophy rooted in "my voice in my history" (CH64), if the idea is to make or allow this voice speak for others—for all others: for the human? How can universalizing of the voice not take place at the expense of the singular and irreducible—that is, at the cost not just of the voices of others but of "my voice in my history"? This would be a question that Levinas might have put to Cavell.[23] If the answer is that this universalizing is what philosophy requires, since what philosophy requires is the universal and the necessary, then one might be inclined to say: so much the worse for philosophy. (So much the worse, Levinas might have said, for all of *us*.)

A reply might go as follows: In normal philosophical circumstances (Hegel's, for example), universalizing is a movement of ascension, but in Cavell's case the direction of the universalizing use of the voice appears to be lateral rather than subsumptive, as if something were being passed from hand to hand (like the moment of speaking in a conversation). As Cavell takes pains to emphasize, there is no fact about Wittgenstein's voice that authorizes it to speak for others—that is, there is nothing different in this voice from what there is in the voice of any one of us. This, if I understand, is the upshot of "the argument of the ordinary," namely that any ordinary voice has the same authority as any other to say what we would say in response to what any situation calls for. The authority does not repose in a universal—my grasp of a rule or concept, for example—much less in an office (being a "guardian of rationality," e.g.); rather, the authority reposes in me. Cavell is quite blunt about this: "what justifies what I do and say is, I feel like saying, *me*" (CH77).

This is perhaps Cavell's way of staying faithful (after all these years) to Kant. There are perhaps various stages of fidelity. In the earliest, in his essay "Must We Mean What We Say?," Cavell interprets Kant's categorical imperative as a description rule, that is, as a description of what we ordinarily do when we are moral rather than a theory of what we must do in order to be morally justified: "when we (you) act morally, we act in a way we would regard as justified universally, justified no matter who had done it. . . . The Categorical Imperative does not tell you what you *ought* to do *if* you want to be moral (and hence is untouched by the feeling that no imperative can really be *categorical*, can bind us no matter what); it tells you (part of) what you in fact do when you are moral" (MW24–25). This seems to locate the Categorical Imperative at the level of autobiographical accounting rather than where we would normally expect to find it, namely at the level of rules and principles. At a somewhat later stage Cavell takes recourse to Kant's conception of aesthetic judgment, whose claim to universality runs up against the limits of other people in a way that ethical claims do not (not ever?): "understanding from inside a view you are undertaking to criticize is sound enough practice whatever the issue. But in the philosophy which proceeds from ordinary language, understanding from the inside is methodologically fundamental. Because the way you must rely on yourself as a source of what is said when, demands that you grant full title to others as sources of that data—not out of politeness, but because the nature of the claim you make for yourself is repudiated without that acknowledgment: it is a claim that no one knows better than you whether and when a thing is said, and if this is not to be taken as a claim to expertise (a way of taking it which repudiates it) then it must be understood to mean that you know no better than others what you claim to know."[24]

So the universal is, in some strong sense, historicized, or (better) localized. What are the consequences of this? What are the risks? It is interesting that for Cavell the risks are to the self, not to others.[25]

In "The Argument of the Ordinary" Cavell supplies the following commentary (of sorts) on Wittgenstein's remark that "Commanding, questioning, recounting, chatting [in other words, speaking a language—and also doing philosophy], are as much a part of our natural history, as walking, eating, drinking, playing" (PI§25):

> Suppose one day I start sliding my feet one after the other rather than lifting them (lots of people more or less do that now), or start skipping or hopping or goose-stepping or whirling once around on the toes of each foot in succession. If you question me about this perhaps I answer: "I've always

meant to do this, you just did not know," or, "I didn't know what moving along the ground could be until now, the inclination is powerful and the results are wonderful." But suppose I answer: "I don't know what has come over me, I don't want this, the inclination is not mine, it mortifies me." Or just: "I'm doing the same as I have always done, the same as you do, making measured moves in a given direction under my own steam. I am not moving faster than walking, we are comfortably keeping up with one another—not like our acquaintance far back there who takes a step once a minute and calls that walking." Wittgenstein's comment seems to be in place here: "It would now be no use to say: 'But can't you see . . . ?'—and repeat the old examples and explanations" (§185). That is, I surely know everything about walking that you do. What you respond to as deviant behavior in me is a threat to me; what I do smacks a little of insanity and I will soon be kept, at least, out of most public places. You might put tremendous pressure on me to conform—do you think I do not know intolerance? I know very well the normativeness of the way things are done—and not just in this society (as though the normativeness were merely something justified by custom and morality); I know of no society that enjoys, or deplores the fact that it engages in, walking as I do, though I might explore for one. (CH85)

The moral of this story seems to be that the universal (what counts as walking, talking, doing philosophy—or being human) is internal to the human form of life, where reasons come to an end, or where everything (how anything is done) depends on recognition and acceptance—or on how one is situated vis-à-vis other people (or vis-à-vis one's culture [CR125]). In "The Availability of Wittgenstein's Later Philosophy," Cavell writes: "the question is: Why are some claims about myself expressed in the form 'We . . . '? About what can I speak for others on the basis of what I have learned about myself? (This is worth comparing with the question: About what can I speak for others on the basis of what I decide to do? When you vote, you speak for yourself; when you are voted in you speak for others.) Then suppose it is asked: 'But how do I know others speak as I do?' About some things I know they do not; I have some knowledge of my idiosyncrasy. But if the question means 'How do I know at all that others speak as I do?' then the answer is, I do not. I may find out that the most common concept is not used by us in the same way" (MW67). So I might find myself a stranger, or a bit mad (or a monster), vis-à-vis other people. This seems the point of the lines quoted from the passage about walking oddly. Or as Wittgenstein writes: "one human being can be a complete enigma to another. We learn this when we come into a strange country with entirely strange traditions; and, what is more, even given a mastery of the country's language. We do not *understand* the people. (And not because of not knowing what they are saying to themselves.) We cannot find our feet with them" (PI2:223).

The question is perhaps not how to overcome the enigma of being human, but how to live with it (or inhabit it). Part of the answer lies in what Cavell calls "the absolute responsibility of the self to itself," where responsibility takes the form of making oneself intelligible to others (CHxvii). Having a voice is a condition of such intelligibility. But such a condition is hedged by limits—or, more exactly, dangers: "I do not picture my everyday knowledge of others as confined but as exposed" (CR432).

3. A Phenomenology of the Monstrous

Earlier I asked in passing about what is entailed in Cavell's notion of the ordinary. It looks like the question of the ordinary goes to the heart of the romantic in Cavell's philosophy.[26] For example, romanticism presupposes, and often celebrates, a rather fully developed conception of the sublime, or of the transcendental, which it also, however, often approaches in the spirit of diagnosis and critique. The sublime, after all, is not just (as in Kant) a category of excessive experience; it is a definition of reality that grips us in a certain irreversible way—once in the grip of this definition, nothing that doesn't conform to it can seem real. If reality is sublime, it is by definition beyond our reach, certainly impalpable, too large to take in, outside our capacities for knowing it. Skepticism is, on Cavell's understanding, an expression of our disappointment with this state of affairs, our disappointment in being merely human and therefore no match for sublime reality, but also our disappointment with whatever in the world fails to live up to the test (or criterion) of sublimity. By contrast, romanticism (of a certain Wordsworthian/Thoreauvian kind) desires intimacy with things; it is a desire for the nonsublime or for the near and the palpable.[27] It is, moreover, a certain way of acting on this desire—for example, by not repudiating what doesn't measure up to sublimity, which means, of course, reorienting ourselves with respect to the world.[28] (Here would be the place to cite Wittgenstein on the "tendency to sublime the logic of our language, as one might put it" [PI§38]; and also section 89: "In what sense is logic something sublime?"— "For there seemed to pertain to logic a peculiar depth—a universal significance. Logic lay, it seemed, at the bottom of the sciences.—For logical investigation explores the nature of all things. It seeks to see to the bottom of things." So seeing is never just seeing what is there; it wants to be a species of divining. Hence "the [often tragic] difficulty of seeing the obvious" [MW310]).

In what sense are we to "reorient ourselves with respect to the world"? Recall the earlier mention of listening and responsiveness as—what? Not alternatives to rationality but a turning of the rational so that it becomes "the exercise not of power but of reception" (SW135). Listening and responsiveness, being drawn to things, being next to them as against "clutching at them" (NY86–88), receiving as against penetrating, allows for an "intimacy with existence" (SW145): this is what the concept of the ordinary seems to come down to. The ordinary is not a category of reality but a description of our proximity to it. The ordinary is what reality is, not so much when it is known as such (it is unknowable in this sense, as per Kant) as when it is inhabited (and inhabited by others as well as by oneself).[29]

The quest for the ordinary is meant to answer (or, as Cavell might prefer, interpret) the problem of human separateness—separateness from others and from the world, which is sometimes a natural, sometimes a philosophical condition, as in Cavell's figure of the Outsider, which is what we are when, as cognitive agents, we reduce the world to a concept or theme (CR416–20). It is perhaps what we are in relation to ourselves (e.g., when, Descartes-like, we ask not "who" but "what" we are—thinking things without need of bodies). In part 4 of The Claim of Reason Cavell uses the word "romanticism" as a name for the experience of the difficulty of being human—that is, the difficulty of being human for sure, without doubt, or perhaps without fear, including the fear of not being human or human enough for others, not to say for oneself. This is an experience of human separateness, an experience that philosophy seems to exacerbate. It is the experience of being so sealed off from others that my existence carries with it the implacable suspicion that I cannot know, for example, that the other is in pain; or that, worse yet, the other cannot know that I am in pain, cannot recognize my pain when I feel it. The question naturally follows: what else can't the other recognize? For Cavell, pain is, if not a criterion, then at least a synecdoche for being human (another synecdoche is fear). Recognizing another's pain is symmetrical with recognizing another's humanness. Being human has no other foundation—no other possibility—than this recognition. A philosopher might ask: what is it that inspires me to grant (or withhold) this recognition? What could cause me to doubt whether another is human? Someone like Franz Kafka would ask: what is it about me that causes this doubt in others? Possibly that I am just like no one else: I think, act, look, talk, walk, do philosophy like no one else. At some point I fall off the edge of your world.

Cavell's Rousseau interpretation in The Claim of Reason provides some perspective on these matters. In Rousseau's origin-of-language story, for example, my initial encounter with another fills me with fear—I find the other frightening (call him "Giant"); but subsequent encounters reveal him to be (at the least) no bigger or stronger (no more fearsome) than I am: in other words, just like me (fearful of others). But this would mean that I am, without meaning to be, frightening to others. What is it about me that causes this reaction in others? This was Rousseau's Kafka-like experience and his dread. ("Could I in my good sense have supposed that one day I, the same man that I was, the same that I still am, would . . . pass for and be taken as a monster?")[30] Hence the Confessions, which is Rousseau's response to his experience of his separateness, that is, his fear of becoming unknowable, unrecognizable, not recognizably human—in short, monstrous. Imagine autobiography as a genre of madness: a form of writing prompted by the experience of subjectivity as something sublime—unknowable, inexpressible, outside the limits of reason and therefore something unrestrainable, savage, a horror to itself as well as to others.

Cavell's romanticism, or one stage of it, might be described as a phenomenology of the monstrous ("the horror of the human" [QO57]). What is it like not to be experienced as human—to be experienced as monstrous? Being human is an ethical relation that calls for acknowledgment of one to the other. I am in this respect responsible for another's humanity—a responsibility that is, rather awfully, prior to my being human. Acknowledgment, it appears, is an asymmetrical relation; that is, it is not a reciprocal arrangement, not a contract or mutual agreement to call ourselves human (it is, after all, in the nature of such agreements to be exclusionary). The ethical relation is a responsibility that leaves me pretty much in the open, exposed on the heath. ("I do not picture my everyday knowledge of others as confined but as exposed" [CR432].) The difficulty of being human begins here, exposed to others, in danger of being taken for a monster, but also, I should imagine, in danger of being one. But a monster of what sort?

In *The Claim of Reason* Cavell asks about being horrified. What causes horror? "Fear is of danger; terror is of violence, of the violence I might do or that might be done me. I can be terrified of thunder, but not horrified by it. And isn't it the case that not the human horrifies me, but the inhuman, the monstrous? Very well. But only what is human can be inhuman. —Can only the human be monstrous? If something is monstrous, and we do not believe that there are monsters, then only the human is a candidate for the monstrous" (CR418). But in what way, by what series of events, does the human grow monstrous? Of being human Wittgenstein says: "it comes to this: only of a living human being and what resembles (behaves like) a living human being can one say: it has sensations; it sees; is blind, is deaf; is conscious or unconscious" (PI§281). That is, only to human beings, or what resembles them, can one ascribe subjectivity. Subjectivity is implicated in the definition (or at least recognition) of the human. So the monstrous would be a state of affairs in which it no longer made sense to ascribe subjective states to human beings—a state of affairs that, as Cavell sees it, Emerson and Thoreau were among the first to analyze.

4. Turning Human

Recall the famous line that concludes Foucault's *Les Mots et le choses*: "as the archeology of our thought shows, man is an invention of recent date, and one perhaps nearing its end."[31] Cavell calls this possibility (the end of romanticism) "the vanishing of the human" (CR468):

> Is this new [romantic, subjective] form of civilization being replaced by another [i.e., postromantic, postsubjective]? In particular, is it being replaced by one in which nothing that happens any longer strikes us as the objectification of subjectivity, as the act of an answerable agent, as the expression and satisfaction of human freedom, of human intention and desire? What has a beginning can have an end. If this future (civilization?) were effected its members would not be dissatisfied. They would have lost the concept of satisfaction. Then nothing would (any longer) give them the idea that living beings, human things, could feel. So they would not (any longer) be human. They would not, for example, be frightened upon meeting others—except in the sense, or under circumstances, in which they would be frightened upon encountering bears or storms, circumstances under which bears would be frightened. And of course particular forms of laughter and amazement would also no longer be possible, ones which depend upon clear breaks between, say, machines and creatures. (CR468)

Cavell says he is thinking here of science, or more exactly of the fact that human subjectivity is invisible to empirical research (as both cognitive science and the neurosciences in particular attest); but he could just as well have been thinking of Foucault and the early poststructuralists (and now the social constructionists), with their conception of the subject as constituted by language, culture, ideology, and so on.[32]

After *The Claim of Reason*, however, Cavell comes to think of "the vanishing of the human" in terms of the early democratic culture against which Emerson and Thoreau rebelled. Here was a culture that had constituted itself as a democracy but had not, so to speak, constituted any democratic selves—because, after all, the self cannot be constituted, or at all events not as anything human; it can only form itself out of itself by taking responsibility for its own discourse (a self is not a subject, as Foucault himself came to see).[33] The exercise of this responsibility is what Cavell means by moral or Emersonian perfectionism, which is an ethical practice that is rooted, Cavell says, in two things: "(1) A hatred of moralism—of what Emerson calls 'conformity'—so passionate and ceaseless as to seem sometimes to amount to a hatred of morality altogether. (Nietzsche calls himself the first antimoralist; Emerson knows that he will seem antinomian, a refuser of any law, including the moral law.) (2) An expression of disgust with or a disdain for the present state of things so complete as to require not merely reform, but a call for a transformation of things, and before all a transformation of the self—a call that seems so self-absorbed and obscure as to make morality impossible" (CH46). (Note *seems* self-absorbed, but perhaps is not?) So on the one hand perfectionism is (notably) a rejection of a morality of rules; and on the other it is an unsatisfiable self-criticism, a restlessness with respect to oneself that never allows one to remain the same. Possibly to be human is to stand in need of transformation (Cavell sometimes prefers the term "transfiguration" [NY44]); otherwise one is closed off to the future, or to others, or to life. The motto of perfectionism is: "I know change is called for and to be striven for, beginning with myself" (CH112).

The goal of Emersonian perfectionism is not a perfect self but rather some- thing that Cavell calls the *next self* (CH9; cf. SW108–9). The "next self," Cavell emphasizes, is outside the categories of true and false, ideal and real, and even self and other. The term is first of all meant to ward off "any fixed, metaphysical interpretation of the idea of a self" (CHxxxi) as something given in advance (a posit). The Emersonian self is non-egocentric; it is, in a sense, not an entity (e.g., a windowless monad, a social product). Rather the project of attaining a self is always on the way, as if our relation to ourselves were one of proximity rather than one of identity.[34] Indeed, having a self at all is a movement—"a process of moving to, and from, nexts" (CH12)—rather than a mode of possession. Perfectionism is, moreover, a universalizing of the self, but—as the term *next self* implies—the movement is, like the movement of universalizing the voice, lateral rather than transcendental. This means averting "the vanishing of the human." One could think of it as a process of peopling the earth anew, changing things into human beings. What this movement looks like at ground level is the subject of, among other things, Cavell's studies of the Hollywood comedies of remarriage, which are about the movement of women out of the isolation of mere objectivity—of being objects for outsiders, beings without subjectivity, voiceless and therefore unknowable as human, like Nora before the end of Ibsen's *A Doll House* ("Do I know more about dolls and statues than I do about human beings?" [CR403] What do outsiders know?). In *Pursuits of Happiness* Cavell calls this movement "the creation of a new woman, or the new creation of a woman"—but also, in the same breath, "a new creation of the human" (PH16)—and the form this movement takes is that of *conversation:* "reciprocity and exchange apart from which separate human individuals cannot acquire the force so much as to name themselves, to create the realm of the private" (PH74).

Some reflection on the private will perhaps help to answer the original question of how the absolute responsibility of the self to itself can square with the ethical exigency of responsiveness to others. The point is that the realm of the private is a place of intimacy, not of isolation, and it appears that only someone's words or voice can open up such a place, which turns out (perhaps against all reason) to be infinitely expansive and inclusive. It is what gives us so much as the idea that living beings, things, can feel. It is therefore the realm of lovers (which for Cavell is allegorical of an unattained but attainable democracy, that is, the realm of freedom (PH152–56): of which, Cavell says, "I cannot reach this realm alone" [PH79]). It is likewise a sojourn at Walden Pond. It is where Emerson sits at the feet of "the common, the mean, and the low." It is where philosophizing occurs, assuming this to be, as Cavell says, where "I have to bring my own life and language to imagination," or autobiography for short (CR125). It is where explanations come to an end and I am thrown back on myself (CR124)—meaning, however, that it is also the human form of life from which lunatics are sometimes removed, or from which, Lear-like, I can and often do withhold myself (CR83–84). It can easily turn into a world without others, what most take privacy to be but which for Cavell is where humanity begins to seem most dubious or where Narcissus fails to recognize himself or where, behind closed doors, the melodrama of the unknown woman plays its matinees. It is therefore a place in need of "some radical change, but as it were from inside, not *by* anything; some say in another birth, symbolizing a different order of natural reactions" (NY44), an order that Cavell sometimes thinks of as democracy considered simply as a realm of talk, a realm adumbrated in the conversation of lovers, as in the comedies of remarriage, and which Cavell, in his argument with John Rawls, calls "a conversation of justice" (CH102).[35]

Basic to Cavell's metaphysics is Kant's bifurcated world—the "two realms," in one of which we are constrained (or, let us say, constituted), in the other free. The one is the natural world, but for Cavell it is also the unredeemed social and political world we happen to inhabit; the other is, well, something like a realm of ecstasy—ecstasy in the sense in which this concept emerged in the third chapter of *The Senses of Walden*, in which Cavell glosses Thoreau's experience of doubleness: "I only know myself as a human entity," Thoreau wrote, "the scene, so to speak, of thoughts and affections; and am sensible of a certain doubleness by which I can stand as remote from myself as from another. However intense my experience, I am conscious of the presence and criticism of a part of me, which, as it were, is not a part of me but a spectator, sharing no experience, but taking note of it, and that is no more I than it is you" (SW102). Cavell's reading is as follows:

> What *we* know as self-consciousness is only our opinion of ourselves, and like any other opinion it comes from outside; it is hearsay, our contribution to public opinion. We must become disobedient to it, resist it, no longer listen to it. We do that by keeping our senses still, listening another way. . . . We are to reinterpret our sense of doubleness as a relation between ourselves in the aspect of indweller, unconsciously building, and in the aspect of spectator, impartially observing. Unity between these aspects is viewed not as a mutual absorption, but as a perpetual nextness, an act of neighboring or befriending. (SW107–8)

Again, our relation with ourselves is one of proximity rather than one of identity; we are beside ourselves in a relation of ecstasy, but notice that ecstasy is critical rather than, say, simply mad. Cavell pictures the indweller and spectator as in "conversation" and as being answerable (responsible) to one another. "The answerability of the self to itself is its possibility of awakening" (SW 109). Awakening to what? The essays and lectures that make up the bulk of Cavell's writings since *The Senses of Walden* endlessly weave together two dimensions of this question, the private and the public, the micro- and macropolitical. The first concerns the self's awakening to its task of self-creation; the second is our awakening to the task of creating the world. In practice, given how and where we are situated, this means bringing the proper name of "America" down to earth, bringing it home, living—indeed, performing—the concept as against merely clarifying it philosophically or procedurally, as in the Rawlsian mode. It means living it as against "living our skepticism," where skepticism, expressing a disappointment with knowledge and a disappointment with the human, is also a despair of politics expressed as disappointment with America, despair of democracy as it stands, with its institution of slavery perhaps only formally dismantled (destroyed on paper but not on the ground, which is striated with aftereffects).[36]

These two dimensions of creation—of the self and of the world—come together in the central place that women have in Cavell's philosophy, and in particular in his conception of women as creatures who come into existence, whose human existence is constituted, through performance. In the comedies of remarriage this performance, as we have seen, takes the form of the conversation of lovers as an image of "the perfected human community" (PS79), but in the melodramas of the unknown woman, as Cavell reads them, the metamorphosis of the woman into a "new human being" occurs through the repudiation of marriage and, more generally, through the repudiation of the world of men, which the woman judges to be, at best, "second-rate" (CT15–16). Men are, it appears, incapable of change, or at all events limited with respect to the kind of transfiguration women are capable of—limited and, in the melodramas of the unknown woman, embodiments of the limits or obstacles that the woman must transcend. What is interesting is that the moment of transcendence is interpreted by Cavell as a moment of transcendental performance, a "theatricalization" of the self that marks the progress of the self from the realm of the private into the public realm of freedom and equality (CT72). Indeed, freedom is not merely a property of subjectivity, an inner freedom hedged by external constraint; on the contrary, freedom is a space or world opened up by the voice or, more exactly, by the voices of women, as if gender, in this instance, were a kind of guarantee that, against all odds—or against the background of the dubious accomplishments of history's men of action—a realm of freedom has been achieved at last.[37]

Notes

Introduction

1. Recall the figure of the philosopher in Kant's "An Answer to the Question: What Is Enlightenment?" See Immanuel Kant, *Kant on History*, trans. Lewis White Beck (Indianapolis: Bobbs-Merrill, 1963), pp. 3–10.

2. See Jürgen Habermas, *The Philosophical Discourse of Modernity*, trans. Frederick G. Lawrence (Cambridge, MA: MIT Press, 1987), p. 208.

3. The "guardian of rationality" is Jürgen Habermas's characterization of the philosopher in "Philosophy as Stand-in and Interpreter," *Moral Consciousness and Communicative Action*, trans. Christian Lenhardt and Shierry Weber Nicholson (Cambridge, MA: Cambridge University Press, 1990), esp. pp. 17–20.

4. See Richard Rorty, "Philosophy as a Kind of Writing: An Essay on Derrida," *Consequences of Pragmatism* (Minneapolis: University of Minnesota Press, 1982), pp. 90–109.

5. See Arthur Danto, "The End of Art," *The Philosophical Disenfranchisement of Art* (New York: Columbia University Press, 1986), pp. 81–115.

6. See Stanley Cavell, "Foreword: An Audience for Philosophy," *Must We Mean What We Say? A Book of Essays* (Cambridge: Cambridge University Press, 1969), pp. xvii–xxix.

7. Ernst Cassirer, *The Philosophy of Symbolic Forms*, trans. Ralph Manheim (New Haven, CT: Yale University Press, 1953), 1:91. Hereafter cited as PSF.

8. Roman Jakobson and Morris Halle, *Fundamentals of Language* (The Hague: Martinus Nijhoff, 1956), p. 76.

9. Friedrich Nietzsche, *The Will to Power*, trans. Walter Kaufman and R. J. Hollingdale (New York: Vintage Books, 1968), p. 267.

10. See Richard Rorty, *Philosophy and the Mirror of Nature* (Princeton, NJ: Princeton University Press, 1979), p. 315. See also Richard Rorty, *Contingency, Irony, and Solidarity* (Cambridge: Cambridge University Press, 1989), esp. the first two chaps., "The Contingency of Language" and "The Contingency of the Self."

11. W. V. O. Quine, *Word and Object* (Cambridge, MA: Harvard University Press, 1960), p. 17. Hereafter cited as WO.

12. W. V. O. Quine, "Two Dogmas of Empiricism," *From a Logical Point of View: Nine Logico-Philosophical Essays* (Cambridge, MA: Harvard University Press, 1953),

p. 44. The classic text on the historicity of science would be Thomas Kuhn, *The Structure of Scientific Revolutions* (Chicago: University of Chicago Press, 1964).

13. See Nelson Goodman, *Ways of Worldmaking* (Indianapolis: Hackett Publishing, 1978), hereafter cited as WWM: "Rather than speak of pictures as true or false we might better speak of theories as right or wrong; for the truth of the laws of a theory is but one special feature and is often, as we have seen, overriden in importance by the cogency and compactness and comprehensiveness, the informativeness and organizing power of the whole system" (p. 19).

14. See Richard A. Schweder, "Anthropology's Romantic Rebellion against the Enlightenment; or, There's More to Thinking Than Reason and Evidence," in *Culture Theory: Essays on Mind, Self, and Emotion*, ed. Richard A. Schweder et al. (Cambridge: Cambridge University Press, 1984), pp. 27–66.

15. See Ludwig Wittgenstein, *Philosophical Investigations*, 3d ed., trans. G. E. M. Anscombe (1953; New York: Macmillan, 1968), §19.

16. Peter Winch, "Understanding a Primitive Society," *Ethics and Action* (London: Routledge & Kegan Paul, 1972), p. 40. Hereafter cited as EA.

17. See Wilhelm Dilthey, "The Construction of the Historical World in the Human Sciences," *Dilthey: Selected Writings*, trans. H. P. Rickman (Cambridge: Cambridge University Press, 1976), pp. 226–28.

18. Here the work of the anthropologist Clifford Geertz needs to be consulted. See, e.g., "Deep Play: Notes on the Balinese Cockfight," in *Interpretive Social Science: A Second Look*, ed. Paul Rabinow and William M. Sullivan (Berkeley: University of California Press, 1987), pp. 195–240.

19. Donald Davidson, "On the Very Idea of a Conceptual Scheme," *Inquiries into Truth and Interpretation* (Oxford: Clarendon Press, 1984), p. 184. Hereafter cited as ITI.

20. See Martin Hollis, "The Social Destruction of Reality," in *Rationality and Relativism*, ed. Martin Hollis and Steven Lukes (Cambridge, MA: MIT Press, 1982), pp. 83–84. The idea that there is in human beings a "core" that "has no history" has been pretty much blown away by the recent work of Joseph Margolis, who is perhaps the only true historicist among contemporary analytic philosophers. See his *Historied Thought, Constructed World: A Primer for the Turn of the Millennium* (Berkeley: University of California Press, 1995), esp. pp. 223–58.

21. Martin Heidegger, *On Time and Being*, trans. Joan Stambaugh (New York: Harper & Row, 1969), pp. 58–59. Hereafter cited as TB.

22. See Max Weber, *Economy and Society*, ed. Guenther Roth and Claus Wittich; trans. Ephraim Fischoff et al. (Berkeley: University of California Press, 1978), 2:956–1005. See also the collection of essays, *The Barbarism of Reason: Max Weber and the Twilight of Enlightenment*, ed. Asher Horowitz and Terry Maley (Toronto: University of Toronto Press, 1994).

23. See John Rawls's classic "procedural approach" to the just and rational

state, *A Theory of Justice* (Cambridge, MA: Harvard University Press, 1971), p. 422. Hereafter cited as TJ.

24. See *Rational Choice*, ed. Jon Elster (Washington Square: New York University Press, 1986), and also Jon Elster, *Ulysses and the Sirens: Studies in Rationality and Irrationality* (Cambridge: Cambridge University Press, 1979), and *Solomonic Judgments: Studies in the Limits of Rationality* (Cambridge: Cambridge University Press, 1989). See also Donald P. Green and Ian Shapiro, *Pathologies of Rational Choice Theory: A Critique of Applications in Political Science* (New Haven, CT: Yale University Press, 1994). For an attempt to apply rational-choice theory to ethics, see David Schmidtz, *Rational Choice and Moral Agency* (Princeton, NJ: Princeton University Press, 1995).

The most instructive and engaging writer on rational choice is Martin Hollis, who thinks that while reason is transcendental and economic it nevertheless only gets interesting when it is returned to ground level where human action is no longer reducible to the systematic operation of a rational actor but involves historical and cultural particulars that theories, models, and generalized examples cannot accommodate, even if reason can. See Martin Hollis, *Models of Man: Philosophical Thoughts on Social Action* (Cambridge: Cambridge University Press, 1977), esp. 143–64; *The Cunning of Reason* (Cambridge: Cambridge University Press, 1987), esp. pp. 146–72; and esp. *Reason in Action: Essays in the Philosophy of Social Science* (Cambridge: Cambridge University Press, 1996), esp. pp. 89–188.

25. Max Horkheimer and Theodor Adorno, *Dialectic of Enlightenment*, trans. John Cumming (1944; New York: Seabury Press, 1972), p. 39. Jürgen Habermas gives a critical account of the development of this problematic in vol. 1 of *The Theory of Communicative Action: Reason and the Rationalization of Society*, trans. Thomas McCarthy (Boston: Beacon Press, 1984), esp. pp. 339–99. See the excellent volume cited above (n. 22), *The Barbarism of Reason: Max Weber and the Twilight of Enlightenment*, esp. the essays of Fred Dallmayr ("Max Weber and the Modern State") and Alkis Kontos ("The World Disenchanted, and the Return of Gods and Demons").

26. See Habermas, *The Philosophical Discourse of Modernity*, esp. pp. 139–40; Heidegger's "critique of modernity is made independent of scientific analysis. [It] renounces all empirical and normative questions that can be treated by social-scientific or historical means, or can be at all handled in argumentative form." Not to put too fine a point on it, it is an irrational critique; it "undermines Western rationalism" and so leaves us helpless once more before the forces of superstition and tyranny that dominated the premodern world. Heidegger's thought is a regression to premodernity or the pre-Enlightenment culture of mystification and unjustified authority.

27. See Rodolphe Gasché, "Postmodernism and Rationality," *Journal of Philosophy* 74 (1988): 528–38.

28. Bernard Williams, *Ethics and the Limits of Philosophy* (Cambridge, MA: Har-

vard University Press, 1985), p. 197. Hereafter cited as ELP. See esp. chap. 10, "Morality, the Peculiar Institution" (pp. 174–96).

29. See Charles Taylor's critique of "the disengaged instrumental mode of life" in *Sources of the Self: The Making of Modern Identity* (Cambridge, MA: Harvard University Press, 1989), pp. 505–13; and Charles Taylor, "The Moral Topography of the Self," in *Hermeneutics and Psychological Theory: Hermeneutic Perspectives on Personality, Psychotherapy, and Psychopathology,* ed. Stanley Messer, Louis Sass, and Robert Woolfolk (New Brunswick, NJ: Rutgers University Press, 1988), pp. 298–320, esp. p. 305.

30. See Charles Taylor, "Overcoming Epistemology," in *Philosophy: End or Transformation?* ed. Kenneth Baynes, James Bohman, and Thomas McCarthy (Cambridge, MA: MIT Press, 1987), pp. 464–88. See Thomas Nagel, *The View from Nowhere* (New York: Oxford University Press, 1986), p. 3: "This book is about a single problem: how to combine the perspective of a particular person inside the world with an objective view of that same world, the person and his viewpoint included." See esp. chap. 9, "Ethics" (pp. 164–88).

31. See Habermas, *The Theory of Communicative Action,* 1:366–99; and Habermas, "An Alternative Way out of the Philosophy of the Subject: Communicative versus Subject-Centered Reason," *The Philosophical Discourse of Modernity,* pp. 294–326.

32. See Karl-Otto Apel, "The A Priori of Communication and the Foundation of the Humanities," in *Understanding and Social Inquiry,* ed. Fred R. Dallmayr and Thomas A. McCarthy (Notre Dame, IN: University of Notre Dame Press, 1977), esp. pp. 294–96.

33. See Richard Rorty, "Solidarity of Objectivity?," in *Post-Analytic Philosophy,* ed. John Rajchman and Cornell West (New York: Columbia University Press, 1985), pp. 3–19, and "Solidarity," *Contingency, Irony, Solidarity,* pp. 189–98; and Cora Diamond, "Losing Your Concepts," *Ethics* 98, no. 2 (January 1988): 255–77. See also Cora Diamond's essay, "Rules: Looking in the Right Place," in *Wittgenstein: Attention to Particulars: Essays in Honour of Rush Rhees,* ed. D. Z. Phillips and Peter Winch (New York: St. Martin's Press, 1989), pp. 12–34.

34. Hans-Georg Gadamer puts the issue clearly: "The question at stake is, What is the relation of rationality as rigorous science to the rationality of life?" His answer is that the one is internal to the other, and that the other is characterized by participation rather than foundation, the give-and-take among human beings as against "the apodictic evidence of self-consciousness." See Gadamer, "The Hermeneutics of Suspicion," in *Hermeneutics: Questions and Prospects,* ed. Gary Shapiro and Alan Sica (Amherst: University of Massachusetts Press, 1984), pp. 62–64. See also the very useful volume of essays edited by Evan Simpson, *Antifoundationalism and Practical Reason: Conversations between Hermeneutics and Analysis* (Edmondton, AB: Academic Printing & Publishing, 1987), esp. the essay by Barry Allen, "Groundless

Goodness," which contains this sentence: "Really to be an antifoundationalist is to oppose the appearance that rationality (whether in belief or in choice) depends on the presence or absence of something. Call it God or call it wide reflective equilibrium, a ground is a ground, and what faces us is the need to be good without grounds" (p. 191). See also Joseph Margolis, *Life without Principles: Reconciling Theory and Practice* (Oxford: Basil Blackwell, 1995), pp. 172–206.

35. See Bernard Williams, "Morality and the Emotions," *Problems of the Self* (Cambridge: Cambridge University Press, 1972), p. 223.

36. See, e.g., D. Z. Phillips, *Interventions in Ethics* (Albany: SUNY Press, 1992), esp. "What Can We Expect from Ethics?," pp. 86–109.

37. Peter Winch, "Particularity and Morals," *Trying to Make Sense* (Oxford: Basil Blackwell, 1987), p. 173. Cf. D. Z. Phillips, "Some Limits of Moral Endeavor," *Through a Darkening Glass* (Notre Dame, IN: University of Notre Dame Press, 1982), esp. pp. 37–38.

38. See Stanley Cavell, *The Senses of Walden: An Expanded Edition* (San Francisco: North Point Press, 1981), pp. 106–7n.

39. Thompson Clarke, "The Legacy of Skepticism," *Journal of Philosophy* 69 (1972): 761.

40. See Cora Diamond, "The Importance of Being Human," in *Human Beings*, ed. David Cockburn (Cambridge: Cambridge University Press, 1991), pp. 35–63.

41. In "Philosophy and the Heterogeneity of the Human," D. Z. Phillips rightly argues (pace Cora Diamond) that there is no such thing as *the* concept of the human. There are (as literature shows) multiple and heterogeneous such conceptions. Philosophy at ground level may need to cure itself of the need for the universal and the necessary. See Phillips, *Interventions in Ethics*, pp. 250–71.

42. In *Modern Poetry and the Idea of Language* (New Haven, CT: Yale University Press, 1974), I argued that poetry cannot be brought under the description of a single theory; rather we need (at least) two theories, which I dubbed the "orphic" and the "hermetic." On the orphic theory, poetry opens up a world for us to inhabit; on the hermetic theory, poetry constructs a world of words sealed off from anything outside of it. The orphic and the hermetic are not genres or poetic types; they are limit-concepts, that is, they define the boundaries within which poetry (and, of course, not just poetry) gets written. Neither are they binary concepts: they mutually clarify but do not mutually exclude one another, as I think my account of Heidegger's conceptions of art, language, and poetry shows. See my *Heidegger's Estrangements: Language, Truth, and Poetry in the Later Writings* (New Haven, CT: Yale University Press, 1989). The distinction between the orphic and the hermetic has, to be sure, a touching simplicity, but I still take pleasure in the richness and open-endedness of its application, most recently in my *Maurice Blanchot: The Refusal of Philosophy* (Baltimore: Johns Hopkins University Press, 1997).

43. Stanley Cavell, *This New Yet Unapproachable America: Lectures after Emerson after Wittgenstein* (Albuquerque, NM: Living Batch Press, 1989), p. 109.

44. See Jean-Paul Sartre, *Being and Nothingness,* trans. Hazel E. Barnes (New York: Washington Square Press, 1956), pp. 340–404. Sartre, however, understands very well the limits, or incompleteness, of any description of the look that is worked out merely "on the level of the *cogito*" (p. 358).

45. Emmanuel Levinas, "Substitution," *Otherwise Than Being or Beyond Essence,* trans. Alphonso Lingis (The Hague: Martinus Nijhoff, 1981), p. 102. Hereafter cited as OTB.

46. In an essay on "Language and Proximity," Levinas says that the "relation of proximity . . . is the original language, a language without words or propositions, pure communication." *Collected Philosophical Papers,* trans. Alphonso Lingis (The Hague: Martinus Nijhoff, 1987), p. 119. Hereafter cited as CPP. Language is not a function or instrument of the assertorial speaking subject; it is "contact," that is, before language articulates itself in words it is a mode of sensibility, a "touching." "Consciousness," says Levinas, "consists in thematizing across a multiplicity, and in thus manifesting being by proclaiming its unity and its identity." It is a conceptual reduction. "But language as contact touches the neighbor in its non-ideal unity," that is, in its singularity (CPP119). See also *Closeness: An Ethics,* ed. Harald Jodalen and Arne Johan Vetlesen (Oslo: Scandinavian University Presses, 1997).

47. Cf. Stanley Cavell, who takes up the problem of the other in part 4 of *The Claim of Reason: Wittgenstein, Skepticism, Morality, and Tragedy* (New York: Oxford University Press, 1979): "I do not picture my everyday knowledge of others as confined but as exposed" (p. 432). A Levinasian might rewrite this as: "I do not picture myself in relation to others as confined to my position as a knowing subject but as exposed like a corporeal subject."

Chapter 1

1. The following works by William James are cited in this essay: *Essays in Radical Empiricism* (New York: Longmans, Green, 1912), hereafter cited as ERE; *Pragmatism: A New Name for Some Old Ways of Thinking* (Cambridge, MA: Harvard University Press, 1975), cited as P; *Varieties of Religious Experience: A Study of Human Nature* (New York: Longman's, Green, 1902), cited as V; *Writings of William James,* ed. John J. McDermott (Chicago: University of Chicago Press, 1977), cited as WWJ.

2. For James, a true statement, one that we are justified in making, works like a "true" (that is, just) law. See "Pragmatism and Humanism" (P105–7).

3. See Martin Heidegger, *Being and Time,* trans. John Macquarrie and Edward Robinson (New York: Harper & Row, 1962), pp. 188–95.

4. As we have seen, for Heidegger "all sight is grounded primarily in under-standing" (*Being and Time*, p. 187). There is no such thing as "pure intuition," except in the derivative sense that he explicates in sec. 33 of *Being and Time*.

5. In "The One and the Many," James writes: "Things tell a story. Their parts hang together so as to work out a climax. They play into each other's hands expressively. Retrospectively, we can see that although no definite purpose presided over a chain of events, yet the events fell into a dramatic form, with a start, a middle, and a finish. In point of fact all stories end; and here again the point of view of a many is the more natural one to take. The world is full of partial stories that run parallel to one another, beginning and ending at odd times. They mutually interlace and interfere at points, but we cannot unify them completely in our minds" (P64). And in "Pragmatism and Humanism," distinguishing between pragmatists and rationalists, he says:

> On the pragmatist side we have only one edition of the universe, unfinished, growing in all sorts of places, especially in the places where thinking beings are at work.
>
> On the rationalist side we have a universe in many editions, one real one, the infinite folio, or *édition de luxe*, eternally complete; and then various finite editions, full of false readings, distorted and mutilated each in its own way. (P113–14)

6. Although it is doubtful whether James would go so far as to say that our self-relation is social, constituted from the outside, all the way down. "The spaces and times of your imagination, the objects and events of your daydreams are not only more or less incoherent *inter se*, but are wholly out of definite relation with the similar contents of any one else's mind" (P70). As Stanley Cavell will later develop it, we must never lose sight of our creatureliness. There was a time when we believed ourselves to be creatures of God; but the death of God alters our relation to our creatureliness. What or whom are we creatures of? There are only two alternatives remaining. We are, on the one hand, cultural constructions, products of historical processes, material conditions, social forces, genetic accidents, family romances, and so on to no definite term. But Cavell insists, against the whole stream of social constructionism, that we are responsible for our creating ourselves. In "Being Odd, Getting Even" (1986), Cavell construes Descartes's *cogito* as a performative: the "I think" is an enactment of my existence in the sense that "saying or thinking may create that existence." See Stanley Cavell, *In Quest of the Ordinary* (Chicago: University of Chicago Press, 1988), pp. 106–12. Cavell reads Emerson as one who says that if I do not think, then I do not exist; rather I merely haunt the world like a ghost, one of the undead. I remain, at all events, uncreated. "Emerson calls the mode of uncreated life 'conformity'" (p. 111). William James seems saturated with

this Emersonian sense that we are not given in advance, not fixed or fated, not controlled from the outside, but responsible for ourselves.

7. Cornell West, *The American Evasion of Philosophy: A Genealogy of Pragmatism* (Madison, WI: University of Wisconsin Press, 1989), esp. pp. 64–67.

8. William James, *Talks to Teachers on Psychology; and to Students and Some of Life's Ideals* (New York: W. W. Norton, 1958), p. 155.

9. Bertrand Russell, "William James's Conception of Truth," *Philosophical Essays* (New York, 1966), pp. 112–30.

10. See Stanley Cavell, "An Emerson Mood," *The Senses of Walden: An Expanded Edition* (San Francisco: North Point Press, 1981), p. 141.

Chapter 2

1. The following texts by Donald Davidson are cited in this essay: "James Joyce and Humpty Dumpty," in *Philosophy and the Arts*, ed. Peter A. French, Theodore E. Uehling, Jr., and Howard K. Wettstein, Midwest Studies in Philosophy 16 (Notre Dame, IN: University of Notre Dame Press, 1991), hereafter cited as PA; *Inquiries into Truth and Interpretation* (Oxford: Clarendon Press, 1984), cited as ITI; "The Second Person," in *The Wittgenstein Legacy*, ed. Peter A. French, Theodore E. Uehling, Jr., and Howard K. Wettstein, Midwest Studies in Philosophy 17 (Notre Dame, IN: University of Notre Dame Press, 1992), cited as WL; "A Nice Derangement of Epitaphs," in *Philosophical Grounds of Rationality: Intentions, Categories, Ends*, ed. Richard E. Grandy and Richard Warner (Oxford: Clarendon Press, 1986), cited as PGR. There are also several references to *Truth and Interpretation: Perspectives on the Philosophy of Donald Davidson*, ed. Ernest LePore (Oxford: Basil Blackwell, 1986), cited as TI.

2. W. V. O. Quine, *Word and Object* (Cambridge, MA: Harvard University Press, 1960), pp. 26–30.

3. Donald Davidson, "Radical Interpretation," *Inquiries into Truth and Interpretation*, p. 137. Cf. pp. 168–69: "But of course it cannot be assumed that speakers never have false beliefs. Error is what gives belief its point. We can, however, take it as given that *most* beliefs are correct. The reason for this is that a belief is identified by its location in a pattern of beliefs; it is this pattern that determines the subject matter of the belief, what the belief is about. Before some object in, or aspect of, the world can become part of the subject matter of a belief (true or false) there must be endless true beliefs about the subject matter. . . . What makes interpretation possible, then, is the fact that we can dismiss a priori the chance of massive error."

4. Richard Rorty, *Contingency, Irony, Solidarity* (Cambridge: Cambridge University Press, 1989), esp. pp. 73–95.

5. ITI245–64; first published in *Critical Inquiry* 5 (Autumn 1978): 29–45, and in *On Metaphor,* ed. Sheldon Sacks (Chicago: University of Chicago Press, 1979), pp. 29–45.

6. Paul Ricoeur, *Interpretation Theory: Discourse and the Surplus of Meaning* (Fort Worth, TX: Texas Christian University Press, 1976), p. 50.

7. See Paul Ricoeur, "Metaphor and the Central Problem of Hermeneutics," *Hermeneutics and the Human Sciences,* trans. John B. Thompson (Cambridge: Cambridge University Press, 1981), pp. 169–70.

8. Thus John Searle thinks that how a metaphor works is "a special case of the general problem of . . . how speaker's meaning and sentence or word meaning come apart." *Expression and Meaning: Studies in the Theory of Speech Acts* (Cambridge: Cambridge University Press, 1979), p. 76. See also p. 113: "Stated very crudely, the mechanism by which irony [or metaphor] works is that the utterance, if taken literally, is obviously inappropriate to the situation. Since it is grossly inappropriate, the hearer is compelled to reinterpret it in such a way as to render it appropriate, and the most natural way to interpret [it is] as meaning the opposite of its literal form."

9. H. P. Grice, "Utterer's Meaning, Sentence Meaning, Word-Meaning," *Foundations of Language* 4 (1968), pp. 225–42.

10. See Davidson, "Meaning and Truth," ITI17–36.

11. See Richard Rorty, "Hesse and Davidson on Metaphor," *Objectivism, Relativism, and Truth* (Cambridge, Cambridge University Press, 1991), pp. 162–72, esp. pp. 169–70. In "Thought and Talk" Davidson introduces the idea of "the autonomy of meaning": "Once a sentence is understood, an utterance of it may be used to serve almost any extra-linguistic purpose" (ITI164). Under the category of "extra-linguistic" comes the idea that sentences can be "socially true," whatever they may be otherwise. Davidson says: "Someone who knows under what conditions his sentences are socially true cannot fail to grasp, and avail himself of, the possibilities of dishonest assertion—or for joking, story-telling, goading, exaggerating, insulting, all the rest of the jolly crew" (ITI165). If fights break out between philosophers and literary critics it is probably over where (what to call it?) logico-empirical truth leaves off and social truth begins, with philosophers aiming for a sharp line and critics dubious about whether anything can be separated from the social. The whole idea of truth conditions begins to cloud up with thoughts of social truth, for reasons that Charles Taylor tries to develop in "Theories of Meaning," *Philosophical Papers* (Cambridge: Cambridge University Press, 1985), 1:248–92, esp. 252–54.

12. See Frank B. Farrell, "Metaphor and Davidsonian Theories of Meaning," *Canadian Journal of Philosophy* 17, no. 3 (September 1987): 625–42. Farrell says: "It is odd, given the importance for Davidson of taking the sentence as the primary unit of meaning, that he rarely in the essay talks of the meaning of metaphorical sentences or of the possible semantic location such sentences might have relative

to other sentences in the language. . . . His treatment of metaphor is almost entirely at the subsentential level" (p. 636). A similar puzzlement (why can't radical interpretation save metaphor's truth?) was registered by David Novitz, "Metaphor, Derrida, and Davidson," *Journal of Aesthetics and Art Criticism* 45, no. 4 (Summer 1985): 101–14, esp. 110–11. The problem is a technical one about truth theories for literal statements not having application to metaphors. See Jeffrey Buechner's response to Novitz, "Radically Misinterpreting Radical Interpretation," *Journal of Aesthetics and Art Criticism* 45, no. 4 (Summer 1987): 409–10.

13. Richard Rorty, "Unfamiliar Noises: Hesse and Davidson on Metaphor," *Objectivity, Relativism, and Truth* (Cambridge: Cambridge University Press, 1991): 168–71.

14. The distinction between observing and inhabiting is developed by Charles Taylor, "Theories of Meaning," *Philosophical Papers* 1, esp. p. 255.

15. Ludwig Wittgenstein, *Philosophical Investigations*, 3d ed., trans. G. E. M. Anscombe (New York: Macmillan, 1968), §193e.

16. I side with those who don't see where the line is to be drawn between truth and fiction. David K. Gidden has a paragraph that I admire in his "The Elusiveness of Moral Recognition," which also appears in the *Philosophy and Arts* volume that contains Davidson's "James Joyce and Humpty Dumpty" (see n. 1). Glidden writes:

> Once whatever story is told, it is recorded history, whether it happened or not, whether it be a memoir or a novel. It could be a history bracketed within a novel, such as the tale of *David Copperfield* or it could be a history bracketed within a life, lived in and out of fiction, the memoirs of Virginia Woolf. Reflecting on these histories increases the repertoire of scenes our own imagination can concoct in painting pictures of our own. All such histories, novels, diaries, reflect the condition humanity is in. Consequently, they often do connect with lives and real situations, even when they are fictions, even if the stories are not our own. Stories enrich our ability to see, to recognize the right thing to be done, stories that we tell ourselves or stories others tell us, told of them or even us. (P. 129)

17. See Donald Davidson, "The Structure and Content of Truth," *Journal of Philosophy* 87, no. 6 (June 1990): 312n14: "There is one intention not touched on by a theory of truth which a speaker must intend an interpreter to perceive, the *force* of the utterance. An interpreter must, if he is to understand a speaker, be able to tell whether an utterance is intended as a joke, an assertion, an order, a question, and so forth. I do not believe there are rules or conventions that govern this essential aspect of language. It is something language users can convey to hearers and hearers can, often enough, detect; but this does not show that these abilities can be regimented. I think there are sound reasons for thinking nothing

like a serious theory is possible concerning this dimension of language. Still less are there conventions or rules for creating or understanding metaphors, irony, humor, etc."

18. Martin Heidegger, *Satz vom Grund* (Pfullingen: Günther Neske, 1957), p. 89.

19. See Paul Ricoeur, *The Rule of Metaphor: Multidiscipinary Studies of the Creation of Meaning in Language*, trans. Robert Czerny, Kathleen McLaughlin, and John Costello (Toronto: University of Toronto Press, 1977), esp. pp. 256–313.

20. See Marcia Cavell on Davidson's theory of metaphor, "Metaphor, Dream-work, Irrationality," in *Truth and Interpretation*, pp. 495–507. Metaphor is outside of rationality, but not so far outside as fantasy since, unlike fantasy, metaphor is not inimical to reason, rather it is madness that knows itself as such. J. E. Malpas links Davidson and Heidegger explicitly in *Donald Davidson and the Mirror of Meaning: Holism, Truth, Interpretation* (Cambridge: Cambridge University Press, 1992), esp. pp. 262–77.

21. Jacques Derrida, "Proverb: 'He that would pun . . . ,'" in John P. Leavey, *GLASsary* (Lincoln: University of Nebraska Press, 1986), p. 18. Compare Michel Foucault, "The Discourse on Language," trans. Rupert Swyer, *Social Science Information* 10, no. 2 (April 1971): 7–30; reprinted in Michel Foucault, *The Archeology of Knowledge*, trans. A. W. Sheridan Smith (New York: Harper & Row, 1972), pp. 215–37. See Jean-Jacques Lecercle, *Philosophy through the Looking-Glass: Language, Nonsense, Desire* (La Salle, IL: Open Court, 1985).

22. See Gilles Deleuze and Félix Guattari, *A Thousand Plateaus: Capitalism and Schizophrenia*, trans. Brian Massumi (Minneapolis: University of Minnesota Press, 1987), pp. 75–110 ("November 20, 1923: Postulates of Linguistics") and esp. pp. 100–1:

Since everybody knows that language is a heterogeneous, variable reality, what is the meaning of the linguists' insistence on carrying out a homogeneous system in order to make a scientific study possible? It is a question of extracting a set of constants from the variables, or of determining constant relations between variables. . . . But the scientific model taking language as an object of study is one with the political model by which language is homogeneous, centralized, standardized, becoming a language of power, a major or dominant language. Linguistics can claim all it wants to be a science, nothing but pure science—it wouldn't be the first time that the order of pure science was used to secure the requirements of another order. What is grammatically, and the sign S, the categorical symbol that dominates statements? It is a power marker before it is a syntactical marker, and Chomsky's trees establish constant relations between power variables. Forming grammatically correct sentences is for the normal individual the prerequisite for any submission to social laws. No one is supposed to be ignorant of grammaticality; those who are belong in special institutions. The unity of language is fundamentally political. There is no mother tongue, only a power takeover by a dominant language that at times advances along a broad front, and at times swoops down on diverse centers simultaneously.

23. Donald Davidson, "A Nice Derangement of Epitaphs," p. 162. What is in question is the idea that linguistic competence means having a system for interpreting what someone says.

You might think of this system as a machine which, when fed an arbitrary utterance (and certain parameters provided by the circumstances of the utterance), produces an interpretation. One model for such a machine is a theory of truth, more or less along the lines of a Tarski truth definition. It provides a recursive characterization of the truth conditions of all possible utterances of a speaker, and it does this through an analysis of utterances in terms of sentences made up from the finite vocabulary and the finite stock of modes of composition. I have frequently argued that command of such a theory would suffice for interpretation. (PGR162–63)

24. See Julia Kristeva, "Within the Microcosm of 'The Talking Cure,'" trans. Thomas Gora and Margaret Waller, *Interpreting Lacan* (New Haven, CT: Yale University Press, 1983), pp. 33–48. See Gerald L. Bruns, "The Otherness of Words: Joyce, Bakhtin, Heidegger," in *Postmodernism: Philosophy and the Arts*, ed. Hugh Silverman (London: Routledge & Kegan Paul), pp. 120–36.

25. See Bjørn T. Ramberg on "The Hermeneutics of Radical Interpretation," in his *Donald Davidson's Philosophy of Language: An Introduction* (London: Basil Blackwell, 1989), pp. 138–41.

26. See M. M. Bakhtin, "Discourse in the Novel," *The Dialogic Imagination: Four Essays by M. M. Bakhtin*, trans. Caryl Emerson and Michael Holquist (Austin: University of Texas Press, 1981), p. 282.

27. Ibid.

28. See Ian Hacking's response to Davidson's essay, "A Parody of Conversation," *Truth and Interpretation*, ed. LePore, pp. 454–56.

29. See Daniel Dummett, "Comments on Davidson and Hacking," *Truth and Interpretation*, ed. LePore, p. 462.

30. See Jacques Derrida, introduction to *Edmund Husserl's "Origin of Geometry"* (Stony Brook, NY: Nicolas Hays, 1978), pp. 102–3.

31. Jacques Derrida, *Memoires for Paul de Man* (New York: Columbia University Press, 1986), p. 15.

32. See Deleuze and Guattari, *A Thousand Plateaus*, pp. 92–100.

33. See Hans-Georg Gadamer, *Truth and Method*, 2d rev. ed., trans. Joel Wein-sheimer and Donald G. Marshall (New York: Crossroad Publishing, 1989), p. 320. Davidson's theory of passing theories might be symmetrical with Gadamer's notion of play, where play is not a rule-governed activity but an event, a give-and-take, into which we are taken up as participants. I can only understand a game by playing it, not by decoding it according to a protocol or following a set of directions. Likewise I can only understand another by "playing along with" the other in an activity that is irreducible to the other's subjectivity or mental operations. Gadamer applies this concept with great originality to the problem of making sense of modernist art and literature (Cubism, twelve-tone music, the late poems of Paul Celan: he might well have mentioned *Finnegans Wake*). See Gadamer, "The Relevance of the Beautiful" (1977), in *The Relevance of the Beautiful and Other Essays*, trans. Nicholas Walker, ed. Robert Bernasconi (Cambridge: Cambridge University Press, 1986), pp. 22–31.

34. Davidson seems to think not. See "Knowing One's Own Mind," *Proceedings and Addresses of the American Philosophical Association* (Newark, DE: American Philosophical Association, 1987), pp. 441–58.

35. See, e.g., Cavell on Kripke's reading of Wittgenstein, *Conditions Handsome and Unhandsome: The Constitution of Emersonian Perfectionism* (Chicago: University of Chicago Press, 1990), esp. pp. 80–83.

36. Paul Valéry, "Concerning 'Le Cimitière Marin,'" *The Art of Poetry*, trans. Denise Folliot (New York: Vintage Books, 1961), p. 148. We will have understood Valéry's poem if we understand how it is made.

37. See Cavell, "Aesthetic Problems of Modern Philosophy," *Must We Mean What We Say? A Book of Essays* (Cambridge: Cambridge University Press, 1976), pp. 82–84.

38. Noam Chomsky, *Aspects of a Theory of Syntax* (Cambridge, MA: MIT Press, 1965), p. 4.

39. See Stephen Fredman, *Poet's Prose: The Crisis in American Verse* (Cambridge: Cambridge University Press, 1983), esp. pp. 134–47.

40. See Steve McCaffery, "Language Writing: From Productive to Libidinal Economy" and "Writing as a General Economy," *North of Intention: Critical Writings, 1973–86* (New York: Roof Books; Toronto: Nightwood Editions, 1986), pp. 143–58 and 201–21.

41. McCaffery, "Lyric's Larynx," *North of Intention*, p. 179.

Chapter 3

1. Ronald Dworkin, *A Matter of Principle* (Cambridge, MA: Harvard University Press, 1985), hereafter cited as MP, and *Law's Empire* (Cambridge, MA, and London: Harvard University Press, 1986), hereafter cited as LE.

2. Peter Goodrich, *Reading the Law: A Critical Introduction to Legal Method and Techniques* (London: Basil Blackwell, 1986), p. 20. Hereafter cited as RL.

3. See Peter Goodrich, *Legal Discourse: Studies in Linguistics, Rhetoric, and Legal Analysis* (New York: St. Martin's Press, 1987), pp. 177–78. Hereafter cited as LD.

4. See Owen Fiss, "Objectivity and Interpretation," *Stanford Law Review* 34 (April 1982): 739–63.

5. Roberto Unger, *The Critical Legal Studies Movement* (Cambridge, MA, and London: Harvard University Press, 1986), p. 17. One ought to take note of the diifference between Goodrich and Unger on how the word "critical" is to be understood. It has some resemblance to the difference between deconstructive and Marxist critique. The one is skeptical and satirical, whereas the other is comic or romantic and utopian.

6. See Hans-Georg Gadamer, *Truth and Method*, trans. Joel Weinsheimer and Donald G. Marshall (Crossroad Publishing, 1989), p. 297; see also pp. 285–90 and esp. pp. 324–41. Gadamer's interest in legal hermeneutics is, of course, not a technical one, and what he has to say on the subject is not meant as a theory or method of legal interpretation but is concerned with the place of self-understanding in any interpretative event, and on this point the law serves him as a particularly rich area of hermeneutical reflection. His idea is that the law is a written code whose original meaning is determinable but incomplete, because the code is general in its language but historical in its mode of existence and singular in its application. Legal hermeneutics is what occurs in the give-and-take—the dialogue—between meaning and history. The historicality of the law means that its meaning is always supplemented whenever the law is understood. This understanding is always situated, always an answer to some unique question that needs deciding, and so is different from the understanding of the law in its original meaning, say the understanding a legal historian would have in figuring the law in terms of the situation in which it was originally handed down. Supplementation always takes the form of self-understanding, that is, it is generated by the way we understand ourselves—how we see and judge ourselves—in light of the law. But this self-understanding throws its light on the law in turn, allowing us to grasp the original meaning of the law in a new way. The present gives the past its point. It is far from clear whether this way of thinking, with its heavy emphasis on historicality, is at all translatable into the terms of analytic jurisprudence, with its picture of the law as proposition and its narrow, subjectivist notions of legal interpretation as discretionary judgment.

7. See, e.g., Gadamer's essays collected in *Reason in the Age of Science*, trans. Frederick G. Lawrence (Cambridge, MA: MIT Press, 1981), esp. pp. 69–138. Gadamer's thinking has been fruitfully developed by social theorists and political philosophers—one thinks of Fred Dallmayr and Richard Bernstein. See, e.g., Ronald Beiner, *Political Judgment* (Chicago: University of Chicago Press, 1983).

By contrast, the idea of a non-epistemic, nontechnical rationality seems to have little meaning in legal theory, which is perhaps one reason it is so difficult for legal scholars to defend the legitimacy of legal decisions. See Steven Burton, *An Introduction to Law and Legal Reasoning* (New York: Little, Brown and Co., 1985), esp. pp. 188–93. There is a serene and pretty standard discussion of the analogical and deductive forms of legal reasoning. But surely no one believes that legal practice bears the least resemblance to the picture Burton gives us, or that legal practice could stand up under the critique of instrumentalist and managerial reasoning that is now commonplace in Continental and poststructuralist thinking. In our technological and bureaucratic culture, the function of the law appears to be essentially administrative and regulatory. Its logic is the logic of social management. Possibly this is as it should be, but in practice this means that the best we can hope for from the law is greater operational efficiency. Due process, fairness, legitimacy: these things are becoming too much to ask for. See John D. Caputo, *Radical Hermeneutics: Repetition, Deconstruction, and the Hermeneutic Project* (Bloomington: Indiana University Press, 1987), pp. 209–94, for an account of what a "Postmetaphysical Rationality" might look like. See esp. pp. 212–13:

> The real obstacle to understanding human affairs lies in the tendency to believe that what we do—whether in building scientific theories or in concrete ethical life—admits of formulation in hard and irrevocable rules. It is precisely this claim that human life is rule-governed which brings hermeneutics . . . out of its corner and into the fight. Hermeneutics pits itself against the notion that human affairs can finally be formalized into explicit rules which can or should function as decision-procedure, whether in scientific theory building or in ethics. An important part of the hermeneutics of play is to deconstruct, to undo that myth.

A "hermeneutics of play" is very close to what Gadamer means by *phronesis*. Gadamer would say that, like existence itself, play is the sort of thing that requires *phronesis*. I had thought that *phronesis* cannot be made intelligible within the conceptual outlook of analytical philosophy, but Martha Nussbaum makes a go of it in her attempt to recover Aristotle for analytic moral philosophy. See her account of "nonscientific deliberation" in *The Fragility of Goodness* (Cambridge: Cambridge University Press, 1985), esp. pp. 300–306.

8. See Gerald L. Bruns, "What Is Tradition?" in *Hermeneutics Ancient and Modern* (New Haven, CT: Yale University Press, 1992), pp. 195–212.

9. See Hans-Georg Gadamer, *Truth and Method*, pp. 440–56; and also Supplement 2, "To What Extent Does Language Preform Thought?," pp. 542–49. Gadamer starts out with Wilhelm von Humboldt's idea that language is a web in which every culture is woven, so that there is nothing that is not linguistical; but Gadamer

takes von Humboldt several steps back from Kant. For him, the web is porous, loose, open-ended, intersecting contingently with other webs. It never adds up, or reduces, to a conceptual scheme, whose metaphor is that of a tightly woven fabric or network of systematically interlaced elements. Gadamer's idea is that linguisticality needs to be emancipated from "the dogmatism of the grammarians" (p. 401). In contrast to prison-house theories, Gadamer insists on the unruly or anarchic nature of linguisticality. Perhaps (groping for metaphors) it were better to say that linguisticality is structured more like the weather than like the total, overarching linguistic, semiotic, or ideological system of the grammarians. We can make sense of the weather by studying its patterns, but only up to a point, since these patterns are more anarchic than lawlike. See John Gleick, *Chaos: Making a New Science* (New York: Viking Press, 1987).

10. See Stanley Cavell, *The Claim of Reason: Wittgenstein, Skepticism, Morality, and Tragedy* (New York: Oxford University Press, 1979), pp. 168–90: "Excursus on Wittgenstein's Vision of Language," where Wittgenstein's vision is close to what Gadamer would think of as *Sprachlichkeit*. Cavell's idea, or version of Wittgenstein's idea, is that language is not rule-governed or determined by universals, but neither is it irrational. Cavell speaks of "the fierce ambiguity of ordinary language" (p. 180), but this ambiguity is not to be raised to the status of rule or deep structure, either. What to say, then? Trying to explain the rationality of language is full of traps or double binds or bottomless pits. As Cavell says, "We begin to feel, ought to feel, terrified that maybe language (and understanding, and knowledge) rests upon very shaky foundations—a thin net over an abyss. . . . Perhaps we feel the foundations of language to be shaky when we look for, and miss, foundations of a particular sort, and look upon our shared commitments and responses—as moral philosophers in our liberal tradition have come to do—as more like particular agreements than they are" (p. 178).

11. Martin Heidegger, "On the Way to Language," trans. Peter Hertz, *The Way to Language* (New York: Harper & Row, 1971), p. 134. See Gerald L. Bruns, *Heidegger's Estrangements: Language, Truth, and Poetry in the Later Writings* (New Haven, CT, and London: Yale University Press, 1989). For a somewhat similar view—I mean the idea that modern theories of language and meaning are "nonsense all the way down"—developed from inside analytic philosophy of language, see G. P. Baker and P. M. S. Hacker, *Language, Sense, and Nonsense* (London: Basil Blackwell, 1984).

12. See Roberto Unger's critique of "deep-structure" thinking in *Social Theory: Its Situation and Its Task* (Cambridge: Cambridge University Press, 1987), pp. 87–119. See also his (ironic) distinction between super-theorists and ultra-theorists (pp. 165–70). The "ultra-theorist," Unger says, disbelieves in such things as foundations, frameworks, systems, schemes, paradigms, prison-houses, superstructures, "scripted histories" and other deep-logic theories of culture and society. The ultra-theorist denies the need for "any general theory of frameworks [and] wants, instead,

to nurture an imagination of the particular that does not depend on the pretense of a comprehensive knowledge or of a privileged vantage point. He remembers, he anticipates, and he defies, but he does not claim to disclose secret and fundamental knowledge" (pp. 167–68). The ultra-theorist is animated by a historical sympathy for "repressed solutions, yesterday's missed opportunities, today's forgotten anomalies, and tomorrow's unsuspected possibilities. The ultra-theorist sees a connection between insight into social reality and sympathetic interest in losers" (p. 167). Unger would probably dismiss hermeneutics as unstructured "ultra-theory," merely ad hoc reflection incapable of any vision of ideal social life. On this point he is correct. Hermeneutics is not engaged in the construction of social theories but is rather more interested in what sort of thinking goes into such construction in our current intellectual situation. What it is interesting is the way Unger has intervened in this situation with his critiques and visions. Possibly we have something to learn from Unger about the nature of *phronesis*, or practical wisdom, and the way it is informed and challenged (Gadamer would say "summoned") by theory. The pathos of theory is that it is always excessive with respect to practice. Visionaries always leave us gasping, "How on earth . . . ?" If we knew how to respond to visionaries we wouldn't need them. Unger regards himself as a "super-theorist," someone who also sees the emptiness of deep-structure analysis but who wants to retain the idea of "a countervailing formative context" in which to develop alternative possibilities (visions) of social existence.

13. See Heidegger's essay, "Words," in *On the Way to Language*, esp. pp. 144–48.

14. As a limit case, of course, the *Wake* has inspired critics and grammarians to double their deep-structuring efforts. See Umberto Eco, "The Semantics of Metaphor," trans. John Snyder, in *Semiotics: An Introductory Anthology*, ed. Robert E. Innis (Bloomington: Indiana University Press, 1985), pp. 250–71. Eco takes the *Wake* as "a model of language in general," that is, as "a metaphor for the process of unlimited semiosis" (p. 252). I'm not sure how this works, but the upshot is that the *Wake* is as law-governed as anything despite its crazy surface.

15. For a deep-structured view of the law, see Bernard S. Jackson, *Legal Semiotics* (London: Routledge & Kegan Paul, 1985).

16. The first thing that someone interested in hermeneutics notices about legal theory is its indifference to the questions of language that bedevil Continental thinking and poststructuralist theory. Most inquiries into the subject of law and language are precritical. See David Mellinkoff, *The Language of the Law* (Boston and Toronto: Little, Brown and Co., 1963). This is basically an empirical study of the question, "What is the language of the law?" Legal theory is only now making its linguistic turn. James Boyd White's writings, which derive from ordinary language philosophy and the later Wittgenstein rather than from hard-core analytical philosophy of language, are valuable for the way they loosen up our thinking about texts and meaning. See James Boyd White, "Law as Language: Reading Law

and Reading Literature," *Texas Law Review* 60 (March 1982): 415–45, and esp. 434–
35 on "checking the text," where "the lawyer is engaged in a continuous argument
the terms of which are always changing, in an interaction between the particular
document and its larger world" (p. 435); and James Boyd White, "Constituting a
Culture of Argument: The Possibilities of American Law," *When Words Lose Their
Meaning: Constitutions and Reconstitutions of Language, Character, and Community* (Chicago
and London: University of Chicago Press, 1984), pp. 231–74. Goodrich's *Reading
the Law* may be the first attempt at a critical and theoretical inquiry into the law
that addresses the difficulties that the question of language (still an open one)
poses for legal theory. How we think of the law depends on how we think of
language. The opposite has more often been true: how we think of language is
frequently determined by our scientific notions of what a law is. It appears that
we need to think of language as lawlike for the same reason that we need to think
of the law as rational (or what we think of as rational: namely, rule-governed) all
the way down. But it is not enough to think this way, even though any other way
seems anarchic—as, e.g., in books like Jean-Jacques Lecercle's *Philosophy through
the Looking-Glass: Language, Nonsense, Desire* (La Salle, IL: Open Court, 1985), which
explores "the dark side of language" (p. 57). Granted, Lecercle says, that language
is rule-governed, a total system or system of systems immanent in its effects; but
the uncanny thing about language is the way it escapes totalization, transgresses its
own laws, remains irreducible to a calculus. Language that escapes its own system
is called, after Jacques Lacan, *lalangue*. Its discourse or *parole* is called *délire. Langue* is
the conception of the *logic* of language. "*Lalangue* is the absence, in any given text, of
coherent structure, or rather the proliferation of structures: those which the linguist
analyses, but also those which he rejects (anagrams, homophonic relationships,
tropes). It is the pattern of points where the system fails (this is why the term
'infelicity' is so apt)" (p. 82). It is in the region of *lalangue* that the later Heidegger
wanders. See also Jacques Derrida on the idea that, with respect to any theory
of language, James Joyce must always be there with Edmund Husserl, in *Edmund
Husserl's "Origin of Geometry": An Introduction*, trans. John P. Leavey, Jr. (Stony Brook,
NY: Nicolas Hays, 1978), pp. 100–105.

17. Gillian Rose, *Dialectic of Nihilism: Post-Structuralism and Law* (London: Basil
Blackwell, 1985).

18. Reiner Schürmann, *Heidegger on Being and Acting: From Principles to Anarchy*,
trans. Christine-Marie Gros and Reiner Schürmann (Bloomington: Indiana University Press, 1987). Schürmann might be an example of what Roberto Unger calls
an "ultra-theorist." See n. 12 above.

19. Plato, Seventh Letter, 342e.

20. The locus classicus here might be Roland Barthes, "From Work to Text,"
The Rustle of Language, trans. Richard Howard (New York: Hill and Wang, 1986),
pp. 56–64, but esp. pp. 59–61 on the "plurality" of text.

21. The most obvious or immediate example of this weakness is the pun, the most transgressive and illegal of all discursive forms. It is well known that puns are not the product of *poiesis* or intention; that is, they are not made the way sentences are made. They just happen—so many instances of the excessiveness of meaning. They are going on all the time in language, and linguistic competence consists in bringing them under control, preventing them from happening, so that we aren't always having to say, "No pun intended." Rational discourse consists in speaking strictly, holding fast to the propositional attitude. Puns are not consistent with this attitude; the pun is the basic figure of outlaw discourse (*jouissance*). Punning is an essentially satiric, anarchic, irrepressible event—one could not get farther away from the legal utterance than by way of the pun. See Jacques Derrida, "Proverb: 'He that would pun . . . ,'" in John P. Leavey, Jr., *GLASsary* (Lincoln: University of Nebraska Press, 1987), p. 18: "In the name of what does one condemn these deviations [*écarts*] that are *Witz*, wordplay, spirit, *pun*? Why does one do it most often in the name of knowledge, in the academic institutions that feel themselves responsible for the seriousness of science and philosophy, by supposing that one has nothing to learn from a pun? Better still, or worse, by supposing that the pun must be morally condemned and as such proscribed, for the pun signals some malice [*malignité*], a perverse tendency to transgress the laws of society? The critics are also guardians of these laws, whether they declare it or not. As such, and in their traditional function, they must denounce those who take to the pun."

22. See Jean-Jacques Lecercle, *Philosophy through the Looking-Glass*: "*Délire* . . . is a form of discourse, which questions our most common conceptions of *language* (whether expressed by linguists or philosophers), where the old philosophical question of the emergence of sense out of *nonsense* receives a new formulation, where the material side of language, its origin in the human body and *desire*, are no longer eclipsed by its abstract aspect (as an instrument of communication or expression). Language, nonsense, desire: *délire* accounts for the relations between these three terms" (p. 6). *Délire* marks the borderline of the law and the legal text; it is the region of what psychoanalysts call "borderline discourse." The question is whether the law is able to seal itself off from the transgressions of its boundaries, or whether these transgressions do not belong to the deepest chambers and inner sanctum of the thing itself.

23. See Jacques Derrida, "Comment ne pas parler: *Dénégations*" (1986), *Psyché: Inventions de l'autre* (Paris: Gallimard, 1987), pp. 535–95.

24. The main text for study here is Bakhtin's "Discourse in the Novel," *The Dialogic Imagination: Four Essays by M. M. Bakhtin*, ed. Michael Holquist, trans. Caryl Emerson and Michael Holquist (Austin: University of Texas Press, 1981), pp. 259–452. Hereafter cited as DI.

25. It turns out that this is also Derrida's line. See Jacques Derrida, "The *Retrait* of Metaphor," trans. F. Gasdner et al., *Enclitic* 2 (1978): 5–33.

26. According to Harold Berman, *Law and Revolution: The Formation of the Western Legal Tradition* (Cambridge, MA: Harvard University Press, 1983), unitary forces are winning: "The source and supremacy of law in the plurality of legal jurisdictions and legal systems within the same legal order is threatened in the twentieth century by the tendency within each country to swallow up all the diverse jurisdictions and systems in a single central program of legislation and administrative regulation. . . . Blackstone's concept of two centuries ago that we live under a considerable number of different legal systems has hardly any counterpart in contemporary legal thought" (pp. 38–39). Berman's attempt to make sense of the law historically rather than theoretically is very appealing from a hermeneutical standpoint, because it is testimony to the multiple and heterogeneous reality of the law; but for Berman it is nevertheless true that this heterogeneity is only the surface of the law, and that the "Western tradition" is rooted in a homogeneity of "postulates" that have survived intact until the present time. This is closer to Ronald Dworkin's way of thinking than, say, to Hans-Georg Gadamer's. Berman's notion of tradition is more monumental and idealist than Gadamer's historicized conception. Berman's history of law is eschatological rather than genealogical. It looks forward to a time when the heterogeneity of legal systems will be embraced by "a common legal language for mankind" (p. 45). Gadamer's idea would be that "common languages" can only be worked out in particular historical situations and in response to the contingencies of events. The idea of a common language in the sense of a totalist scheme is just historically implausible.

27. Catharine MacKinnon, "Feminism, Marxism, Method, and the State: Toward Feminist Jurisprudence," *Signs: Journal of Women in Culture and Society* 8 (1983): 635–58.

28. Ibid., p. 645.

29. See Frank Burton and Pat Carlen, *Official Discourse* (London: Routledge & Kegan Paul, 1979), pp. 57–58, 69.

30. Stanley Cavell, *The Claim of Reason*, p. 241.

Chapter 4

1. Martin Heidegger, *Being and Time*, trans. John Robinson and Edward Macquarrie (New York: Harper & Row, 1959), p. 63; translation slightly amended.

2. See *Midwest Studies in Philosophy* 13, ed. Peter A. French, Theodore E. Uehling, Jr., and Howard Wettstein (Notre Dame, IN: University of Notre Dame Press, 1988). See also *Identity, Character, and Morality: Essays in Moral Psychology*, ed. Owen Flanagan and Amélie Oksenberg Rorty (Cambridge, MA: MIT Press, 1990), esp. Gary Watson's essay, "On the Primacy of Character" (pp. 449–70).

3. See Alasdair MacIntyre, *After Virtue: A Study in Moral Theory* (Notre Dame, IN: University of Notre Dame Press, 1981), hereafter cited as AV; *Whose Justice? Which Rationality?* (Notre Dame, IN: University of Notre Dame Press, 1988), hereafter cited as WJ; and *Three Rival Versions of Moral Inquiry* (Notre Dame, IN: University of Notre Dame Press, 1990), hereafter cited as TRV.

4. Cf. Peter Winch, "The Universalizability of Moral Judgments," *Ethics and Action* (London: Routledge & Kegan Paul, 1972), pp. 151–70.

5. On the lack of complexity in MacIntyre's theory, see D. Z. Phillips, "After Virtue?" *Interventions in Ethics* (Albany, NY: SUNY Press, 1992), pp. 42–60, esp. pp. 59–60.

6. Charles Taylor makes a useful distinction between ancient and modern conceptions of the subject in his book *Hegel* (Cambridge: Cambridge University Press, 1975), p. 6: "The essential difference can perhaps be put in this way: the modern subject is self-defining, where on previous views the subject is defined in relation to a cosmic order." The modern subject is a disengaged rational ego, external to the world and responsible for its shaping; the ancient subject occupies a place within an order of things. In effect, MacIntyre wants to restore the ancient conception of the human subject. A very valuable essay is Taylor's "The Moral Topography of the Self," *Hermeneutics and Psychological Theory: Interpretive Perspectives on Personality, Psychotherapy, and Psychopathology,* ed. Stanley B. Messer et al. (New Brunswick, NJ, and London: Rutgers University Press, 1988), pp. 298–320. See also Taylor's "Self-Interpreting Animals," *Philosophical Papers,* vol. 1, *Human Agency and Language* (Cambridge: Cambridge University Press, 1985), pp. 45–76.

7. See Robert Langbaum, *The Poetry of Experience: The Dramatic Monologue in Modern Literary Tradition* (New York: W. W. Norton, 1963), p. 160: "For it is because they had lost sight of that traditional ethos from which the Enlightenment separates us that nineteenth-century readers read Shakespeare as they read the literature of their own time. They read him not as drama in the traditional Aristotelian sense, not in other words as a literature of external action in which the events derive meaning from their relation to a publicly acknowledged morality, but as literature of experience, in which the events have meaning inasmuch as they provide the central character with an occasion for experience—for self-expression and self-discovery. What such a reading suggests is that drama depends for its structure on belief in a single objective moral system, and dissolves without that belief into monodrama—into the nineteenth-century's substitute for poetic drama, the dramatic monologue."

8. J. Hillis Miller, *The Forms of Victorian Fiction* (Notre Dame, IN: University of Notre Dame Press, 1968), p. 2.

9. See particularly Eric A. Havelock, "The Socratic Self As It Is Parodied in Aristophanes' *Clouds*," *Yale Classical Studies* 22 (1972): 1–18.

10. See Aristotle, *Nicomachean Ethics* 1128a, where he himself acknowledges these traditions. Hereafter cited as A.

11. Robert Musil, *The Man without Qualities*, trans. Eithne Wilkins and Ernst Kaiser (New York: Perigree Books, 1953), p. 34.

12. Hannah Arendt, *The Human Condition* (Chicago: University of Chicago Press, 1958), p. 184.

13. See Wilhelm Dilthey, "The Construction of the Historical World through the Human Sciences," *Dilthey: Selected Writings*, trans. H. P. Hickman (Cambridge: Cambridge University Press, 1976), p. 235. Dilthey says: "Meaning is the comprehensive category through which life can be understood," and "the category of meaning is the relationship, inherent in life, of parts of a life to the whole." Moreover, the category of meaning is, for Dilthey, superior to the concept of purpose, or *telos*: "The category of purpose, or of good, which considers life as directed towards the future, presupposes that of value. But the connectedness of life cannot be established from this category either, for the relations of purposes to each other are only those of possibility, choice, and subordination. Only the category of meaning overcomes mere to co-existence of the subordinating of the parts of life to each other" (p. 216). And as Dilthey explains in several places, e.g., in his remarks on autobiography, the primacy of the category of meaning means the primacy of narrative (pp. 214–16).

14. See W. V. O. Quine, "Two Dogmas of Empiricism," *From a Logical Point of View: Nine Logico-Philosophical Essays* (Cambridge, MA: Harvard University Press, 1953), pp. 42–45.

15. It would be interesting to try to fit what MacIntyre says about narrative into a volume like *Interpretation and Narrative*, ed. Vario J. Valdés and Owen J. Miller (Toronto, Buffalo, London: University of Toronto Press, 1978), in which teleology, e.g., is no longer a concept with any force or application. See esp. J. Hillis Miller's contribution, "Ariadne's Thread: Repetition and the Narrative Line" (pp. 148–66).

16. Iris Murdoch, "Against Dryness: A Polemical Sketch," *Revisions: Changing Perspectives in Moral Philosophy*, ed. Stanley Hauerwas and Alasdair MacIntyre (Notre Dame, IN: University of Notre Dame Press, 1983), pp. 46–47. Hereafter cited as AD.

17. Alasdair MacIntyre, "Relativism, Power, and Philosophy," *Relativism: Interpretation and Confrontation*, ed. Michael Krausz (Notre Dame, IN: University of Notre Dame Press, 1989), pp. 193–94. Hereafter cited as RIC.

18. See Gerald L. Bruns, "The Interpretation of Character in Jane Austen," *Inventions: Writing, Textuality, and Understanding in Literary History* (New Haven, CT: Yale University Press, 1982), pp. 111–24.

19. Emmanuel Levinas gives us an ethical theory which is based on biblical models of exposure to time and history as against Greek models of *eudaimonia* or the wholeness of life. See in particular Levinas's essay, "Substitution," *Otherwise Than*

Being or Beyond Essence, trans. Alphonso Lingis (The Hague: Martinus Nijhoff, 1971), pp. 99–129.

20. Alasdair MacIntyre, "Epistomological Crises, Dramatic Narrative, and the Philosophy of Science," *The Monist* 60, no. 4 (October 1977): 454–55; hereafter cited as EC. See also WJ22.

21. Cora Diamond, "Losing Your Concepts," *Ethics* 98, no. 2 (January 1988): 268–69.

22. See RIC, p. 196: On "the nature of the historical process which made the language of modernity what it is": "A central feature of that process had to be . . . the detachment of the language-in-use from any particular set of canonical texts; and an early stage in that history was the gradual accumulation in the culture of so many different, heterogeneous, and conflicting bodies of canonical texts from so many diverse parts of the cultural past that every one of them had to forego any exclusive claim to canonical status and thereby, it soon became apparent, any claim to canonical status at all." Derrida's idea would be that, with modernity's surplus or excess of languages and narratives, one gains in freedom what one loses in justification.

23. See Martin Heidegger, "The End of Philosophy and the Task of Thinking," *On Time and Being,* trans. Joan Stambaugh (New York: Harper & Row, 1969), pp. 55–73. Hannah Arendt, *The Human Condition* (Chicago: University of Chicago Press, 1958), pp. 22–78.

24. See Richard Rorty, *Contingency, Irony, and Solidarity* (Cambridge: Cambridge University Press, 1989). Hereafter cited as CIS.

25. The main texts in this dispute are available in *Rationality,* ed. Bryan R. Wilson (New York: Harper & Row, 1970): Peter Winch, "The Idea of a Social Science" (pp. 1–17); MacIntyre, "Is Understanding Religion Compatible with Believing It?" (pp. 62–77); Winch, "Understanding a Primitive Society" (pp. 78–111); and MacIntyre, "The Idea of a Social Science" (pp. 112–30).

26. The problem here is one that Joseph Margolis tries to engage in *Texts without Referents: Reconciling Nature and Narrative* (London: Basil Blackwell, 1989), namely the problem of whether a rationality applicable to physical reality can be equally applicable to cultural reality. Are meanings within the same ordinance of explanation as causes? See esp. pp. 187–234.

27. On the moral questionableness of a moral community, see John D. Caputo, *Against Ethics* (Bloomington: Indiana University Press, 1990).

28. W. B. Yeats, *A Vision* (New York: Macmillan, 1965), pp. 279–80.

29. Mikhail Bakhtin, "From the Prehistory of the Novel," *The Dialogue Imagination: Four Essays by M. M. Bakhtin,* trans. Caryl Emerson and Michael Holquist (Austin: University of Texas Press, 1981), p. 52. Hereafter cited as DI.

30. The best place to begin thinking through the sometimes incommensurable values of justice and freedom is the work of the political theorist William Connolly. See *The Ethos of Pluralization* (Minneapolis: University of Minnesota Press, 1995);

Identity/Difference: Democratic Negotiations of Political Paradox (Ithaca, NY: Cornell University Press, 1991); *Political Theory and Modernity* (Ithaca, NY: Cornell University Press, 1988); and, esp. with respect to MacIntyre, *The Augustinian Imperative: A Reflection on the Politics of Morality* (New York: Sage Books, 1992).

31. See two excellent studies that examine the social and political complexity of the so-called vernacular revolutions in the Renaissance: Paula Blank, *Broken English: Dialects and the Politics of Language in Renaissance Writings* (London: Routledge, 1996), and Judith Anderson, *Words That Matter: Linguistic Perception in Renaissance English* (Stanford, CA: Stanford University Press, 1996).

32. John McCumber, *Poetic Interaction: Language, Freedom, Reason* (Chicago and London: University of Chicago Press, 1989), p. 1. Hereafter cited as PI.

Chapter 5

1. Stanley Cavell, *The Claim of Reason: Wittgenstein, Morality, Skepticism, and Tragedy* (New York and Oxford: Oxford University Press, 1979), p. 496. This essay originated as a paper for a conference entitled "Neurobiology and Narrative" held at the University of Notre Dame in April 1991. Linking neurobiology and narrative together caught a lot of people, mainly philosophers and literary critics, by surprise. Interestingly, a lot of neuroscientists present were not surprised but had already made "narrative" part of their vocabulary. I did not understand very clearly what the word meant to them, especially since so many present were "eliminativists" committed to the abolition of "folk psychology" (or literature for short) in favor of physiological descriptions of how the brain works. Evidently narrative is a metaphor for the brain's capacity to improvise combinations as against the capacity it shares with computers for calculation and representation. As a mostly uncritical reader of Heidegger, I naturally liked very much the turn that the scientists seemed to be taking away from calculative and conceptual rationality, the modes of thinking that Heidegger singled out as marking the triumph (and therefore the end) of philosophy. My sense of narrative, however, having been shaped (not by Heidegger but) by *The Life and Opinions of Tristram Shandy*, was and remains something very different from a process of combination. I prefer the anarchic theory that narrative puts things together only in order to serve as a medium for their coming apart, or as an occasion for them to register their ontological refusal to connect with other things whether similar or different. Pursuing this thought one becomes a champion of singularity, non-identity, alterity, and other postmodern values. I should mention that I've been seeking support for my anarchism from the French writer Maurice Blanchot, the philosopher of fragments. His writings have helped me to realize that the basic unit of reality (or, one might say, of history) is the interruption. See,

e.g., his essay, "Interruption (as on a Riemann surface)," *The Infinite Conversation*, trans. Susan Hanson (Minneapolis: University of Minnesota Press, 1993), pp. 75–79. The interruption, according to Blanchot, is not simply a blank or gap in a continuity; it is a change in form or structure—"A change such that to speak (to write) is *to cease thinking solely with a view toward unity*, and to make the relations of words an essentially dissymmetrical field governed by discontinuity; as though, having renounced the uninterrupted force of a coherent discourse, it were a matter of drawing out a level of language where one might gain the power not only to express oneself in an intermittent manner, but also to allow intermittance itself to speak: a speech that, non-unifying, is no longer content with being a passage or a bridge—a non-pontificating speech capable of clearing the two shores separated by an abyss, but without filling in the abyss or reuniting its shores: a speech without reference to unity" (pp. 77–78). Anyhow the interruption is what narratives (worlds) are made of. The following essay doesn't so much try to justify this belief as use it to scare some philosophers who think that narrative is a species of propositional discourse serving, for cognitive or edifying purposes, the usual function of mediation. Of course, this theory of narrative can be made immensely complex and attractive, as a recent collection of very interesting essays shows. See *Narrative in Culture: The Uses of Storytelling in the Sciences, Philosophy, and Literature*, ed. Christopher Nash (London: Routledge, 1990), esp. the essay by Donald McCloskey, "Storytelling in Economics" (pp. 5–22), as well as the editor's contribution, "Slaughtering the Subject: Literature's Assault on Narrative" (pp. 199–218).

2. A short checklist of relevant titles would include the following: Paul Ricoeur, *Time and Narrative*, 3 vols. (Chicago: University of Chicago Press, 1984–89); Alasdair MacIntyre, *After Virtue: A Study in Moral Theory* (Notre Dame, IN: University of Notre Dame Press, 1981), hereafter cited as AV; D. Z. Phillips, *Through a Darkening Glass: Philosophy, Literature, and Cultural Change* (Notre Dame, IN: University of Notre Dame Press, 1982), and *Interventions in Ethics* (Albany: SUNY Press, 1992); Jerome Bruner, *Actual Minds, Possible Worlds* (Cambridge, MA: Harvard University Press, 1986), *Acts of Meaning* (Cambridge, MA: Harvard University Press, 1990), esp. pp. 43–65, and "The Narrative Construction of Reality," *Critical Inquiry* 18, no. 1 (Autumn 1991): 1–21; Anthony Kerby, *Narrative and the Self* (Bloomington: Indiana University Press, 1991); Roy Schafer, *Retelling a Life: Narration and Dialogue in Psychoanalysis* (New York: Basic Books, 1992); Cora Diamond, "On the Importance of Being Human," in *Human Beings*, ed. David Cockburn (Cambridge: Cambridge University Press, 1991), pp. 35–62.

3. Antonio Damasio, *Descartes' Error: Reason, Emotion, and the Human Brain* (New York: Avon Books, 1994), pp. 242–43.

4. Alasdair MacIntyre, *Whose Justice? Which Rationality?* (Notre Dame, IN: University of Notre Dame Press, 1988), p. 352.

5. Richard Rorty, *Contingency, Irony, and Solidarity* (Cambridge: Cambridge

University Press, 1989), hereafter cited as CIS; see p. 19: "Positivist history of culture . . . sees language as gradually shaping itself around the contours of the physical world. Romantic history of culture sees language as gradually bringing Spirit to self-consciousness. Nietzschean history of culture, and Davidsonian philosophy of language, see language as we now see evolution, as new forms of life constantly killing off old forms—not to accomplish a higher purpose, but blindly." On my reading, Rorty tinkers with this scheme by seeing the constant killing off of old forms of life by the new as a method of emancipation.

6. Alasdair MacIntyre, "Epistemological Crises, Dramatic Narrative, and the Philosophy of Science," *The Monist* 60, no. 4 (October 1977): 459; and AV 190–209.

7. Richard Rorty, "Inquiry as Recontextualization: An Anti-Dualist Account of Interpretation," *Objectivity, Relativism, and Truth* (Cambridge: Cambridge University Press, 1991), p. 93.

8. Ibid., p. 110.

9. See Jorge Luis Borges, "The Garden of the Forking Paths," which is the story about Ts'ui-Pên, a connoisseur of labyrinths, who leaves behind him when he dies an unreadable novel entitled *The Garden of the Forking Paths*. Someone explains: "In all fictional works, each time a man is confronted with several alternatives, he chooses one and eliminates the others; in the fiction of Ts'ui-Pên, he chooses— simultaneously—all of them. *He creates*, in this way, diverse futures, diverse times which themselves also proliferate and fork" (p. 26). The novel is said to be "an incomplete, but not false, image of the universe as Ts'ui-Pên conceived it. In contrast to Newton and Schopenhauer, your ancestor did not believe in uniform, absolute time. He believed in an infinite series of times, in a growing, dizzying net of divergent, convergent, and parallel lines. This network of times which approached one another, forked, broke off, or were unaware of one another for centuries, embraces *all* possibilities of time" (p. 28). See Gary Saul Morson's study of complex temporalities of narrative, *Narrative and Freedom: The Shadows of Time* (New Haven, CT: Yale University Press, 1994), esp. 117–72 (on "sideshadowing"). One could speculate that the difference between literary history and the history of philosophy (or science) is that the one is structured like a novel by Ts'ui-Pên, whereas the other practices "eliminativism" in the belief that too many stories makes justifiable true beliefs impossible.

10. Jean-François Lyotard, "Wittgenstein 'After,'" *Political Writing*, trans. Bill Readings and Kevin Paul (Minneapolis: University of Minnesota Press, 1993), p. 21.

11. Peter Winch, "Moral Integrity," *Ethics and Action* (London: Routledge & Kegan Paul, 1972), p. 182.

12. The classic argument is Paul Churchland's in "Eliminative Materialism and the Propositional Attitudes," *Journal of Philosophy* 78, no. 2 (1981), rpt. as *A Neurocomputational Perspective: The Nature of Mind and the Structure of Science* (Cambridge,

MA, and London: MIT Press, 1989), pp. 1–22; see also pp. 111–29, where Churchland gives the gist of the eliminativist argument:

> [Neuroscience] is unlikely to find "sentences in the head" or anything else that answers to the structure of individual beliefs and desires. On the strength of this shared assumption, I am willing to infer that folk psychology is false, and that its ontology is chimerical. Beliefs and desires are of a piece with phlogiston, caloric, and the alchemical sciences. We therefore need an entirely new kinematics and dynamics with which to comprehend human cognitive activity, one drawn, perhaps, from computational neuroscience and connectionist AI. Folk psychology could then be put aside in favor of this descriptively more accurate and explanatorily more powerful portrayal. Certainly, it will be put aside in the lab and in the clinic, and eventually, perhaps, in the marketplace as well. (P. 125)

See also Stephen Stich, *From Folk Psychology to Cognitive Science* (Cambridge, MA: MIT Press, 1983), p. 229, where folk theory is said to be "screamingly false"; and Patricia Churchland, *Neurophilosophy: Toward a Unified Science of the Mind/Brain* (Cambridge, MA: MIT Press, 1986), pp. 277–313, esp. pp. 299–310 and p. 302.

My sense is that most neuroscientists, neurophilosophers, and so on, do not realize or understand that there is any link (or, really, identity) between folk psychology and literature, and that getting rid of the one would mean, practically speaking, getting rid of the other (e.g., no longer teaching it in school). My informal conversations with neuroscientists (maybe three) indicates that they would reject with horror the practical consequences of their views, which if pursued with scientific rigor would amount to the burning of books and the censorship of nonscientific disciplines. They have no conception of folk psychology except as something that tried to be good science and failed.

The underdescription of folk psychology by neurophilosophers like the Churchlands is itself a nice anthropological problem. The Harvard psychologist Jerome Bruner thinks of himself as defending folk psychology in *Acts of Meaning*, pp. 33–65, where he describes it as an "instrument of culture," or culture's way of keeping itself under rational control. Bruner's is a functional theory of folk psychology (or of narrative, or of literature, or—for that matter—of religion): the task of narrative is to organize experience into hierarchies of coherence, thereby giving us an intelligible world to inhabit. Bruner speaks of "some human 'readiness' for narrative" comparable to our "readiness to convert the world of visual input into figure and ground" (p. 45). Basically this is a Kantian theory of narrative to which everyone subscribes more or less. The details of the theory have been worked out with specific attention to Kant by Claudia Brodsky, *The Imposition of Form: Studies in Narrative Representation and Knowledge* (Princeton, NJ: Princeton University

Press, 1987), esp. pp. 21–87. A non-Kantian theory of narrative would, in all likelihood, be a theory of the fragment, or a theory of what it is in narratives that resists the imposition of form. Here one would have to begin consulting studies of language and propositional attitudes by psychoanalytically inclined theorists. The most compelling of these is Jean-Jacques Lecercle, author of *Philosophy through the Looking-Glass* (La Salle, IL: Open Court, 1985), and *The Violence of Language* (London: Routledge, 1990).

13. Richard Rorty, "In Defense of Eliminative Materialism," *Review of Metaphysics* 24, no. 1 (September 1970): 120.

14. See Jürgen Habermas, "Philosophy as Stand-In and Interpreter," *Moral Consciousness and Communicative Action*, trans. Christian Lenhardt and Shierry Weber Nicholson (Cambridge, MA: MIT Press, 1990), pp. 1–20. This is an essay about the danger of philosophy "losing its identity" (p. 16) if it cooperates too much with nonphilosophical intellectual practices. Habermas wants to hold on to some version of Kant's idea of philosophy as the monitor of our cultural discourses with a view toward keeping them in line with the propositional standards of philosophical argument. The program here is pretty much that of Plato's *Republic*, with philosophy acting, in Habermas's phrase, as "the guardian of rationality" (p. 17). One gets the full force of this argument in Habermas, *The Philosophical Discourse of Modernity*, trans. Frederick G. Lawrence (Cambridge, MA: MIT Press, 1990).

15. Rorty adapts Bloom to his own theory of redescription in CIS40–42. Perhaps a theory of obsolescence can be extracted from literary history by applying an axiom from art history that not everything is possible at every moment, but the fact that no one any longer does or can write a Homeric epic does not mean that Homeric epics are out of date in the way that the things Homeric heroes believed in are, or appear to be, for most people, out of date. But of course if one takes the *Odyssey* to be simply a web of beliefs, then one can take it that the *Odyssey* is an obsolete text, that is, it is no longer our—anyway no longer your—ownmost web. But one might also take it that the *Odyssey* is, in a variety of ways, excessive to its function as a web of beliefs. Smart policy among philosophers has always been to allegorize Homer so that he will always remain consistent with current beliefs. Horkheimer and Adorno in their *Dialectic of Enlightenment* offer a modern example of how to keep Homer from going out of date.

16. Richard Rorty, "Non-Reductive Physicalism," *Objectivism, Relativism, Truth* (Cambridge: Cambridge University Press, 1991), p. 114.

17. See Joseph Margolis, *Texts without Reference: Reconciling Science and Narrative* (London: Basil Blackwell, 1989), p. 301; and Arthur Danto, "The Artworld," *Journal of Philosophy* 10 (1968): 162.

18. See Cora Diamond, "Losing Your Concepts," *Ethics* 98, no. 2 (January 1988): 255–77.

19. Hubert Dreyfus, "Holism and Hermeneutics," in *Hermeneutics and Praxis*, ed.

Robert Hollinger (Notre Dame, IN: University of Notre Dame Press, 1985), pp. 227–47.

20. "What the Romantics expressed as the claim that the imagination, rather than reason, is the central human faculty was the realization that a talent for speaking differently, rather than for arguing well, is the chief instrument of cultural change" (CIS7).

21. See Diamond, "Losing Your Concepts."

22. William Gass, "The Medium of Fiction," *Fiction and the Figures of Life* (Boston: Nonpareil Books, n.d.), pp. 30, 33. Marble is another of Gass's favorite metaphors for language: what happens when we use language as if it were marble rather than as a system for framing representations?

23. See William Paulson, *The Noise of Culture: Literary Texts in a World of Information* (Ithaca, NY: Cornell University Press, 1988), esp. pp. 80–100.

24. Jurij Lotman, *The Structure of the Artistic Text*, trans. Gail Lenhoff and Ronald Vroon (Ann Arbor: Michigan Slavic Contributions, no. 7, 1977), p. 75.

25. Of noise Michel Serres (*Genesis*, trans. Geneviève James and James Nielson [Ann Arbor: University of Michigan Press, 1995]) writes:

> Background noise may well be the ground of our being. It may be that our being is not at rest, it may be that it is not in motion, it may be that our being is disturbed. The background noise never ceases; it is limitless, continuous, unending, unchanging. It has itself no background, no contradictory. . . . Noise cannot be a phenomenon; every phenomenon is separated from it, a silhouette on a backdrop, like a beacon against the fog, as every message, every cry, every call, every signal must be separated from the hubbub that occupies silence, in order to be, to be perceived, to be known, to be exchanged. As soon as a phenomenon appears, it leaves the noise; as soon as a form looms up or pokes through, it reveals itself by veiling noise. So noise is not a matter of phenomenology, so it is a matter of being itself. It settles in subjects as well as in objects, in hearing as well as in space, in the observers as well as in the observed, it moves through the means and the tools of observation, whether material or logical, hardware or software, constructed channels or languages; it is part of the in-itself, part of the for-itself; it cuts across the oldest and surest philosophical divisions, yes, noise is metaphysical. It is the complement to physics, in the broadest sense. (P. 13)

26. Churchland, *A Neurocomputational Perspective*, p. 8.

27. Jorge Luis Borges, "The Library of Babel," *Labyrinths* (New York: New Directions, 1961), p. 54.

28. In *Contingency, Irony, and Solidarity* Rorty makes this interesting distinction, that "whereas the Romantic sees Yeats as having gotten at something which nobody

had previously gotten at, expressed something which had long been yearning for expression, the Davidsonian sees him as having hit upon some tools which enabled him to write poems which were not just variations on the poems of his precursors. Once we had Yeats's later poems in hand, we were less interested in reading Rossetti's" (pp. 19–20). But this is just to map the history of science onto literary history, missing, as if it were a barn door, Yeats's lesson that he *was*, in a certain way of putting it, writing variations on the poems of his precursors, among whom ("I was in all things Pre-Raphaelite") he numbered Dante Gabriel Rossetti.

29. Alasdair MacIntyre, *Relativism: Interpretation and Confrontation*, ed. Michael Krausz (Notre Dame, IN: University of Notre Dame Press, 1989), p. 196.

30. MacIntyre thus supplies a reason why, as Lyotard says in a famous thesis, our metanarratives are no longer credible; they've been swallowed up by a culture that rules nothing out.

31. On the normative character of the history of physics, see Alasdair MacIntyre, *Three Rival Versions of Moral Enquiry: Encyclopaedia, Genealogy, and Tradition* (Notre Dame, IN: University of Notre Dame Press, 1990), pp. 150–51.

32. Laurence Sterne, *The Life and Opinions of Tristram Shandy, Gentleman*, vol. 1, bk. 14.

33. See Gerald L. Bruns, "Toward a Random Theory of Prose," introduction to Viktor Shlovsky, *Theory of Prose*, trans. Benjamin Sher (Elmwood Park, IL: Dalkey Archive Press, 1990), pp. ix–xiv. Cf. Anthony Cascardi, "Narrative and Totality," *The Philosophical Forum* 21, no. 3 (Spring 1990): esp. 290:

> [Consider] the novel as an attempt to construct a totality in an otherwise "detotalized" world [a totality would be what MacIntyre looks for in narratives]. On the one hand, narration in the novel displays a preoccupation with reality that is coincident with the goals of philosophical enlightenment in securing the rationality of the world. Yet on the other hand, the novel responds to a need for the (conscious, historical) mediation of experience and for the articulation of desires as the bases of a vision of personal identity that cannot always be centered with respect to a social whole. At the same time, novelistic narration must balance the coherence and continuity required of a story against a variety of threats to the integrity of the whole. These threats often take the form of details, digressions, and apparent distractions from the principal story line or plot, and may be likened to what Bataille described as the "heterogeneous" elements at work within culture as a whole. Beginning with Cervantes, and in a remarkable way with Sterne, the tensions between continuity and digression, between narrative distraction and the will to conclude, constitute the twin poles of narration, and the fundamental energies of the novel may be seen to derive from them. The "waywardness" of the novel is fueled by the unpredictability of desire and by the introduction of various forms of disruption, often configured as desire or lack. . . .

This captures an important historical point that gets ignored in what one might call cognitive approaches to narrative, as in the collection *Narrative Thought and Narrative Language,* ed. Bruche Britton and A. D. Pellegrini (Hillsdale, NJ: Lawrence Erlbaum Associates, 1990), which gathers papers from a very interesting conference in 1987 organized by the Institute for Behaviorial Research at the University of Georgia.

34. See Daniel Dennett, *Consciousness Explained* (New York: Little, Brown & Co., 1991), p. 135. See Rorty's review of Daniel Dennett's *Consciousness Explained* in the *London Review of Books* 13, no. 22 (November 21, 1991): 3–6. There is also an interesting volume of critical responses to Dennett, *Dennett and His Critics,* ed. Bo Dahlbom (London: Routledge, 1993). See in particular the editor's contribution, "Mind Is Artificial," pp. 161–83, which is a very persuasive argument against the premise (on which the whole of neuroscience and neurophilosophy is based) that the brain is a biological entity. In an essay entitled "The Growing Philosophical Neglect of History and Culture," *Philosophical Forum* 28–29 (Summer/Fall 1977), Joseph Margolis writes: "Certainly, it follows as a direct consequence that *if* the mind is a socially 'constructed' site of competences embedded in historically emergent collective practices, then physicalism, reductive or eliminative, cannot but be completely false" (p. 292).

35. See Daniel Dennett, "Why Everyone Is a Novelist," *Times Literary Supplement* (September 16–22, 1988).

36. See Andy Clark, *Microcognition: Philosophy, Cognitive Science, and Parallel Distributed Processing* (Cambridge, MA: MIT Press, 1989), esp. pp. 83–106.

37. There is, e.g., no such thing as the Bible; there are only multiple and heterogeneous versions of endlessly redacted, wildly disseminated, relentlessly reinterpreted sacred texts irreducible to anything like a single, authoritative, universally canonical Scripture. See Gerald Bruns, "Secrecy and Understanding," *Inventions: Writing, Textuality, and Understanding in Literary History* (New Haven, CT: Yale University Press, 1982), pp. 17–43, esp. pp. 24–30.

38. Jerome McGann, "History, Herstory, Theirstory, Ourstory," in *Theoretical Issues in Literary History,* ed. David Perkins (Cambridge, MA: Harvard University Press, 1991), p. 197.

39. Gilles Deleuze and Félix Guattari, *Mille plateaux* (Paris: Editions de minuit, 1980), pp. 31–32; *A Thousand Plateaus,* trans. Brian Massumi (Minneapolis: University of Minnesota Press, 1987), p. 21.

Chapter 6

1. Martha Nussbaum, "Flawed Crystals: James's *The Golden Bowl* and Literature as Moral Philosophy," *Love's Knowledge: Essays on Philosophy and Literature* (New York and Oxford: Oxford University Press, 1990), p. 139; hereafter cited as LK. See

also Martha Nussbaum, *The Fragility of Goodness: Luck and Ethics in Greek Tragedy and Philosophy* (Cambridge: Cambridge University Press, 1986), pp. 14–15; hereafter cited as FG.

2. In this stress on particularity Nussbaum is anticipated and, in many ways, exceeded by the so-called Welsh school of ethical theory, principally Peter Winch and D. Z. Phillips, who reject the idea that moral philosophy consists in the discovery of rules to show how in general people should act; rather, moral philosophy consists in the study of how moral judgments actually take place against the background of the heterogeneity and complexity of moral beliefs, practices, and situations. See J. L. Stocks, *Morality and Purpose* (London: Routledge & Kegan Paul, 1970); Peter Winch, *Ethics and Action* (London: Routledge & Kegan Paul, 1972), and *Trying to Make Sense* (Oxford: Basil Blackwell, 1987), esp. the chap. "Particularity and Morals," pp. 167–80; D. Z. Phillips, *Interventions in Ethics* (Albany: SUNY Press, 1992); and the essays by various hands in *Wittgenstein: Attention to Particulars: Essays in Honour of Rush Rhees*, ed. D. Z. Phillips and Peter Winch (New York: St. Martin's Press, 1989).

3. Emmanuel Levinas, *Totality and Infinity*, trans. Alphonso Lingis (Philadelphia: Duquesne University Press, 1961), p. 39. Hereafter cited as TI.

4. Emmanuel Levinas, *Otherwise Than Being or Beyond Essence*, trans. Alphonso Lingis (The Hague: Martinus Nijhoff, 1981), p. 48. Hereafter cited as OTB.

5. See Martha Nussbaum, "The Discernment of Perception: An Aristotelian Conception of Private and Public Rationality," LK54–105.

6. This matter is complicated in interesting ways. In her superb analysis of James's *Ambassadors*, Nussbaum raises the question of whether the intimacy of others does not constitute the limit of a morality of perception. The case is that of Strether as a moral agent confronting the intimacy of Chad and Mme. de Vionnet. "What Strether senses is that what he calls the 'deep deep truth' of sexual love is at odds with the morality of perception, in two ways. It asks for privacy, for others to avert their gaze; and on the inside it asks that focus be averted from all else that is outside. Lovers see, at such times, only one another; and it is not really deep if they *can* carefully see around and about them. That vision excludes general attention and care, at least at that moment. And this intimacy is a part of the world that demands *not* to be in the eyes of the perceiving, recording novelist—at least not in all of its particularity" (LK188–89). To which Nussbaum adds: "Perception as a morality enjoins trust in responsive feeling; but its feelings are the feelings of a friend. . . . There is reason to suppose that the exclusivity and intensity of personal love would in fact impede the just and general responsiveness that these gentler feelings assist. And if they impede that, they impede the perceiver's contribution to our moral project, to our communal effort to arrive at perceptive equilibrium. But the recognition that there is a view of the world from passion's point of view,

and that this view is closed to the perceiver, shows us that perception is, even by its own lights, incomplete" (LK189).

7. In *Otherwise Than Being* Levinas acknowledges that his notion of ethical responsibility as exposure cannot be made intelligible and defensible in the traditional language of ethics. It arises, as he says, from "non-philosophical experiences" (OTB120)—e.g., the biblical experience of being called, of being sent into exile, of persecution without reason, but also the experience of the Holocaust.

8. See Levinas, *Nine Talmudic Readings*, trans. Annette Aronowicz (Bloomington: Indiana University Press, 1990), esp. p. 35.

9. Charles Taylor, *Sources of the Self: The Making of Modern Identity* (Cambridge, MA: Harvard University Press, 1989), pp. 160, 174–75.

10. Martin Heidegger, *Introduction to Metaphysics*, trans. Ralph Manheim (Garden City, NY: Doubleday, 1961), pp. 124–32, 142–45.

11. See Hans-Georg Gadamer, "On the Hermeneutic Relevance of Aristotle," *Truth and Method*, 2d rev. ed., trans. Joel Weinsheimer and Donald G. Marshall (New York: Crossroad, 1988), pp. 312–24. Hereafter cited as TM. On hermeneutical experience, see pp. 346–62. I give an account of this conception in my "On the Tragedy of Hermeneutical Experience," *Hermeneutics Ancient and Modern* (New Haven, CT: Yale University Press, 1992), pp. 179–94.

12. See Stanley Cavell, "Thinking of Emerson," *The Senses of Walden: An Expanded Edition* (San Francisco: North Point Press, 1981), p. 133.

13. Levinas says: "Thematization and conceptualization, which moreover are inseparable, are not peace with the other but suppression or possession of the other. For possession affirms the other, but within a negation of its independence. 'I think' comes down to 'I can'—to an appropriation of what is, to an exploitation of reality. Ontology as first philosophy is a philosophy of power. It issues in the State and in the non-violence of the totality, without securing itself against the violence from which this non-violence lives, and which appears in the tyranny of the State. Truth, which should reconcile persons, here exists anonymously. Universality presents itself as impersonal; and this is another inhumanity" (TI46).

14. Martha Nussbaum's answer to this would be that, well, of course, it's to be assumed that responsiveness to complexities of experience includes responsiveness to the other in Levinas's sense of openness and exposure or in Cavell's sense of acknowledgment and acceptance. But it seems to me that her analysis excludes exactly what Cavell and Levinas are trying to get at in their reflections on our ethical relation to the other. Nussbaum is still trying to conceptualize this relation in terms of knowledge, that is, as a kind of knowing. I read both Levinas and Cavell as arguing that this sort of reduction is morally disastrous in its consequences. See particularly Cavell's reading of *Othello* at the end of *The Claim of Reason: Wittgenstein, Skepticism, Morality, and Tragedy* (New York: Oxford, 1979), pp. 481–96; hereafter

cited as CR. For Nussbaum, "the truth of skepticism" as Cavell tries to tell it seems not to have any force.

15. Gadamer's point about *phronesis* in *Truth and Method* is that it is always *situated* knowledge and cannot be adequately figured on the model of seeing. Of course, Aristotle appears to figure it precisely on this model (*Nicomachean Ethics*, 1109b, where the word for perception is *aisthesis*). Gadamer's idea is that the philosophical career of *aisthesis* since antiquity blocks our sense of what Aristotle is getting at. For that, we need to think of *phronesis* in terms of dialogue, of knowing what a situation calls for in the way of right action: "it is a knowledge of the particular situation that completes moral knowledge, a knowledge that is nevertheless not a perceiving by the senses. For although it is necessary to see from a situation what it is asking of us, this seeing does not mean that we perceive in the situation what is visible as such, but that we learn to see it as the situation of action and hence in the light of what is right. . . . This is confirmed by what constitutes the antithesis to this kind of seeing. The antithesis to the seeing of what is right is not error or deception, but blindness" (TM322). The difference between responding to a call and perceiving something is not merely metaphorical, because what defines the moral situation—and it is Levinas above all who makes this emphatic—is our involvement with other people and the claims this involvement imposes on us.

16. See Hans-Georg Gadamer, *The Idea of the Good in Platonic-Aristotelian Philosophy*, trans. P. Christopher Smith (New Haven, CT, and London: Yale University Press, 1986), esp. pp. 33–62 and 165–68.

17. The crucial passage in Nussbaum's account is the following:

Aristotle has, then, attacked the *techne* conception of practical reason (or its Platonic development) on several fronts. He has insisted upon anthropocentricity, denied the commensurability of the values, shown both the limits (and also the positive contribution) of the general, placed the allegedly ungovernable "irrational parts" at the heart of rational deliberation. He has developed further a conception of practical reasoning we saw adumbrated in the *Antigone*, in which receptivity and the ability to yield flexibly to the "matter" of the contingent particular were combined with a reverence for a plurality of values, for stable character, and for the shared conventions of which character, through moral education, is the internalization. He can claim to have a techne of practical reason just in the sense and to the degree that Protagoras can also make this claim: for Aristotelian practical wisdom is, up to a point, both general and (both through the early moral education and through reflective material like the *Nicomachean Ethics*) teachable. And this art will in a sense expand our control over uncontrolled *tuche*: for Aristotle reminds us that we, like archers, will be more likely to hit our target if we try through reflection to get a clearer view of it. But Aristotle warns against pressing such an aim too far: for he shows that each of the strategies used to make practical wisdom more scientific and more in control than this leads to a distinct impoverishment of the world of practice. (FG309–10)

Of course, it is possible that all that Nussbaum means by a *"techne* of practical reason" is that people need some sort of moral training or guidance, a *paideia,* since left to ourselves we aren't likely to be anything but trouble to others. But it's notoriously arguable whether *phronesis* is teachable in the sense meant by the word *techne.* So Gadamer, e.g., thinks of *phronesis* as something that presupposes a certain richness of experience—in the strong sense of experience that he develops in *Truth and Method,* that is, hermeneutical experience, not empirical or inductive experience nor even the Hegelian concept of *Erlebnis* but rather *Erfahrung,* experience that transforms us into people of wisdom. See Gadamer's account of hermeneutical experience, TM310–25. My sense is that Martha Nussbaum is trying too hard to defend the rationality of *phronesis* against the narrow criteria of rationality that characterize logical empiricism.

18. Winch, *Ethics and Action,* pp. 179–80, 182.

19. See John Rawls on deliberative rationality in *A Theory of Justice* (Cambridge, MA: Harvard University Press, 1971), pp. 407–23.

20. See Stanley Cavell, *Disowning Knowledge in Six Plays by Shakespeare* (Cambridge: Cambridge University Press, 1987), hereafter cited as DK.

21. Susanne Langer, *Feeling and Form* (New York: Scribner's, 1961), p. 331.

22. See Martha Nussbaum, *"The Golden Bowl* as Moral Philosophy":

Any view of deliberation that holds that it is, first and foremost, a matter of intuitive perception and improvisatory response, where a fixed antecedent ordering or ranking among values is to be taken as a sign of immaturity rather than of excellence; any view that holds that it is the job of the adult agent to approach a complex situation responsively, with keen vision and alert feelings, prepared, if need be, to alter his or her prima facie conception of the good in the light of the new experience, is likely to clash with certain classical aims and assertions of moral philosophy, which has usually claimed to make progress on our behalf precisely by extricating us from this bewilderment in the face of the present moment, and by setting us up in a watertight system of rules or a watertight procedure of calculation which will be able to settle troublesome cases, in effect, before the fact. Philosophers who have defended the primacy of intuitive perception are few. And when they have appeared, they have naturally also concluded—as does, for example, Aristotle—that moral theory cannot be a form of scientific knowledge that orders "the matter of the practical" into an elegent antecedent system. In fact, Aristotle makes it very clear that his own writing provides at most a "sketch" or an "outline" of the good life, whose content must be given by experience, and whose central claims can be clarified only by appeal to the life and to works of literature. (LK154)

"*The Golden Bowl* as Moral Philosophy" first appeared in *New Literary History* 15, no. 1 (Autumn 1983): 179–202. Hilary Putnam (pp. 203–7) responded to Nussbaum by objecting to her (apparent) displacement of rules as the proper concern of moral philosophy. Nussbaum's response was to find a place for rules in her ethics of particularity—the project of "Perceptive Equilibrium: Literary Theory and Ethical Theory" (LK168–94), which tries to split the difference between Henry James and John Rawls. See Peter Jones, "Philosophy, Interpretation, and the Golden Bowl," in *Philosophy and Literature*, ed. A. Phillips Griffiths (Cambridge: Cambridge University Press, 1984), pp. 211–28.

23. I take up this subject in my *Heidegger's Estrangements: Language, Truth, and Poetry in the Later Writings* (New Haven, CT, and London: Yale University Press, 1989).

24. As an example of this recoil, see Martha Nussbaum's response to an earlier version of this chapter, "Reply to Bruns," *Soundings: An Interdisciplinary Journal* 72 (1989): 771–81. Nussbaum thinks my conception of poetry is too simple, which of course is what I think about the Aristotelian reduction of literature to a logic of description. The impasse between us might be resolved, at least some way, by trying to think of poetry as a limit-concept as well as a genre description. Much of what I've written about poetry over the last thirty years has tried to clarify this distinction. My most recent attempt is in *Maurice Blanchot: The Refusal of Philosophy* (Baltimore: Johns Hopkins University Press, 1997), esp. chap. 2.

25. See Jacques Derrida, "Proverb: 'He that would pun . . . ,'" in John P. Leavey, Jr., *GLASSsery* (Lincoln: University of Nebraska Press, 1987), p. 18.

26. See Martin Heidegger, *What is Called Thinking?*, trans. J. Glenn Gray (New York: Harper & Row, 1968), pp. 127–30; and Jacques Derrida, introduction to *Edmund Husserl's "Origin of Geometry,"* trans. John P. Leavey, Jr. (Stony Brook, NY: Nicolas Hays, 1978), pp. 100–104.

27. See Jacques Derrida, *Glas* (Paris: Editions Galilée, 1974). See also Derrida, "Two Words for Joyce," in *Post-Structuralist Joyce*, ed. Derek Attridge and Daniel Ferrer (Cambridge: Cambridge University Press, 1984), p. 150. *Glas*, says Derrida, is "a sort of Wake."

28. On the conflict, or anyhow difference, between Platonists and Aristotelians on the question of poetry, see Bruns, "Against Poetry: Heidegger, Ricoeur, and the Originary Scene of Hermeneutics," *Hermeneutics Ancient and Modern* (New Haven, CT: Yale University Press, 1992), pp. 229–46.

29. Geoffrey Hartman, *Criticism in the Wilderness: The Study of Literature Today* (New Haven, CT, and London: Yale University Press, 1980), p. 135.

30. See Cora Diamond, "Missing the Adventure: Reply to Martha Nussbaum," *The Realistic Spirit: Wittgenstein, Philosophy, and the Mind* (Cambridge, MA: MIT Press, 1990), pp. 309–18.

31. So one wonders whether there isn't some internal connection between philosophy and aestheticism, where aestheticism is a bracketing or enframing of human life that allows us to adopt the standpoint of the detached observer. There is a sense in which Aristotle's admiration for tragedy depends on his getting outside of or beyond it. What he shows us is how to produce a philosophical reduction of tragedy, which is a sort of alternative to Plato's exclusionary approach; but the philosopher as sealed-off subject is common to both. What this comes down to is whether there is not some fundamental incompatibility between philosophy and the moral life that still remains to be addressed. See Jacques Derrida's essay on Levinas, "Violence and Metaphysics," *Writing and Difference*, trans. Alan Bass (Chicago: University of Chicago Press, 1978). Derrida quotes this line from Levinas's *Totality and Infinity*: "Solipsism is neither observation nor sophism; it is the very structure of reason." And he comments: "Therefore, there is a soliloquy of reason and a solitude of light. Incapable of respecting the Being and meaning of the other, phenomenology and ontology would be philosophies of violence. Through them, the entire philosophical tradition, in its meaning and at bottom, would make common cause with oppression and with the totalitarianism of the same. The ancient clandestine friendship between light and power, the ancient complicity between theoretical objectivity and technico-political possession" (p. 91).

Chapter 7

1. William Carlos Williams, "Kora in Hell: Improvisations" (1920), *Imaginations*, ed. Webster Schott (New York: New Directions, 1970), p. 70.

2. The term "aesthetics of nondifferentiation" belongs to Hans-Georg Gadamer, who argues that "the being of art cannot be defined as an object of aesthetic consciousness," that is, one cannot tell whether a thing is art just by looking at it. There are no formal features that set the work of art apart from nonaesthetic objects; the work is not external to the world that it represents. A good deal of contemporary North American poetry and poetics can be read as, in effect, the working out of Gadamer's critique of aesthetics: "The work of art cannot simply be isolated from the 'contingency' of the chance conditions in which it appears, and where this isolation occurs, the result is an abstraction that reduces the actual being of the work. It itself belongs to the world to which it represents itself." Hans-Georg Gadamer, *Wahrheit und Methode* (Tübingen: J. C. B. Mohr, 1975), p. 111; *Truth and*

Method, 2d rev. ed., trans. Joel Weinsheimer and Donald G. Marshall (New York: Crossroad, 1989), pp. 116–17. As Gadamer remarks in passing, his analysis leaves open the question of what counts as art. Gadamer doesn't try to close this question but rather takes it as a pretext for developing a nonobjective conception of art in which art is no longer a work but an event in which we are caught up as in the playing of a game. Art history, in Gadamer's view, is just such a game in which the artist is often far in advance of our ability to play so that we are frequently left not knowing what art is.

3. William Carlos Williams, *Paterson* (New York: New Directions, 1963), pp. 261–62.

4. David Antin, *talking at the boundaries* (New York: New Directions, 1976), p. 20.

5. Stephen Fredman, *Poet's Prose: The Crisis in American Verse* (Cambridge: Cambridge University Press, 1983), p. 135.

6. Antin, *talking at the boundaries,* pp. 211–12.

7. Antin builds a talk poem around this event. See "what it means to be avant-garde," *Formations* 2, 2 (1985): 53–71; rpt. in *what it means to be avant-garde* (New York: New Directions, 1993), pp. 41–64.

8. Sherman Paul, *In Search of the Primitive: Rereading David Antin, Jerome Rothenberg, and Gary Snyder* (Baton Rouge: Louisiana State University Press, 1986), p. 62.

9. See Fredman, *Poet's Prose,* pp. 140–48; Fredric Jameson, "Postmodernism, or the Logic of Late Capitalism," *New Left Review* 146 (1984): 53–92; Marjorie Perloff, "The Word as Such: L=A=N=G=U=A=G=E Poetry in the Eighties," *The Dance of the Intellect: Studies in the Poetry of the Pound Tradition* (Cambridge: Cambridge University Press, 1985), pp. 215–38; Lee Bartlett, "What Is Language Poetry?," *Critical Inquiry* 12 (Summer 1986): 741–52; George Hartley, *Textual Politics and the Language Poets* (Bloomington: Indiana University Press, 1989); Jeffrey Nealon, "Politics, Poetics, and Institutions: 'Language Poetry,'" *Double Reading: Postmodernism after Deconstruction* (Ithaca, NY: Cornell University Press, 1993), pp. 132–59.

10. David Bromige, "Lines," in "The L=A=N=G=U=A=G=E Poets," ed. Charles Bernstein, *Boundary* 2 14, nos. 1–2 (Fall 1985/Winter 1986): 70.

11. Tina Darragh, "Raymond Chandler's Sentence," *Striking Resemblance: Work, 1980–86* (Providence, RI: Burning Deck, 1989), p. 32.

12. Arthur Danto, *The Transfiguration of the Commonplace: A Philosophy of Art* (Cambridge, MA, and London: Harvard University Press, 1981), p. 78. Hereafter cited as TC. Danto developed his arguments further in the essays collected in his *The Philosophical Disenfranchisement of Art* (New York: Columbia University Press, 1986), hereafter cited as PD. See particularly the title essay, pp. 1–22.

13. See William Camfield's account of the short, possibly violent career of Duchamp's *Fountain,* "Marcel Duchamp's *Fountain:* Its History and Aesthetics in the

Context of 1917," in *Marcel Duchamp: Artist of the Century*, ed. Rudolf E. Kuenzli and Francis M. Naumann (Cambridge, MA: MIT Press, 1989), pp. 64–94.

14. Williams, in his prologue to *Kora in Hell*, has this wonderful anecdote: "We returned to Arensberg's sumptuous studio where he gave further point to his remarks by showing me what appeared to be an original of Duchamp's famous 'Nude Descending the Staircase.' But his, he went on to say, is a full-sized photographic print of the first picture, with many new touches by Duchamp himself" (*Imaginations*, pp. 8–9).

15. Arthur Danto, "The Artworld," *Journal of Philosophy* 61, no. 19 (October 1964): 581.

16. See Stanley Cavell, *The Claim of Reason: Wittgenstein, Skepticism, Morality, Tragedy* (New York: Oxford University Press, 1979), pp. 180–90.

17. This supposition was articulated very straightforwardly years ago by the Chicago Aristotelian, Elder Olson: "In the order of our coming to know the poem, it is true, the words are all-important; without them we could not know the poem. But when we grasp the structure we see that in the poetic order they are the least important element; they are governed by everything else in the poem. We are in fact far less moved by the words as mere words than we think." "William Empson, Contemporary Criticism, and Poetic Diction," *Critics and Criticism*, ed. R. S. Crane et al. (Chicago: University of Chicago Press, 1952), p. 34.

18. See David Lewis, "Truth in Fiction," *Philosophical Papers* (New York and Oxford: Oxford University Press, 1983), esp. 1:266–70.

19. See Paul Ricoeur, *Hermeneutics and the Human Sciences*, trans. John B. Thompson (Cambridge, MA: MIT Press, 1981), esp. pp. 141–44. See the discussion of Ricoeur's hermeneutics in my *Hermeneutics Ancient and Modern* (New Haven, CT: Yale University Press, 1992), pp. 229–46. Cf. Fredric Jameson's Marxist and utopian hermeneutics as developed in *Marxism and Form: Twentieth-Century Dialectical Theories of Literature* (Princeton, NJ: Princeton University Press, 1971), esp. pp. 116–59, and *The Political Unconscious: Narrative as a Socially Symbolic Act* (Ithaca, NY, and London: Cornell University Press, 1982), esp. pp. 74–75. Like Habermas, Ricoeur, et al., Jameson draws the line at discourse that interferes with the project of worldmaking. See "Postmodernism, or the Cultural Logic of Late Capitalism," *New Left Review* 146 (July/August, 1984): 53–91, where Jameson compares the writing of language poets to schizophrenic discourse. For Jameson, narratives are forestructures for understanding the world, where understanding means entering the world and changing it. Marxism, on Jameson's account of it, is the forestructure in which texts are approached in this way, call it the "right" way of getting into the hermeneutical circle. So a text is not (not just) a piece of ideological recital to be excoriated or burned but a window or threshold onto the future: a looking-glass. Reading on this view is not consumption but action (action turns texts into prophecies, as the ancients knew). Danto thinks that the reason why the history of art is the history

of censorship is that every work of art stands the chance of coming true if enough people act on it: the work of art is a project that opens the future in a certain way by projecting possibilities, and so at the very least it gives us a standpoint that cannot help being critical with respect to the world we inhabit (now, at this moment). See the title essay in Danto, *The Philosophical Disenfranchisement of Art*, esp. pp. 5–18.

20. Michael Davidson, "The Prose of Fact," *Hills* 6–7 (Spring 1980): 166.

21. Jean-François Lyotard, *The Postmodern Condition*, trans. Geoff Bennington and Brian Massumi (Minneapolis: University of Minnesota Press, 1984), p. 5.

22. Theodor Adorno, *Aesthetic Theory*, trans. C. Lenhardt (London and New York: Routledge & Kegan Paul, 1984), p. 179.

23. David Bromige, "My Poetry," in *In the American Tree*, ed. Ron Silliman (Orono, ME: National Poetry Foundation, 1986), p. 217.

24. See Charles Bernstein, *Content's Dream: Essays, 1975–1984* (New York: Sun & Moon Press, 1986), pp. 13–33, and Silliman, *The New Sentence* (New York: Roof Books, 1987), pp. 7–18.

25. Charles Bernstein, "Artifice of Absorption," *Paper Air* 4 (1987): 63–64, rpt. in his *Poetics* (Cambridge, MA: Harvard University Press, 1992), pp. 86–87.

26. Stanley Cavell, *The Senses of Walden: An Expanded Edition* (San Francisco: North Point Press, 1981), p. 33. Hereafter cited as SW.

27. Ron Silliman, "The Chinese Notebook," *The Age of Huts* (New York: Roof Books, 1986), p. 49.

28. See Hugh Kenner, *The Counterfeiters* (Garden City, NY: Anchor Books, 1973), pp. 57–90.

29. Stanley Cavell, *Must We Mean What We Say? A Book of Essays* (Cambridge: Cambridge University Press, 1969), pp. 188–89. Hereafter cited as MW.

30. Behind this link between the work of art and a person is Wittgenstein's notion that a thing (a word, e.g.) is meaningful if it has a place in our life. Cora Diamond has a nice account of how this is to be understood in "Rules: Looking in the Right Place," in *Wittgenstein: Attention to Particulars: Essays in Honour of Rush Rhees*, ed. D. Z. Phillips and Peter Winch (New York: St. Martin's Press, 1989), pp. 12–34. One might think of language poetry as a way of responding to the place words have in our lives.

31. See Cavell, *The Claim of Reason*, p. 241. Compare *Must We Mean What We Say?*, p. 324: "The world is to be accepted; as the presentness of other minds is not to be known, but acknowledged." On the concept of acknowledgment, see also Cavell, *In Quest of the Ordinary: Lines of Skepticism and Romanticism* (Chicago: University of Chicago Press, 1988), p. 8: "I do not propose the idea of acknowledging as an alternative to knowledge but rather as an interpretation of it"—a way of taking knowledge differently: no longer as grasping something but now as responding to something; no longer as possessing something but now as being with something.

32. Emmanuel Levinas, *De l'existence à l'existant* (Paris: Fontaine, 1946), p. 90;

Existence and Existents, trans. Alfonso Lingis (The Hague: Martinus Nijhoff, 1978), p. 56.

33. Ludwig Wittgenstein, *Philosophical Investigations*, trans. G. E. M. Anscombe, 3d ed. (New York: Macmillan, 1968), §129.

34. Ron Silliman, *The New Sentence* (New York: Roof Books, 1987), pp. 63–93.

35. Barrett Watten, "Complete Thought," in *In the American Tree*, ed. Silliman, pp. 43–47.

36. Lyn Hejinian, "My Life," in *In the American Tree*, ed. Silliman, p. 51.

37. Silliman, "The Chinese Notebook," *The Age of Huts*, p. 50.

38. Adorno, in *Aesthetic Theory*, speaks of the "open form" underwritten by aesthetic nominalism, or the idea that form is always singular and unrepeatable, that it can never be objectified but is always internal and specific to the individual work—in short, the rejection of the universal or what Fredric Jameson, in a happy phrase, calls "single-shot" definitions of the work of art (Fredric Jameson, *Late Marxism: Adorno, or, the Persistence of the Dialectic* (London and New York: Verso, 1990), p. 159. Aesthetic nominalism not only "spells the end of any universal aesthetics or doctrine of aesthetic invariables, the tendency even goes so far as to challenge the very conception of aesthetic unity and of the closure of the work itself" (p. 160). Hence the appeal of the Williams tradition to the metaphor of the open. For Jameson, language poetry is an example of aesthetic nominalism invading subjectivity itself and producing a kind of schizophrenia. See "Postmodernism, or the Cultural Logic of Late Capitalism," *New Left Review* 146 (July–August 1984): 53–92. From the standpoint of traditional aesthetics, Williams, Charles Olson, and the language poets would be aesthetic nominalists who think that "the work of art is supposed to organize itself from below rather than submit to ready-made principles of organization foisted on it from above. But this [says Adorno] is impossible. No work that is left to its own devices has the power of self-organization and self-limitation, and the attempt at endowing it with such powers must end in fetishism. In aesthetics, nominalism unchained is destructive of all forms. . . . It literally ends in facticity, which is irreconcilable with art," that is, the distinction between art and non-art, or in other words the whole Kantian idea of aesthetic differentiation, becomes now impossible to uphold (Theodor Adorno, *Aesthetic Theory*, ed. Gretel Adorno and Rolf Tiedemann, trans. Robert Hullot-Kentor [Minneapolis: University of Minnesota Press, 1997], pp. 313–14). The language poets might be thought of as taking up the challenge of a nominalist poetics. Language poets are in love with facticity.

39. Bob Perelman, *a.k.a.* (Great Barrington, MA: The Figures, 1984), p. 1.

40. Ron Silliman, *The New Sentence* (Berkeley, CA: The Figures, 1981), p. 90.

41. Ron Silliman, *Tjanting* (Berkeley, CA: The Figures, 1981), p. 201.

42. Wittgenstein, *Philosophical Investigations*, §19.

43. As if ethics constituted the limits of reason (Levinas).

44. See Cavell, *The Claim of Reason*, p. 177: "In 'learning language' you learn not merely what the names of things are, but what a name is; not merely what the form of expression is for expressing a wish, but what a wish is; not merely what the word for 'father' is, but what a father is. . . . In learning language, you do not merely learn the pronunciation of sounds, and their grammatical orders, but the 'forms of life' which make those sounds the words they are, do what they do—e.g., name, call, point, express a wish or affection, indicate a choice or an aversion, etc." See also pp. 189–90.

45. See Williams, *Paterson*, p. 164. Daniel Tiffany would disagree: "Language poetry," he says, "should . . . be understood as a belated contribution to a persistent, modernist rhetoric of materiality, whose utopian desire is to extract the word from its semiotic and ideological matrix, in order to plunge it into the *jouissance* of pure materiality." See Daniel Tiffany, "The Rhetoric of Materiality," *Sulfur* 22 (Spring 1988): 203. But perhaps a good example of the materiality I have in mind is Charles Bernstein's "I and The" (*The Sophist* [Los Angeles: Sun & Moon Press, 1987], pp. 59–80), a poem (he says) that "was compiled from *Word Frequencies in Spoken American English*, by Hartvig Dahl (Detroit: Verbatim/Gale Publishing, 1979). Dahl's sample was based on transcripts of 225 psychoanalytic sessions involving twenty-nine generally middle-class speakers with an average age in the late twenties. These speakers, twenty-one of whom were men, used a total of 17,871 different words in the session. In the poem, frequency is presented in descending order"—beginning with:

> I and the
> to that you
> it of a
>
> know was uh
> in but is
> this me about
>
> just don't my
> what I'm like
> or have so . . .

and ending with:

> plain joke carried
> future ground hang
> help picking nine

blow value advantage
closer attempt silence
park punishes cousin

relevant independence shot
glasses support magazine
courses pardon results

46. Marjorie Perloff, "Poetry and the Common Life," *Sulfur* 12 (1984): 160–64.

47. Louis Simpson, "26th Precinct Station," in ibid., p. 162.

48. Kenneth Rexroth, "The Signatures of All Things," in ibid., p. 163.

49. Stanley Cavell, *Pursuits of Happiness: The Hollywood Comedy of Remarriage* (Cambridge, MA: Harvard University Press, 1981), p. 41.

50. Gerald Burns, "Letters to Obscure Men," *Letters to Obscure Men* (Quincy, IL: Salt Lick Press, 1975), p. 2.

51. Michael Davidson, "After the Dancers," *The Prose of Fact* (Berkeley: The Figures, 1981), p. 34.

52. Martin Heidegger, "Logos (Heraclitus Fragment 50)," *Early Greek Thinking*, trans. David Farrell Krell and Frank A. Capuzzi (New York: Harper & Row, 1975), p. 66. See Heidegger, *Being and Time*, esp. §26 on "being-with" as a description of our relation to world and to others in it: "The world of Dasein is a *with-world* [*Mitwelt*]. Being-in [the world] is *Being-with* Others" (p. 155). In §34 Heidegger says that discourse *(Rede)* is a mode of being-in-the-world, and that listening and keeping silent are as much modes of discourse as speaking. In particular: "Listening-to . . . is Dasein's existential way of Being-open as Being-with for Others" (p. 206). Similarly, in §§31–32 Heidegger characterizes our relation to the world, or being in it, as one of understanding *(Verstehen)*, where understanding is a mode of practical involvement rather than theoretical cognition capable of being laid out in statements and descriptions from an observer's standpoint.

53. Heidegger, *Early Greek Thinking*, p. 67, but contrast *Being and Time*, §34, where Heidegger characterizes listening in terms of "hearing the voice of the friend" (p. 206).

54. Ron Silliman, *What* (Great Barrington, MA: The Figures, 1988), p. 66.

55. Bernstein, "Artifice of Absorption," p. 38.

56. Steve McCaffery, "Lyric's Larynx," *North of Intention* (New York: Roof Books; Toronto: Nightwood Editions, 1986), p. 178. See my *Heidegger's Estrangements*, pp. 144–46.

57. Ibid., p. 170.

58. Eliot Weinberger, review of *In the American Tree*, *Sulfur* 20 (Fall 1987): 196–97. Interestingly, Weinberger complains that language poetry does not (often) include translations from poetry in other languages. In the same way, perhaps,

what might fail to survive the translation of a language poem into another tongue would not be anything linguistic; that is, if a language poem is untranslatable, it would not be for the reasons normally given for untranslatability of poetry, e.g., the ineffability of it, or that its meaning is so embedded in its words that it cannot be transported apart from them. What is not transportable is context: language poetry foregrounds the speech of its own everyday environment, which is to say a form of life that, as H. L. Mencken would say, is not English, nor does it exhibit any recognizable intellectual or cultural refinement that would lift its better portion to a more accessible plane—it seems unredeemed in every sense: the unmemorable, entirely forgettable, erasable locution is what is most likely to make its way into a language poem, as if in defiance of the very idea of criteria. This doesn't have to mean that language poetry is confined to its environment. See Marjorie Perloff, *"Traduit de l'américain:* French Representations of the 'New American Poetry,'" *Poetic License: Essays on Modernist and Postmodernist Lyric* (Evanston, IL: Northwestern University Press, 1990), pp. 53–69. Heidegger, in his Aristotelian period, would have put it that language poetry, being "mere talk" *(Gerede),* mere "gossiping and passing the word along," is "inauthentic" because nothing is disclosed in such talk, nothing matters to it, nothing is worth taking to heart. ("And indeed this idle talk is not confined to vocal gossip, but even spreads to what we write, where it takes the form of 'scribbling' [das 'Geschreibe']" *[Being and Time,* p. 212].) Imagine language poetry trying to express the genius of inauthenticity.

59. See Max Horkheimer and Theodor Adorno, *Dialectic of Enlightenment,* trans. John Cumming (New York: Seabury Press, 1972), p. 156; and Cavell, *Pursuits of Happiness,* pp. 41–42, 73–80.

60. Quoted by Cavell, *The Senses of Walden,* p. 142.

61. Williams, "Kora in Hell," *Imaginations,* p. 9.

62. Gordana P. Crnković, "Utopian America and the Language of Silence," in *John Cage: Composed in America,* ed. Marjorie Perloff and Charles Junkerman (Chicago: University of Chicago Press, 1994), pp. 167–87, esp. pp. 168–69. It is precisely the verticality of American culture that the language poets attack in their writings— and of course not just the language poets, as the ongoing controversies surrounding the National Endowment for the Arts make quite plain.

63. Stephen Fredman, *The Grounding of American Poetry: Charles Olson and the Emersonian Tradition* (Cambridge: Cambridge University Press, 1993), esp. pp. 139– 49.

64. Allen Ginsberg, "Beginning of a Poem of These United States," *Fall of America* (San Francisco: City Lights, 1972), p. 1.

65. See Louis Marin, "Disneyland: A Degenerate Utopia," *Glyph* 1 (Baltimore and London: Johns Hopkins University Press, 1977), pp. 50–66, and esp. p. 54:

Disneyland is the representation realized in a geographical space of the imaginary relationship which the dominant groups of American society maintain with their real conditions of existence or, more precisely, with the real history of the United States and with the space outside of its borders. Disneyland is a fantasmatic projection of the history of the American nation, of the way in which this history was conceived with regard to other peoples and to the natural world. Disneyland is an immense and displaced metaphor of the system of representations and values unique to American society.

66. "For a man who no longer has a homeland, writing becomes a place to live." Theodor Adorno, *Minima Moralia: Reflections from a Damaged Life*, trans. E. F. N. Jephcott (London: New Left Books, 1974), p. 87.

67. So Wittgenstein: "What is common to them all?—Don't say: 'There must be something common, or they would not be called "games"'—but *look and see* whether there is anything common to them all.—For if you look at them you will not see something that is common to them *all*, but similarities, relationships, and a whole series of them at that" (*Philosophical Investigations*, §66). See Stanley Cavell, *In Quest of the Ordinary*, p. 13.

68. Charles Olson, "PROJECTIVE VERSE," *Charles Olson: Selected Writings* (New York: New Directions, 1966), p. 16. See Robert Creeley, "A Note on Poetry," *A Quick Graph: Collected Notes & Essays* (San Francisco: Four Seasons Foundation, 1970), p. 26: "The sonnet says, in short, we must talk, if you want, with another man's mouth, in the peculiar demands of that 'mouth,' and can't have our own."

69. Bernstein, *Content's Dream*, p. 17.

70. Antin, *talking at the boundaries*, p. 1.

71. Stanley Cavell, *Conditions Handsome and Unhandsome: The Constitution of Emersonian Perfectionism* (The Carus Lectures, 1988) (Chicago and London: University of Chicago Press, 1990), p. 85.

72. Robert Creeley, *Was That a Real Poem & Other Essays* (Bolinas, CA: Four Seasons Foundation, 1979), p. 106.

73. Robert Creeley, "Waiting," *The Collected Poems of Robert Creeley* (Berkeley and Los Angeles: University of California Press, 1982), p. 270.

74. Ron Silliman, "Canons and Institutions: New Hope for the Disappeared," in *The Politics of Poetic Form: Poetry and Public Policy*, ed. Charles Bernstein (New York: Roof Books, 1990), pp. 150, 156.

75. John Matthias, "The Stefan Batory Poems" ("Five: the library"), *Crossing* (Chicago: Swallow Press, 1979), pp. 81–82. *Crossing* has this bibliographical note appended to it: "I am indebted, as in *Turns* and *Bucyrus* [Matthias's earlier volumes], to an odd assortment of books and authors for facts, fancies, passages of verse or of prose, translations, information, scholarship and scandal which I have had occasion in these poems to quote, plagiarize, willfully ignore, tactfully modify,

stupidly misconstrue, or intentionally travesty" (p. 121). There follows a list of about fifty or so texts which form the discursive background to *Crossing*.

76. See John Matthias, *Turns* (Chicago: Swallow Press, 1975), p. 57; and *Crossing*, pp. 48–49. A difficulty of habitation is what Maurice Blanchot thinks of as poetry's "originary experience": "The poem is exile, and the poet who belongs to it belongs to the dissatisfaction of exile. He is always lost to himself, outside, far from home; he belongs to the foreign, to the outside which knows so intimacy or limit, and to the separation which Hölderlin names when in his madness he sees rhythm's infinite space." See Maurice Blanchot, *The Space of Literature*, trans. Ann Smock (1955; Lincoln: University of Nebraska Press, 1982), p. 237.

77. See Stanley Cavell, *This New Yet Unapproachable America: Lectures after Emerson after Wittgenstein* (Albuquerque, NM: Living Batch Press, 1989), p. 91: ""Why is this new America said to be unapproachable? There are many possibilities"—the first being that one dwells there, "but is unable to experience it."

78. John Matthias, "Places and Poems: A Self-Reading and a Reading of the Self in the Romantic Context from Wordsworth to Parkman," in *The Romantics and Us: Essays on Literature and Culture*, ed. Gene W. Ruoff (New Brunswick, NJ, and London: Rutgers University Press, 1990), p. 54.

79. John Matthias, *A Gathering of Ways* (Athens, OH: Swallow Press/Ohio University Press, 1991), pp. 43–44.

Chapter 8

1. Wallace Stevens, "An Ordinary Evening in New Haven," *Collected Poems* (New York: Knopf, 1954), p. 129. Hereafter cited as CP.

2. See Kenneth Schmitz, "Toward a Metaphysical Restoration of Natural Things," in *An Etienne Gilson Tribute*, ed. Charles O'Neill (Milwaukee: Marquette University Press, 1959), pp. 245–52.

3. See, e.g., J. Hillis Miller, *The Linguistic Moment from Wordsworth to Stevens* (Princeton, NJ: Princeton University Press, 1985), pp. 390–422.

4. Wallace Stevens, *Opus Posthumous*, ed. Samuel French Morse (New York: Alfred Knopf, 1957), p. 158. Hereafter cited as OP.

5. The first phrase is from OP167, the second from CP259.

6. Hugh Kenner, *A Homemade World* (New York: William Morrow, 1975), p. 75.

7. M. M. Bakhtin, *The Dialogic Imagination: Four Essays by M. M. Bakhtin*, trans. Caryl Emerson and Michael Holquist (Austin: University of Texas Press, 1981), p. 296. Hereafter cited as DI.

8. Harold Bloom, *Wallace Stevens: The Poems of Our Climate* (Ithaca, NY, and London: Cornell University Press, 1977), p. 387 (Bloom's italics).

9. Geoffrey Hartman, *Saving the Text* (Baltimore: Johns Hopkins Press, 1981), pp. 123–26.

10. Ibid., pp. 123–36.

11. Emmanuel Levinas, *Otherwise Than Being or Beyond Essence*, trans. Alphonso Lingis (The Hague: Martinus Nijhoff, 1987), p. 48.

12. See Jack Goody, *The Domestication of the Savage Mind* (Cambridge: Cambridge University Press, 1976), pp. 36–51.

13. Arthur Danto, "Philosophical Writing and Actual Experience," in *Beyond Representation: Philosophy and Poetic Imagination*, ed. Richard Eldridge (Cambridge: Cambridge University Press, 1996), pp. 101–2.

14. Stanley Cavell, *Themes out of School: Effects and Causes* (San Francisco: North Point Press, 1984), p. 48.

15. Hartman, *Saving the Text*, p. 122. Cf. Charles Bernstein's "Writing and Method": "One vision of a constructive writing practice I have, and it can be approached in both poetry and philosophy, is of a multidiscourse text, a work that would involve many different types and styles and modes of language in the same 'hyperspace.' Such a textual practice would have a dialogic or polylogic rather than monologic method" (*Content's Dream: Essays, 1975–1984* [New York: Sun & Moon Press, 1986], p. 227).

16. See Gerald Bruns, *Modern Poetry and the Idea of Language* (New Haven, CT: Yale University Press, 1974), pp. 101–17, on the Mallarméan text.

17. Jürgen Habermas, *The Philosophical Discourse of Modernity*, trans. Frederick G. Lawrence (Cambridge, MA: MIT Press, 1987), p. 203.

Chapter 9

1. The following works by Stanley Cavell are cited in this chapter: *The Claim of Reason: Wittgenstein, Skepticism, Morality, Tragedy* (New York: Oxford University Press, 1979), cited as CR; *Disowning Knowledge in Six Plays by Shakespeare* (Cambridge: Cambridge University Press, 1987), cited as DK; *Must We Mean What We Say? A Book of Essays* (Cambridge: Cambridge University Press, 1969), cited as MW; *In Quest of the Ordinary: Lines of Skepticism and Romanticism* (Chicago: University of Chicago Press, 1988), cited as QO; *The Senses of Walden: An Expanded Edition* (San Francisco: North Point Press, 1981), cited as SW; *Themes out of School: Effects and Causes* (San Francisco: North Point Press, 1984), cited as TO.

2. Cavell's discussion of *Othello* comes at the close of *The Claim of Reason* and is reprinted in *Disowning Knowledge* as "*Othello* and the Stake of the Other," pp. 125–42.

3. See Cavell, "The Uncanniness of the Ordinary" (QO153–78).

4. Thompson Clarke, "The Legacy of Skepticism," *Journal of Philosophy* 69 (1972): 761.

5. Paul Alpers, "*King Lear* and the Theory of the Sight Pattern," in *In Defense of Reading*, ed. Reuben Brower and Richard Poirier (New York: E. P. Dutton, 1963), pp. 133–52.

6. See Stanley Cavell, "Knowing and Acknowledging" (MW238–66) and "The Philosopher in American Life" (QO8). The idea is that in forgoing knowing one is not giving up reason, good sense, or even, on a certain view, philosophy. One is rather simply resituating oneself with respect to the world, or to other people, in a new, or perhaps just ordinary, way.

7. See Stanley Cavell, "Skepticism and a Word about Deconstruction" (QO 130–36). In "Politics as Opposed to What?," Cavell comments on the deconstructionists' misreading of J. L. Austin (TO41–48); see also Cavell's "What Did Derrida Want of Austin?," *Philosophic Passages: Wittgenstein, Emerson, Austin, Derrida* (London: Basil Blackwell, 1995), pp. 42–65.

8. See Emmanuel Levinas, *Totality and Infinity: An Essay on Exteriority*, trans. Alphonso Lingis (Pittsburgh: Duquesne University Press, 1969), hereafter cited as TI; and *Otherwise Than Being or Beyond Essence*, trans. Alphonso Lingis (The Hague: Martinus Nijhoff, 1978), hereafter cited as OTB.

9. Levinas, OTB48.

10. On romantic hermeneutics, see Gerald L. Bruns, "The Interpretation of Character in Jane Austen," in *Inventions: Writing, Textuality, and Understanding in Literary History* (New Haven, CT, and London: Yale University Press, 1982), pp. 111–24, and "Wordsworth at the Limits of Romantic Hermeneutics," in *Hermeneutics Ancient and Modern* (New Haven, CT: Yale University Press, 1992), pp. 159–78.

11. See Martha Nussbaum, *The Fragility of Goodness: Luck and Ethics in Greek Tragedy and Philosophy* (Cambridge: Cambridge University Press, 1985), esp. pp. 378–94.

12. James Joyce, *Ulysses* (New York: Random House, 1961), p. 18, and *Ulysses*, ed. Hans Gabler (New York: Random House, 1986), p. 15; hereafter citations will be first to the 1961 edition and second to Gabler's 1986 computer-embellished edition (e.g., U18/15).

13. Not surprisingly, Molly Bloom associates Stephen with Bloom's statue of Narcissus ("theres real beauty and poetry for you" [U776/638]).

14. See Hans-Georg Gadamer, *Truth and Method*, 2d rev. ed., trans. Joel Weinsheimer and Donald G. Marshall (New York: Crossroad, 1989), pp. 341–79. Hereafter cited as TM.

15. See Gerald L. Bruns, "On the Tragedy of Hermeneutical Experience," *Hermeneutics Ancient and Modern*, pp. 179–94. It is important to emphasize, since the point is frequently missed even by careful readers of Gadamer, that what gets restructured is not simply one's subjectivity, one's private self-relation, but also, in the nature of the case, the world that one inhabits. From a hermeneutical standpoint, at any rate, tragedy is never simply an event in the tragic hero's subjective situation.

16. See Hans-Georg Gadamer, "Text and Interpretation," in *Hermeneutics and Modern Philosophy*, ed. Brice Wachterhauser (Albany: SUNY Press, 1987). "The mere presence of the other before whom we stand helps us to break up our own bias and narrowness even before he opens his mouth to make a reply. What becomes a dialogical experience for us here is not restricted to the sphere of arguments and counterarguments the exchange and unifications of which may be the end meaning of every confrontation. Rather, as the experiences that have been described above indicate, there is something else in this experience, namely, a potentiality for otherness [*Andersseins*] that lies beyond every coming to agreement about what is common" (pp. 383–84). The text inscribes this "something else" in the form of its own resistance to clarification. This resistance is not simply a problem to be solved. The text is not simply a philological object; phenomenologically, it makes its appearance in the form of a resistance that brings our ability to understand and interpret up short. With respect to the text we are always in a state of crisis between alienation and appropriation, translation and conversion. The temptation to revise the text runs up against the need to revise ourselves.

17. See Gerald Bruns, *Heidegger's Estrangements: Language, Truth, and Poetry in the Later Writings* (New Haven, CT: Yale University Press, 1989), pp. 116–49.

Chapter 10

1. The following works by Cavell are discussed in this essay: *Conditions Handsome and Unhandsome: The Constitution of Emersonian Perfectionism* (Chicago: University of Chicago Press, 1990), hereafter cited as CH; *The Claim of Reason: Wittgenstein, Skepticism, Morality, and Tragedy* (New York: Oxford University Press, 1979), cited as CR; *Contesting Tears: The Hollywood Melodrama of the Unknown Woman* (Chicago: University of Chicago Press, 1996), cited as CT; *Disowning Knowledge in Six Plays of Shakespeare* (Cambridge: Cambridge University Press, 1987), cited as DK; *Must We Mean What We Say? A Book of Essays* (Cambridge: Cambridge University Press, 1969), cited as MW; *This New Yet Unapproachable America: Lectures after Emerson after Wittgenstein* (Albuquerque, NM: Living Batch Press, 1989), cited as NY; *Pursuits of Happiness: The Hollywood Comedy of Remarriage* (Cambridge, MA: Harvard University Press, 1981), cited as PH; *A Pitch of Philosophy: Autobiographical Exercises* (Cambridge, MA: Harvard University Press, 1994), cited as PP; *Philosophical Passages: Wittgenstein, Emerson, Austin, Derrida* (London: Basil Blackwell, 1995), cited as PhP; *In Quest of the Ordinary: Lines of Skepticism and Romanticism* (Chicago: University of Chicago Press, 1988), cited as QO; *The Senses of Walden: An Expanded Edition* (San Francisco: North Point Press, 1981), cited as SW; *Themes out of School: Effects and Causes* (San Francisco: North Point Press, 1984), cited as TO.

2. See Emmanuel Levinas, *Totality and Infinity: An Essay on Exteriority*, trans. Alphonso Lingis (Pittsburgh: Duquesne University Press, 1969); and *Otherwise Than Being or Beyond Essence*, trans. Alphonso Lingis (The Hague: Martinus Nijhoff, 1981), esp. pp. 9–11.

3. Compare Zygmunt Bauman's work, which also tries to think of the moral subject as constituted by responsibility rather than by rules. See esp. Bauman, *Postmodern Ethics* (London: Basil Blackwell, 1993), and *Life in Fragments: Essays in Postmodern Morality* (London: Basil Blackwell, 1995). Likewise Paul Ricoeur's recent work is an attempt to develop an ethics of the self in which the self is not an ego that posits itself but is constituted through a relation to the otherness of other people. See Ricoeur, *Oneself as Another*, trans. Kathleen Blamey (Chicago: University of Chicago Press, 1992), esp. pp. 329–56.

4. Ludwig Wittgenstein, *Philosophical Investigations*, 3d ed., trans. G. E. M. Anscombe (New York: Macmillan, 1968), §283; hereafter cited as PI with section number.

5. In "Something out of the Ordinary," Cavell remarks in passing that "in the modern period of the arts . . . the great arts together with their criticism increasingly take on the self-reflective condition of philosophy." *Proceedings and Addresses of the American Philosophical Association* 71, no. 2 (1997): 27.

6. Friedrich Schlegel, "Athenäum Fragments," nos. 116, 238, *Philosophical Fragments*, trans. Peter Firchow (Minneapolis: University of Minnesota Press, 1991), pp. 31–32, 50–51.

7. Cavell's "Kierkegaard's *On Authority and Revelation*" contains an account of the dilemma of the modern artist that could stand as an excellent summary of romantic poetics:

> I do not suppose Kierkegaard meant to suggest that a genuine author has to have, or claim, God's authority for his work, but a description of the apostle's position characterizes in detail the position I take the genuine modern artist to find himself in: he is pulled out of the ranks by a message which he must, on pain of loss of self, communicate; he is silent for a long period, until he finds his way to saying what it is he has to say (artistically speaking, this could be expressed by saying that while he may, as artists in former times have, begin and for a long time continue imitating the work of others, he knows that this is merely time-marking—if it is preparation, it is not artistic preparation—for he knows that there are no techniques at anyone's disposal for saying what he has to say); he has no proof of his authority, or genuineness, other than his own work (artistically speaking, this is expressed by the absence of conventions within which to compose) . . . ; finally, the burden of being called to produce it is matched by the risk of accepting it. . . . Art produced

under such spiritual conditions will be expected to have a strange, unheard of *appearance.* (MW177)

Compare CR123 and "Aesthetic Problems of Modern Philosophy," MW82–86.

    8. Samuel Taylor Coleridge, *Biographia Literaria,* ed. J. Shawcross, 2 vols. (Oxford: Oxford University Press, 1912), II:32.

    9. Ron Silliman, *The New Sentence* (New York: Roof Books, 1989), pp. 63–93.

    10. In "Emerson, Coleridge, Kant," Cavell promises that one day he will explain what he means when he says that Coleridge's *Biographia Literaria,* which has certain formal affinities with Laurence Sterne's *The Life & Opinions of Tristram Shandy,* is "composed essentially without digression" (QO42). It is not easy to imagine what such an explanation would look like, but it might well amount to Cavell's apology for his own prose style. Cavell provides this hint: "To say that the book is composed without digression means accordingly that if it has some end, the approach to it is followed in as straightforward a path as the terrain permits. This suggests that the end is, or requires, continuous self-interruption. But then this will be a way of drawing the consequences of philosophy's self-description as a discourse bearing endless responsibility for itself. And this could be further interpreted as a matter of endless responsiveness to itself—which might look to be exactly irresponsible" (QO42–43). This is a fairly typical sequence of Cavellian sentences (adding up to a short paragraph). If I understand, the idea is that a book composed without digression is not necessarily linear or consecutive in its progression. It depends on the terrain, which may (if indeed there is some end) require a good deal of backtracking, or the necessity of covering the ground more than once, keeping in touch with where one is. What leaps from the page is the following piece of Shandyism: "This suggests that the end is, or requires, continuous self-interruption." One would like to know more about what this means, since the phrase "continuous self-interruption" captures exactly the distinctive feature of Cavell's prose and describes the progress of sentences in this paragraph in particular; but, as ever, Cavell does not pause to clarify, nor do the sentences that follow follow straightforwardly as if carrying something (an argument, say) forward: the prose is, classically, anarchic, but also, for this reason, musical, with many dissonances sounding at once. What sort of end is it that "is, or requires self-interruption," and what is its connection with "philosophy's self-description as a discourse bearing endless responsibility for itself"? One imagines a prose alerted to itself and checking itself, making sure what and where its words are before drawing itself further along, the way the word "responsibility" is checked so that (on a whim or a cue?) it "could be further interpreted as a matter of endless responsiveness to itself." Which in turn "might look to be exactly irresponsible," as wordplay often does, or as if one were just making things up as one went along, not really knowing or possibly even caring where one might end up, so long as one left nothing unsaid or left no

variation untried. Fear of inexpressiveness does that to one's writing sometimes; I mean it expands it exponentially like a balloon. One could certainly argue that this paragraph "is composed without digression," since nothing is turned aside (or everything is), but nevertheless it has what Deleuze and Guattari would recognize as a rhizomatic rather than arboreal structure; that is, it resembles crabgrass rather than a tree with roots growing to a point.

11. Cavell divides *The Senses of Walden* into three parts: "Words," "Sentences," and "Portions," but not as if he were integrating things into larger units; he says near the end of "Sentences" that Thoreau writes sentences, but we supply the contexts for taking them now this way, now that (SW66–67), as if contexts were local, contingent, and autobiographical; in a certain sense we are responsible for the meaning of Thoreau's sentences—perhaps on the principle, as Luther thought, that the meaning of a Scriptural text is its application to one's life. *Walden*, Cavell says, is meant to be taken on the model of Scripture (SW14).

12. See, e.g., Arthur Danto's recent "Philosophical Writing and Actual Experience," in *Beyond Representation: Philosophy and Poetic Imagination*, ed. Richard Eldridge (Cambridge: Cambridge University Press, 1996), pp. 90–106. Against Cavell's idea that a philosopher's philosophy is articulated at the level of the individual voice, Danto argues that "the voice does not really penetrate the philosophy; the philosophy is the argument. . . . This is the bottom-line view of philosophy, that philosophy does not vary in any significant way depending on whose fingers it comes out of or out of whose mouth it issues. The bottom-line view of philosophy . . . means suppressing whatever does not . . . belong to philosophy. And that means . . . the suppression of voice" (pp. 101–2).

13. Gertrude Stein, "Composition and Explanation," *Selected Writings of Gertrude Stein*, ed. Carl Van Vechten (New York: Vintage Books, 1962), p. 518; and see *Pursuits of Happiness*, where Cavell remarks on Gertrude Stein's writing, "the hallmark of which is its repeatings" (PH241), which is also true of Cavell's writing. This is the place, incidentally, where Cavell issues his "promissory remark" that one day he will "go back to Stein's work" (PH242). The promise still needs to be made good.

14. Gerald L. Bruns, "Poethics: John Cage and Stanley Cavell at the Crossroads of Ethical Theory," in *John Cage: Composed in America*, ed. Marjorie Perloff and Charles Junkerman (Chicago: University of Chicago Press, 1994), pp. 206–25.

15. The art historian Michael Fried's influence on Cavell would be worth investigating in this connection. See Fried's polemic, "Art and Objecthood," *Artforum* (Summer 1967). Compare Marjorie Perloff's recent book, which situates Wittgenstein's writing in the context of both early and contemporary avant-garde poetics, *Wittgenstein's Ladder: Poetic Language and the Strangeness of the Ordinary* (Chicago: University of Chicago Press, 1996), esp. pp. 181–218.

16. "It seems to me that the puzzle of the Emersonian sentence must find a

piece of its solution in a theory of the fragment: maintaining fragmentariness is part of Emerson's realization of romanticism" (Cavell, NY21).

17. See *The L=A=N=G=U=A=G=E Book*, ed. Bruce Andrews and Charles Bernstein (Carbondale and Edwardsville: Southern Illinois University Press, 1984), an anthology of theoretical and critical writings by contemporary American poets.

18. See Martin Heidegger, *On the Way to Language*, trans. Peter Hertz (New York: Harper & Row, 1971), p. 57.

19. See Jürgen Habermas, "Philosophy as Stand-In and Interpreter," *Moral Consciousness and Communicative Action*, trans. Christian Lenhardt and Sheirry Weber Nicholsen (Cambridge, MA: MIT Press, 1990), pp. 17–20. Contrast Cavell's remark, in "Aversive Thinking": "However glad we may be to think of ourselves as intellectually fastidious, I do not suppose we relish the idea of ourselves as intellectual police" (CH35).

20. In "The Availability of Wittgenstein's Later Philosophy," Cavell remarks that "there is virtually nothing in the *Investigations* that we should ordinarily call reasoning; Wittgenstein asserts nothing which could be proved, for what he asserts is either obvious (§126)—whether true or false—or else concerned with what conviction, whether by proof or evidence or authority—would consist in. Otherwise there are questions, jokes, parables, and propositions so striking (the way lines are in poetry) that they stun mere belief. (Are we asked to believe that 'if a lion could talk we could not understand him'?) (II, p. 223). Belief is not enough. Either the suggestion penetrates past assessment and becomes part of the sensibility from which assessment proceeds, or it is philosophically useless" (MW71).

21. See Cavell, "Thinking of Emerson," SW131–32.

22. One could compare here Levinas's notion of my passivity in the face of the other [*Autrui*], whose claims on me remove me from the position of the rational subject exercising conceptual control. This passivity is also understood as sensibility, that is, vulnerability or exposure to suffering or affection (*Otherwise Than Being*, pp. 63–64). See Simon Critchley's account of the Heideggerian critique of the subject and its philosophical consequences, "Prolegomena to Any Post-Deconstructive Subjectivity," in *Deconstructive Subjectivities*, ed. Simon Critchley and Peter Dews (Albany: SUNY Press, 1996), pp. 13–46.

23. It is a question implicit in Ewa Ziarek's critique of Cavell's notion of community in *The Rhetoric of Failure: Deconstruction of Skepticism, Reinvention of Modernism* (Albany: SUNY Press, 1996), pp. 37–53.

24. MW239–40; cf. "Aesthetic Problems of Modern Philosophy" (MW86–96) and "Emerson's Constitutional Amending" (PhP34–36).

25. For example, Cavell risks the rebuke of feminist thinkers by repeatedly, almost obsessively, speaking for the film heroines he studies, most egregiously in "Ugly Duckling, Funny Butterfly," where he speaks for (of all people) Bette Davis. See CT132, where Cavell addresses this issue; but see also the chapter on *Stella*

Dallas, in which Cavell allegorizes (I had almost said, "impersonates") Stella Dallas as a nonconformist who embodies Emersonianism in response to "the feminine side" of the "demand for thinking," namely "thinking as reception" (CT220–21).

26. On Cavell's romanticism, see Russell Goodman, *American Philosophy and the Romantic Tradition* (Cambridge: Cambridge University Press, 1990), chap. 1.

27. George Leonard gives an excellent account of Wordsworth as a poet of "mere real things" in *Into the Light of Things: The Art of the Commonplace from Wordsworth to John Cage* (Chicago: University of Chicago Press, 1994).

28. This is the theme of *The Senses of Walden,* "The Avoidance of Love," pt. 4 of *The Claim of Reason,* and the early essays on Emerson, to mention only these.

29. In "Thinking of Emerson," Cavell says that the writing of Emerson and Thoreau is "the accomplishment of inhabitation" (SW134), but inhabitation is not appropriation, that is, not possession or ownership; on the contrary, it is continuous with "abandonment" (SW136–38), which echoes Heidegger's "being on the way" *(Unterwegssein)* and also, perhaps more exactly, his notion of *Gelassenheit,* letting-be, which means being open and responsive to things as opposed to grasping them conceptually. Abandonment is also an Emersonian concept of freedom, where (as in the essay "Circles") the self learns to live without foundations, or is always excessive with respect to the categories and distinctions that it constructs in order to make sense of experience, as if a true interpretation were one that allowed the self to remain open to experience, not one that captured it in a description. "Circles" at any rate suggests a self that inhabits the world but does not settle it; on the contrary, the idea is to unsettle it, keep it loose and unconstrained—this is what motivates "aversive thinking." It is not merely a lucky guess that leads Cavell to characterize Emerson finally as a "philosopher of freedom" (PhP41).

30. Jean-Jacques Rousseau, *Reveries of a Solitary Walker,* trans. Charles E. Butterworth (New York: Harper & Row, 1979), p. 2.

31. Michel Foucault, *The Order of Things: An Archaeology of the Human Sciences* (New York: Vintage Books, 1973), p. 387.

32. See Manfred Frank, *What Is Neostructuralism?,* trans. Sabine Wilke and Richard Gray (Minneapolis: University of Minnesota Press, 1989). See also *Who Comes after the Subject?,* ed. Eduardo Cadava, Peter Connor, and Jean-Luc Nancy (London: Routledge, 1991), esp. p. 5.

33. In a late interview Foucault remarked that the difficulty in developing an ethics not based on rules is that we "cannot find any other ethics than an ethics founded on so-called scientific knowledge of what the self is, what desire is, what the unconscious is, and so on." But the self is not a "what"; it is neither a subject nor an object of knowledge. The self is accessible only in the form of care or concern, and for Foucault ethics is the expression of this care for the self *(le souci de soi).* See Michel Foucault, "On the Genealogy of Ethics: An Overview of a Work in Progress," *The Foucault Reader,* ed. Paul Rabinow (New York: Pantheon Books,

1984), p. 343. The history of this ethical practice is the subject of the third volume of Foucault's *History of Sexuality,* and it is evident that what he is studying is exactly the tradition of moral perfectionism in which Cavell situates Emerson, Thoreau, and himself, and which he summarizes in terms of "the absolute responsibility of the self to itself" (CHxxvii). See Foucault, *The Care of the Self,* vol. 3 of *The History of Sexuality,* trans. Robert Hurley (New York: Vintage Books, 1986), esp. pp. 37–68. What is worth noticing is that, for both Cavell and Foucault, care or responsibility for the self is linked to writing in a fundamental way. For example, Foucault remarks that keeping notebooks *(hypomnemata)* was from ancient times a form of self-government aimed at constituting oneself as a free moral agent. "Into them one entered quotations, fragments of works, examples, and actions to which one had been witness or of which one had read the account, reflections or reasonings which one had heard or which had come to mind. They constituted a material memory of things read, heard, or thought, thus offering these as an accumulated treasure for rereading and later mediation. They also formed a raw material for the writing of more systematic treatises in which were given arguments and means by which to struggle against some defect (such as anger, envy, gossip, flattery) or to overcome some difficult circumstance (a mourning, an exile, downfall, disgrace)" (*The Foucault Reader,* p. 364). We recognize this as (already) the tradition of writing (local, contingent, autobiographical) in which Emerson and Thoreau excelled. It is possible to criticize this conception of self-perfection by means of writing on the grounds that writing is less real than live action or intervention in the world. See Richard Shusterman's critique of Cavell's moral perfectionism in his *Practicing Philosophy: Pragmatism and the Philosophical Life* (New York and London: Routledge, 1997), pp. 99–110. But possibly writing, finding one's voice, is what live action and intervention in the world are for human beings—this is how Cavell interprets Wittgenstein's notion of "forms of life" (NY40–44). "Is the gasping of the human voice, say sobbing or laughing, the best proof of the human?" (CR477). Supposing proof to be necessary, a laugh or cry will serve.

34. Cf. Paul Ricoeur's distinction between two kinds of identity, *idem* and *ipse,* the same and the self. The one is categorical, whereas the other is an identity that persists over time without ever remaining the same. It is only through narrative that the identity of a self is accessible. See Ricoeur, *Oneself as Another,* pp. 2–3, 140–68, and consider the importance Cavell places on autobiography as enacting one's existence (QO108–9).

35. See Cavell, *Pursuits of Happiness* (pp. 17–18): "Our films may be understood as parables of the development of consciousness at which the struggle is for reciprocity or equality of consciousness between a woman and a man, a study of the conditions under which this fight for recognition (as Hegel put it) or demand for acknowledgment (as I have put it) is a struggle for mutual freedom, especially of the views each holds of the other. This gives the films of our genre a utopian cast.

They harbor a vision which they know cannot fully be domesticated, inhabited, in the world we know."

36. See Simon Critchley's critique of Cavell's attachment to America in *Very Little . . . Almost Nothing: Death, Philosophy, Literature* (London: Routledge, 1997), pp. 125–31.

37. See Schusterman's critique of Cavell's notion of writing as self-creation in *Practicing Philosophy: Pragmatism and the Philosophical Life*, pp. 99–110. The complaint is that such self-creation as voice or writing never gets outside of language, much less outside the text: it falls short of "robust praxis" of the kind we associate with social action and political struggle: "Though Cavell's ethics of democracy is not reducible to a mere textual aestheticism, it leaves itself too vulnerable to such an interpretation through its extreme emphasis on writing and neglect of other important dimensions of democratic philosophical life. For isn't there more to knowing how to live than knowing how to read and write, even in the special, more demanding, perfectionist sense that Cavell gives these textual terms?" (p. 108). But if one couches writing against the historical background of suppressed voices and enforced privacy, one can see in the performance of voice and writing something like the constitution of a world which at last one can inhabit.

Bibliography

Adorno, Theodor. *Aesthetic Theory*. Ed. Gretel Adorno and Rolf Tiedemann. Trans. Robert Hullot-Kentor. Minneapolis: University of Minnesota Press, 1997.

———. *Minima Moralia: Reflections from a Damaged Life*. Trans. E. F. N. Jephcott. London: New Left Books, 1974.

Allen, Barry. "Groundless Goodness." In *Antifoundationalism and Practical Reason: Conversations between Hermeneutics and Analysis*. Ed. Evan Simpson. Edmondton, AB: Academic Printing & Publishing, 1987.

Alpers, Paul. "*King Lear* and the Theory of the Sight Pattern." In *In Defense of Reading*. Ed. Reuben Brower and Richard Poirier. New York: E.P. Dutton, 1963.

Anderson, Judith. *Words That Matter: Linguistic Perception in Renaissance English*. Stanford: Stanford University Press, 1996.

Andrews, Bruce, and Charles Bernstein, eds. *The L=A=N=G=U=A=G=E Book*. Carbondale and Edwardsville: Southern Illinois University Press, 1984.

Antin, David. *talking at the boundaries*. New York: New Directions, 1976.

———. *what it means to be avant-garde*. New York: New Directions, 1984.

Apel, Karl-Otto. "The A Priori of Communication and the Foundation of the Humanities." In *Understanding and Social Inquiry*. Ed. Fred R. Dallmayr and Thomas A. McCarthy. Notre Dame, IN: University of Notre Dame Press, 1977.

Arendt, Hannah. *The Human Condition*. Chicago: University of Chicago Press, 1958.

Bakhtin, M. M. *The Dialogic Imagination: Four Essays by M. M. Bakhtin*. Trans. Caryl Emerson and Michael Holquist. Austin: University of Texas Press, 1981.

Barthes, Roland. "From Work to Text." *The Rustle of Language*. Trans. Richard Howard. New York: Hill and Wang, 1986.

Bartlett, Lee. "What Is Language Poetry?" *Critical Inquiry* 12 (Summer 1986): 741–52.

Bauman, Zygmunt. *Life in Fragments: Essays in Postmodern Morality*. London: Basil Blackwell, 1995.

———. *Postmodern Ethics*. London: Basil Blackwell, 1993.

Beiner, Ronald. *Political Judgment*. Chicago: University of Chicago Press, 1983.

Berman, Harold. *Law and Revolution: The Formation of the Western Legal Tradition*. Cambridge, MA: Harvard University Press, 1983.

Bernstein, Charles. *Content's Dream: Essays, 1975–1984*. New York: Sun & Moon Press, 1986.

————. *Poetics*. Cambridge, MA: Harvard University Press, 1992.

————. *The Sophist*. Los Angeles: Sun & Moon Press, 1987.

————, ed. "The L=A=N=G=U=A=G=E Poets." *Boundary* 2 14:1–2 (Fall 1985/ Winter 1986).

————, ed. *The Politics of Poetic Form: Poetry and Public Policy*. New York: Roof Books, 1990.

Blanchot, Maurice. *The Infinite Conversation*. Trans. Susan Hanson. Minneapolis: University of Minnesota Press, 1993.

————. *The Space of Literature*. Trans. Ann Smock. Lincoln: University of Nebraska Press, 1982.

Blank, Paula. *Broken English: Dialects and the Politics of Language in Renaissance Writings*. London: Routledge, 1996.

Bloom, Harold. *Wallace Stevens: The Poems of Our Climate*. Ithaca, NY, and London: Cornell University Press, 1977.

Britton, Bruche, and A. D. Pellegrini, eds. *Narrative Thought and Narrative Language*. Hillsdale, NJ: Lawrence Erlbaum Associates, 1990.

Brodsky, Claudia. *The Imposition of Form: Studies in Narrative Representation and Knowledge*. Princeton, NJ: Princeton University Press, 1987.

Bromige, David. "My Poetry." In *In the American Tree*. Ed. Ron Silliman. Orono, ME: National Poetry Foundation, 1986.

Bruner, Jerome. *Acts of Meaning*. Cambridge, MA: Harvard University Press, 1990.

————. *Actual Minds, Possible Worlds*. Cambridge, MA: Harvard University Press, 1986.

————. "The Narrative Construction of Reality." *Critical Inquiry* 18:1 (Autumn 1991): 1–21.

Bruns, Gerald. *Heidegger's Estrangements: Language, Truth, and Poetry in the Later Writings*. New Haven, CT: Yale University Press, 1989.

————. *Hermeneutics Ancient and Modern*. New Haven, CT: Yale University Press, 1992.

————. *Inventions: Writing, Textuality, and Understanding in Literary History*. New Haven, CT, and London: Yale University Press, 1982.

————. *Maurice Blanchot: The Refusal of Philosophy*. Baltimore: Johns Hopkins University Press, 1997.

————. *Modern Poetry and the Idea of Language*. New Haven, CT: Yale University Press, 1974.

————. "The Otherness of Words: Joyce, Bakhtin, Heidegger." In *Postmodernism: Philosophy and the Arts*. Ed. Hugh Silverman. London: Routledge & Kegan Paul, 1990.

————. "Poethics: John Cage and Stanley Cavell at the Crossroads of Ethical Theory." In *John Cage: Composed in America*. Ed. Marjorie Perloff and Charles Junkerman. Chicago: University of Chicago Press, 1994.

————. "Toward a Random Theory of Prose." Intro. to Viktor Shlovsky, *Theory of Prose*. Trans. Benjamin Sher. Elmwood Park, IL: Dalkey Archive Press, 1990.

Buechner, Jeffrey. "Radically Misinterpreting Radical Interpretation." *Journal of Aesthetics and Art Criticism* 45:4 (Summer 1987): 409–10.

Burns, Gerald. *Letters to Obscure Men*. Quincy, IL: Salt Lick Press, 1975.

Burton, Frank, and Pat Carlen. *Official Discourse*. London: Routledge & Kegan Paul, 1979.

Burton, Steven. *An Introduction to Law and Legal Reasoning*. New York: Little, Brown and Co., 1985.

Cadava, Eduardo, Peter Connor, and Jean-Luc Nancy, eds. *Who Comes After the Subject?* London: Routledge, 1991.

Camfield, William. "Marcel Duchamp's *Fountain*: Its History and Aesthetics in the Context of 1917." In *Marcel Duchamp: Artist of the Century*. Ed. Rudolf E. Kuenzli and Francis M. Naumann. Cambridge, MA: MIT Press, 1989.

Caputo, John D. *Against Ethics*. Bloomington: Indiana University Press, 1990.

————. *Radical Hermeneutics: Repetition, Deconstruction, and the Hermeneutic Project*. Bloomington: Indiana University Press, 1987.

Cascardi, Anthony. "Narrative and Totality." *The Philosophical Forum* 21:3 (Spring 1990).

Cassirer, Ernst. *The Philosophy of Symbolic Forms*. Trans. Ralph Mannheim. New Haven, CT: Yale University Press, 1953.

Cavell, Marcia. "Metaphor, Dreamwork, Irrationality." *Truth and Interpretation: Perspectives on the Philosophy of Donald Davidson*. Oxford: Basil Blackwell, 1986.

Cavell, Stanley. *The Claim of Reason: Wittgenstein, Skepticism, Morality, and Tragedy*. New York: Oxford University Press, 1979.

————. *Conditions Handsome and Unhandsome: The Constitution of Emersonian Perfectionism*. Chicago: University of Chicago Press, 1990.

————. *Contesting Tears: The Hollywood Melodrama of the Unknown Woman*. Chicago: University of Chicago Press, 1996.

————. *Disowning Knowledge in Six Plays of Shakespeare*. Cambridge: Cambridge University Press, 1987.

————. *Must We Mean What We Say? A Book of Essays*. Cambridge: Cambridge University Press, 1969.

————. *Philosophical Passages: Wittgenstein, Emerson, Austin, Derrida*. London: Basil Blackwell, 1995.

————. *A Pitch of Philosophy: Autobiographical Exercises*. Cambridge, MA: Harvard University Press, 1994.

————. *Pursuits of Happiness: The Hollywood Comedy of Remarriage*. Cambridge, MA: Harvard University Press, 1981.

————. *In Quest of the Ordinary: Lines of Skepticism and Romanticism*. Chicago: University of Chicago Press, 1988.

———. *The Senses of Walden: An Expanded Edition.* San Francisco: North Point Press, 1981.

———. "Something out of the Ordinary." *Proceedings and Addresses of the American Philosophical Association* 71:2 (1997).

———. *Themes out of School: Effects and Causes.* San Francisco: North Point Press, 1984.

———. *This New Yet Unapproachable America: Lectures after Emerson after Wittgenstein.* Albuquerque, NM: Living Batch Press, 1989.

Chomsky, Noam. *Aspects of a Theory of Syntax.* Cambridge, MA: MIT Press, 1965.

Churchland, Patricia. *Neurophilosophy: Toward a Unified Science of the Mind/Brain.* Cambridge, MA: MIT Press, 1986.

Churchland, Paul. *A Neurocomputational Perspective: The Nature of Mind and the Structure of Science.* Cambridge, MA, and London: MIT Press, 1989.

Clark, Andy. *Microcognition: Philosophy, Cognitive Science, and Parallel Distributed Processing.* Cambridge, MA: MIT Press, 1989.

Clarke, Thompson. "The Legacy of Skepticism." *Journal of Philosophy* 69 (1972).

Connolly, William. *The Augustinian Imperative: A Reflection on the Politics of Morality.* New York: Sage Books, 1992.

———. *The Ethos of Pluralization.* Minneapolis: University of Minnesota Press, 1995.

———. *Identity/Difference: Democratic Negotiations of Political Paradox.* Ithaca, NY: Cornell University Press, 1991.

———. *Political Theory and Modernity.* Ithaca, NY: Cornell University Press, 1988.

Creeley, Robert. *The Collected Poems of Robert Creeley.* Berkeley and Los Angeles: University of California Press, 1982.

———. "A Note on Poetry." *A Quick Graph: Collected Notes & Essays.* San Francisco: Four Seasons Foundation, 1970.

———. *Was That a Real Poem & Other Essays.* Bolinas, CA: Four Seasons Foundation, 1979.

Critchley, Simon. "Prolegomena to Any Post-Deconstructive Subjectivity." *Deconstructive Subjectivities.* Ed. Simon Critchley and Peter Dews. Albany: SUNY Press, 1996.

———. *Very Little . . . Almost Nothing: Death, Philosophy, Literature.* London: Routledge, 1997.

Crnkovié, Gordana. "Utopian America and the Language of Silence." In *John Cage: Composed in America.* Ed. Marjorie Perloff and Charles Junkerman. Chicago: University of Chicago Press, 1994.

Dahlbom, Bo. "Mind is Artificial." In *Dennett and His Critics.* Ed. Bo Dahlbom. London: Routledge, 1993.

Dallmayr, Fred. "Max Weber and the Modern State." *The Barbarism of Reason: Max Weber and the Twilight of Enlightenment.* Toronto: University of Toronto Press, 1994.

Damasio, Antonio. *Descartes' Error: Reason, Emotion, and the Human Brain*. New York: Avon Books, 1994.

Danto, Arthur. "The Artworld." *Journal of Philosophy* 10 (1968).

———. *The Philosophical Disenfranchisement of Art*. New York: Columbia University Press, 1986.

———. "Philosophical Writing and Actual Experience." In *Beyond Representation: Philosophy and Poetic Imagination*. Ed. Richard Eldridge. Cambridge: Cambridge University Press, 1996.

———. *The Transfiguration of the Commonplace: A Philosophy of Art*. Cambridge, MA, and London: Harvard University Press, 1981.

Darragh, Tina. *Striking Resemblance: Work, 1980–86*. Providence, RI: Burning Deck, 1989.

Davidson, Donald. *Inquiries into Truth and Interpretation*. Oxford: Clarendon Press, 1984.

———. "James Joyce and Humpty Dumpty." *Philosophy and the Arts*. Ed. Peter A. French, Theodore E. Uehling, Jr., and Howard K. Wettstein. Midwest Studies in Philosophy 16. Notre Dame, IN: University of Notre Dame Press, 1991.

———. "Knowing One's Own Mind." *Proceedings and Addresses of the American Philosophical Association*. Newark, NJ: American Philosophical Association, 1987.

———. "A Nice Derangement of Epitaphs." *Philosophical Grounds of Rationality: Intentions, Categories, Ends*. Ed. Richard E. Grandy and Richard Warner. Oxford: Clarendon Press, 1986.

———. "The Second Person." *The Wittgenstein Legacy*. Ed. Peter A. French, Theodore E. Uehling, Jr., and Howard K. Wettstein. Notre Dame, IN: University of Notre Dame Press, 1992.

———. "The Structure and Content of Truth." *Journal of Philosophy* 87:6 (June 1990).

Davidson, Michael. "The Prose of Fact." *Hills* 6–7 (Spring 1980).

Deleuze, Gilles, and Félix Guattari. *A Thousand Plateaus: Capitalism and Schizophrenia*. Trans. Brian Massumi. Minneapolis: University of Minnesota Press, 1987.

Dennett, Daniel. *Consciousness Explained*. New York: Little, Brown & Co., 1991.

———. "Why Everyone Is a Novelist." *Times Literary Supplement* (September 16–22, 1988).

Derrida, Jacques. "Comment ne pas parler: *Dénégations*." *Psyché: Inventions de l'autre*. Paris: Gallimard, 1987.

———. "Introduction." *Edmund Husserl's Origin of Geometry*. Stony Brook, NY: N. Hays, 1978.

———. *Memoires for Paul de Man*. New York: Columbia University Press, 1986.

———. "Proverb: ' . . . He that would pun . . . '." *GLASsery*. John P. Leavey, Jr. Lincoln: University of Nebraska Press, 1987.

———. "The *Retrait* of Metaphor." Trans. F. Gasdner et al., *Enclitic* 2 (1978): 5–33.

———. "Two Words for Joyce." *Post-Structuralist Joyce.* Ed. Derek Attridge and Daniel Ferrer. Cambridge: Cambridge University Press, 1984.

———. "Violence and Metaphysics." *Writing and Difference.* Trans. Alan Bass. Chicago: University of Chicago Press, 1978.

Diamond, Cora. "The Importance of Being Human." In *Human Beings.* Ed. David Cockburn. Cambridge: Cambridge University Press, 1991.

———. "Losing Your Concepts." *Ethics* 98:2 (January 1988): 255–77.

———. "Missing the Adventure: Reply to Martha Nussbaum." *The Realistic Spirit: Wittgenstein, Philosophy, and the Mind.* Cambridge, MA: MIT Press, 1990.

———. "Rules: Looking in the Right Place." *Wittgenstein: Attention to Particulars: Essays in Honour of Rush Rhees.* Ed. D. Z. Phillips and Peter Winch. New York: St. Martin's Press, 1989.

Dilthey, Wilhelm. *Dilthey: Selected Writings.* Trans. H. P. Rickman. Cambridge: Cambridge University Press, 1976.

Dreyfus, Hubert. "Holism and Hermeneutics." In *Hermeneutics and Praxis.* Ed. Robert Hollinger. Notre Dame, IN: University of Notre Dame Press, 1985.

Dummett, Daniel. "Comments on Davidson and Hacking." *Truth and Interpretation: Perspectives on the Philosophy of Donald Davidson.* Oxford: Basil Blackwell, 1986.

Dworkin, Ronald. *Law's Empire.* Cambridge, MA: Harvard University Press, 1985.

———. *A Matter of Principle.* Cambridge, MA, and London: Harvard University Press, 1986.

Eco, Umberto. "The Semantics of Metaphor." Trans. John Snyder. In *Semiotics: An Introductory Anthology.* Ed. Robert E. Innis. Bloomington: Indiana University Press, 1985.

Elster, Jon, ed. *Rational Choice.* Washington Square: New York University Press, 1986.

———. *Solomonic Judgments: Studies in the Limits of Rationality.* Cambridge: Cambridge University Press, 1989.

———. *Ulysses and the Sirens: Studies in Rationality and Irrationality.* Cambridge: Cambridge University Press, 1979.

Farrell, Frank B. "Metaphor and Davidsonian Theories of Meaning." *Canadian Journal of Philosophy* 17:3 (September 1987): 625–42.

Fiss, Owen. "Objectivity and Interpretation." *Stanford Law Review* 34 (April 1982): 739–63.

Foucault, Michel. *The Care of the Self.* Vol. 3 of *The History of Sexuality.* Trans. Robert Hurley. New York: Vintage Books, 1986.

———. "The Discourse on Language." Trans. Rupert Swyer. *Social Science Information* 10:2 (April 1971): 7–30. Reprinted in *The Archeology of Knowledge.* Trans. A. W. Sheridan Smith. New York: Harper & Row, 1972.

———. "On the Genealogy of Ethics: An Overview of a Work in Progress." In *The Foucault Reader.* Ed. Paul Rabinow. New York: Pantheon Books, 1984.

————. *The Order of Things: An Archeology of the Human Sciences.* New York: Vintage Books, 1973.

Frank, Manfred. *What Is Neostructuralism?* Trans. Sabine Wilke and Richard Gray. Minneapolis: University of Minnesota Press, 1989.

Fredman, Stephen. *The Grounding of American Poetry: Charles Olson and the Emersonian Tradition.* Cambridge: Cambridge University Press, 1993.

————. *Poet's Prose: The Crisis in American Verse.* 2d ed. Cambridge: Cambridge University Press, 1990.

French, Peter A., Theodore E. Uehling, Jr., and Howard Wettstein, eds. "Ethical Theory: Character and Virtue." *Midwest Studies in Philosophy.* Notre Dame, IN: University of Notre Dame Press, 1988.

Gadamer, Hans-Georg. "The Hermeneutics of Suspicion." In *Hermeneutics: Questions and Prospects.* Ed. Gary Shapiro and Alan Sica. Amherst: University of Massachusetts Press, 1984.

————. *The Idea of the Good in Platonic-Aristotelian Philosophy.* Trans. P. Christopher Smith. New Haven, CT, and London: Yale University Press, 1986.

————. *Reason in the Age of Science.* Trans. Frederick G. Lawrence. Cambridge, MA: MIT Press, 1981.

————. *The Relevance of the Beautiful and Other Essays.* Trans. Nicholas Walker. Ed. Robert Bernasconi. Cambridge: Cambridge University Press, 1986.

————. "Text and Interpretation." In *Hermeneutics and Modern Philosophy.* Ed. Brice Wachterhauser. Albany: SUNY Press, 1987.

————. *Truth and Method.* 2d ed. Trans. Joel Weinsheimer and Donald G. Marshall. New York: Crossroad Publishing, 1989.

Gasché, Rodolphe. "Postmodernism and Rationality." *Journal of Philosophy* 74 (1988): 528–38.

Gass, William. "The Medium of Fiction." *Fiction and the Figures of Life.* Boston: Nonpareil Books, 1971.

Geertz, Clifford. "Deep Play: Notes on the Balinese Cockfight." In *Interpretive Social Science: A Second Look.* Ed. Paul Rabinow and William M. Sullivan. Berkeley: University of California Press, 1987.

Ginsberg, Allen. "Beginning of a Poem of These United States." *Fall of America.* San Francisco: City Lights, 1972.

Gleick, John. *Chaos: Making a New Science.* New York: Viking Press, 1987.

Glidden, David K. "The Elusiveness of Moral Recognition." In *Philosophy and the Arts.* Ed. Peter A. French, Theodore E. Uehling, Jr., and Howard K. Wettstein. Midwest Studies in Philosophy 16. Notre Dame, IN: University of Notre Dame Press, 1991.

Goodman, Nelson. *Ways of Worldmaking.* Indianapolis: Hackett Publishing, 1978.

Goodman, Russell. *American Philosophy and the Romantic Tradition.* Cambridge: Cambridge University Press, 1990.

Goodrich, Peter. *Legal Discourse: Studies in Linguistics, Rhetoric, and Legal Analysis.* New York: St. Martin's Press, 1987.

――――. *Reading the Law: A Critical Introduction to Legal Method and Techniques.* London: Basil Blackwell, 1986.

Goody, Jack. *The Domestication of the Savage Mind.* Cambridge: Cambridge University Press, 1976.

Green, Donald P. and Ian Shapiro. *Pathologies of Rational Choice Theory: A Critique of Applications in Political Science.* New Haven, CT: Yale University Press, 1994.

Habermas, Jürgen. *Moral Consciousness and Communicative Action.* Trans. Christian Lenhardt and Shierry Weber Nicholson. Cambridge: Cambridge University Press, 1990.

――――. *The Philosophical Discourse of Modernity.* Trans. Frederick G. Lawrence. Cambridge, MA: MIT Press, 1987.

――――. *The Theory of Communicative Action: Reason and the Rationalization of Society.* Trans. Thomas McCarthy. Boston: Beacon Press, 1984.

Hacking, Ian. "A Parody of Conversation." *Truth and Interpretation: Perspectives on the Philosophy of Donald Davidson.* Oxford: Basil Blackwell, 1986.

Hartley, George. *Textual Politics and the Language Poets.* Bloomington: Indiana University Press, 1989.

Hartman, Geoffrey. *Criticism in the Wilderness: The Study of Literature Today.* New Haven, CT, and London: Yale University Press, 1980.

――――. *Saving the Text.* Baltimore: Johns Hopkins Press, 1981.

Havelock, Eric A. "The Socratic Self As It Is Parodied in Aristophanes' *Clouds.*" *Yale Classical Studies* 22 (1972): 1–18.

Heidegger, Martin. *Being and Time.* Trans. John Macquarrie and Edward Robinson. New York: Harper & Row, 1962.

――――. *Early Greek Thinking.* Trans. David Farrell Krell and Frank A. Capuzzi. New York: Harper & Row, 1975.

――――. *Introduction to Metaphysics.* Trans. Ralph Manheim. Garden City, NY: Doubleday, 1961.

――――. *On Time and Being.* Trans. Joan Stambaugh. New York: Harper & Row, 1969.

――――. *On the Way to Language.* Trans. Peter Hertz. New York: Harper & Row, 1971.

――――. *Satz vom Grund.* Tübingen: Gunther Neske Pfullingen, 1957.

――――. *What Is Called Thinking?* Trans. J. Glenn Gray. New York: Harper & Row, 1968.

Hollis, Martin. *The Cunning of Reason.* Cambridge: Cambridge University Press, 1987.

――――. *Models of Man: Philosophical Thoughts on Social Action.* Cambridge: Cambridge University Press, 1977.

――――. *Reason in Action: Essays in the Philosophy of Social Science.* Cambridge: Cambridge University Press, 1996.

————. "The Social Destruction of Reality." In *Rationality and Relativism*. Ed. Martin Hollis and Steven Lukes. Cambridge, MA: MIT Press, 1982.

Horkheimer, Max, and Theodor Adorno. *Dialectic of Enlightenment*. Trans. John Cumming. New York: Seabury Press, 1972.

Horowitz, Asher, and Terry Maley, eds. *The Barbarism of Reason: Max Weber and the Twilight of Enlightenment*. Toronto: University of Toronto Press, 1994.

Jakobson, Roman, and Morris Halle. *Fundamentals of Language*. The Hague: Martinus Nijhoff, 1956.

James, William. *Essays in Radical Empiricism*. New York: Longman's, Green, 1912.

————. *Pragmatism: A New Name for Some Old Ways of Thinking*. Cambridge, MA: Harvard University Press, 1975.

————. *Talks to Teachers on Psychology; and to Students on Some of Life's Ideals*. New York: W. W. Norton, 1958.

————. *Varieties of Religious Experience: A Study of Human Nature*. New York: Longman's, Green, 1902.

————. *Writings of William James*. Ed. John J. McDermott. Chicago: University of Chicago Press, 1977.

Jameson, Fredric. *Marxism and Form: Twentieth-Century Dialectical Theories of Literature*. Princeton, NJ: Princeton University Press, 1971.

————. *The Political Unconscious: Narrative as a Socially Symbolic Act*. Ithaca, NY, and London: Cornell University Press, 1982.

————. "Postmodernism, or the Logic of Late Capitalism." *New Left Review* 146 (1984): 53–92.

Jodalen, Harald, and Arne Johan Vetlesen, eds. *Closeness: An Ethics*. Oslo: Scandinavian University Presses, 1997.

Jones, Peter. "Philosophy, Interpretation, and the Golden Bowl." *Philosophy and Literature*. Ed. A. Phillips Griffiths. Cambridge: Cambridge University Press, 1984.

Kant, Immanuel. "An Answer to the Question: What Is Enlightenment?" *Kant on History*. Trans. Lewis White Beck. Indianapolis: Bobbs-Merrill, 1963.

Kenner, Hugh. *The Counterfeiters*. Garden City, NY: Anchor Books, 1973.

————. *A Homemade World*. New York: William Morrow, 1975.

Kerby, Anthony. *Narrative and the Self*. Bloomington: Indiana University Press, 1991.

Kontos, Alkis. "The World Disenchanted, and the Return of Gods and Demons." *The Barbarism of Reason: Max Weber and the Twilight of Enlightenment*. Toronto: University of Toronto Press, 1994.

Kristeva, Julia. "Within the Microcosm of 'The Talking Cure.'" *Interpreting Lacan*. Trans. Thomas Gora and Margaret Wailer. New Haven, CT: Yale University Press, 1983. Langbaum, Robert. *The Poetry of Experience: The Dramatic Monologue in Modern Literary Tradition*. New York: W. W. Norton, 1963.

Langer, Susanne. *Feeling and Form*. New York: Scribner's, 1961.

Leavey, John P. GLASsary. Lincoln: University of Nebraska Press, 1986.

Lecercle, Jean-Jacques. Philosophy through the Looking-Glass: Language, Nonsense, Desire. La Salle, IL: Open Court, 1985.

———. The Violence of Language. London: Routledge, 1990.

Leonard, George. Into the Light of Things: The Art of the Commonplace from Wordsworth to John Cage. Chicago: University of Chicago Press, 1994.

Levinas, Emmanuel. Collected Philosophical Papers. Trans. Alphonso Lingis. The Hague: Martinus Nijhoff, 1987.

———. Existence and Existents. Trans. Alfonso Lingis. The Hague: Martinus Nijhoff, 1978.

———. Nine Talmudic Readings. Trans. Annette Aronowicz. Bloomington: Indiana University Press, 1990.

———. Otherwise Than Being or Beyond Essence. Trans. Alphonso Lingis. The Hague: Martinus Nijhoff, 1981.

———. Totality and Infinity. Trans. Alphonso Lingis. Pittsburgh: Duquesne University Press, 1964.

Lewis, David. "Truth in Fiction." Philosophical Papers. New York and Oxford: Oxford University Press, 1983.

———. Totality and Infinity. Trans. Alphonso Lingis. Pittsburgh: Duquesne University Press, 1964.

Lotman, Jurij. The Structure of the Artistic Text. Trans. Gail Lenhoff and Ronald Vroon. Ann Arbor: Michigan Slavic Contributions, no. 7, 1977.

Lyotard, Jean-François. Political Writings. Trans. Bill Readings and Kevin Paul. Minneapolis: University of Minnesota Press, 1993.

McCumber, John. Poetic Interaction: Language, Freedom, Reason. Chicago and London: University of Chicago Press, 1989.

MacIntyre, Alasdair. After Virtue: A Study in Moral Theory. Notre Dame, IN: University of Notre Dame Press, 1981.

———. "Epistemological Crises, Dramatic Narrative, and the Philosophy of Science." Monist 60:4 (October 1977): 459.

———. Relativism: Interpretation and Confrontation. Ed. Michael Krausz. Notre Dame, IN: University of Notre Dame Press, 1989.

———. Three Rival Versions of Moral Enquiry: Encyclopaedia, Genealogy, and Tradition. Notre Dame, IN: University of Notre Dame Press, 1990.

———. Whose Justice? Which Rationality? Notre Dame, IN: University of Notre Dame Press, 1988.

MacKinnon, Catharine. "Feminism, Marxism, Method, and the State: Toward Feminist Jurisprudence." Signs: Journal of Women in Culture and Society 8 (1983): 635–58.

Malpas, J. E. Donald Davidson and the Mirror of Meaning: Holism, Truth, Interpretation. Cambridge: Cambridge University Press, 1992.

Margolis, Joseph. *Texts without Reference: Reconciling Science and Narrative.* Oxford: Basil Blackwell, 1989.

———. *Historied Thought, Constructed World: A Conceptual Primer for the Turn of the Millennium.* Berkeley: University of California Press, 1995.

———. *Life without Principles: Reconciling Theory and Practice.* Oxford: Basil Blackwell, 1995.

Marin, Louis. "Disneyland: A Degenerate Utopia." *Glyph* 1 (1977): 50–66.

Matthias, John. *Crossing.* Chicago: Swallow Press, 1979.

———. *A Gathering of Ways.* Athens, Ohio: Swallow Press/Ohio University Press, 1991.

———. "Places and Poems: A Self-Reading and a Reading of the Self in the Romantic Context from Wordsworth to Parkman." In *The Romantics and Us: Essays on Literature and Culture.* Ed. Gene W. Ruoff. New Brunswick, NJ, and London: Rutgers University Press, 1990.

———. *Turns.* Chicago: Swallow Press, 1975.

McCaffery, Steve. *North of Intention: Critical Writings, 1973–86.* New York: Roof Books; Toronto: Nightwood Editions, 1986.

McCloskey, Donald. "Storytelling in Economics." In *Narrative in Culture: The Uses of Storytelling in the Sciences, Philosophy, and Literature.* Ed. Christopher Nash. London: Routledge, 1990.

McGann, Jerome. "History, Herstory, Theirstory, Ourstory." In *Theoretical Issues in Literary History.* Ed. David Perkins. Cambridge, MA: Harvard University Press, 1991.

Mellinkoff, David. *The Language of the Law.* Boston and Toronto: Little, Brown and Co., 1963.

Miller, J. Hillis. "Ariadne's Thread: Repetition and the Narrative Line." In *Interpretation and Narrative.* Ed. Vario J. Valdés and Owen J. Miller. Toronto, Buffalo, London: University of Toronto Press, 1978.

———. *The Form of Victorian Fiction.* Notre Dame, IN: University of Notre Dame Press, 1968.

———. *The Linguistic Moment from Wordsworth to Stevens.* Princeton, NJ: Princeton University Press, 1985.

Morson, Gary Saul. *Narrative and Freedom: The Shadows of Time.* New Haven, CT: Yale University Press, 1994.

Murdoch, Iris. "Against Dryness: A Polemical Sketch." In *Revisions: Changing Perspectives in Moral Philosophy.* Ed. Stanley Hauerwas and Alasdair MacIntyre. Notre Dame, IN: University of Notre Dame Press, 1983.

Nagel, Thomas. *The View from Nowhere.* New York: Oxford University Press, 1986.

Nash, Christopher. "Slaughtering the Subject: Literature's Assault on Narrative." In *Narrative in Culture: The Uses of Storytelling in the Sciences, Philosophy, and Literature.* Ed. Christopher Nash. London: Routledge, 1990.

Nealon, Jeffrey. "Politics, Poetics, and Institutions: 'Language Poetry.'" *Double Reading: Postmodernism after Deconstruction*. Ithaca, NY: Cornell University Press, 1993.

Nietzsche, Friedrich. *The Will to Power*. Trans. Walter Kaufmann and R. J. Hollingdale. New York: Vintage Books, 1968.

Novitz, David. "Metaphor, Derrida, and Davidson." *Journal of Aesthetics and Art Criticism* 45:4 (Summer 1985): 101–14.

Nussbaum, Martha. *The Fragility of Goodness*. Cambridge: Cambridge University Press, 1985.

———. *Love's Knowledge: Essays on Philosophy and Literature*. New York and Oxford: Oxford University Press, 1990.

———. "Reply to Bruns." *Soundings: An Interdisciplinary Journal* 72 (1989).

Olsen, Elder. "William Empson, Contemporary Criticism, and Poetic Diction." In *Critics and Criticism*. Ed. R. S. Crane et al. Chicago: University of Chicago Press, 1952.

Olson, Charles. "PROJECTIVE VERSE." *Charles Olson: Selected Writings*. New York: New Directions, 1966.

Paulson, William. *The Noise of Culture: Literary Texts in a World of Information*. Ithaca, NY: Cornell University Press, 1988.

Perelman, Bob. *a.k.a.* Great Barrington, MA: The Figures, 1984.

Perloff, Marjorie. *The Dance of the Intellect: Studies in the Poetry of the Pound Tradition*. Cambridge: Cambridge University Press, 1985.

———. *Poetic License: Essays on Modernist and Postmodernist Lyric*. Evanston, IL: Northwestern University Press, 1990.

———. "Poetry and the Common Life." *Sulfur* 12 (1984): 160–64.

———. *Wittgenstein's Ladder: Poetic Language and the Strangeness of the Ordinary*. Chicago: University of Chicago Press, 1996.

Phillips, D. Z. *Interventions in Ethics*. Albany: SUNY Press, 1992.

———. *Through a Darkening Glass: Philosophy, Literature, and Cultural Change*. Notre Dame, IN: University of Notre Dame Press, 1982.

Phillips, D. Z., and Peter Winch, eds. *Wittgenstein: Attention to Particulars: Essays in Honour of Rush Rhees*. New York: St. Martin's Press, 1989.

Quine, W. V. O. *From a Logical Point of View: Nine Logico-Philosophical Essays*. Cambridge, MA: Harvard University Press, 1989.

———. *Word and Object*. Cambridge: Cambridge University Press, 1960. Ramberg, Bjørn T. *Donald Davidson's Philosophy of Language: An Introduction*. London: Basil Blackwell, 1989.

Rawls, John. *A Theory of Justice*. Cambridge, MA: Harvard University Press, 1971.

Ricoeur, Paul. *Hermeneutics and the Human Sciences*. Trans. John B. Thompson. Cambridge: Cambridge University Press, 1981.

—. *Interpretation Theory: Discourse and the Surplus of Meaning.* Fort Worth: Texas Christian University Press, 1976.

—. *Oneself as Another.* Trans. Kathleen Blarney. Chicago: University of Chicago Press, 1992.

—. *The Rule of Metaphor: Multidisciplinary Studies of the Creation of Meaning in Language.* Trans. Robert Czerny, Kathleen McLaughlin, and John Costello. Toronto: University of Toronto Press, 1977.

—. *Time and Narrative.* 3 vols. Chicago: University of Chicago Press, 1984–89.

Rorty, Richard. *Consequences of Pragmatism.* Minneapolis: University of Minnesota Press, 1982.

—. *Contigency, Irony, and Solidarity.* Cambridge: Cambridge University Press, 1989.

—. "In Defense of Eliminative Materialism." *Review of Metaphysics* 24:1 (September 1970).

—. *Objectivism, Relativism, and Truth.* Cambridge: Cambridge University Press, 1991.

—. *Philosophy and the Mirror of Nature.* Princeton, NJ: Princeton University Press, 1979.

—. "Review of Daniel Dennett's *Consciousness Explained.*" *London Review of Books* 13:22 (21 November 1991): 3–6.

—. "Solidarity or Objectivity?" In *Post-Analytic Philosophy.* Ed. John Rajchman and Cornell West. New York: Columbia University Press, 1985.

Rose, Gillian. *Dialectic of Nihilism: Post-Structuralism and Law.* London: Basil Blackwell, 1984.

Russell, Bertrand. "William James's Conception of Truth." *Philosophical Essays.* New York, 1966. Sartre, Jean-Paul. *Being and Nothingness.* Trans. Hazel E. Barnes. New York: Washington Square Press, 1956.

Schafer, Roy. *Retelling a Life: Narration and Dialogue in Psychoanalysis.* New York: Basic Books, 1992.

Schmidtz, David. *Rational Choice and Moral Agency.* Princeton, NJ: Princeton University Press, 1995.

Schmitz, Kenneth. "Toward a Metaphysical Restoration of Natural Things." In *An Etienne Gilson Tribute.* Ed. Charles O'Neill. Milwaukee: Marquette University Press, 1959.

Schürmann, Reiner. *Heidegger on Being and Acting: From Principles to Anarchy.* Trans. Christine-Marie Gros and Rainer Schurmann. Bloomington: Indiana University Press, 1987.

Schweder, Richard A. "Anthropology's Romantic Rebellion against the Enlightenment; or, There's More to Thinking Than Reason and Evidence." In *Culture Theory: Essays on Mind, Self, and Emotion.* Ed. Richard A. Schweder et al. Cambridge: Cambridge University Press, 1984.

Searle, John. *Expression and Meaning: Studies in the Theory of Speech Acts.* Cambridge: Cambridge University Press, 1979.

Serres, Michel. *Genesis.* Trans. Geneviève James and James Nielson. Ann Arbor: University of Michigan Press, 1995.

Shusterman, Richard. *Practicing Philosophy: Pragmatism and the Philosophical Life.* New York and London: Routledge, 1997.

Silliman, Ron. *The Age of Huts.* New York: Roof Books, 1986.

———. *The New Sentence.* New York: Roof Books, 1987.

———. *Tjanting.* Berkeley, CA: The Figures, 1981.

Stevens, Wallace. *Collected Poems.* New York: Knopf, 1954.

———. *Opus Posthumous.* Ed. Samuel French Morse. New York: Alfred Knopf, 1957.

Stich, Stephen. *From Folk Psychology to Cognitive Science.* Cambridge, MA: MIT Press, 1983.

Stocks, J. L. *Morality and Purpose.* London: Routledge & Kegan Paul, 1970.

Taylor, Charles. *Hegel.* Cambridge: Cambridge University Press, 1975.

———. "The Moral Topography of the Self." In *Hermeneutics and Psychological Theory: Hermeneutic Perspectives on Personality, Psychotherapy, and Psychopathology.* Ed. Stanley Messer, Louis Sass, and Robert Woolfolk. New Brunswick, NJ: Rutgers University Press, 1988.

———. "Overcoming Epistemology." In *Philosophy: End or Transformation.* Ed. Kenneth Baynes, James Bohman, and Thomas McCarthy. Cambridge, MA: MIT Press, 1987.

———. *Philosophical Papers.* Vol. 1: *Human Agency and Language.* Cambridge: Cambridge University Press, 1985.

———. *Philosophical Papers.* Vol. 2: *Philosophy and the Human Sciences.* Cambridge: Cambridge University Press, 1985.

———. *Sources of the Self: The Making of Modern Identity.* Cambridge, MA: Harvard University Press, 1989.

Tiffany, Daniel. "The Rhetoric of Materiality." *Sulfur* 22 (Spring 1988).

Unger, Roberto. *The Critical Legal Studies Movement.* Cambridge, MA, and London: Harvard University Press, 1986.

———. *Politics: A Work in Constructive Social Theory.* Cambridge: Cambridge University Press, 1987.

———. *Social Theory: Its Situation and Its Task.* Cambridge: Cambridge University Press, 1987.

Valdés, Mario J., and Owen J. Miller, eds. *Interpretation and Narrative.* Toronto, Buffalo, London: University of Toronto Press, 1978.

Valéry, Paul. "Concerning 'Le Cimitiere Marin.'" *The Art of Poetry.* Trans. Denise Folliot. New York: Vintage Books, 1961.

Watson, Gary. "The Primacy of Character." In *Identity, Character, and Morality:*

Essays in Moral Psychology. Ed. Owen Flanagan and Amélie Oksenberg Rorty. Cambridge, MA: MIT Press, 1990.

Weber, Max. *Economy and Society.* Ed. Günther Roth and Claus Wittich. Trans. Ephraim Fischoff et al. Berkeley: University of California Press, 1978.

Weinberger, Eliot. Review of *In the American Tree. Sulfur* 20 (Fall 1987): 196–97.

West, Cornell. *The American Evasion of Philosophy: A Genealogy of Pragmatism.* Madison: University of Wisconsin Press, 1989.

White, James Boyd. "Law as Language: Reading Law and Reading Literature." *Texas Law Review* 60 (March 1982): 415–45.

———. *When Words Lose Their Meaning: Constitutions and Reconstitutions of Language. Character and Community.* Chicago and London: University of Chicago Press, 1984.

Williams, Bernard. *Ethics and the Limits of Philosophy.* Cambridge, MA: Harvard University Press, 1985.

———. *Problems of the Self.* Cambridge: Cambridge University Press, 1972.

Williams, William Carlos. "Kora in Hell: Improvisations." In *Imaginations.* Ed. Webster Schott. New York: New Directions, 1970.

———. *Paterson.* New York: New Directions, 1963.

Wilson, Bryan R., ed. *Rationality.* New York: Harper & Row, 1970.

Winch, Peter. *Ethics and Action.* London: Routledge & Kegan Paul, 1972.

———. *Trying to Make Sense.* Oxford: Basil Blackwell, 1987.

Wittgenstein, Ludwig. *Philosophical Investigations.* 3d ed. Trans. G. E. M. Anscombe. New York: Macmillan, 1968.

Ziarek, Ewa. *The Rhetoric of Failure: Deconstruction of Skepticism, Reinvention of Modernism.* Albany: SUNY Press, 1996.

Name Index

Adorno, Theodor, 12, 142, 154, 221n.25, 258n.22, 259n.38, 262n.59, 263n.66
Allen, Barry, 222–23n.34
Alpers, Paul, 185, 266n.5
Althusser, Louis, 5
Anderson, Judith, 242n.31
Antin, David, 135–37, 148, 256n.4, 256n.6, 256n.7, 263n.70
Apel, Karl-Otto, 13, 222n.32
Aquinas, Thomas, 88
Arendt, Hannah, 76, 240n.12
Aristotle, 1, 3, 73, 75–76, 81, 90, 120, 128–29, 139–40, 190, 233n.7, 240n.10, 251n.14, 252–53n.17, 253–54n.22
Arnold, Matthew, 73, 91
Ashbery, John, 149
Austen, Jane, 76, 80
Austin, J. L., 185, 199

Baker, G. P., 234n.11
Bakhtin, Mikhail, 47, 48, 59, 63–64, 79, 90–92, 170–73, 230n.26, 237n.24, 241n.29, 264n.7
Barthes, Roland, 144, 236n.20
Bartlett, Lee, 256n.9
Bataille, Georges, 55
Bauman, Zygmunt, 268n.3
Beckett, Samuel, 41, 74, 79, 80, 206
Beiner, Ronald, 232–33n.7
Benveniste, Émile, 144

Berman, Harold, 238n.26
Bernstein, Charles, 142, 153, 158, 258n.24, 258n.25, 260–61n.45, 261n.55, 263n.69, 265n.15
Black, Max, 45
Blanchot, Maurice, 141, 242–43n.1, 264n.76
Blank, Paula, 242n.31
Bloom, Harold, 97, 136, 171–72, 246.n15, 264n.8
Borges, Jorge Luis, 102, 244n.9, 247n.27
Bradley, A. C., 185, 192
Brodsky, Claudia, 245–46n.12
Bromige, David, 137, 142, 146, 256n.10, 258n.23
Bruner, Jerome, 243n.2, 245n.12
Buechner, Jeffrey, 228n.12
Burns, Gerald, 150–51, 261n.50
Burton, Frank, 238n.29
Burton, Steven, 233n.7
Butterick, George, 136

Cage, John, 55, 93, 101, 151, 204
Camfield, William, 256–57n.13
Capra, Frank, 154
Caputo, John D., 233n.7, 241n.27
Carlyle, Thomas, 24, 73
Cascardi, Anthony, 248n.33
Cassirer, Ernst, 4–5, 8, 219n.7
Cather, Willa, 156
Cavell, Marcia, 229n.20

203, 206, 209, 211, 216, 219n.1,
245n.12
Keats, John, 178
Kenner, Hugh, 143, 167, 264n.6
Kerby, Anthony, 243n.2
Kontos, Alkis, 221n.25
Kripke, Saul, 208, 231n.35
Kristeva, Julia, 47, 230n.24
Kuhn, Thomas, 220n.12

Lacan, Jacques, 5, 47, 236n.16
Langbaum, Robert, 239n.7
Langer, Susanne, 122–23, 253n.21
Lecercle, Jean-Jacques, 229n.21,
236n.16, 246n.12
Leonard, George, 272n.27
Levinas, Emmanuel, 1, 16–18, 109–11,
118, 122, 143–44, 173, 186–88,
200–1, 298, 224n.45, 224n.46,
240–41n.19, 250n.3, 250n.4,
251n.7–8, 251n.13, 255n.31,
258–59n.32, 265n.11, 266n.8,
268n.2, 271n.22
Lévi-Strauss, Claude, 8
Lewis, David, 140, 257n.18
Lotman, Jurij, 101, 247n.24
Lyotard, Jean-François, 96, 141–42,
244n.10, 258n.21

MacIntyre, Alasdair, xi–xii, 72–92, 94–
103, 239n.3, 240n.15, 240n.17,
241n.20, 248n.30
MacKinnon, Catharine, 66, 238n.27
Mallarmé, Stéphane, 133, 141, 146,
149, 175, 205
Margolis, Joseph, xi, 98, 220n.20,
223n.34, 241n.26, 246n.17
Marin, Louis, 262–63n.65
Matthias, John, 160–63, 263–64n.75,
264n.76, 264n.78, 264n.79

McCaffery, Steve, 55–56, 153–54,
231n.40, 231n.41, 261n.56,
261n.57
McCloskey, Donald, 243n.1
McCumber, John, 92, 242n.32
McGann, Jerome, 106, 249n.38
Mellinkoff, David, 235n.16
Mill, John Stuart, 30
Miller, J. Hillis, 74, 166, 172, 239n.8,
264n.3
Morson, Gary Saul, 244n.9
Murdoch, Iris, 78, 83, 240n.16
Musil, Robert, 76, 240n.11

Nagel, Thomas, 222n.30
Nealon, Jeffrey, 256n.9
Nietzsche, Friedrich, 6, 83–84, 88,
114, 157, 214, 219n.9
Novitz, David, 228n.12
Nussbaum, Martha, xi, 92, 108–29,
190, 206, 233n.7, 249–50n.1,
250n.5, 251–52n.14, 253–54n.22,
254n.24, 266n.11

Olson, Charles, 155, 157–58, 160,
263n.68
Olson, Elder, 257n.17

Parkman, Francis, 162
Pater, Walter, 118
Paul, Sherman, 136, 256n.8
Paulson, William, 101, 247n.23
Perelman, Bob, 146, 259n.39
Perloff, Marjorie, 136, 149–50, 256n.9,
261n.46, 262n.58, 270n.15
Phillips, D. Z., xi, 223n.36, 223n.41,
239n.5, 243n.2, 250n.2
Plato, 2, 62, 71, 74, 90, 95, 114–17,
126, 195, 236n.19, 246n.14
Poe, Edgar Allan, 206–7
Pope, Alexander, 202

Subject Index